AF412232

A STORY OF
AUSTRALIAN
PAINTING

Mary Eagle was born in 1944. She is the Senior Curator of Australian Art at the National Gallery of Australia. Her other books include *The George Bell School* (1981), *Australian Modern Painting Between the Wars* (1989), *The Art of Rupert Bunny* (1991) and *The Oil Paintings of Arthur Streeton in the National Gallery of Australia* (1994).

John Jones is a freelance curator and historian working in Melbourne. He is a former school master, National Gallery of Victoria education officer and Curator of Australian Paintings and Sculptures at the Australian National Gallery. In the late 1980s he worked at Deutscher Fine Art, there becoming involved with the ICI Collection of Australian Art. His principal area of concern is with Australian colonial art.

A STORY OF
AUSTRALIAN PAINTING

MARY EAGLE AND
JOHN JONES

MACMILLAN
AUSTRALIA

First published in Macmillan by Pan Macmillan Publishers
Australia 1994, a division of Pan Macmillan Australia Pty Limited
63-71 Balfour Street, Chippendale, Sydney

Every endeavour has been made to contact copyright holders to
obtain the necessary permission for use of illustrative material.
Any person who may have been inadvertently overlooked should
contact the publisher.

Copyright © ICI Australia Ltd 1994

All rights reserved. No part of this book may be reproduced
or transmitted in any form or by any means, electronic or
mechanical, including photocopying, recording or by any
information storage and retrieval system, without prior
permission in writing from the publisher.

National Library of Australia
cataloguing-in-publication data:

Eagle, Mary, 1944–
A story of Australian painting.

ISBN 0 7329 0778 0.

1. ICI Australia—Art collections. 2. Painting, Australian. 3.
Painting, Modern—19th century—Australia. 4. Painting,
Modern—20th century—Australia. 5. Painting—Private
collections—Victoria—Melbourne. I. Jones, John (John James).
II. ICI Australia

759.994

Typeset in 11½/13½ Andover by Midland Typesetters
Printed in Singapore by Kyodo Printing

CONTENTS

FOREWORD

The ICI Australia collection of Australian paintings was assembled over a period of some thirty-five years, commencing in the 1950s at the time of construction of the Company's head office building in Melbourne.

ICI House was completed in 1958. It was the first of the utilitarian glass tower blocks to be built in the city and is widely recognised as one of the most significant post-war buildings in the country. A fountain by the sculptor Gerald Lewers was commissioned for the courtyard and the Company began selectively purchasing Australian paintings and sculptures by other artists of the time. The originator of the collection was Chairman of the Company, Kenneth Begg.

Under successive chairmen, most recently Milton Bridgland, the collection has been strengthened and enriched. His special contribution was the assembling, with historical and evolutionary perspective, representative works of artists and art movements of both the nineteenth and twentieth centuries; particularly items by artists who have made significant contributions to the development and reputation of Australian painting.

Over the years the collection has had a number of advisers, including the former Director of the National Gallery of Victoria, Sir Daryl Lindsay, and Dr Ursula Hoff (then Senior Curator of Prints and Drawings at the Gallery). Throughout, various artists and art dealers have also assisted with the collection. Clifton and Judith Pugh, Joseph Brown, Chris Deutscher and John Jones have all had a significant influence on the structure and quality of the collection.

No collection of this kind is ever complete, but in 1992 it was seen to be reasonably well rounded and capable of portraying and illustrating an outline history of the development of Australian painting from the early nineteenth century. The collection ends with the 1960s generation of painters extending into the 1980s. The important recent history of contemporary Aboriginal art, beginning in the 1970s, and the emergence of a new generation of artists in the 1980s are significant newer developments beyond the scope of this collection.

In 1991, reviewing its collection, the Company turned attention to how it might serve the public. Individual works from the collection are regularly lent to public institutions for inclusion in exhibitions. The Company decided to bring the ICI Collection of Australian Art to the people of Australia through a publication with the object of providing a richly illustrated and accessible text for the benefit of art lovers and students within the wider community.

It is hoped that this book will bring pleasure to many art lovers and inspiration to students, from among whom will emerge the leading Australian artists of the future.

Colin Short
Chairman, ICI Australia Limited

PREFACE

John Jones was curator of the ICI collection in 1991 when the company decided to bring the art collection to the people of Australia through a publication. The company employed him to write the book with Mary Eagle of the National Gallery of Australia. These two had worked together as curators at the National Gallery and shared a similar outlook on art. John Jones had already created extensive research files on the paintings and had done most of the time-consuming labour of preparing a scholarly catalogue. In the event he was also responsible for writing the chapter 'Vitality'.

The writers started their project by looking at the paintings chronologically. Through a preliminary discussion of each of the paintings in turn, their subject, style, artist and the social circumstances in which they were painted, a structure emerged for the book that reflected the works of art. A title, *A Story of Australian Painting*, was chosen to indicate that there are many histories rather than a single one: the story in this book would be the histories of the paintings interpreted (inevitably) from the writers' late twentieth-century perspective.

For the book to be representative of both authors there had to be collaboration in the actual writing as well as in the preparation. The chapter to be written was discussed, there was extra research, then came the writing, most of it by Mary Eagle. This was followed by a period of revision and preparation for the next chapter. The authors relied on the many well-researched publications now available on Australian art and culture.

Mary Eagle and John Jones

WAYS OF SEEING

1788–1830s

The idea of Australia, the land down under at the end of the world, has often amused writers and artists from the northern hemisphere. Little was known about the country except that it was the home of nomadic Aborigines and entered western history only in the late eighteenth century when it became a prison colony of Great Britain.

One can see from the first images in this book how unfamiliar the landscape and its people were to the British settlers. Whereas white Australians now have behind them a complex history of many generations of people looking at and responding to the landscape and climate, the country was then largely unexplored and unmapped. The soldiers and convicts – among them some artists – brought little to this country apart from memories, some skills learned in Europe, and hazy intentions.

The first artists mostly took the stance of science, adopting its method of describing and analysing. Some of their interpretations have come to seem unfamiliar – different from the ways our country has been seen since. Later came a moral science, with nature elevated to a sublime statement of God's great creation. That theme was finally worked through by the 1870s, leaving the way free for the 1880s' and 1890s' expression of a relaxed intimacy of the people with their natural setting. The transition from unfamiliarity to familiarity took as long as a century.

John Lewin (1770–1819) was the first free artist to come to the colony specifically to make art. Trained by his ornithologist father in the science of drawing and engraving birds and other examples of 'natural history', Lewin seized the opportunity offered by the settlement of the southern continent to explore an entirely new field of natural history. He arrived in Sydney on the *Minerva* in January 1800, armed with letters of recommendation from aristocratic patrons who were interested in the fashionable new natural sciences. During the next two years the artist accompanied an expedition to the Hunter River and another to the Pacific island of Tahiti before settling on a 100-hundred acre grant of land at Parramatta. Between 1803 and 1808 Lewin collaborated with his artist wife Maria in collecting specimens and making drawings and engravings for two publications about the 'Natural History of Lepidopterous Insects of New South Wales' and the 'Birds of New Holland'. These, the Lewins' only publications, were printed in London by John's brother in 1805 and 1808 respectively.

Lewin's opportunities in the colony were greater than they would have been back home. Instead of returning to England, he settled permanently in Sydney, became a farmer, and took a variety of commissions for works of art from successive colonial governors and wealthy settlers. In the new colony he stood out as one of the few artists capable of extending his repertoire to the highest category of eighteenth-century art: history painting. For Governor Macquarie's birthday ball in 1812 he was commissioned to paint a transparency. Back home in England paintings on transparent silk, lit dramatically from behind, had been a feature of festivals and incidentally a source of some of the most interesting experimentation in late eighteenth-century art. Lewin chose to paint a corroboree and afterwards, working on the project on and off for two years, produced a 15 by 18 feet (4.6 m x 5.5 m) painting of the subject. He taught himself to paint in oils, again on a large scale, and produced a number of still-life paintings and at least one large historical subject in the oil medium. Judging from the many hundreds of drawings that remain, however, most of Lewin's time was given to his first professional interest, natural history.

The opossum 1807 (plate 1), neat in drawing and unfaded in colour, is a handsome example of his art. As a natural science draughtsman, Lewin was trained to record all the details of the possum: its feet, tail, eyes and snout, the texture of hair and the transition to soft skin, the musculature and bone structure. If equipped with the knowledge to do so, the more sophisticated artist of scientific ambition would venture further in describing

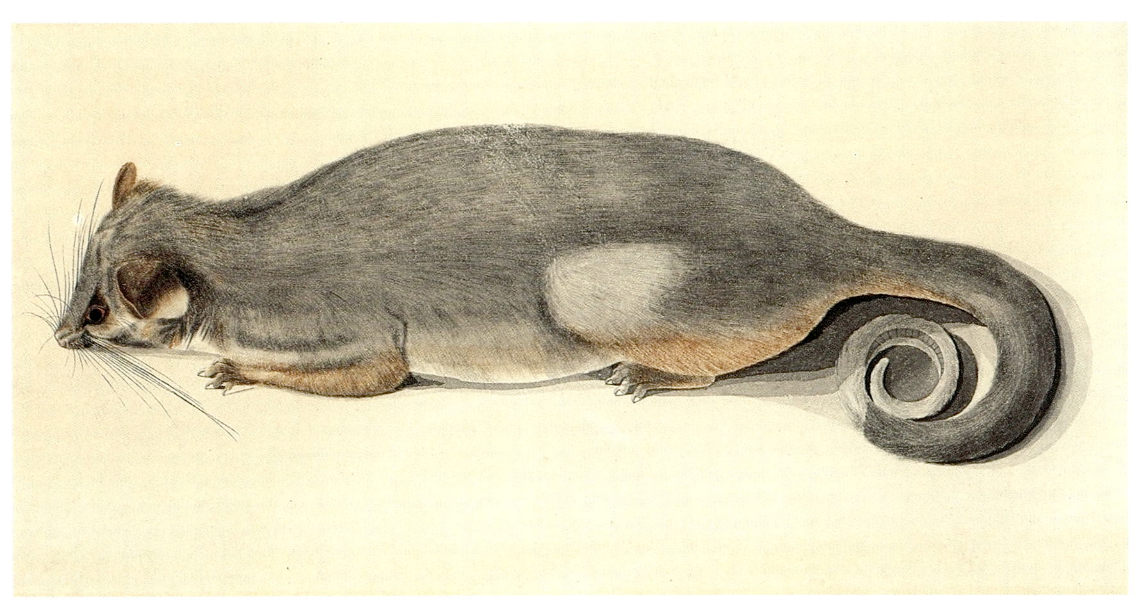

1   J.W. Lewin
1770–1819
(*The opossum*) 1807
watercolour on paper
25.0 × 47.0 cm

the possum in its family and social arrangements, habitat and diet. Lewin sometimes included information about the social world of his creatures. More often ignoring the information he had acquired in collecting specimens of natural history, he showed the creature in deathlike isolation. In a letter to an English patron, Dru Drury, for whom he collected insects, Lewin revealed that he had been reproached for not supplying adequate information about his finds.[1]

The question is sometimes asked how the art history of Australia would have differed if the country had been settled when contact was made by a succession of Dutch sailors in the seventeenth century: Willem Janszoon (in 1604 and 1619), Dirk Hartog (in 1616), Haevik Claeszoon van Hillegom (1618), Frederik de Hourman (1619), Jan Carstensz (1625), François Thijssen (1627) and others after him. After the Dutch East India Company in 1615 recommended that its trading vessels sailed east from the Cape of Good Hope at a southerly parallel, contact with Australia was inevitable and frequent.[2] What if, instead of British convicts, the European settlers had been Dutch burghers or Portuguese traders? Because Australia was settled at the end of the eighteenth century, its art for the first half-century reflected an aesthetic that was consciously rational. In the classificatory mode then prevailing in Europe, the functions, media, styles and imagery of high art, genre studies and natural history (including topography) were each and all of them separately determined. The categories were understood and honoured as a necessary communication: not for nothing was the eighteenth century the age of reason, the era of the dictionary!

Another historical factor determining Australia's early art history was the control exerted by the British armed forces and colonial office over the penal colony's establishment and development. Officers of the British armed forces were trained in the accurate recording of geography, flora and fauna. The fashion for scientific art had a lasting effect on the European-style art produced in Australia. Not only was the beginning of western-style art in this country determined by the official exercise of faithfully recording the geography and natural phenomena, the tendency was lasting. Observation of nature became the dominant mode of Australian art almost into the present.

This pictorial history picks up again forty years after British settlement, in the penal settlement of Newcastle, north of Sydney. Appropriately, the image is of an Aboriginal man, *Burgun* c. 1814–20 (plate 2).[3] We see immediately that this stately man holding spear and shield was alien: remarkably foreign to the artist Richard Browne (1776–1824). Browne has been attentive to the details of shield, spear, grass and other body ornaments. He is altogether the detached scientist, drawing this – one of his several images of Burgun – with fine and careful hand. We could assume from the starkness of the image alone that the exercise in portraying an Aboriginal involved an unusual cultural confrontation. One culture is appraised by another. Browne, like many others facing the same challenge, avoided showing the ambiguities, misreadings and tentative guesses that were necessarily involved in analysing something foreign. His evasive method of coping with the task of describing the indescribable was to reduce art to its craft, a simplifying outline, and chastely reduced colour. The crispness of Browne's style reflects his selection of what to look for and what to describe. The orderly method belonged within the discipline of the 'natural sciences' rather than within the tradition of European portraiture – though Browne has included decorative details in excess of ethnography, such as the wisps of hair brushed like a halo around Burgun's head.

From our point of view in the late twentieth century it seems that the simplicity of Browne's style disguises his lack of knowledge. In watercolours produced over almost twenty years Browne described not only Aborigines in this manner but also the birds and beasts of Australia. In these images the only hint or acknowledgment of imaginative shyness on the part of the artist is the shadowy withdrawal of each body within its outline: a negative presence offset by an outline so wryly articulate, so vivid, in every drawing that the outline actually seems to leap with life. The suggestion of a live presence within the silhouettes makes Browne's images unforgettable. *If Browne looked to an English tradition of silhouette portraiture, it was left far behind in his unconventional exercise of the genre.*

Burgun, or 'Burgon', or 'Long Jack', was a native of the tribe that owned the country around Lake Macquarie. The

Newcastle penal settlement had been established on the Hunter River near Lake Macquarie in 1801. Ironically, Burgun was employed as a jailer and tracker of escaped convicts and paid in tobacco, corn and blankets (not in rum as were many ex-convicts). According to the Reverend Samuel Leigh, a Wesleyan missionary working at Newcastle, Burgun was 'a sensible and intelligent man . . . very active in apprehending the runaways from that settlement'. He 'brought back in triumph' a number of escaped convicts. Leigh reported Burgun as a rescuer of lost men, describing his tracking of 'Bush Rangers' as an act of mercy, 'preventing them from perishing from want in the bush or perpetrating new crimes to lengthen out a miserable existence'. It was said that Burgun treated escapees 'with kindness and was never known to use any needless violence in securing them'. In a letter of November 1821 Leigh recorded the murder of Burgun 'a few months back whilst on an excursion of the above kind . . . cruelly stabbed to the heart by a Bush Ranger [one of the convict escapees] who has since been apprehended, tried and convicted of the murder and executed for the same'.

Irony of ironies, the portraitist Richard Browne was himself a convict at Newcastle who had official employment as an artist. He worked for Lieutenant Thomas Skottowe, commandant at the Newcastle secondary penal station where Browne served most of his sentence, recording the fauna of the Newcastle and Lake Macquarie region for Skottowe's unpublished manuscript 'Specimens from Nature' (1813). Browne was employed as well by Leigh to take portraits of the Aborigines of the region. Hence he knew Burgun in two capacities, as one of his jailers and as the subject for a portrait commissioned by the Reverend Leigh.

The grave portrayal of Aboriginal Burgun by convict Browne may be seen in the light of their comparable situations: an image of one displaced and propertyless person by another man equally homeless and dependent. The social equivalence of artist and subject, and missionary Leigh's story of Burgun as kindly jailer and hero, stands in opposition to the more recent popular notion that the Aborigines were invariably downtrodden and despised by the British settlers. As a consequence of British settlement the Aborigines lost their lands, their inheritance and

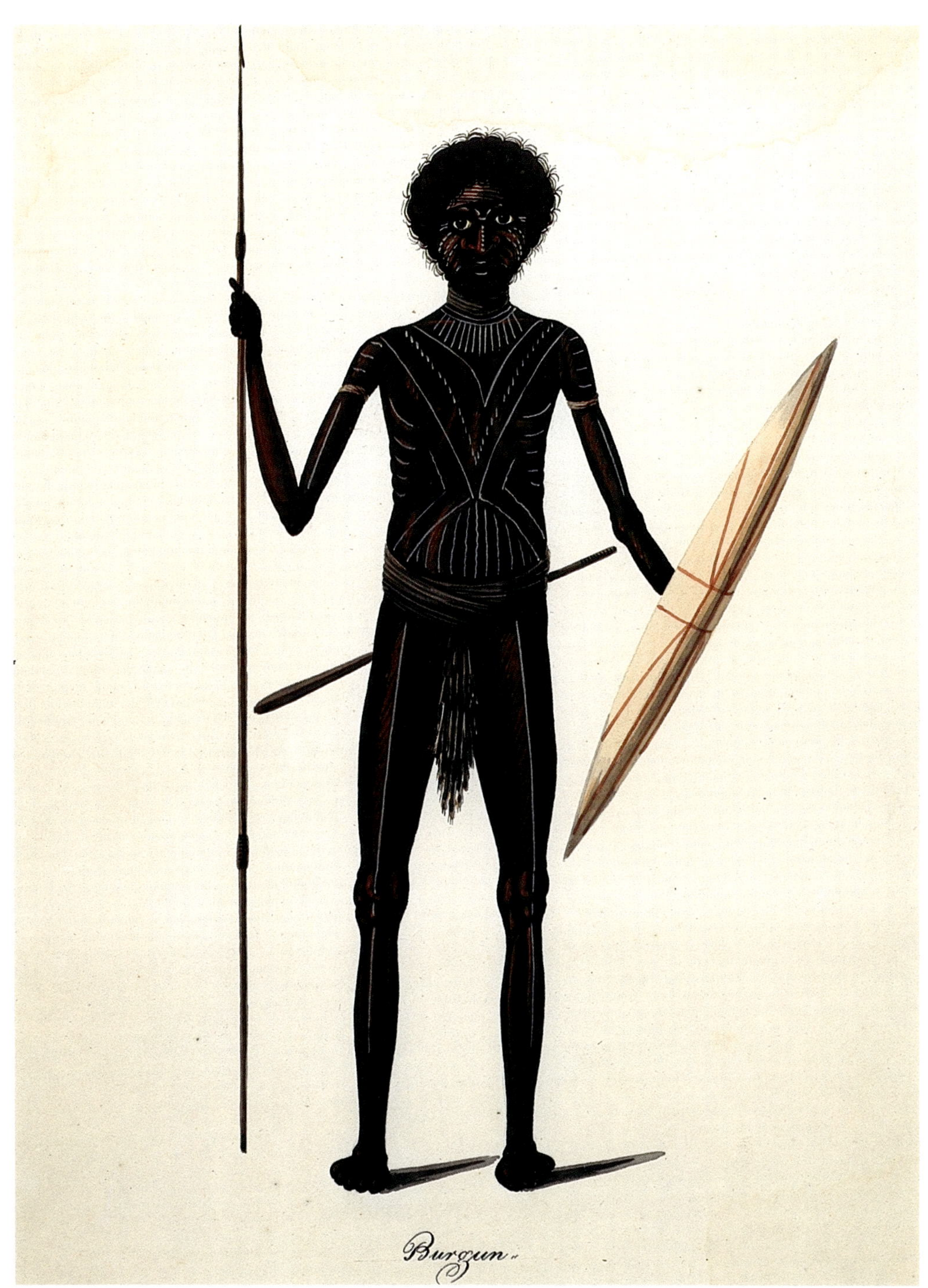

2   Richard Browne
1776–1824
Burgun (1814–20)
watercolour on paper
29.6 × 24.0 cm

a large part of their culture. It may be said that the philosophical and scientific treatises and the art of the period were basically as disregardful of the property rights and independent culture of the Aborigines as were the settlers: the superiority of the British and their right to rule was assumed. Nonetheless the official, paternal, Government line was clear, as for example in the 1816 *Proclamation to the Aborigines* of Lieutenant Governor Davey, which declared that black and white were equal before the law and this equality was to be observed in the most full and ample manner. And Governor Macquarie had proposed that Aborigines were eligible for small grants of land and that native reserves be established for Aborigines to live undisturbed by European vagrants.

For the incoming landscape painters of European birth and training, it was as if they had encountered 'a country without geography, and a race of men without a history'.[4] Despite the geology of the land, this, the world's oldest continent with a very long history of human habitation, was assumed to be new because it was new to the settlers. Joseph Lycett (c.1775–1828) painted *The Sugarloaf Mountain near Newcastle* (plate 3) in 1822, the year after Burgun's death. In effect, he showed Burgun's country, and Burgun's relatives. Like virtually every other early European landscapist, he completely ignored the Aborigines' forms of occupancy, both their practical uses of the land and their visual representations of it. Though he painted his view from land that was part of an 'Aboriginal Grant to the London Missionary Society' of 10 000 acres on the eastern shore of Lake Macquarie, he overlooked the official recognition that it was Aboriginal territory. Some years later he advertised the landscape as a site for British settlement, writing beside the engraved version of the image that 'Many settlers have recently taken up their grants of Land in this delightful part of the Island'.[5]

Lycett believed in the *art*lessness of the virgin Australian landscape. He began an 'Advertisement' for his *Views in Australia* (published in London in instalments in 1824 and 1825) with a suggestive image of creative beginnings:

> Among all the various occurrences which constitute the history of human affairs, there are perhaps none calculated to excite such universal interest as the

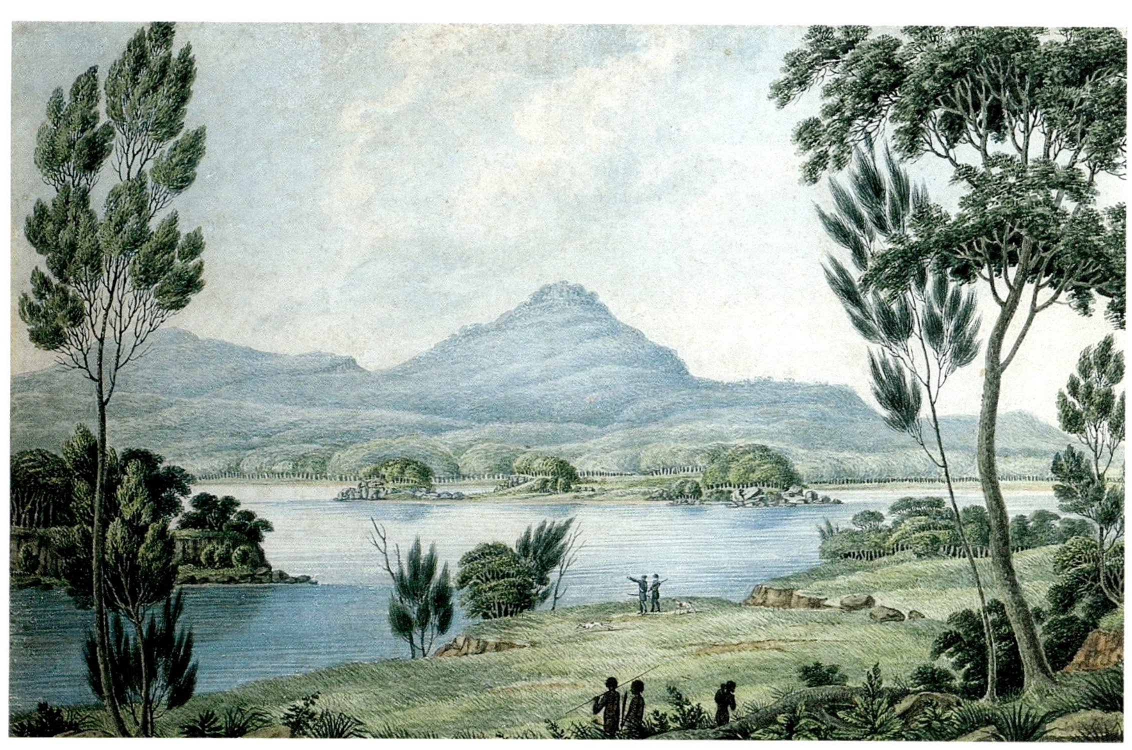

3   Joseph Lycett
c. 1775–1828
The Sugarloaf Mountain near Newcastle (1822)
watercolour on board
17.4 × 27.4 cm

DISCOVERY OF UNKNOWN COUNTRIES, and the progress of art upon the soil and people, which NATURE, on such occasions, resigns from her own creative hand to the care and culture of their civilised discoverers . . .[6]

Lycett's text beside the engraved version of *The Sugarloaf Mountain near Newcastle* described a landscape waiting to be born. 'The scenery here depicted presents itself to the Spectator', wrote Lycett. 'The country here becomes beautifully picturesque', she is 'pristine', she is 'new'.

He gave his subject a conventional European composition of classical symmetry and majestic movement. As in the Augustan poetry of Alexander Pope, we have woods nodding to woods within a picturesque view. All in nature is apparently serene and well-ordered. The colouring, fresh, green and rain-washed, is as English as the composition. In the foreground two Europeans gesture towards the view: these figures were a conventional inclusion in painted views. But, as well, Lycett included Aborigines. Their representation in a non-Aboriginal landscape – one which has all the appearance of being an English fantasy – compares with a much later image by Eugene von Guérard showing the fertile plains of the Western District of Victoria settled by Europeans and the displaced Aborigines inhabiting the dark and rock-strewn high country of the Grampians (plate 17).

Lycett's claim to be an artist–creator of the Australian landscape was reasonable given the role he adopted of persuasive interpreter. He, and other artist–discoverers, departed from the role of the ideal natural historian who would record without bias the vegetation, geographical formations and weather conditions of this unfamiliar country, to manufacture meanings for the landscape. Lycett saw himself as the creator of a valuable landscape property.

His primary purpose in producing these *Views in Australia* was to advertise the country to prospective British farmers. Like a modern real-estate agent he presented the landscape as lush, picturesque, peaceful, potentially productive and open to free settlement. The advertisement was successful. By 1828 over 400 000 acres of this land recently opened for settlement had been taken up and parish areas named after well-known places back home, 'Ravensworth', 'Barnard Castle', 'Kelso', 'St Boswells',

'Jedburgh', 'St Aubyn', 'Hexham', 'Butterwick', 'Lemington', 'Hartwhistle'.[7]

In 1826, when twenty-year-old Frederick Garling had his portrait painted (plate 4) by Augustus Earle (1793–1838), the colony of New South Wales was over thirty years of age and had produced its first generation of young men and women. The colonists naturally copied the forms and graces of social life back in Great Britain. Stately homes had been built. Plush furnishings had been imported. Cabinet-makers and gilders, silversmiths, engravers and artisans of all kinds were busily employed in satisfying the needs of the prosperous mercantile, professional and military classes such as the Garlings (his father was the Colony's Crown Solicitor). Whereas colonial taste followed the British mode, adhering closely to the published 'pattern books', there were modifications reflecting a warmer climate, the high expense of importing furniture from Great Britain, and an Indian-Asian pattern of trade. Such were the addition of verandahs to Georgian-style buildings, the separation of the kitchen from the rest of the house, the drapery of Indian cotton cloths, cane chairs, venetian blinds, floor coverings of grass matting, unpapered walls and the spartan lack of clutter in colonial interiors.[8] There were adaptations relating to the local social climate as well. All prominent visitors to the colony commented on the topsy-turvy family arrangements, whereby jailers would marry their prisoners, and emancipated convicts would become wealthy and powerful members of colonial society.

The art of painting flourished in Sydney though there were few practitioners of longstanding. Family portraits were commissioned from the Richard Reads, senior and junior, delicate watercolourists in the tradition of the major English watercolourist of the period, Richard Dighton. With the arrival of Augustus Earle, more by accident than intention, in May 1825, Sydney had its first competent portraitist in oils. Earle, a world-travelling British artist of American descent, had arrived in Hobart on 18 January 1825, after being abandoned for some months on the windswept island of Tristan da Cunha.[9]

Earle's portrait of Frederick Garling, in its succulent oil medium, sombre palette of greys, black and creams and sensitive modelling of face and costume, is a serious yet graceful interpretation of a well-bred young man. Part of its appeal is its physical presence: a solid and capable work of moderate size, painted in oils on canvas. The Georgian tradition of portraiture in oils was more assertive than the intimate tradition of miniaturist portraits in watercolour which prevailed in the colony. Earle, who painted many portraits during the two years he was in Sydney (on and off), established the oil medium as a desirable alternative to portrait drawing. His images were of two sorts, grand, full-length, rhetorical statements, and the smaller, half-length portraits of the type he produced of Frederick Garling Junior. Earle had a penetrating intelligence (demonstrated slyly in his images of Australian life) and had gained an unusually wide repertoire of styles and subjects from his Royal Academy training, from working as a painter with members of his family, which included two prominent Anglo-American painters, and from his own considerable travels around the world. He was by far the most sophisticated artist to visit Sydney during the colonial period.

In Sydney, Earle set up a miniature art gallery in his rooms at 10 George Street, the first venture of the kind in the colony. According to one resident it 'was much visited by the youths of the colony and must have had considerable influence in promoting good taste'.[10] In August 1826 in the Sydney *Monitor* he advertised art materials for sale and proffered his services as an art instructor.[11] This was around the time he accepted the commission to paint young Frederick Garling, whose ambition was to become a professional artist. Garling had grown up in Governor Macquarie's Sydney where he arrived, aged nine, with his family in August 1815. Given that Earle was offering art lessons, knew the Garling family and had received a commission to paint young Frederick's portrait, it is highly likely that the young man took lessons from Earle, which would make Frederick Garling Australia's first locally trained artist. Early in 1827 Garling was appointed official artist on Stirling's expedition to the Swan River in Western Australia. That expedition was to ascertain the suitability of Western Australia for settlement and so Garling's illustrations of the Swan River, like Lycett's *Views in Australia*, were drawn with a specific, practical purpose in mind.

The convicts in the colonies were mostly British working-class victims of hard luck. But not all. The genteel

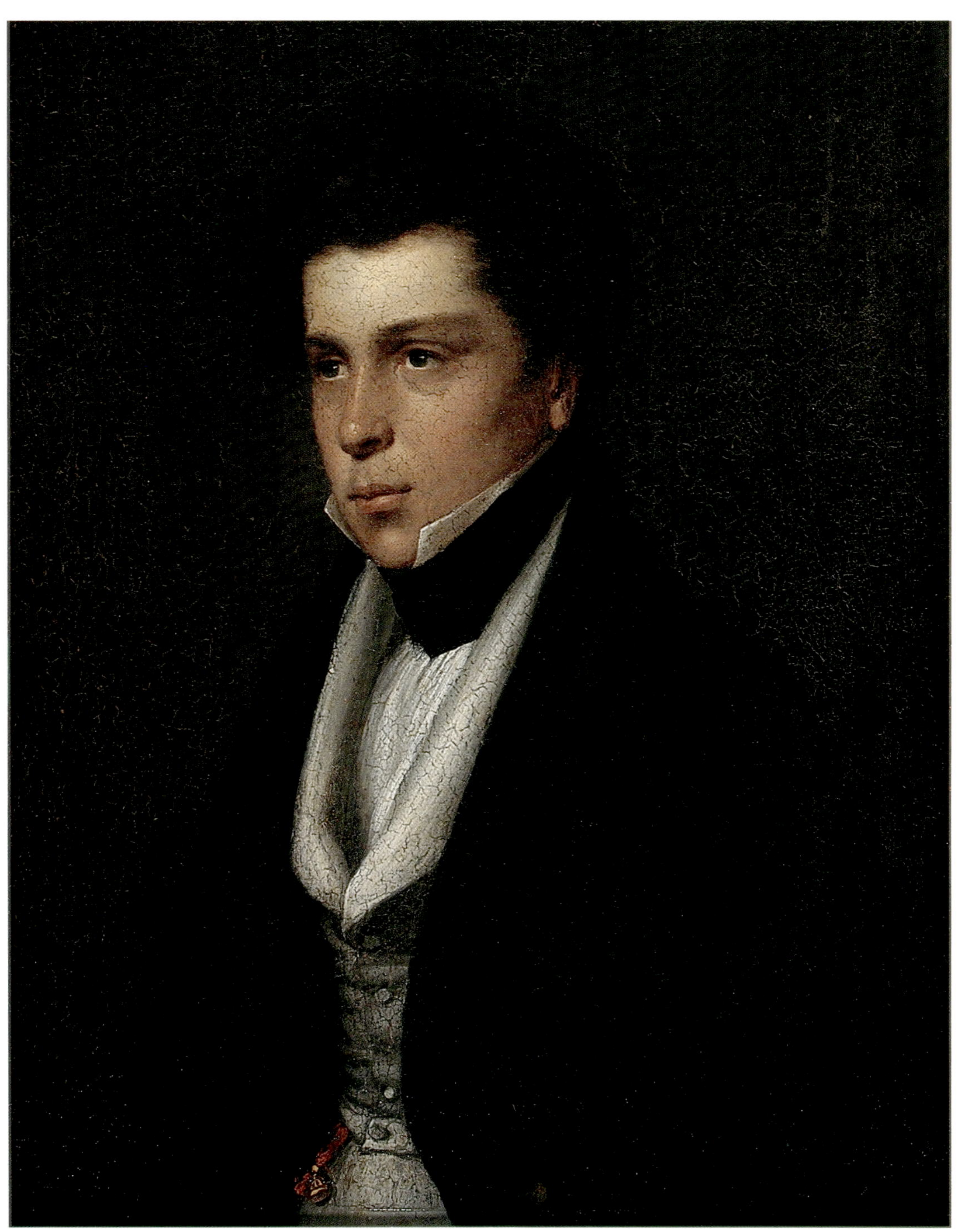

4   Augustus Earle
1793–1838
Frederick Garling (1826)
oil on cedar panel
34.0 × 26.5 cm

German artist Charles Rodius (1802–60) was convicted in London in 1829 for stealing a purse 'containing a handkerchief, a smelling bottle, an opera-glass and two opera tickets' from Lady Laura Meyrick as she was leaving the Royal Opera House. *The Times* called him 'a young foreigner, dressed in a most fashionable style'. Rodius was occupied in London teaching art to the children of the rich. It would appear that he had a habit of stealing young ladies' handkerchiefs.[12]

In Sydney he was employed for a couple of years as artist and architect by the Department of Public Works and on the side continued to give lessons to the children of middle-class colonists. He obtained exemption from government employment in June 1832 and a ticket of leave in February 1834, the year the last of his lithographic *Portraits of Australian Aborigines* were published by J.G. Austin.[13]

So far as art was concerned, Rodius was a realist. When an engraved drawing of Sydney by Rodius was published in February 1834 it was noted:

> this view surpasses in correctness of external objects
> and precision of drawing, anything we have yet seen
> of this kind produced in the Colony. The great defect
> of all the engravings of New South Wales Scenery
> hitherto brought out, has been a want of verisimilitude.[14]

Likewise, his many portraits of white and black subjects were drawn without prejudice. The bias in most depictions of Aborigines was revealed in one review praising 'an excellent likeness' by Rodius, in which 'the intelligence of the countenance (unlike the mass of the aborigines) is very happily caught'.[15]

Rodius never worked in the oil medium which would have obliged him to adopt the descriptive conventions of the grand manner. Although Rodius claimed to have studied art in Paris in the 1820s his democratic attitude and observant record of character in the lithographic drawings of 1834, *Neddy Noora* (plate 5) and his wife *Tooban* (plate 6), suggest a German background in scientific drawing. A Paris training, by contrast, would have equipped him with a repertoire of classical allusions in style and story – which were conspicuously absent from his art.

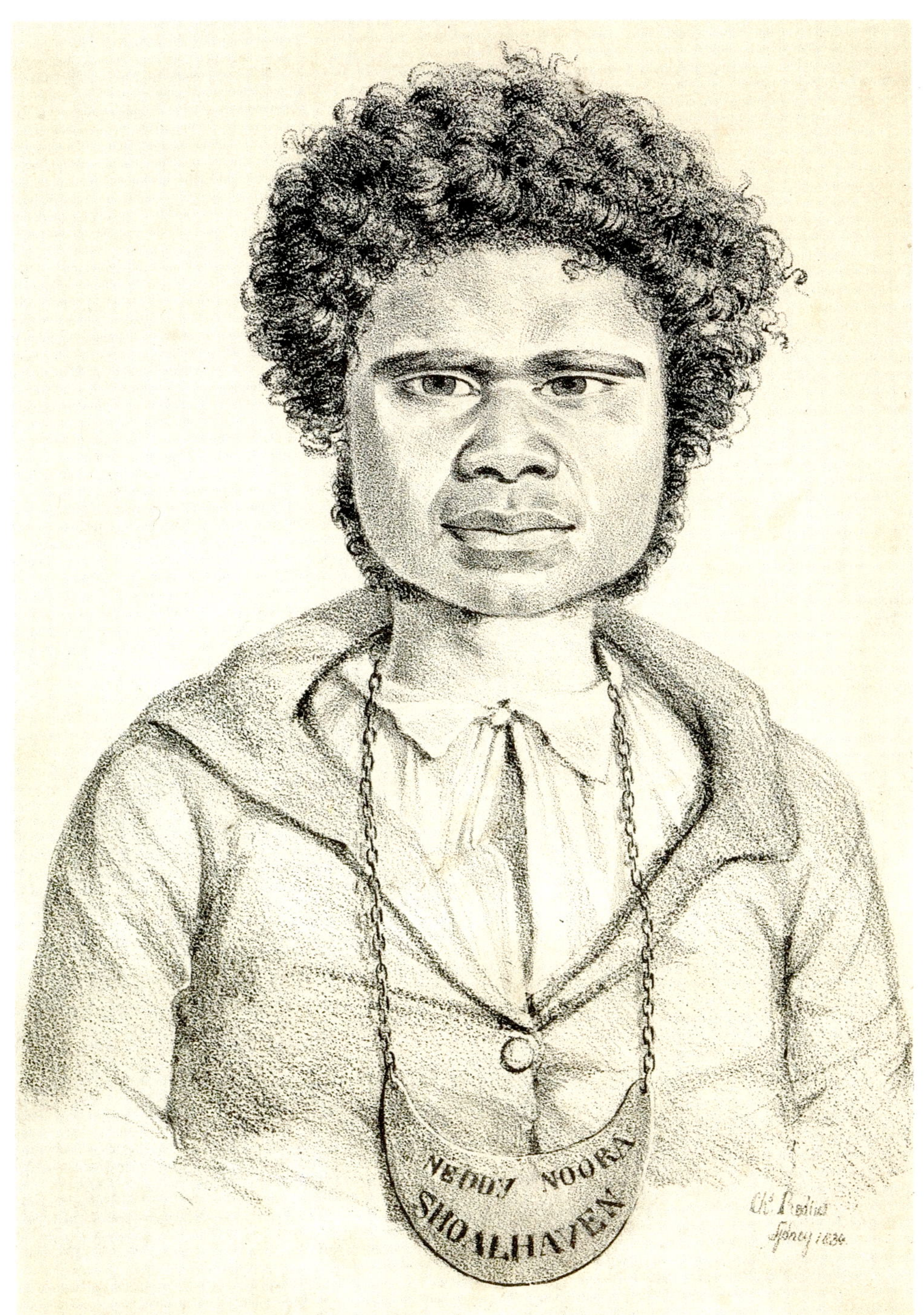

5   Charles Rodius
1802–60
Neddy Noora, Shoalhaven 1834
lithograph on paper
20.7 × 14.8 cm

Rodius' frank attention to the truth of what he saw meant he did not always caricature his portrait subjects; he showed them in everyday dress rather than classical or exotic garb, and positioned them matter-of-factly, close to him, in a good light, and in full face or characterful profile. In many respects a better ethnographer than Lewin was a natural history draughtsman, he included as part of his portrait the name, family (or tribe) and address (region) of his subjects, and the date and place of the drawing. Thus Neddy Noora and Tooban of Shoalhaven were drawn 'from Nature and on Stone' [that is, lithographic stone] in Sydney in 1834.

Having achieved a reputation for the accuracy of his modest portrait drawings Rodius, in the 1840s and 1850s, faced the competition of photography, which offered even greater scientific accuracy.

The painter John Glover (1767–1849) brought another set of expectations and attitudes to the Australian landscape. He was an older man – aged sixty-four when he came to Van Diemen's Land in 1831. He was a free settler and, most important for the way he looked at Australian scenery, he was a reputable English artist in oils within a tradition to which he was not subservient, having actually helped its establishment. He was one of three artists – the others were Richard Wilson[16] and George Smith – who had been given the appellation of the English Claudes – after Claude Lorraine.

Glover's *Dinas Brann near Llangollen* 1837 (plate 7), a memory of Welsh scenery, was painted in Van Diemen's Land from notes and imagination, and invites comparison with the painter's milder Australian views. Here is a wilderness landscape, wild and mountainous, with sunlit peaks and a deep shadowy vale. The impression of wildness is conveyed through a dramatic marriage of storm cloud, sunlight and shadow.

To contemporaries, Glover's Welsh landscape would be recognised as being in the rugged style of Salvator Rosa. Rosa, a seventeenth-century paragon, was emulated in eighteenth-century England for this savage interpretation, just as other seventeenth-century 'masters' Jacob van Ruysdael and Aelbert Cuyp, from the Netherlands, were emulated for expressions of rustic peace, and Claude Lorraine for the expression of classical grace in landscape. From the point of view of the Australian landscape

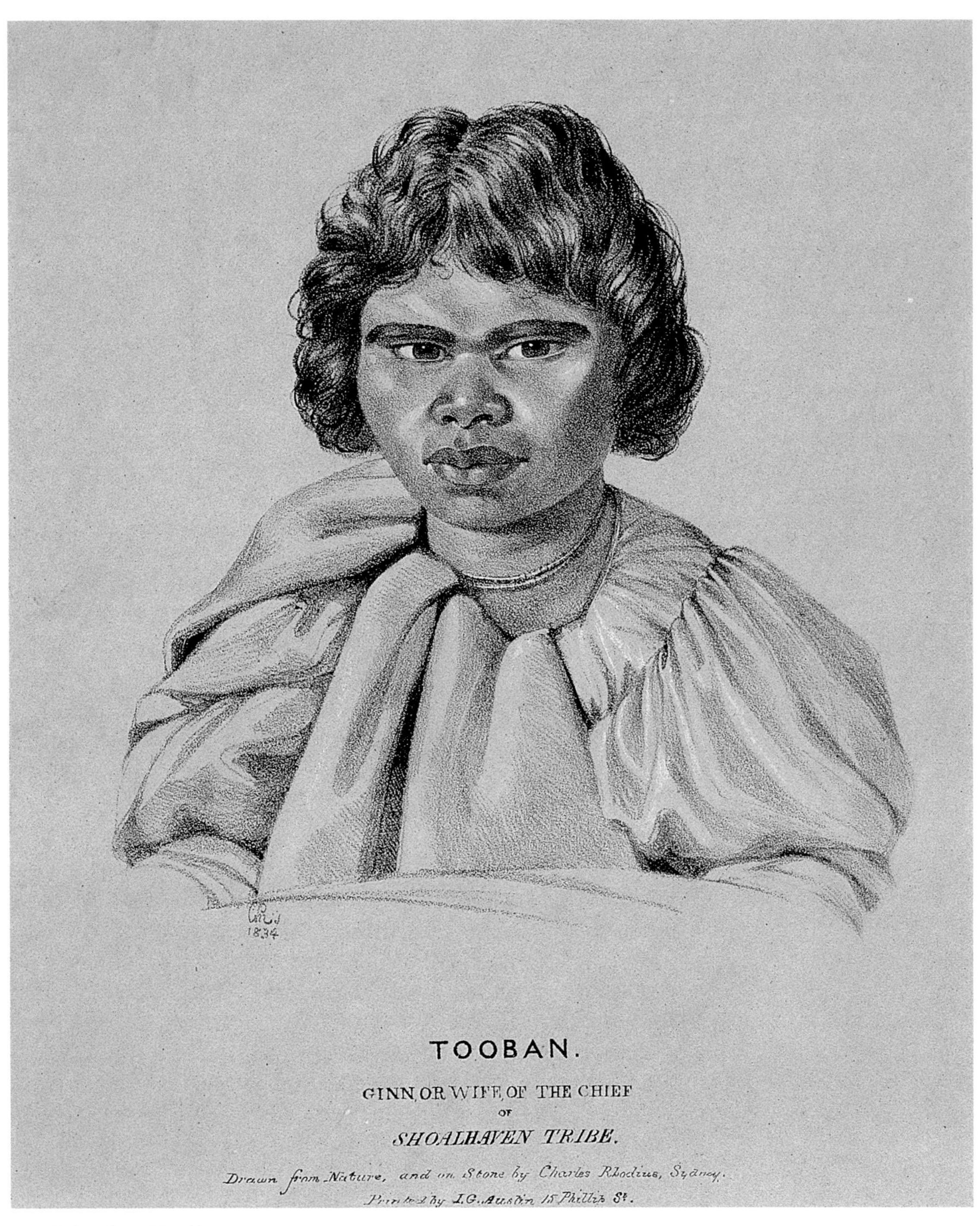

6   Charles Rodius
1802–60
Tooban, gin or wife of the Chief of the Shoalhaven Tribe 1834
lithograph on paper
24.0 × 20.0 cm

tradition, it is significant that the European landscapists who were exemplars had never imagined a 'wilderness' outside the reach of human occupancy.[17] Salvator Rosa, the specialist in wilderness landscapes, was known for his picturesque bandits. In Glover's otherwise forbidding Welsh scene there are resting cattle, a distant sunlit village and castle ruins.

Significantly for Australian art, Glover chose not to use the wilderness rhetoric for his scenes of Van Diemen's Land, even though he had suitable subjects in abundance. He painted Mount Wellington looming in mist and rain but softened the effect by incorporating a rainbow. He painted Aboriginal corroborees but made them picnics. Of Glover's contemporary colonial critics, Dr Lhotsky at least was displeased at his mild interpretation, objecting that the 'eminent' artist had 'not endeavoured to select a really primitive and original Australian nature'.[18] Typically, Glover treated the valley landscapes around his farm at Patterdale as quiet pastorals. Aborigines, shepherds, the figure of the artist himself, were peaceful inhabitants of the landscapes. His exemplars for these domestic idylls were the seventeenth-century Dutch painters rather than the tempestuous Italians. Why this gentler artistic possession of the Australian landscape? Was it because, as a farmer-settler, Glover wanted to see his land in the best light? Instead of perpetuating the wilderness he made a garden. That nurturing of the landscape, which was literally Glover's occupation in creating a flourishing garden at Patterdale, was also true of Glover's artistic appropriation of the new country.

Paradoxically, most of Glover's Australian landscapes were painted for an English market, whereas for colonial consumption he recalled the well-tried European subjects of Claude Lorraine and Salvator Rosa.

'Untutored' is one thing colonial landscapes were not. Whether the landscapes of first encounter were awkwardly topographical, or occasionally 'sublime' or, more usually, pleasantly 'picturesque', whether they were intended as scientific description or as persuasive advertisement, almost invariably they were painted to recipe. It happened that Australia was settled and its landscapes explored in the years from the late eighteenth century to the middle of the nineteenth century when European teaching and practice of the visual arts carefully

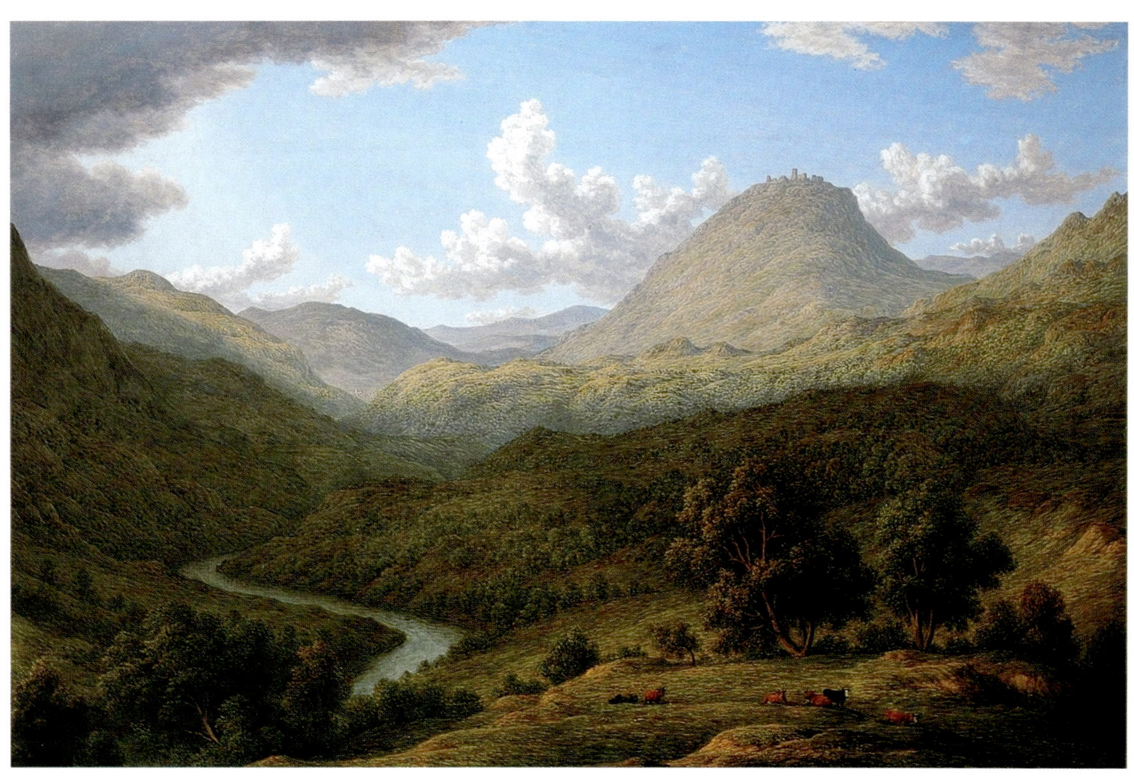

7   John Glover
1767–1849
Dinas Brann near Llangollen 1837
oil on canvas
76.0 × 114.0 cm

imitated the past. It was an age remarkable for classification and typology. The application of European models to a new geography was inevitable within the practice of visual art. It was unavoidable for another reason too – the practical need to have a visual language to record what one saw.

1 See letter published in Bernard Smith (ed.), *Documents on Art and Taste in Australia: The Colonial Period 1770–1914*, Oxford University Press, Melbourne, 1975, pp. 18–24.
2 Kenneth Gordon McIntyre, *The Secret Discovery of Australia: Portuguese Ventures Two Hundred Years Before Captain Cook*, Souvenir Press, Australia, 1977, argues that the Portuguese navigator Cristovao Mendonça came ashore on the east coast of Australia in 1521 or 1522, before Willem Janszoon (see p. 236). See also Graeme Aplin, S.G. Foster and Michael McKernan, (eds), *Australians: Events and Places*, in the Bicentennial series *Australians: A Historical Library*, Fairfax, Syme & Weldon Associates, Sydney, 1987, p. 175.
3 For a larger discussion of how the Aborigines were first seen see Ian Donaldson and Tamsin Donaldson (eds), *Seeing the First Australians*, George Allen & Unwin, Sydney, 1985, and Geoffrey Dutton, *White on Black: The Australian Aborigine Portrayed in Art*, Macmillan, Melbourne, 1974.
4 George Hamilton, *Experiences of a Colonist Forty Years Ago*, Adelaide, 1880, p. 38, quoted in Paul Carter, *The Road to Botany Bay: An Essay in Spatial History*, Faber and Faber, London, 1987, p. 70.
5 Joseph Lycett, text accompanying the plate *The Sugar-Loaf Mountain, near Newcastle, New South Wales*, no. 13 in his *Views in Australia, or New South Wales and Van Diemen's Land Delineated*, J. Soutier, London 1824–5; See *Map of the River Hunter and its Branches*, published to accompany Henry Dangar's *Index and Directory to Map of the Country Bordering upon River Hunter*, London, 1828, redrawn for the *Newcastle Herald*, 1 November 1984, p. 6.
6 Lycett, 'Advertisement', foreword to his *Views in Australia, or New South Wales and Van Diemen's Land Delineated*.
7 See *Map of the River Hunter and its Branches*.
8 Frederick Garling junior in the 1850s made watercolours of some of the brilliant interiors and social occasions of the 1820s, for example, *Guests in the Dome Room of Captain Piper's Mansion at Point Piper*, c. 1856, *Sloper Cox's Wedding at Hobartville, Richmond*, c. 1856. For details of early Australian architecture and interior decoration, see J.M. Freeland, *Architecture in Australia: A History*, F.W. Cheshire, Melbourne, 1968, and Terence Lane and Jessie Serle, *Australians at Home: A Documentary History of Australian Domestic Interiors from 1788 to 1914*, Oxford University Press, Melbourne, 1990.
9 See Augustus Earle, *Narrative of a Residence in New Zealand, Journal of a Residence in Tristan da Cunha*, E.H. McCormick (ed.), Clarendon Press, Oxford, 1966, introduction to the 1832 edition, p. 50, and *Sydney Gazette*, 10 May 1825.
10 *Sydney Gazette*, 28 July 1829, p. 3.

11 *Monitor*, Sydney, 18 August 1826, p. 112, repeated 25 August 1826. See also *Monitor* 8 September 1826. William Dixon, 'Notes on Australian Artists: Part 1, Augustus Earle', *Royal Australian Historical Society*, vol. v, 1919, pp. 287–92.

12 This is from the entry on Charles Rodius in Joan Kerr (ed.), *The Dictionary of Australian Artists: Painters, Sketchers, Photographers and Engravers to 1870*, Oxford University Press, Melbourne, 1992. See also Eve Buscombe, *Artists in Early Australia and their Portraits to 1850*, Eureka Research, Sydney, 1979, pp. 70–82, 201.1–215.1.

13 *Portraits of Australian Aborigines Drawn from Nature and on Stone by Charles Rodius*, printed by J.G. Austin, Sydney, 1831–4. Rodius published further portraits of Aborigines in the 1840s.

14 *Australian*, Sydney, 3 February 1834. Rodius described himself as an architect and appears to have been occupied in Paris as an architectural draughtsman.

15 *Bell's Life in Sydney*, 24 March 1849, quoted by Buscombe in *Artists in Early Australia*, p. 78.

16 Richard Wilson also painted Welsh scenes near Dinas Brann (Art Gallery of South Australia).

17 The discussion of landscape painting is indebted to recent reappraisals of landscape painting from the mid-eighteenth to the mid-nineteenth centuries, for example by Ann Bermingham, *Landscape and Ideology: The English Rustic Tradition 1740–1860*, University of California Press, Berkeley, 1986, and U.C. Knoepflmacher and G.B. Tennyson (eds), *Nature and the Victorian Imagination*, University of California Press, Berkeley, 1977.

18 Dr John Lhotsky, 'The State of the Arts in New South Wales and Van Diemen's Land', *Art Union*, London, July 1839, pp. 99–100, republished in Smith, *Documents on Art and Taste in Australia*, pp. 71–6.

AN OUTPOST OF EMPIRE

Sydney in the 1840s

Before mid-century the colony's most notable landscape painter was Conrad Martens (1801–78) who arrived in Australia in April 1835 and had a prolific career as a watercolourist in Sydney up to his death. Martens held empirical description at arm's length, rating imagination higher.

Road across the Blue Mountains with Mount Tomah in the distance c. 1845 (plate 8), is small yet sublime, an epic of exploration and expansion along the lines of William Woolls' visionary 'Australia: A Moral and Descriptive Poem' of 1833:

> Careless of fear the bold surveyor strides
> Thro' boundless woods, or o'er the mountain tides.
> Hill, stream or valley, own alike his sway,
> And in smooth surface form the level way;
> The hills fall prostrate, and the vallies rise,
> High rears the arch above the precipice!
> While with consistent path, for many a mile
> The level causeway soothes the traveller's toil.
> Thus as the Arts stretch forth the fav'ring hand,
> Australia rises both by sea and land.[1]

Woolls' poem expressed imperial aspiration through human endeavour and exploration. In a style combining the balanced rotundity of eighteenth-century Augustan rhyming with the no less majestic naturalism of Wordsworthian verse, the poet dealt with his theme expansively. The purely local awareness that an unknown Australian continent awaited discovery became an image for the birth of a nation through the civilising eye of the conquerer.[2] Ordinary ingredients of road, resting travellers and transport symbolised themes of grandeur: more immediately the crossing of a mountain barrier to rich pastures beyond. Its rhetoric suggested the progress of

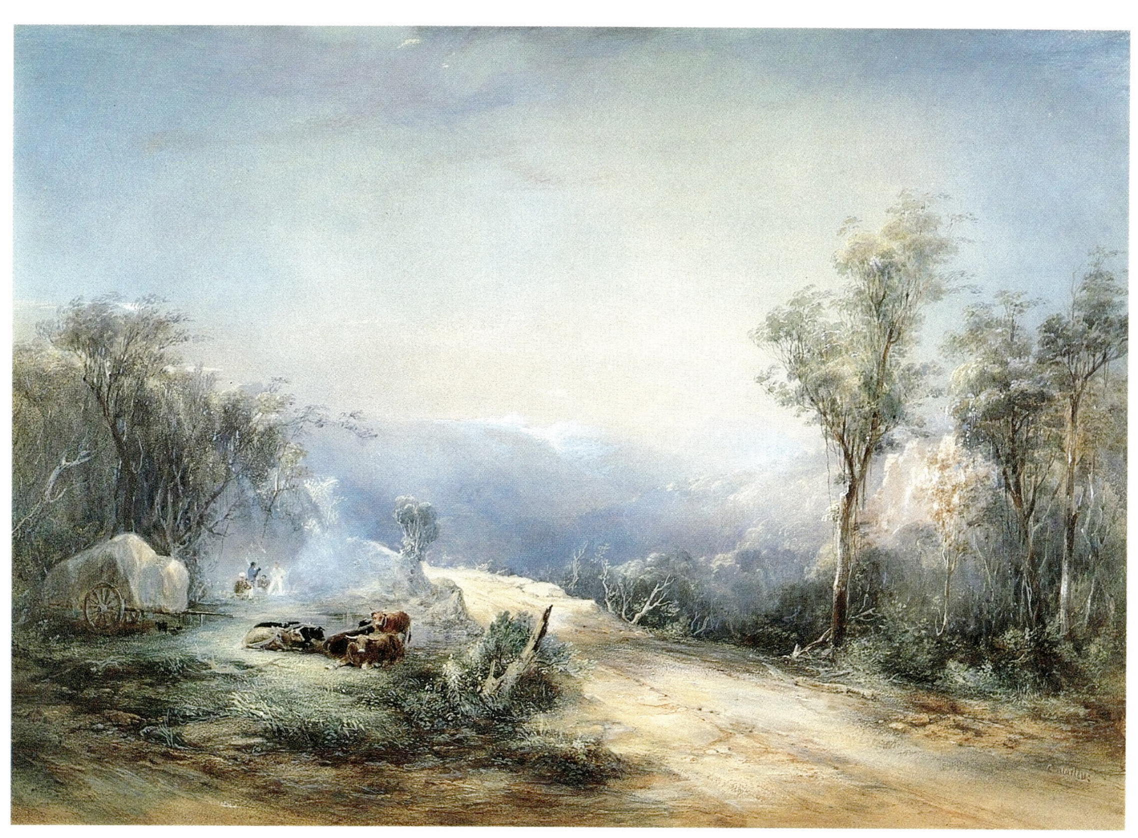

8   Conrad Martens
1801–78
(Road across the Blue Mountains with Mount Tomah in the distance) (1845)
watercolour on paper
45.5 × 65.2 cm

civilisation into the future.

The painter Martens no less than the poet Woolls was aware that his interpretation was rhetorical. 'Knowing what to do in painting may be compared to knowing what to say in writing,' he explained in a lecture delivered to an audience of aspiring Sydney artists in 1856.[3] In other words, while subscribing to his age's faith in nature, Martens felt no contradiction in making the claim that 'it is through the medium of art only that we learn to *see* nature correctly'.[4] Actually to *see* nature was never Martens' ambition. For him, disciplined interpretation (rather than seeing) led to correct perception. The lesson reiterated by him in lectures and conversation was that the culture of versifying, or of drawing and painting, was much more important than seeing. In the 1856 lecture already quoted Martens explained how to work from nature in a controlled way. An outdoor sketch such as originated this watercolour would be produced decisively and rapidly. The artist got a broad effect by drawing a few large accents 'with a firm and unbroken line' and filling the rest of the paper with as many subsidiary forms as seemed suitable: these gave a sense of the place while the sheet of paper set practical limits to the composition. The method, with its strict procedure, guarded the artist against falling into a 'confusion' of undirected visual perceptions. Martens stayed faithful to this one concept of truth in nature, quoting the greatest master of British eighteenth-century painting, Joshua Reynolds, to the effect that fiction was truer than minute imitation and the artist pursuing the goal of simple grandeur 'arrives at his end, even by being unnatural in the confined sense of the word'.

Martens had studied under the English watercolourist Copley Fielding. Another of Fielding's students was the nineteenth-century aesthetician John Ruskin who described the master's disciplined approach to art through recipes: 'Copley Fielding taught me to wash colour smoothly in successive tints, to shade cobalt through pink madder into yellow ochre for skies, to use a broken scraggy touch for the tops of mountains, to represent calm lakes by broad strips of shade with lines of light between them, to produce dark clouds and rain with twelve or twenty successive washes, and to crumble burnt umber with a large brush for foliage and foreground.'[5]

Road across the Blue Mountains . . . is governed by a powerful yet simple opposition of light and shade. Australian skies followed Copley Fielding's recipes for English skies in washes of cobalt, pink madder and yellow ochre. Selective details were brushed in with heavier and darker outlines to indicate their closeness to the viewer compared with forms in the distance which were hazed in a bluish atmosphere. To achieve poetic 'space and grandeur', which in Conrad Martens' view were 'much to be desired, especially in mountain scenery', his mountain view missed out the mid tones, omitted the middle ground, exaggerated the relative scale of forms, and limited the subject to less than half of what could be seen at a glance with one unnaturally fixed eye.[6] In defence of his summary interpretation Martens once more quoted Joshua Reynolds: 'What pretence has the art to claim kindred with poetry, but by its powers over the imagination?'

By contrast with the many artists who studied the geography, flora and fauna of the Australian continent detail by detail, Martens was not at all interested in studying nature in detail. Truthful observation was fine, he said, 'so long as it does not amount to absolute servility'.[7] For him art added poetry to nature (itself inartistic). What Martens himself added may be summed up concisely as a poetic metaphor of natural harmony conspiring with human civilisation.

In Montevideo, South America, in October 1833, Martens had supplanted an ailing Augustus Earle as ship's draughtsman on perhaps the most important scientific expedition of the nineteenth century. For a year he worked with Charles Darwin while that naturalist was in the full flush of his enthusiasm for the theories of the German geographer Alexander von Humbolt. Von Humbolt proposed a universal harmony uniting nature, art and science. 'Nature is a unity in diversity of phenomena; a harmony blending together all created things, however dissimilar in form and attributes; one great whole animated by the breath of life.'[8] So influenced was Martens by the concept of natural harmony that in Australia he portrayed Nature's harmony through what Darwin (following Humbolt) described as her 'most beautiful haze', and without special regard for the other aspect of Humbolt's vision – the expression of natural diversity.

Darwin wrote in his diary, Rio de Janeiro, 1832:

> During the day I was particularly struck with a remark
> of Humbolt's who often alludes to 'the thin vapour
> which, without changing the transparency of the
> air, renders its tints more harmonious, softens its
> effects', etc. This is an appearance which I have never
> observed in the temperate zones. The atmosphere,
> seen through a short space of half or three-quarters
> of a mile, was perfectly lucid, but at a greater distance
> all colours were blended into a most beautiful haze.[9]

Martens was perhaps encouraged in his atmospheric haze by the lack of diversity, some said the monotony, of the Australian geography and flora, and a climate that lacked noticeable seasonal change.

In the already familiar rhetoric of Empire, Martens' positive interpretation was the progress of civilisation in the new world. Upon first sighting Sydney in January 1836, his friend Charles Darwin felt proud of his country's achievement. 'My first feeling was to congratulate myself that I was born an Englishman.' Closer acquaintance brought a more ambivalent response, 'upon seeing more of the town afterwards ... my admiration fell a little', but Darwin's initial response echoed that of many tourists viewing the further outposts of Britain's expanding empire.[10] Some forty-seven years earlier Britain's aspirations for its newest colony had been commemorated by Darwin's grandfather, Erasmus Darwin:

> There shall tall spires, and dome-capt towers ascend,
> And piers and quays their massy structures blend
> While with each breeze approaching vessels glide,
> And northern treasures dance on every tide.

The British Empire, a long time in the building and widely scattered throughout the world, at no stage in its history existed as a sovereign entity. Characteristically, the Crown's control over its diverse colonies was exercised through trade and shipping; trade in the form of markets for British manufacturers was the major reason for Britain's expansion and trade determined the fate of the colonies. The early history of New South Wales and Van Diemen's Land was exceptional in involving direct rule through government. And yet, although an empire style of architecture and city planning was not imposed by centralised authority, the colonial settlements of places as far distant as Vancouver, Karachi, Calcutta, Auckland and Sydney acquired a family resemblance. The reason, again, was trade. For purposes of trade and communication the settlements generally clustered around the seaports, at the mouths of great rivers. The industrial age in the nineteenth century became the age of city building and of stricter town planning. British contemporary models were used for colonial cities around the world. Mid-century in particular saw increasing uniformity as buildings began to spread throughout the colonies and the rate of settlement escalated. Since colonial towns grew through the efforts of people who shared the same functional hierarchy of trade, transport and administration, naturally there were coincidences of architectural style and town planning.

The artist G.E. Peacock (1806–after 1856) celebrated imperial idealism in his tiny souvenirs of 1846: *View of Government House and Fort Macquarie from the Botanical Gardens* (plate 9 c) and *Port Jackson, New South Wales, view up the Harbour near Garden Island* (plate 9 b). His views are of Sydney, however the emphasis is squarely on the imperial theme. More important than Sydney itself in this imperial view-making was Sydney's place in Britain's far-flung Empire, an Empire that embraced Asia, India, Africa and the Antipodes. Peacock's subjects, like Henry Gritten's (1818–73) later *View of Hobart Town from Kangaroo Point* c. 1854 (plate 10), served the larger interpretation and in doing so ignored the less savoury aspects of life in the colonies. In other words he showed something resembling Charles Darwin's first proud view of Sydney but not his revised opinion. As with any number of contemporary tourist mementos from Capetown to Calcutta, the image of a maritime empire was from a visitor's mobile point of view. The view of the port, in its harmony, suggests the safe traffic of shipping, trade and commerce. The settlement of Port Jackson is not depicted for its streets and buildings – which would have had local interest – but as the site of imperial residence: a white palace and a white fort set amidst exotic gardens under a blue sky.

There was a reality behind this pictorial melange. Peacock may have chosen a point of view that put certain

9   G.E. Peacock
1806 – after 1856
A suite of five views
of Sydney (from an
original six)
a   *View of Sydney and
Port Jackson from the
South Head Road,
above Rose Bay* 1846
oil on board
15.5 × 20.8 cm

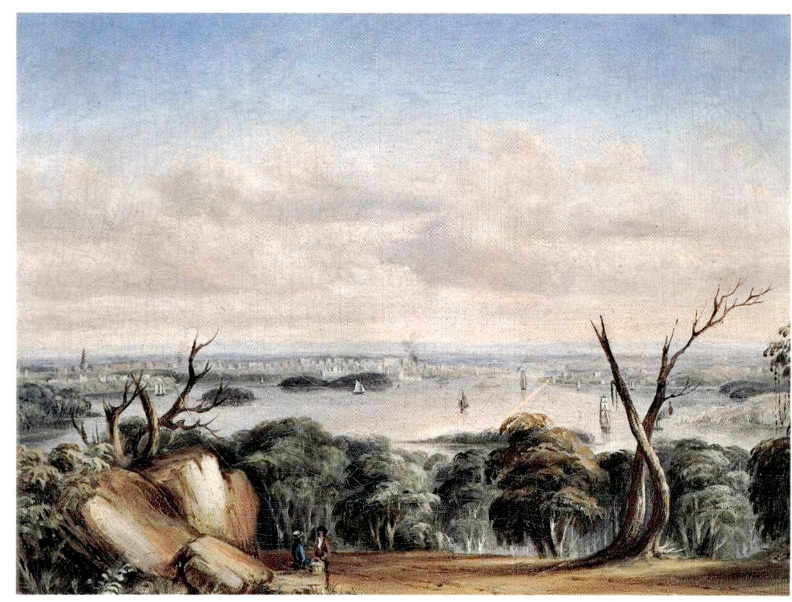

b   *Port Jackson, New
South Wales, view up
the Harbour near
Garden Island* 1846
oil on board
15.5 × 20.8 cm

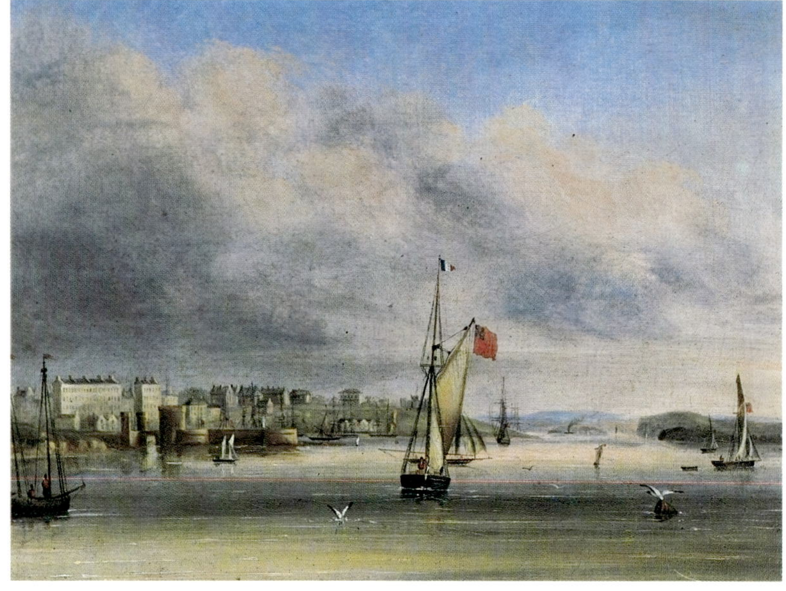

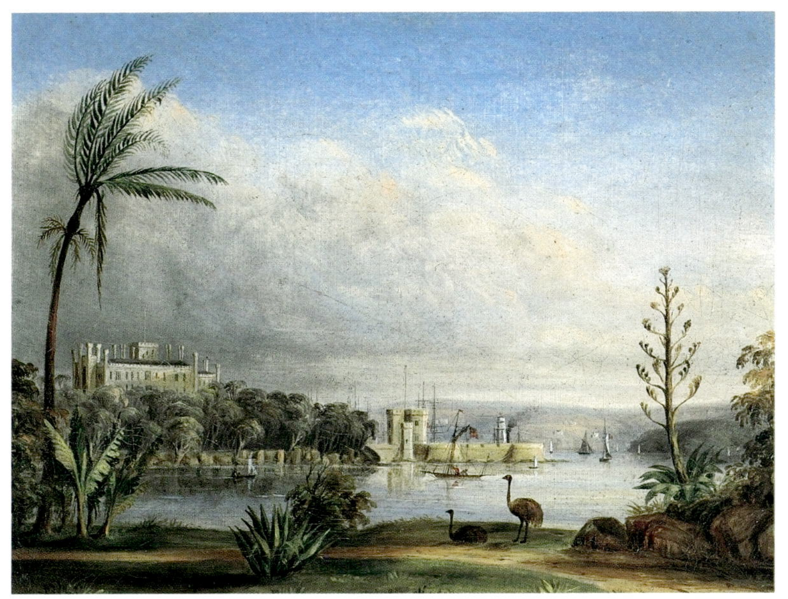

c   *View of Government House and Fort Macquarie from the Botanical Gardens* 1846
oil on board
15.5 × 20.8 cm

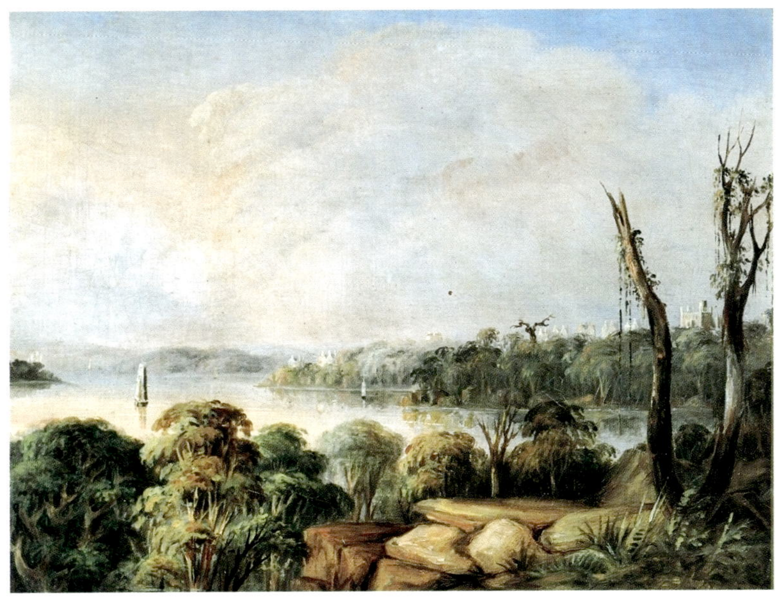

d   *Port Jackson, New South Wales, view East from the back of Government Domain, Woolloomooloo Point, Darling Point and Point Piper in perspective with Clarke's Island* 1846
oil on board
15.5 × 20.8 cm

e *Port Jackson, New
South Wales, North
West view from the
Lady Darling's Point
with Garden Island*
1846
oil on board
15.5 × 20.8 cm

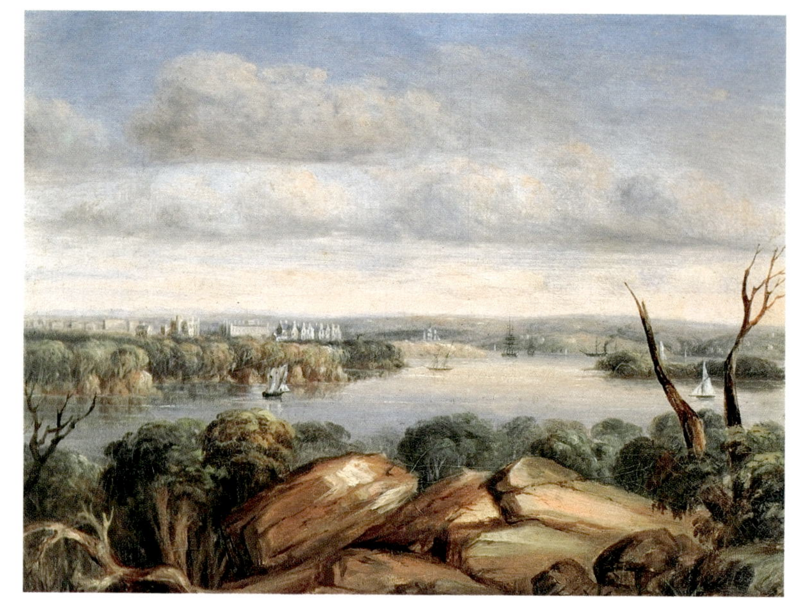

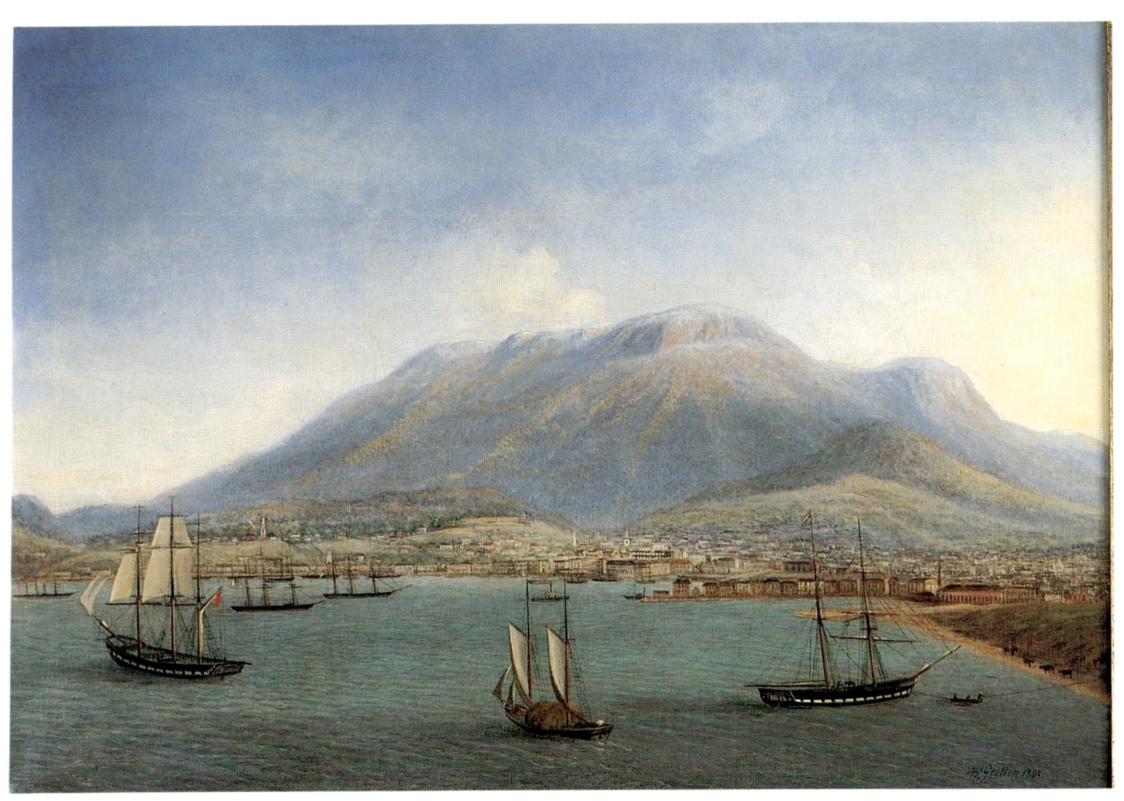

10   Henry Gritten
1818–73
View of Hobart Town from Kangaroo Point (1854)
oil on canvas
36.1 × 53.2 cm

elements in alignment but he was echoing a style that was pursued pragmatically in British government. The Government Houses of the Australian colonies were invariably adjacent to botanic gardens, as if the two went hand in hand. The Sydney Botanical Gardens were planted with palms and joined with the grounds of Government House. The scene was Australian more by the inclusion of two emus than by the style of buildings or the exotic vegetation.

The idea of an architectural style expressive of the British Empire, never previously planned, entered the thoughts of administrators in England in the 1830s. The Government Houses of Sydney (constructed 1837–45), Hobart (1855–8) and Perth (1859–62) were built in the Gothic style. Adelaide's (1839–40) alone was restrained late regency and Melbourne's, not built until the 1870s, vast and superbly Italianate. According to one historian of the British Empire: 'Gothic became the generally established High Victorian idiom, it was eagerly adopted as an imperial medium too. Like an invading army itself, it swept across the British possessions, rearing its pinnacles, turrets and finials wherever the flag flew.'[11] British rule was asserted subtly through this pious and imposing architectural style.

James Morris argues that the mystique of empire came into existence not by conscious plan but gradually, as the machinery was set up to guarantee the safety of British trade. Although the British style of empire was not fully realised until later in the century, from the architecture and town planning of Australian colonies and from images such as these by Peacock, we can see that the major themes were already in existence by the 1840s.[12]

The reality of George Peacock's life was different from the ideal he painted. A young solicitor from an upright, middle-class English family, he committed forgery for which he was sentenced to death in 1836. The sentence having been commuted to transportation, Peacock joined the ranks of convicts in New South Wales. In Sydney he worked under the Government Astronomer James Dunlop and by 1840 was employed as a meteorologist at the Weather Station on South Head. Perhaps his employment studying the weather encouraged him to paint. Certainly his middle-class background explains the elevated sentiments expressed in his art.

1 William Woolls, *Australia: A Moral and Descriptive Poem*, Sydney, 1833, pp. 3-37, quoted in Robert Dixon, *The Course of Empire: Neo-Classic Culture in New South Wales 1788-1860*, Oxford University Press, Melbourne, 1986, p. 79.

2 See Dixon, *The Course of Empire*, pp. 79-119.

3 Conrad Martens' lecture, delivered to the Sydney Sketching Club, Monday 21 July 1856. Reported in the *Sydney Morning Herald* Tuesday 22 July 1856, p. 5, col. 1.

4 ibid.

5 Andrew Sayers, *Drawing in Australia*, Australian National Gallery and Oxford University Press, Melbourne, 1989, p. 47, and Bernard Smith, *European Vision and the South Pacific 1768-1850*, Clarendon Press, Oxford, 1960, p. 233.

6 Conrad Martens' lecture, Monday 21 July 1856.

7 ibid.

8 This quotation is from Alexander von Humbolt, *Cosmos: A Sketch of a Physical Description of the Universe*, (trans. E. C. Otte), 2 vols, London, Henry G Bohm, 1849, vol. 1, pp. 1-24. Von Humbolt's enormous reputation was achieved before 1810 and his philosophy was known from various writings, for example Darwin owned von Humbolt's *Personal Narrative* of his travels in South America (published 1814-19).

9 Charles Darwin, diary, Rio de Janeiro, 1852, quoted in R.D. Keyes, *The Beagle Record*, Cambridge, 1979. See Stephen Jay Gould, 'Church, Humbolt and Darwin: The Tension and Harmony of Art and Science', in F. Kelly, S.J. Gould, J.A. Ryan and D. Rindge, *Frederick Edwin Church*, National Gallery of Art, Washington, 1989. For an earlier authoritative discussion both of the effect of Humbolt's theories on Australian art, and of the art of Conrad Martens, see Bernard Smith, *European Vision and the South Pacific 1768-1850*, Clarendon Press, Oxford, 1960. For an alternative reason for Conrad Martens' interest in atmospheric conditions see Tim Bonyhady, *Images in Opposition*, Oxford University Press, Melbourne, 1985, pp. 92-3.

10 Quoted in James Morris, *Heaven's Command: An Imperial Progress*, Penguin, London, 1979, ch. 7, p. 138.

11 Jan Morris, 'In Quest of the Imperial Style', in *Architecture of the British Empire*, Robert Fermor-Hesketh (ed.), Weidenfeld and Nicolson, London, 1986, p. 25.

12 Morris, *Heaven's Command: An Imperial Progress*.

THE CIVILISED COLONIES

The Mid-Nineteenth Century

Our own age and that of the High Victorians are in surprising agreement about what makes a good story. Both ages have relished a detailed and lively exposition. Both have preferred what is topical, caricatured and observed from that which is personal. Artists of the mid-nineteenth century pictured colonial life in set pieces. More than a century later television soap operas employ the same rhetoric.

A television series documenting Australian history might well introduce the second stage of colonisation with scenes and sounds of domestic life. Carts rattling over cobbled streets, the clink of glasses and voices raised in argument in a pub, the sound of hobble chains, the distant bark of a dog, the thump of an axe, the swish of skirts on a floor. The scene would flit from crinolined children in ferny gardens (children seen and not heard) to an army of young men in moleskins wielding pickaxes at the busy goldfields. From stately city mansions the camera would pass to a crudely constructed slab hut. We would be shown a shepherd on an outback run, tending a campfire at night. There would be images of bushfire, flood, a child lost in the bush. According to this eager perception the Australian colonies, during the first decades of Queen Victoria's reign, were teeming with life and a character all their own.

The exercise of mediating an earlier visual expression into the sound and motion of our own times proves remarkably easy. The similarity is not merely the obsession with types: typical sounds, typical scenes, typical stories. Nor is the likeness simply an extroverted liking for action and a crowded narrative. A more serious connection exists in the voyeurism of both ages. We are, as the Victorians were, eager for entertainment and reluctant for personal involvement.

During the middle years of the century, art in the

colonies concerned itself more with subjects of a domestic nature, looking inward upon life as it was lived in Australia as well as continuing the outward-looking, earlier themes of exploration, discovery, natural science and empire. There were good reasons for the change. The audience at home in Britain had been complemented by a growing audience in the colonies. The question that arises is whether the emergence of domestic imagery – the painting of modern life – was merely a reflection of a contemporary shift in European taste. The industrial revolution brought about a change in European art from patrician subjects and classical references, which served a small aristocratic audience, to an art that was descriptive, literary and modern, which served an expanding middle class. Or are we to think of this period in Australian art as reflecting a second stage within the history of a new country: the stage of social consolidation? The question remains valid despite the impossibility of neatly separating the history of colonial art from developments in the art and social life of Great Britain. Australia's history marched in time with the industrial revolution in Europe, while at the same time it was a small colony – or rather a group of colonies – on the other side of the world. Australia's distance from Europe, the exigencies of pioneering, the social changes brought about by the industrial revolution, all worked upon colonial society and colonial art.

As well as portraits of colonists, the collection includes images dealing explicitly with the social mores of colonial life at mid-century. There is a picture of life in a smart Sydney terrace home and another of conviviality in the taverns of the goldfields. We experience the sad fate of one family (a private tragedy) and the dramatic misfortune of a troupe of actors (public tragedy). The styles of these paintings indicate what sort of story is being told. Each painting cues the viewer's appropriate response.

In 1851 William Nicholas (c.1807–54) painted a small, pretty watercolour portrait, *Masters William, Arthur and Miss Augusta Campbell* (plate 11). It was painted at the children's home, or else at the artist's studio where there was a room set aside for dressing-up in one's elaborate best clothes.[1] An affecting story surrounds the image. The young parents, William and Martha Campbell, commissioned the portrait out of the usual parental feelings of possessive pride in their beautiful, healthy children. Like modern parents commissioning a portrait photograph or family video, they wanted a memento of a certain stage in their family's childhood, to be cherished in future years. William Campbell, a clerk with the Colonial Crown Solicitor's Office in Sydney, had been born in Antrim, Ireland, in 1819 or 1820. His wife Martha was the daughter of one of the first free settlers, William Bear, who had come out to the colony on the *Buffalo* in 1799. The couple married in 1845 and settled into one of the houses designed by James Hume at Fitzroy Terrace, 6–18 Pitt Street, Redfern. It was a smart address in a respectable neighbourhood. Their neighbours in the terrace were Edward Lotze, mercantile clerk, Henry Morgan, gentleman and agent, Captain R. T. Furlong, J.P., Mrs Henry McDermott and Andrew Melville, mercantile clerk.[2] But in June 1852, a year after the children's portraits were painted, this healthy, happy family was destroyed when first William died, and the following day his wife. The cause of their deaths (natural, unnatural?) was not explained in the newspaper announcements.[3] William and Martha left four orphans, the eldest, William, but six years old, and the youngest a baby. This Dickensian story of domestic tragedy had its epilogue in the fates of the children. The baby, Alfred, died six months after his parents, in December 1852. We know nothing of Arthur's fate. William died at sea. Augusta alone lived to marry and have three children. As fate would have it, Nicholas' tranquil portrait in a sun-filled room showed the family at the highest point of its fortune.

The boys, dressed in tartan, stand either side of their young sister Augusta, who sits, bowered in frills, on a purple cushion on a squat regency stool: the lion-clawed legs of this stool, bizarrely anthropomorphic, are the only agitated imagery in the picture. Nicholas has merely sketched in the usual *conversazione* (story picture) in an image of fraternal love. The older boy supports his sister at the shoulder, while Arthur offers her a sprig of silvery leaves – there is a discarded sprig of leaves on the pink carpet.

The *conversazione* tradition of telling a small story in such group portraits of children was in decline with the advent of photography. Although in 1851 the technology of the camera was in its infancy, Nicholas had already responded to the change. (He may have experimented with the

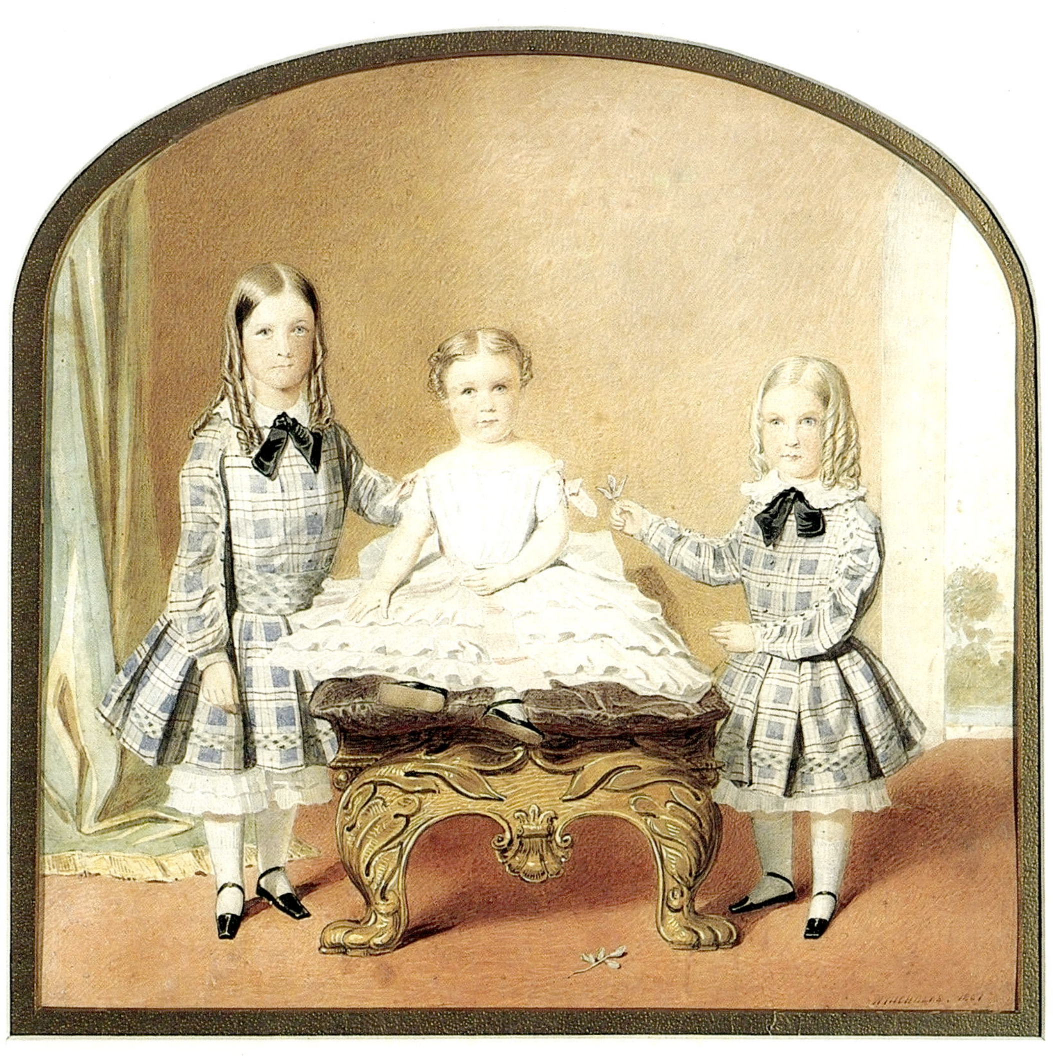

11   William Nicholas
c. 1807–54
Masters William, Arthur and Miss Augusta Campbell 1851
watercolour on paper
26.0 × 27.5 cm (with arched top)

process: certainly his friend, the painter John Rae, explored photography around this time.) In painting the Campbell children the artist was more interested in describing their momentary facial expressions – self-conscious and serious – than in telling a coherent story. Within a few years the sort of image Nicholas painted here of the Campbell family would be produced by photography, but with some things gone from the tradition. A truer likeness would be captured but there would be a loss of poetry.

From mid-century, photography took over the bulk of commissions for portraiture, streetscapes and tourist views, its cheapness, ease and abundance swamping the handmade product. However, until the early twentieth century, photography was not capable of producing the cinematic effects of narrative drama, excitement and pace, or the poetic overtones that were the traditional province of story painting.

Portrait painting offered what frozen-faced photography did not achieve for some decades: an air of naturalness and a reading of character. In Sydney in the 1850s, Charles Rodius, his living threatened by photography, 'respectfully acquainted the public' by newspaper advertisement that, as well as expressing a likeness, he could avoid 'the stiffness which detracts so much from correct expression' in photography.[4]

In Victoria, an 1856 pair of portraits (plates 12 and 13) of the Geelong chemist Charles Kernot and his wife Mary by Robert Dowling (1827–86) were everything mid-century taste asked for. Though quite small, these oil paintings on card are sombrely beautiful, ample in modelling and composition, and photographically realistic. By comparison with Charles Rodius, who made portraits of a young Aboriginal husband and wife twenty years earlier, rendering his subjects in a frank style which stripped most of their social ambience, Dowling found his interpretation in the expression of precisely the social refinement of his sitters. Dowling showed Charles Kernot amused and in command of himself and his circumstances, and Mary as unaffected yet possessing dignity and refinement. Hands, often the weakest aspect of unskilled portraiture, under Dowling's sensitive treatment became an articulate feature as important to the total expression of character as the faces. The conventional triangular composition of waist-length portraiture – the apex at the

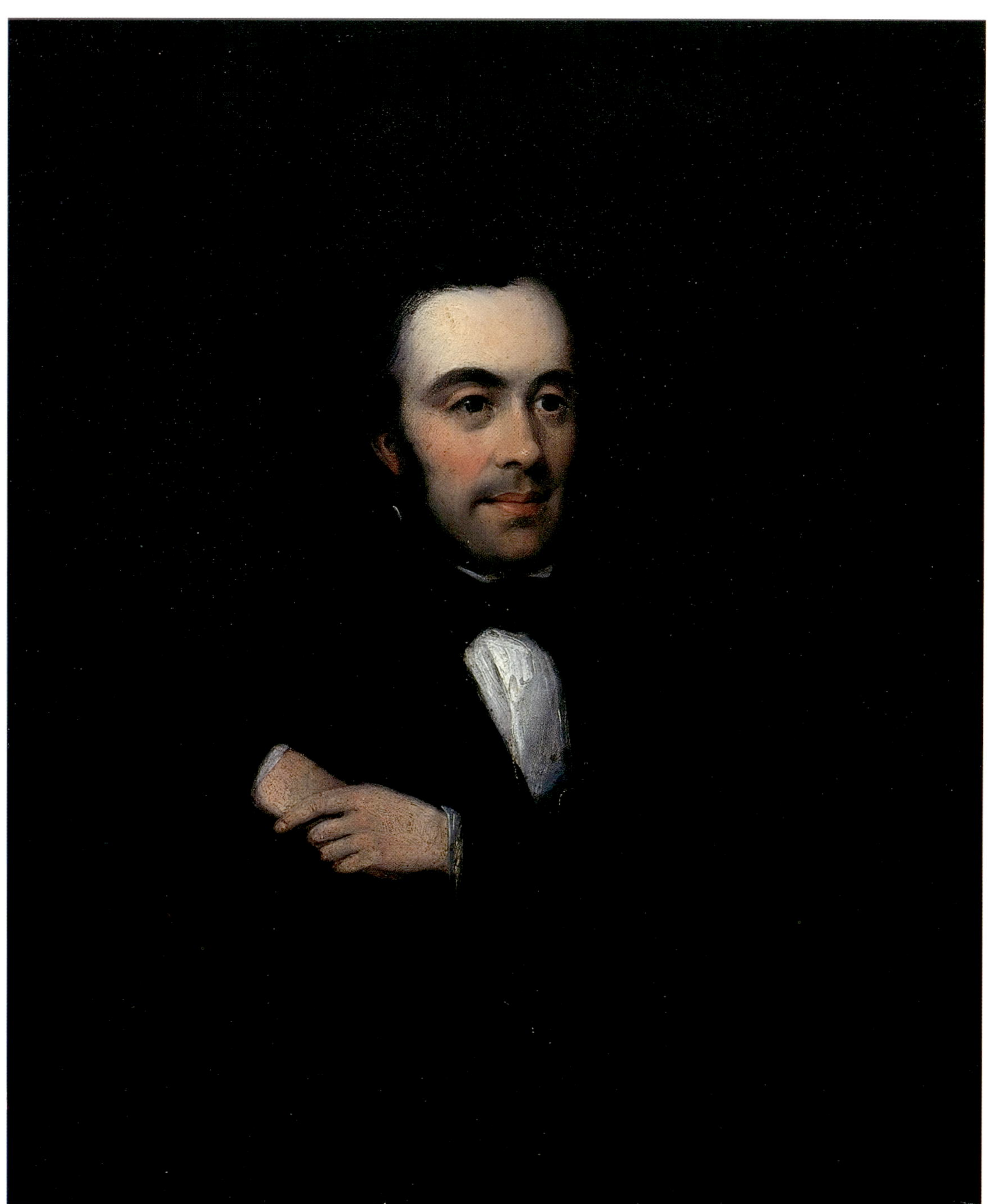

12   Robert Dowling
1827–86
Charles Kernot 1856
oil on board
31.0 × 25.0 cm

head and the base line at hand or waist level – was subtly varied from one portrait to the other. One of Charles' arms rests on a high piece of furniture, lifting the compositional accents of face and hands to the centre of the image. Mary's arms slope more gradually and terminate in the graceful gesture of her hands near the bottom of the canvas. By this simple means Dowling portrayed Charles as the active, Mary as the self-contained, one of the married pair.

The portraits were painted in Geelong, when Robert Dowling stayed there on the way to visit his brother in the Western District of Victoria. The Kernots were friends, Nonconformists like the Tasmanian Dowlings, and shared the same Fabian interests in a range of social and intellectual pursuits. Charles Kernot's sons played a role in the establishment of the University of Melbourne.

Robert Dowling had been brought up in the faith of his father, the Reverend Henry Dowling, a Baptist minister who had brought his family to Van Diemen's Land in 1834 and to Launceston from 1840. He actively espoused the causes of civil and religious liberty, the establishment of an infant school and the cessation of transportation. Among Henry's friends was John West, historian, anti-transportationist and an aesthetic mentor for young Robert. The would-be artist listened to West propound the Ruskinian view of art as truthful, naturalistic and an active moral force for good. In Australia as a young man, and later in England, Dowling produced significant subject paintings of Australian Aborigines.

Robert Dowling and his family left for England in 1857 – the year after he painted the Kernot portraits. Aided in his ambition to become a major painter by a subscription from colonial well-wishers, he settled in London and enrolled at Leigh's Academy in Newman Street. His London career was watched from Australia and he played to this market while also flattering the growing awareness of Empire in England.[5]

The history of nineteenth-century western art is often told as if the conditions for art were the same everywhere. In fact we have to imagine in mid-century Australia the opposite condition for subject painting from that which prevailed in France. What happened in the art of France depended upon a unique social system. There, state patronage and a state bureaucracy ruled the training,

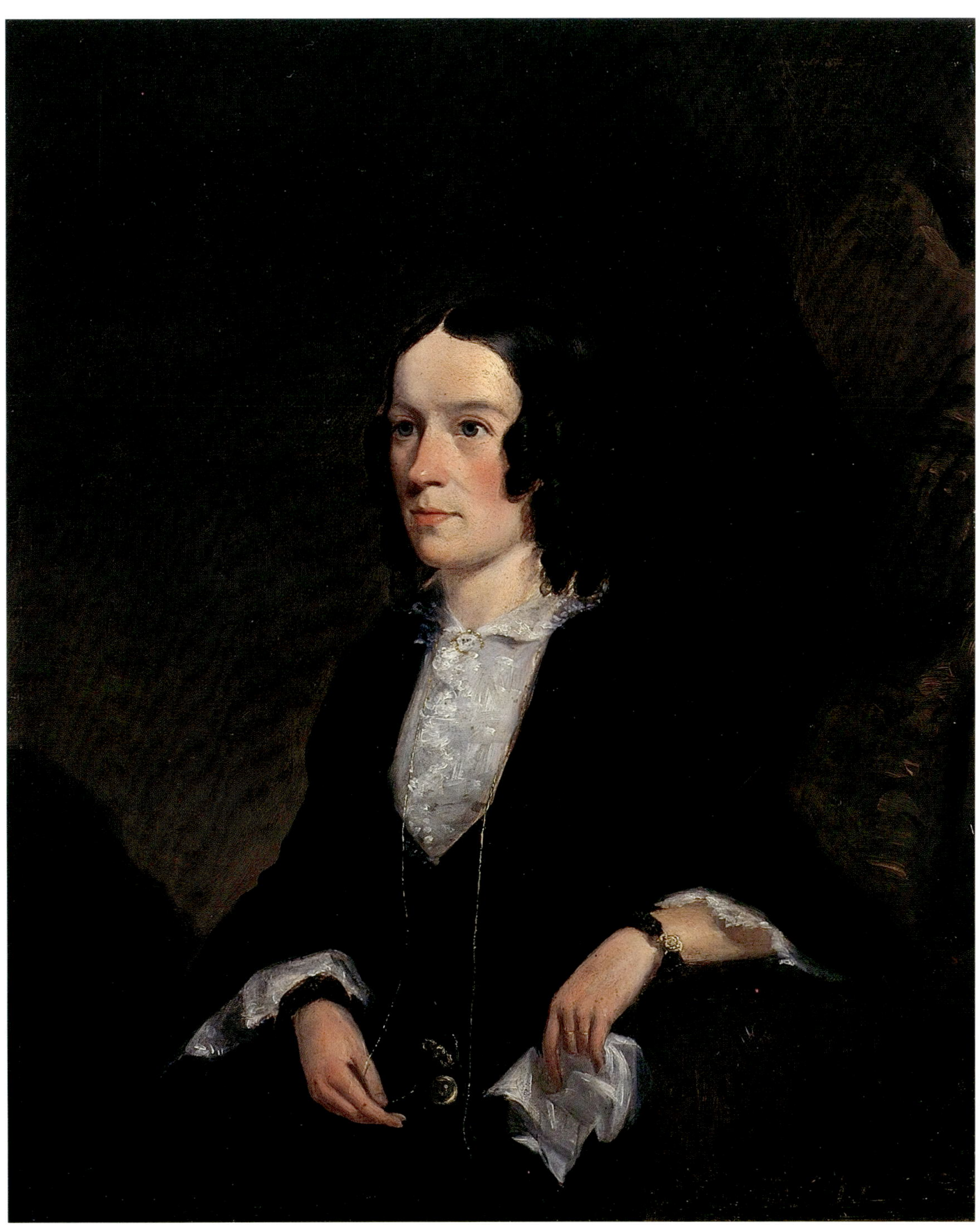

13   Robert Dowling
1827–86
Mary Kernot 1856
oil on board
30.0 × 25.0 cm

exhibition and finances of art. The system was effective, almost the only way of marketing art, until the impressionists in the 1880s discovered an alternative middle-class audience for their modern-life subjects. Because the French system for training artists and exhibiting art was so very constricted, the impressionists in the 1860s and 1870s could appear (and were) revolutionary. Patronage in Britain and Germany was more complex, already influenced by the middle classes more than a century before. Subjects of a comparable modernity to those steam trains, canals and holiday scenes that provoked an artistic explosion in Paris in the 1860s were already hanging, a small minority, in the Royal Academy decades earlier. Australia's story is different again.

In Australia there was never a time when the landscape and scenes of modern life were not painted and, in fact, favoured. Australia's introduction to art had been under the heading of natural science and ethnography, which required a pictorial record of the manners and customs of the people and the architecture, costumes, flora and fauna of the country. Until the population grew large enough and there was sufficient wealth, the various local institutions of art could not flourish. From the 1820s onwards attempts were made to establish art schools, galleries and exhibition venues, all of which came to nothing until after mid-century. New South Wales, settled in 1788, did not support a public art gallery until 1874. The Sydney Mechanics School of Art began in 1843. The New South Wales Academy of Art held its first exhibition in 1872 and was succeeded in 1880 by the Art Society of New South Wales. On the other hand Victoria, though not colonised until 1835 and not declared a separate colony until 1851, benefited from the massive influx of wealth and immigration to the goldfields in the 1850s. The National Gallery of Victoria was established in 1861. The National Gallery of Victoria School was opened in 1870. Mechanics institutes were opened in Victorian towns in the early years of the colony, and technical schools held courses in art from the 1860s. The Victorian Society of Fine Arts held its first exhibition in 1857, the Victorian Academy of Art was launched in 1870 and gave way to the Victorian Artists' Society in 1888.

Those same gold rushes which brought a great surge of wealth and immigration to Victoria in the 1850s were

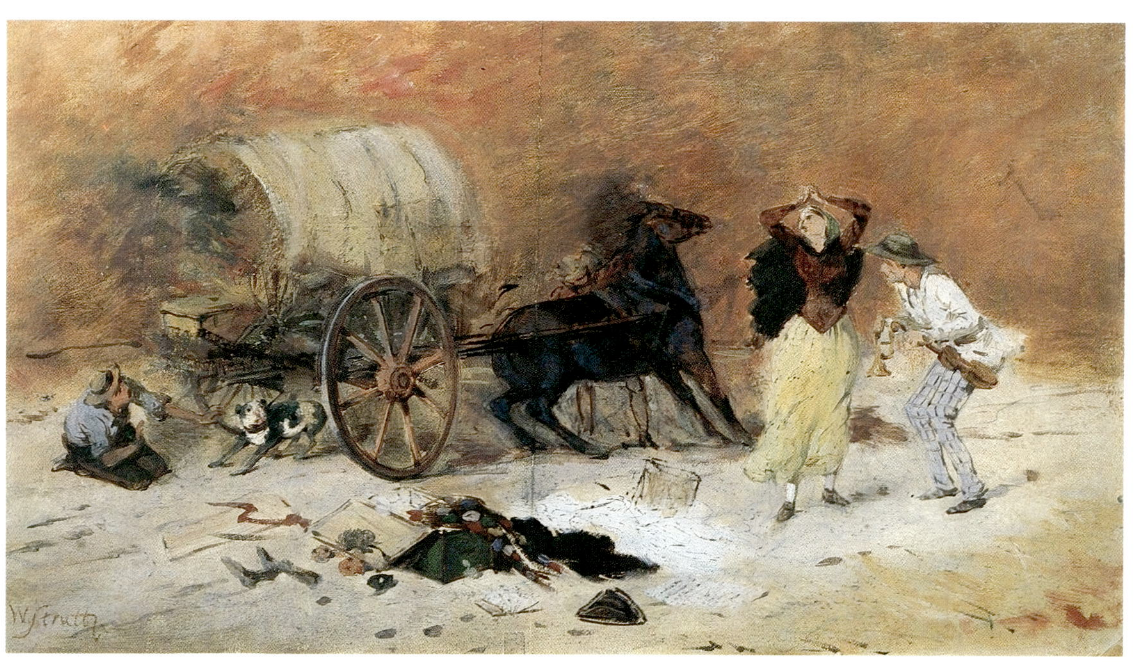

14   William Strutt
1825–1915
The actor's cart, Black Thursday, February 6th 1851 (1863)
oil on paper
22.1 × 39.2 cm

also the cause of an influx of professionally trained English and European artists into Victoria at that time. Culturally, the new colony of Victoria leapt ahead of New South Wales, to a level of sophistication not matched by the older colony until the 1920s.

The artist William Strutt (1825–1915) was one of the victims of gold fever. Arriving in Melbourne in July 1850, he immediately found employment with a new magazine, the *Illustrated Australian Magazine*, published by the Ham brothers. A year later he joined the first gold rushes to Ballarat, failed to succeed, and within a couple of months was back again in Melbourne, working as an illustrator for Thomas Ham before branching out on his own. He undertook commissions for oil portraits, official as well as private. He made drawings of the first Victorian Parliament on 13 November 1851, and of subsequent opening ceremonies, and sketched the Colonial Militia and the departure of the Burke and Wills expedition in 1860. These were made in response to demand but Strutt also had an eye to their future use as the source imagery for major paintings about the founding years of the colony. As a subsidiary source of information for these projected paintings he kept a journal filled with documentary information. But although, both as portraitist and modern history painter, he quickly established a unique reputation, and through the 1850s was the only painter of any consequence within a high art tradition in Melbourne, he did not find a backing in the colony for the ambitious images he wanted to produce. Strutt hoped for better things. In 1862 he sailed for England and almost immediately began working on the heroic Australian history painting *Black Thursday, February 6th, 1851* (completed 1864).

Among his preparatory oil sketches of incidents during the famous fires of 1851 was *The actor's cart, Black Thursday, February 6th 1851* (plate 14). This small oil was not painted in Australia but back in England c. 1863, the year before completing the big picture. It was based on a small watercolour drawing of the subject.[6] Strutt, who had been trained at the Ecole des Beaux Arts to think in terms of suitable subjects for modern history paintings, seems to have immediately recognised the pictorial significance of the fires.

Melbourne certainly participated in the drama of that

1851 Black Thursday, as bushfires flared over the southern half of the state of Victoria between Barwon Heads, near Melbourne, and Mount Gambier, over the South Australian border. Working at Ham's that day, Strutt and the others had to stop work, so dark was the sky. Smoke thick with ashes and burning debris hung over the city. The excitement was intense as people gathered in the streets, watching the sky and waiting for news. In the following Tuesday's paper Strutt read about a troupe of actors caught in the fire, and recounted the story in his journal:

> A company of travelling actors and an actress en route for Sydney, having a cart filled with necessary paraphernalia of their avocation, which they intended following at the various towns upon the journey, became enveloped in the flames on the Big Hill [Pretty Sally Hill, near Kilmore, 48 kilometres north of Melbourne] and the whole of their wardrobe and effects were destroyed, the only articles snatched from the burning being a cornopean [cornet] and violin.[7]

Tragi-comedy and slapstick appealed to the artist. The image has its serious side yet there is humour too, in the actress' theatrical gesture of despair, the actor clutching violin and cornet and the driver coaxing a dog from under the burning cart. (Strutt repeated the figure of the gesticulating actress in *Black Thursday* where her extravagant gesture is in keeping with the intensely theatrical character of the historical drama.)

Actors at the time were popularly thought of as frivolous and slightly risque figures, whose function in life was decorative rather than serious. The insignificant troupes of performers who toured the goldfields and traipsed from town to town did not even have the advantage of being respected for their professional skill, unlike those theatrical companies which came to the colony on the wings of Culture. In choosing actors as his protagonists Strutt recognised that whereas an ordinary settler caught in the bushfire would apppeal to sentiments of pathos, an actor in the same plight was fair game for half-humorous treatment. We see a similar ribald treatment of music-hall culture in S.T. Gill's watercolour *Night concert, Main*

Road, Ballarat c. 1854 (plate 15).

S.T. Gill (1819-80) was another sort of artist from Strutt, whose one colonial rival for an urbane and knowledgeable style was the sculptor Charles Summers. Strutt could regard his achievement as greater than that of the painters Gilfillan, Marshall Claxton, and Chester Earles, who attempted a similar mode. But S.T. Gill had an altogether different métier. He specialised in journalistic subjects, exploration and adventure in the colonies, the hurly-burly of the goldfields, humorous scenes of low-life and modest, honest depictions of the Australian landscape. In this genre, a clear description and entertainment mattered more than the flourishes of a high style. Gill's pictorial style, of simple outlines and flat colours, as well as his topical subjects, fitted within a robust English pictorial tradition that went back through George Cruikshank, James Gillray and Thomas Rowlandson to William Hogarth.

Genre painting in Queen Victoria's time was synonymous with morality. The first message of a storytelling picture was its type of morality, whether elevated, poetic (emotional, morally evasive), broad (suited to masculine tastes), or merely vulgar. Gill's vulgar but attractive image of a sly grog shanty in Main Road, Ballarat, compares with Louisa Meredith's prayerful revulsion from the dirty sights of the same street a year later. Ballarat was, she said, 'more irredeemably hideous than the blackest mining village in any English coal or iron district'. Weary of slipping in the mud of the main road, she waited for her husband at one of the shops. For a woman of her middle-class upbringing to be loitering in the main street of the dirty, primitive township would be an impropriety: it was imperative to be occupied and so she filled in the time by sketching the buildings across the street. The subject taxed her as an artist, more particularly as a woman artist whose given function was to render pleasant subjects in gentle watercolour or orderly pencil, however Louisa Meredith 'temporarily overcame her revulsion, and her picture softens the prayer she recorded about Ballarat in her book *Over the Straits* – "May I never look upon the like again!"'[8]

The symbol of mobility and meeting place for all levels of colonial society was the public house, such as the one Gill painted in Ballarat. Public houses – pubs – were

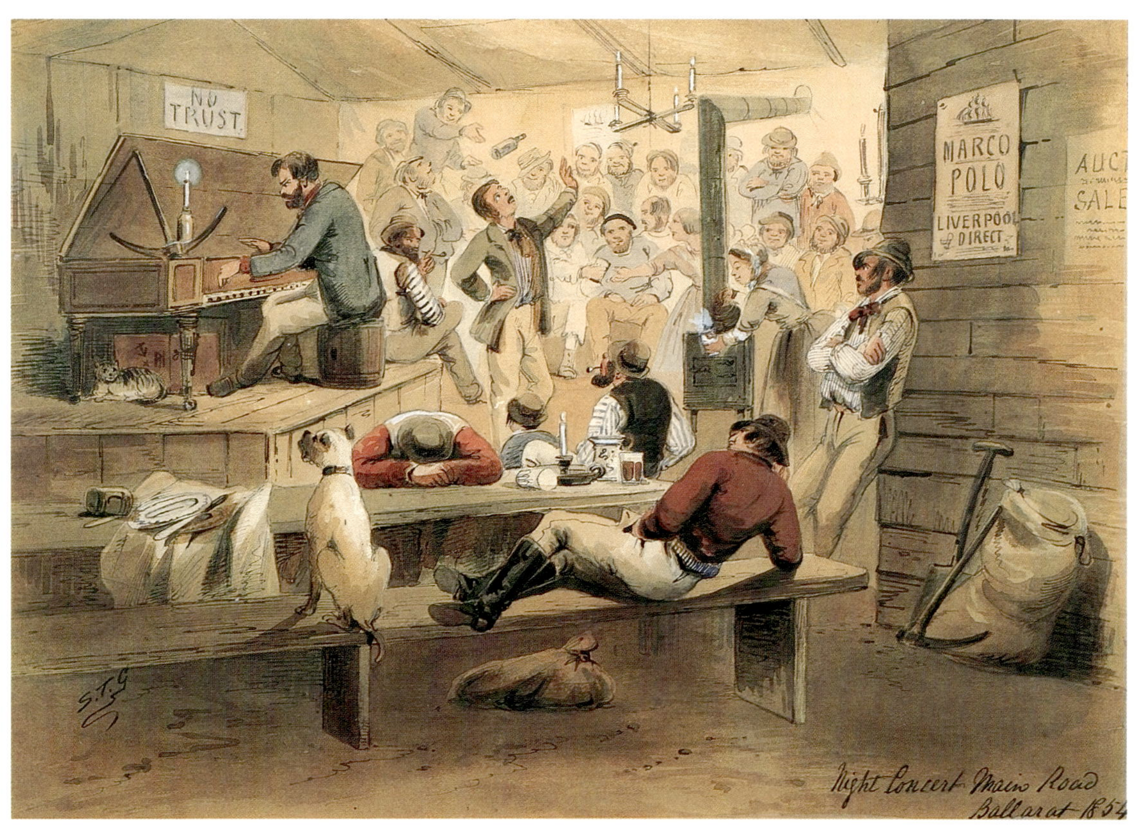

15   S.T. Gill
1819–80
Night concert, Main Road, Ballarat (1854)
watercolour on paper
26.5 × 37.0 cm

necessary for the many travellers in the mobile society that was Australia in the mid-nineteenth century.[9] Pubs provided food, drink, shelter, warmth, light, lavatories, sometimes a bed and, above all, human company for an itinerant population. 'Even those with a home met in the public houses to talk, sing, dance, dice, play cards and plan most of the other activities of common life in the colonies.'[10]

Those all-round theatres of entertainment, the public houses, were the stage for Australia's strolling players. The only upright observer of Gill's *Night concert* is a dog at centre image. Everyone else sprawls, slouches, turns a back or hurls a bottle in response to the singer–actor whose pose is as histrionic as that of the actress in Strutt's bushfire painting. Part of Gill's humour may be directed at the diggers, whose boorish style of behaviour was as carefully cultivated, in its way, as the singer's histrionics. Within the image every detail was a cue for a well-trained response from Gill's colonial patrons. Accordingly there was meaning in the message 'no trust' and in its positioning above a lighted candle; the local aesthetic idiom was announced in the piano-lid supported by a miner's pick; and the gamble for wealth through gold was advertised in two posters in the foreground, one for an auction and the other for a luxurious return to England on board the clipper *Marco Polo*. In the miners' eyes the sumptuous *Marco Polo*, 'the wonder of the age', was synonymous with a mission achieved and a happy departure from the squalor of the diggings to the respectability of Home.[11]

Emigration is the sub-plot of all Australian history. From the outset of settlement until more than half a century later many of the emigrant colonists did not expect to stay. This would be true, for example, of the artists Gould, Nicholas, Strutt and Gill, whose paintings are the subject of this chapter. The gold rushes of the 1850s brought a sudden new influx of short-term immigrants. The surge in population was enormous. Between 1838 and 1854 the colony of Victoria grew from 6000 people to 244 000. The discomforts of coping with their arrival, and their frontier style of behaviour, had the contrary effect of confirming older settlers in their attachment to the new country. Adventurers of the sort Charles Dickens created in the quaint character of Mr

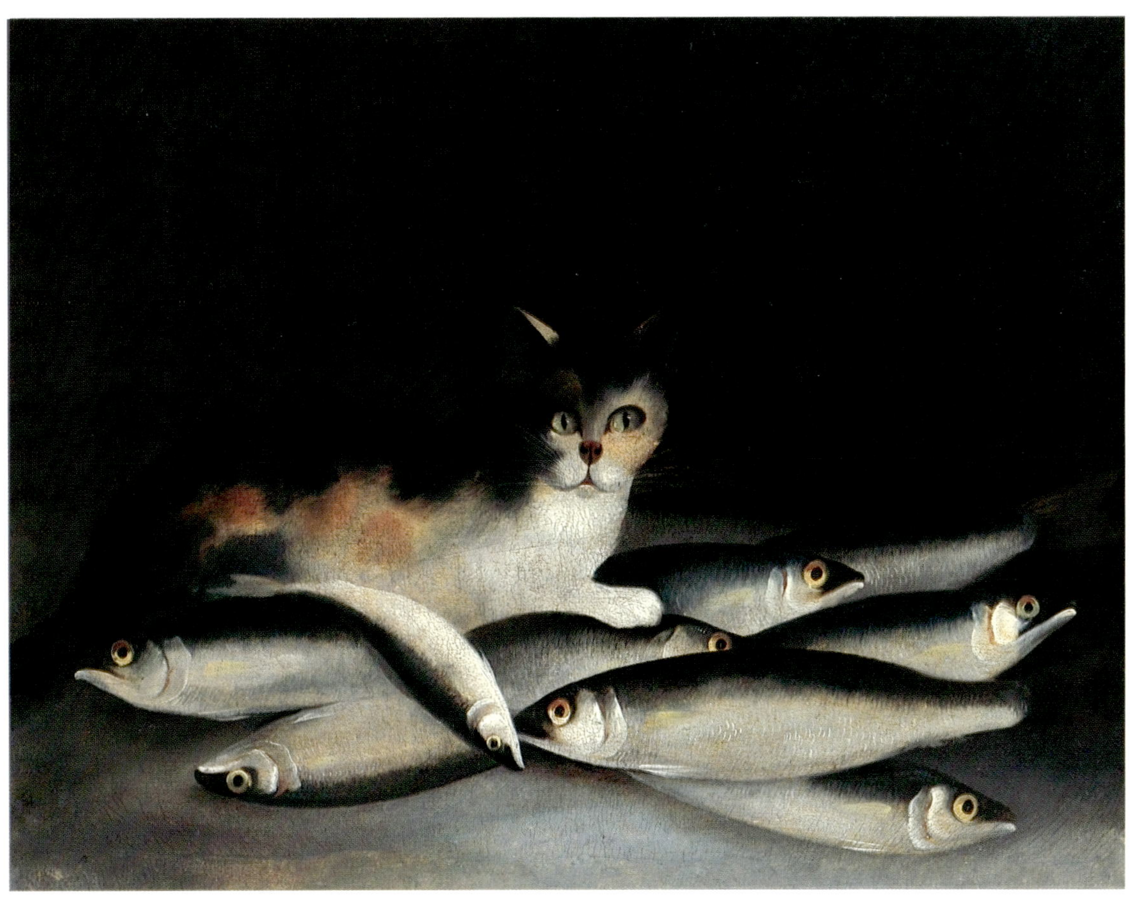

16 W.B. Gould
1803–53
(Still life: cat and fish) 1849
oil on canvas laid down on wood panel
41.5 × 61.0 cm

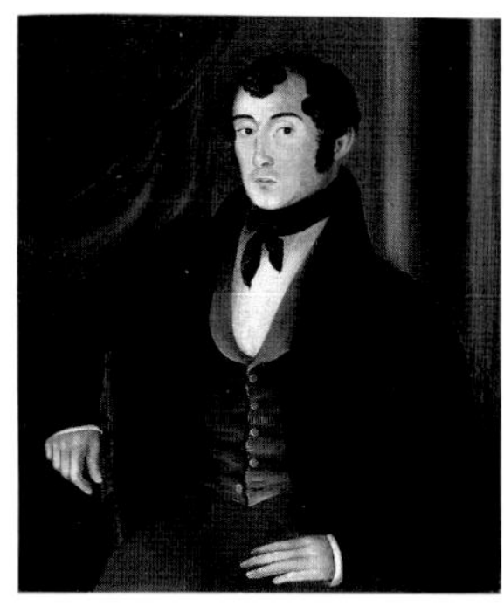

Self portrait of convict artist W.B. Gould painted in 1838.

Collection: Tasmanian Museum and Art Gallery

Micawber – who wanted to make a fortune to take home – did not see themselves, as they have subsequently appeared, as the founding fathers of a new country. There was hostility from the squatters, who deplored the snatch and grab methods of the diggers. Castigating the seekers after gold as mere transients out to get what they could regardless of the public good, the older settlers began to use the rhetoric and to feel the possessive emotion of a social patriarchy. And so the colony, mid-century, had cross-currents of frontier life and cultural consolidation.

Whereas Gill painted scenes of public houses, we are told on the other hand that William Buelow Gould (1803–53), a convict artist 'of very bad character' and 'a very drunken and dangerous person', often painted in the public house.[12] To produce the work-in-kind that would pay for his large consumption of grog and for his gambling debts, hotel keepers resorted to locking up the artist with paint and canvas (or wood panel) until he met his obligations.[13] It has been suggested that this was how, and why, he produced pictures for the walls of pub parlours.

An appropriate subject would be the cat and fish of *Still life, cat and fish* 1849 (plate 16). Gould had a repertoire of such still-life motifs – fish, cockfights, dead game, fruit and flowers – which he rendered in an attractive provincial style. In London he had taken lessons from William Mulready, a Royal Academician who had an interest in seventeenth-century Dutch painting. In Tasmania during the early 1830s Gould had employment for a while with Dr de Little at Macquarie Harbour on the wild west coast, making natural history drawings of fish and other marine life. He capitalised on that research later in painting decorative images of Tasmanian fish, such as the red bait in this work. Not just fish, but botanical specimens, native birds, landscapes and caricatures were part of his subject matter. He found other employment painting devices on carriages, and working as a scene-painter.

By the 1860s the journalistic subjects and style specialised in by S.T. Gill had become the particular province of newspaper and magazine illustration. Their descendants in our own time are the news stories and social documentaries of television. Strutt's rhetorical manner, of an altogether more polite tradition, flourished in Australian literature more than the visual arts, but had its issue in the affecting and pathetic scenes of contemporary Australian history that were painted in the 1880s by George Folingsby's students at the Melbourne National Gallery School. It would be appropriate to place the national themes of the 1890s – Tom Roberts' *The Breakaway* and *Bailed Up* and Streeton's *Fire's On* – within the Australian tradition of great paintings of modern life.

1 Patricia R. McDonald and Barry Pearce, *The Artist and the Patron: Aspects of Colonial Art in New South Wales*, Art Gallery of New South Wales, Sydney, 1988, pp. 45, 70. Nicholas visited the home of one patron to paint likenesses of her children (letter by Mrs Sarah Wentworth), and there is a reference to the artist having a room at his studio for his sitters to use when changing costume (*Sydney Morning Herald*, 6 September 1842, p. 1.)
2 Kevin Fahy, 'Fitzroy Terrace, 6–18 Pitt Street, Redfern, NSW', in *Australiana*, vol. 12, no. 1, February 1990, pp. 9–13.
3 *Sydney Morning Herald Births, Deaths and Marriages Index* (information from Richard Neville). For the children see the family tree of James and Elizabeth Bean.
4 *Bell's Life in Australia*, Sydney, 14 April 1855.
5 See John Jones, entry on Robert Dowling, in Joan Kerr (ed.), *The Dictionary of Australian Artists*.
6 *The actor's cart*, watercolour, 21.0 x 38.7 cm, Dixson Library, Sydney.
7 George Mackaness (ed.), 'The Australian Journal of William Strutt ARA 1850–1862', *Australian Historical Monographs*, vol. xvi (part one of two), Dubbo, 1958, pp. 19–21; *Argus*, Melbourne, 11 February 1851, p. 2.
8 This paragraph is indebted to Weston Bate, *Lucky City: The First Generation at Ballarat 1851–1901*, Melbourne University Press, Melbourne, 1978, p. 98.
9 J.M. Freeland, *The Australian Pub*, Melbourne University Press, Melbourne, 1966.
10 ibid. p. 243.
11 Basil Lubbock, *The Colonial Clippers*, Nautical Press, Glasgow, 2nd edn, 1948, pp. 21–33.
12 *Tasmanian State Archive, Convict Record*, quoted in Eve Buscombe, *Artists in Early Australia and their Portraits to 1850*, Sydney, Eureka Research, 1979, p. 143.
13 William Moore, *The History of Australian Art*, vol. 1, p. 31, from Henry Allport, quoted in Buscombe, p. 148.

GOD IN NATURE

Portraying the Country

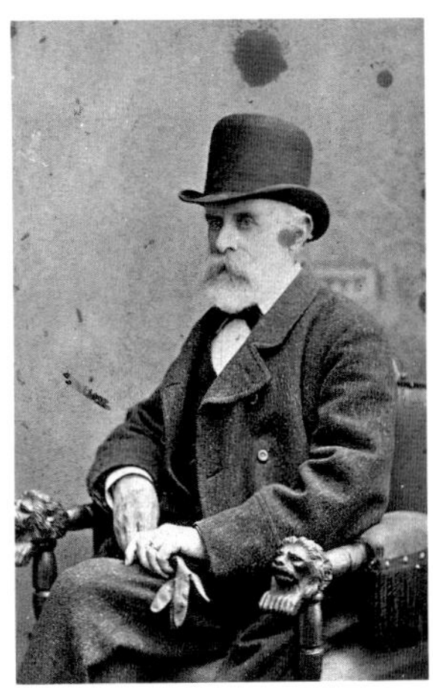

A *carte-de-visite* of
Eugene von Guérard c.
1870.

*Photograph by Stewart and
Company*
*La Trobe Collection, State Library
of Victoria*

In Australia as in the Americas, landscape was the dominant theme of the visual arts throughout the nineteenth century. In Australia it remains a major theme. It is especially noteworthy that a formidable, mythic landscape has ruled not only painting but Australian literature as well, despite the fact that literature is essentially about people. The landscape has dominated Australian poetry and informed the human narratives of many of the country's best-known writers, such as Henry Lawson, Patrick White and Randolph Stow. Two of the most influential novels in the history of Australian literature, Tom Collins' classic *Such is Life* (1903) and Gerald Murnane's *The Plains* (1984), actually have landscape as their central narrative. Human dramas have adhered to the land as if the landscape had the power to determine the fate of its inhabitants: the story told and retold is of puny men, weak women and innocent children who are dependent on a primal landscape. The paintings discussed in this chapter represent a phase in the development of the quintessentially Australian theme.

The German painter Eugene von Guérard (1811–1901), creator of *View of the Wannon Springs in the Grampians, with Mount Abrupt, Colony of Victoria* 1859 (plate 17) did not doubt that his concern with accuracy went hand in hand with his drive to depict beauty and meaning in its highest form.

The viewer of this painting travels from a complex foreground into the serenity of distant plains bathed in the glow of a descending sun. Sun-tipped clouds and two eagles flying in mid-heaven bear witness to a significant moment in the daily pattern of natural existence. Nature's harmonies are palpable in the scene, their divine laws informing the coherence of the image. The smallest plant form in its apparent irregularity of growth is part of a universal system. The eagles lifted high on the evening's

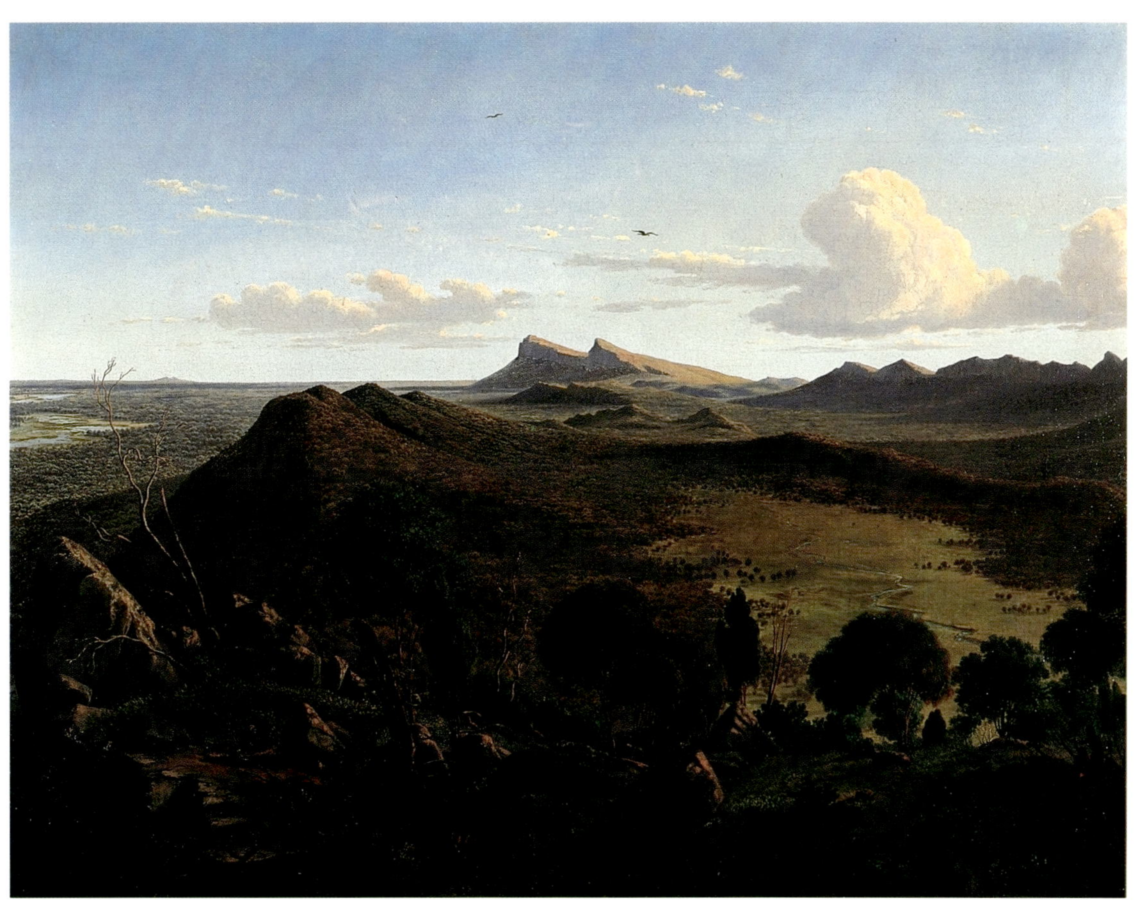

17   Eugene von Guérard
1811–1901
View of the Wannon Springs in the Grampians,
with Mount Abrupt, Colony of Victoria 1859
oil on canvas
56.0 × 73.0 cm

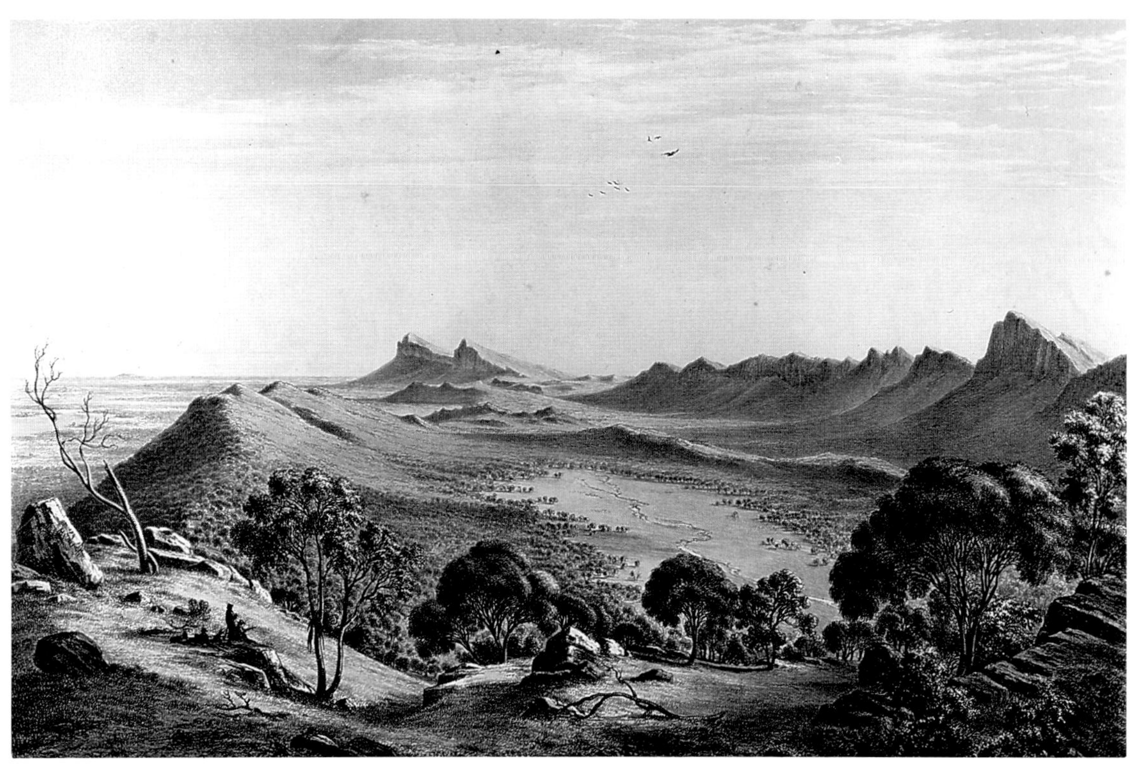

warm currents of air are as significant in the whole truth of nature as the majestic repetition of the pyramidal hills of the Sierra Range on the horizon.

This still land, with its far-off flocks of sheep beside the Wannon River, calls for close observation, otherwise its full meaning is not felt. Von Guérard used metaphors to drive home a message. Between the distant scene painted in such detail and the subdued foreground, two histories are worked out. The plains are the future – the rich pasturelands of an Australia Felix. Stone monoliths and dense shadow in the foreground envelop the past, represented by a small Aboriginal family camp.

In the lithograph version of this same image, produced in 1865, the artist replaced the Aborigines with a group of hunters holding guns, and imagined the hinterland not as here – a Canaan flowing with milk and honey – but as an imaginary inland sea from which Mount Abrupt rises to an altitude of 1000 metres—

> From out the plain
> Heaves like a long-swept wave about to break,
> And on the curl hangs pausing.[1]

Von Guérard had patrons among the Western District pastoralists who, as well as commissioning homestead portraits, asked for landscape views. Having built grand country houses and produced families that were growing up in this new country (though often educated in England), the squatters had begun to look towards a probable future in Australia and to feel a proprietorial interest in the country they had settled. The many poetic images of the Western District by von Guérard – such as this one – fed this newly proud identification with the land. As one contemporary remarked, 'in the treatment of these [subjects] . . . the artist has displayed the feeling of a poet and the touch of a master'.[2] Moreover the combination of scientific description and the poetry of divine power was understood and appreciated: 'The works of this artist forcibly recall a remark of von Humboldt . . . [that] "The grand style in landscapes is the product of a deep comprehension of nature, and their internal mental processes".'[3]

The lengthy volumes of Alexander von Humbolt's *Cosmos* had been published in English translation in 1849. Reading this famous treatise, interested colonists discovered a visionary science in which the patient study of the natural world was linked with a semi-religious philosophy of unity and wonder. Von Humbolt reversed the relation of man and nature: 'We must trace [nature's] image reflected in the mind of man.' This too had been the message of the Romantic poets Wordsworth, Shelley and William Blake. In the revolution Wordsworth brought about in poetry, the description of nature and the nature of poetry – the verse forms and imagery – were driven into irregular new paths, their form taken from the ebb and flow of attraction and repulsion between the self and nature.

An equivalent revolution took place in landscape painting. The great importance of this revolution of the imagination is that it was neither confined to the arts nor contained within science. Scientists like von Humbolt, as well as poets and painters like Wordsworth and Constable, linked the patient study of the natural world with a semi-religious philosophy of unity and amplitude. The most influential British art critic and aesthetic philosopher throughout the entire nineteenth century, John Ruskin, drew a connection between the overwhelming sensation of sublimity and a scientific project such as drawing the minutiae of rocks and foliage. Here was a poetic science; observation in the service of exaltation; the materials of science given a religious structure; a Romantic philosophy of emotion informed by intellect; a greater realism in both art and science. The tension later felt between art and science – which eventually polarised them – was not experienced by the earlier nineteenth-century scientists and artists who subscribed to this natural philosophy.

Australia did not offer von Guérard the best landscape to realise his sublime vision. But across the Tasman lay the geologically new, mountainous landscape of New Zealand. Artists interested in the sublime went there in search of subjects. Von Guérard visited the South Island of New Zealand in 1876, producing two instantly famous and widely exhibited paintings, *Milford Sound with Pembroke Peak and Bowen Falls on the West Coast of Middle Island, New Zealand 1877–9* and *Lake Wakatipu with Mount Earnshaw, Middle Island, New Zealand 1877*. A smaller version of the second, *Wakatipu, with Mount Earnshaw 1878* (plate 18) is in the collection. Symmetry is its organising principle, the echo of reflections in water and the unusual composition of a half-circle. And like a painting by the great American exponent of the Humboltian aesthetic Frederick Church, the geographical span is vast: the distance an everlasting snowscape and the foreground a warm home to tropical plants.

At the time von Guérard achieved this zenith of his ambition, a contemporary painter in Melbourne, Louis Buvelot (1814–88), realised the opposite, intimate vision of Australian landscape that was to be particularly significant for the Heidelberg School in the last fifteen years of the century. His paintings will be discussed at the end of this chapter.

Nicholas Chevalier (1828–1902) was seventeen years younger that von Guérard. Though they arrived in Melbourne within a couple of years of each other, Chevalier's approach to painting was recognised for what it was: a later, younger, less spiritual version of von Guérard's intense style. Marcus Clarke considered him a 'popular' artist.[4] The *Argus* critic James Smith described his style as 'an agreeable paraphrase of von Guérard'.[5] These descriptions made the essential distinction between

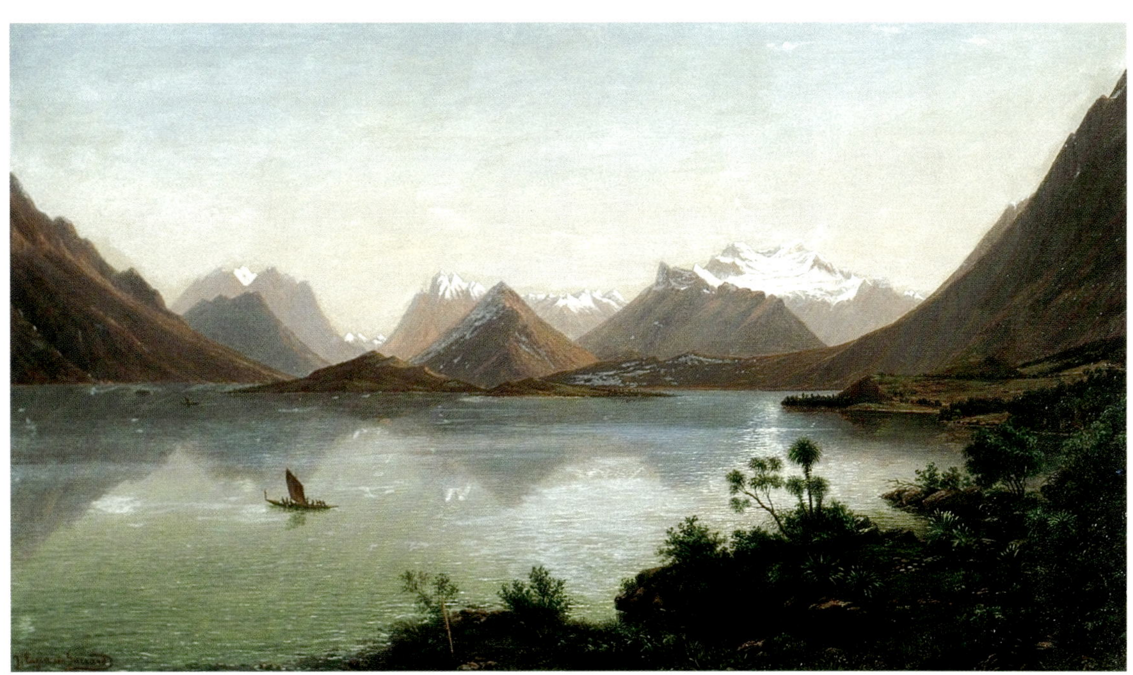

18   Eugene von Guérard
1811–1901
Wakatipu, with Mount Earnshaw 1878
oil on canvas
37.0 × 65.0 cm

von Guérard's elevated style and lofty interpretations and Chevalier's more genial invitation to the viewer to participate in enjoying his imagery. Chevalier's workmanlike brush technique was noticeably less smooth and polished than von Guérard's. The brusque lack of finish was appropriate for a painter of life from the human point of view.

Both artists accompanied the scientist George Neumayer on expeditions in the colony and, characteristically, their interpretations of the scenery differed. Chevalier went with Neumayer to Gippsland between November 1863 and February 1864. An industrious worker, only one month after returning from the expedition he had thirty-seven pictures and sketches for exhibition, most of them painted during and after the Gippsland expedition. Chevalier's 'wilderness paintings' (his term) were more straightforward than those of the older artist. There were no poetic metaphors. The unstressed attractiveness of the paintings was in keeping with Chevalier's personality (he was a likeable, sociable man). To those who did not respond to Chevalier's relaxed manner he appeared a less ambitious artist imaginatively than von Guérard. But there were many who favoured this agreeable type of painting. Queen Victoria was one: she employed Chevalier in later years as a recorder of life at court. The painting *Sealers' Cove, Wilson's Promontory* 1864 (plate 19), one of 'the fruits of his late tour of Gippsland',[6] was bought from the Fourth Annual Exhibition of Fine Arts in Melbourne in 1864 – the year it was painted – by the pastoralist Alexander Dennis as a wedding present for his daughter Mary Wettenhall. Not only was Chevalier well patronised by the colonists, he was the first local artist to have a work purchased by the National Gallery of Victoria.

Chevalier's image transformed the discomfort and uncertainty of bush travel into a fresh and colourful story about adventure in the wilderness. Rather than quelling the viewer by a peremptory style or lofty interpretation, nothing about the picture disturbs. The viewer was invited to explore the image from the comfort of his armchair, perhaps with the book of Neumayer's expedition in his hands. Looking at the painting and reading the published account, he could virtually pinpoint Chevalier's day at Sealers' Cove, the weather and the peaceful incidents. The

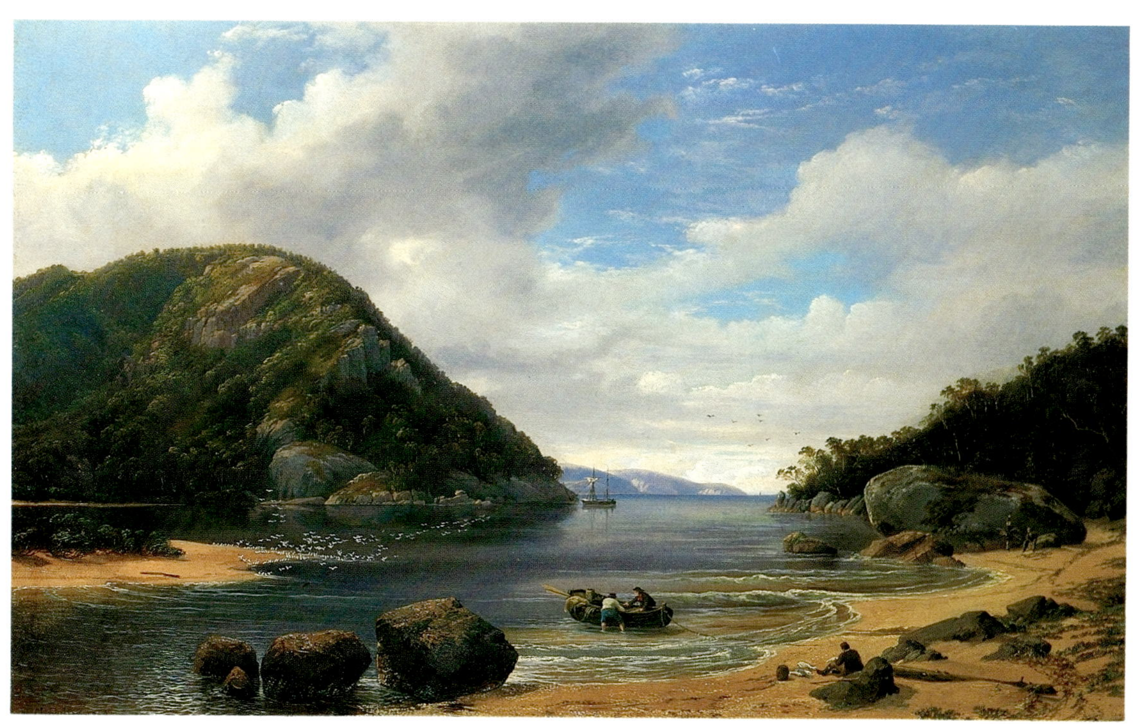

19   Nicholas Chevalier
1828–1902
Sealers' Cove, Wilson's Promontory 1864
oil on canvas
42.9 × 68.6 cm

season is summer, it is midday, the sea is calm, cumulus clouds are blowing up in a blue sky, a ship is moored at the entrance to the cove and a boat has brought men ashore to fish and collect firewood and water from Sealers' Creek. In other words, the owner of the painting (and the less wealthy owners of the chromo-lithograph of it produced by Troedel) had the pleasure of participating in an episode of efficient husbandry after the mode made so popular by Daniel Defoe's *Robinson Crusoe*. The morality of Chevalier's paintings – this and, for example, *The Buffalo Ranges* 1864 (National Gallery of Victoria) – is about the blessings of God on human endeavour rather than the poetry of divinity in nature.

By contrast to the picture of tranquil productivity, Neumayer's written account of the expedition revealed Chevalier as an amusingly incompetent city dweller abroad in the bush. On a not particularly difficult expedition Chevalier insisted on going off alone to sketch on Wilson's Promontory and twice nearly lost his life before rejoining the party. Neumayer, who knew Chevalier's ways, was 'apprehensive' for his feckless companion's safety, and left him a trail of 'instructions' on 'little pieces of paper' suspended from trees, but even so Chevalier 'got off our track and was wandering about on Cape Liptrap for two whole days without food or water, narrowly escaping losing his life, and it was only by finding a few carrots near the old hut that he was enabled to hold out'. Then this victim of his own farce nearly drowned crossing the Powlet River, 'it was only by particularly good luck that he drifted to firm ground'.[7]

The power of science in nineteenth-century art was demonstrated in another way by the painters Haughton Forrest, H.J. Johnstone and W.C. Piguenit, who used photography or, more accurately, the appearance of photography to validate their respectful vision of nature. Nineteenth-century reasoning went like this: the camera could not lie, hence it was the best instrument for a scientific demonstration of natural laws. To create an effect that was as true to life as a photograph, the painter subdued certain aspects of the older painting tradition. For an image to appear relatively uninterpreted it could not sustain metaphor (unlike a painting by von Guérard). To be photographically sublime, its awesomeness must appear the work of nature rather than the subjective interpretation of the artist. Because the nineteeth-century camera produced images that were monochromatic, fixed, without movement, and sharply focussed, the paintings that strove for the appearance of photography would also be more or less tonal, evenly-accented, still, smooth and textureless. They could be, and frequently were, sublimely atmospheric.

W.C. Piguenit (1836–1914) ventured into photography in 1870 with a suite of images sent to the Intercolonial Exhibition in Sydney. In 1873 he travelled with the explorer and politician James R. Scott to Lake St Clair and Lake Petrarch in the Western Highlands of Tasmania. During the previous twenty years of employment as a draughtsman for the Survey Department he had gone with surveyors to make drawings in the landscape. On the expedition with Scott, Piguenit made detailed drawings of Lake St Clair and may have taken photographs. He was most likely already aware of 1860s photographs of Lake St Clair by 'Paul Ricochet', Morton Allport and his wife, Elizabeth (née Ritchie). Piguenit's drawings of Lake St Clair are photographically accurate, and although more vertical in emphasis, correspond in detail with a camera's single-point perspective.[8]

The painting *Lake St Clair – the source of the River Derwent, Tasmania* c. 1887 (plate 20) exists in at least seven versions (two of which are in monochrome). The first was purchased the year it was painted (1875) – bought by enthusiastic public subscription for the proposed Art Gallery of New South Wales. This later version may have been painted after revisiting the area in 1887. Compared with the complexity of von Guérard's description or an image by Chevalier, Piguenit's image is considerably simplified. The clouds wreathing around Mount Olympus and a thin line of white water are the most compelling parts of the image, otherwise the scene is remarkably sombre and immobile – virtually a tonalist image. The drama is of light, which was the only drama the early camera afforded. Piguenit's most memorable images, such as this painting and *The flood in the Darling 1890* 1895 (Art Gallery of New South Wales), are about light on water. Water was favoured both by photographers and by the artists whom they inspired because it mirrored the landscape, gave an effect of amplitude and supplied a natural compositional symmetry. Composed and

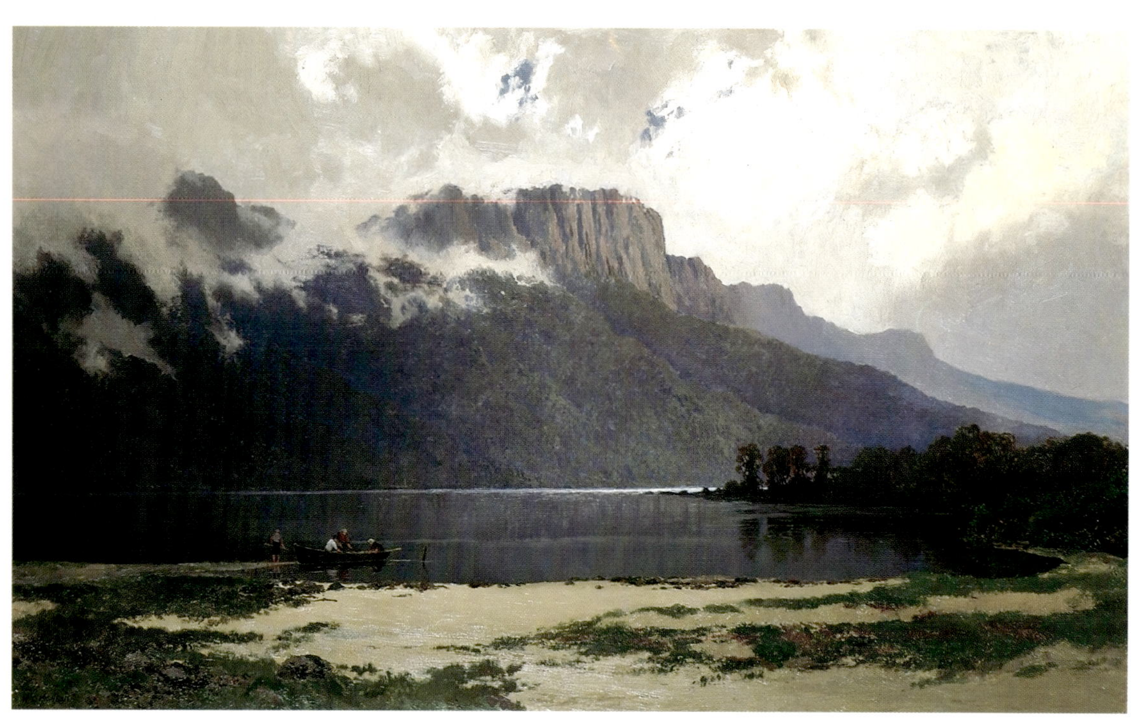

20   W.C. Piguenit
1836–1914
Lake St Clair – the source of the River Derwent,
Tasmania (1887)
oil on canvas
77.7 × 128.0 cm

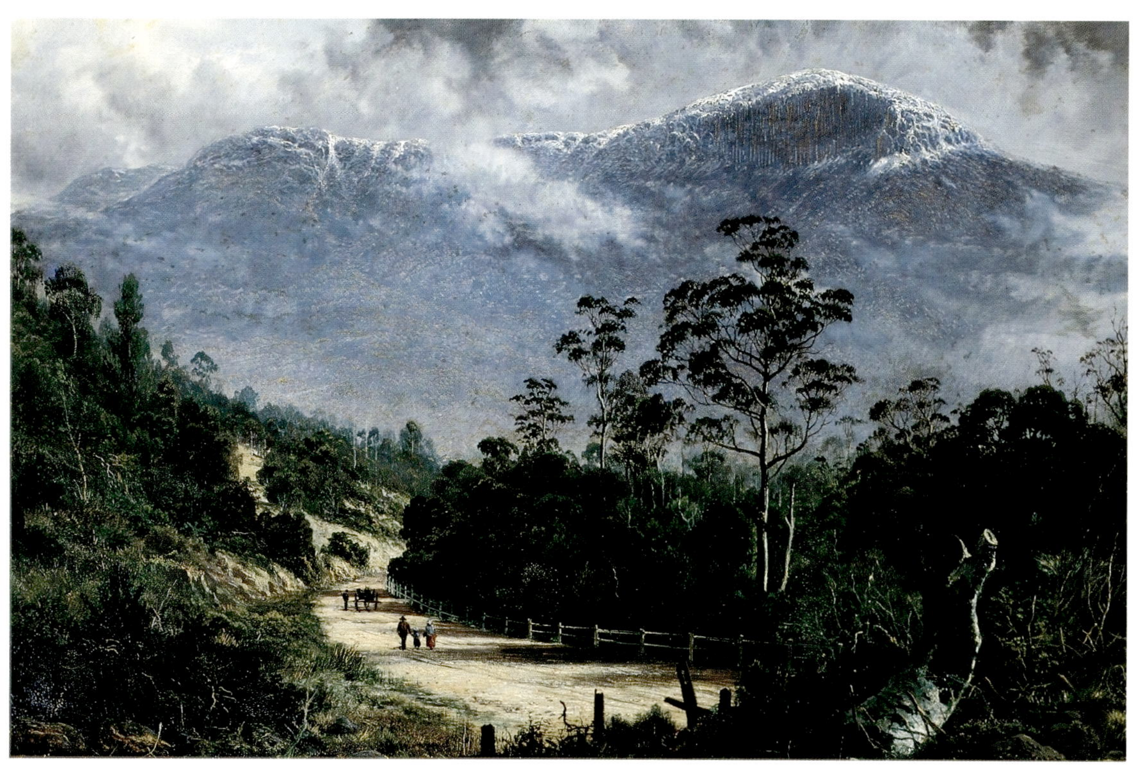

21　Haughton Forrest
1826–1925
Mount Wellington from the Huon Road (1885)
oil on board
31.0 × 47.1 cm

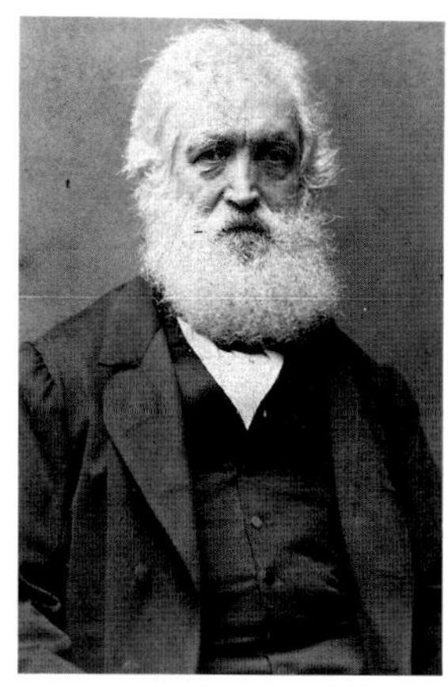

A *carte-de-visite* portrait of Louis Buvelot taken in the last few years of his life (c. 1885).

Photograph by Foster and Martin
La Trobe Collection, State Library
of Victoria

simplified thus, nature declared her perfection.

The photographic appearance of Piguenit's paintings, including *Lake St Clair*, has caused historians to speculate that he used photographs as the source of images. However the painter conflated and altered the topography of some scenes and a photographic source appears unlikely.[9] Rather than simply imitating photography, Piguenit was inspired by its effects. That is to say, his paintings positively declare the aesthetic virtues of the camera. His painted visions of watery landscapes are comparable to British landscape paintings by Keeley Halswelle and Peter Graham (paintings much sought after in Australia) which also followed the style of photographs. From the 1850s, when photography became commercially viable, it was the most popular and readily available of any art medium. Its immense popularity in Australia was reflected in Piguenit's phenomenal success as a prize-winning painter whose works were assiduously pursued by collectors and the trustees of art museums.

The difference between Haughton Forrest (1826–1925), using a traditional image of a distant mountain viewed through a foreground vista of woods and road in his *Mount Wellington from the Huon Road* c. 1885 (plate 21), and Louis Buvelot, using the same basic composition in *Afternoon at Blackwood* 1879 (plate 22), is the great difference between an older convention of picturesque grandeur, by now rather sterile, and a fresh realisation. Buvelot's image is bathed in the low, pink, late-afternoon light of an autumnal April in the southern state of Victoria. A painting such as this shows how and why he was admired by the Heidelberg School artists of the following decade.

The most striking quality of Buvelot's image, after the soft light, is the unpretentiousness of the scene. Instead of soaring mountains we have the rather unspectacular high country of the Great Dividing Range near Melbourne. The bush is open and scrubby and the road not a formal route but a wandering track made by the passage of carts. The intimacy of Buvelot's vision is a long way from sublime impersonality. He arrived in Melbourne in 1865. Australians, who by then were accustomed to images of sombre magnificence, recognised the scenery Buvelot painted but at first did not know whether they unreservedly admired the mild pastoral treatment. One pleased but circumspect critic wrote:

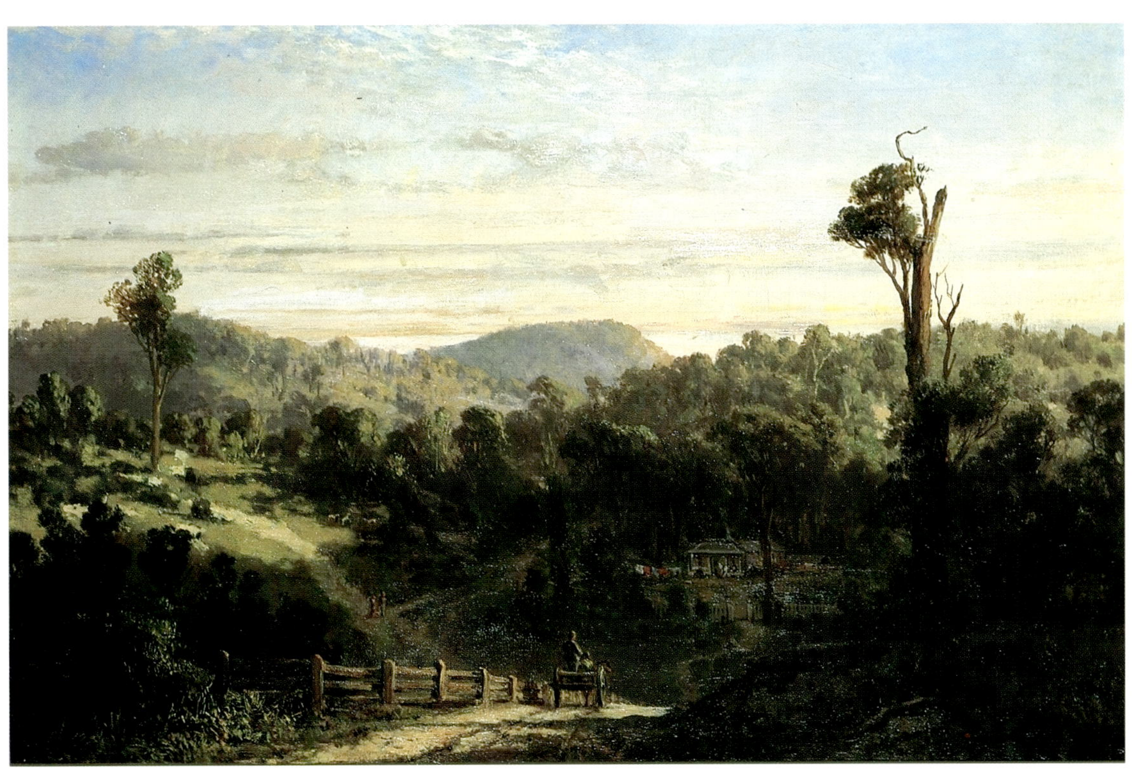

22   Louis Buvelot
1814–88
Afternoon at Blackwood 1879
oil on canvas
46.0 × 68.5 cm

It is really a comfort and a pleasure to look at them, they are so sunny, so pleasant, in a word, nice. Mr. Buvelot's pencil . . . seldom strays many miles from Melbourne: and perhaps that is why it is so comfortable compared with its sombre and magnificent rivals. No mountains, no gum forests, no wildernesses, but snug little nooks, eminently suggestive of noontide meditations, lovemakings and picnics.[10]

If at first the domestic poetry of these quiet pastorals was not appreciated it was because Buvelot's expression of an intimate relationship between human beings and nature was not recognised for what it was. The 1860s and 1870s in Australian art was a time when the eye of the beholder was still overwhelmed by the strident presence of all-powerful Nature in von Guérard's images and the only slightly muted declaration of natural power in paintings by Chevalier, Piguenit and Haughton Forrest.

Buvelot's best paintings weren't from his first years in the colony, but from the late 1870s to the early 1880s, the period of this work. In the decade after his arrival he developed a feeling for how the light revealed the structure of the land and the characteristically open bushland. He was perhaps the first artist to appreciate the geological age of the country, the worn-down ranges, rifts and valleys appearing on a continuous, undulating skin of earth interrupted by low rocky outcrops. Though much more characteristic of Australia, this geology had been bypassed by the proponents of towering mountainscapes.

In its casual sprawl the outdoor pencil drawing for *Afternoon at Blackwood* (National Gallery of Australia) is even more representative than the slightly modified, studio-painted image. In the studio Buvelot added angles, extended and deepened the shadows, and made a motif of a shattered gum tree: taking his image closer to the picturesque convention. His major studio contribution was to give his picture a rustic story that was both conventional and completely in keeping with the scene and the atmosphere of late afternoon. We see a horse and cart approaching a small farmhouse, we see washing on the line, a smoking chimney: our perceptions merge into those of the farmer returning home at the close of day.

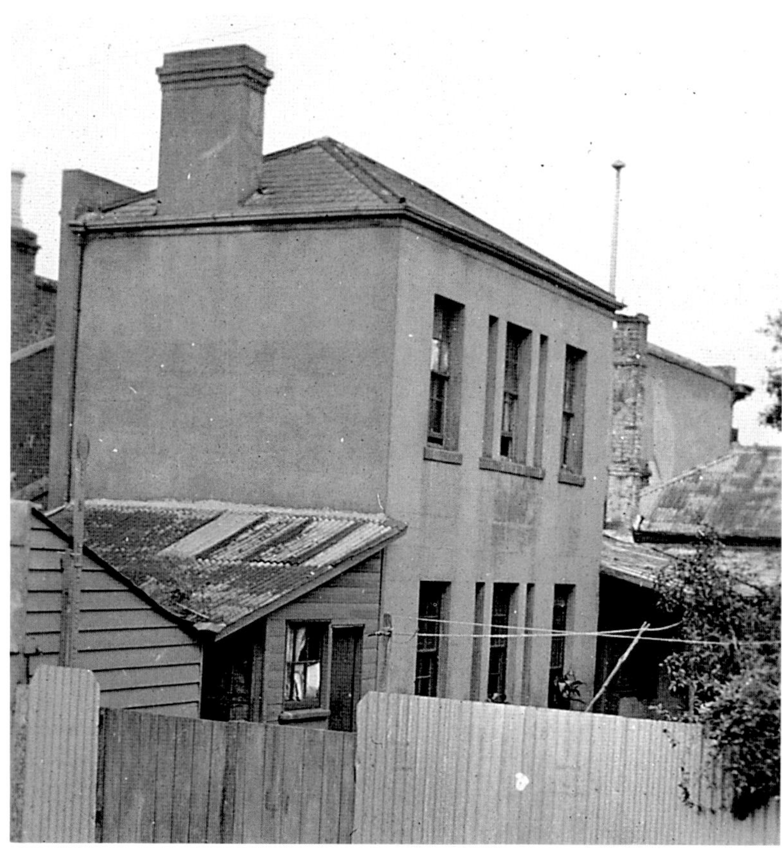

Louis Buvelot's studio in Little George Street, Fitzroy, Melbourne. Built last century this studio, with south-facing windows, can still be seen today.
Photograph by J.K. Moir
La Trobe Collection, State Library of Victoria

Scents and sounds are evoked by the painting, as well as purely visual impressions. The appropriateness and poetry of Buvelot's narratives was noticed and emulated by the Heidelberg School painters in the 1880s and 1890s.

Landscape's pre-eminence reflects the culture of discovery that has prevailed in this country. In Australia, unlike Europe, the landscape was not familiar territory to its inhabitants, but a new frontier. The southern continent was discovered, explored and explained in the light of the new natural sciences that were evolving in Europe. And those sciences embodied a compelling marriage of empiricism and mythic imagination. Natural science made a claim to replace old philosophies with a new religion based on science. The world of man and nature was presented not simply in its parts but as an entirety. Wrote von Humbolt:

> In order to depict nature in its exalted sublimity, we must not dwell exclusively on its external manifesta-

tions, but we must trace its image reflected in the
mind of man, at one time filling the dreaming land
of physical myths with forms of grace and beauty
and at another developing the noble germ of artistic
creations.[11]

Accordingly, when the landscape acquired a powerful
spiritual significance in paintings of the 1850s and 1860s,
the reason for this access of feeling was not merely the
inevitable historical sequence of practical discovery
followed by more leisured enjoyment of the land, though
that applied. The timing was more important. At mid-
century a number of artists arrived who were able to put
the new scientific interpretation into practice. Behind them
lay half a century of a Romantic landscape tradition in
Europe – the dappled English meadows of Constable, the
grandeur of Turner's atmospheric skies, the extremity of
nature in Caspar David Friedrich's images of lonely alpine
travels.

The obvious comparison for Australia is America in the
nineteenth century. In both countries landscape became
a symbol for an imaginative frontier of physical
discovery – map-making and scientific analysis – and of
mental piety. Australia and America had mixed
populations of newcomers. The landscapes were perceived
by these relatively small migrant populations as vast and,
in their complexity, posing possibly insurmountable
obstacles to the understanding. Natural science provided
ways of coping that were both practical and mythic. But
whereas the tradition in America continued to be of
sublime and worshipful naturalism, in Australia that
tradition was expressed wholeheartedly for a
comparatively short period of time. In the long run the
interpretation has been materialistic and pragmatic rather
than mystical. The difference may be explained by the
geography of the countries and by differences of social
history. The puritan fathers left a legacy of American piety
whereas the convicts of the industrial age left a legacy
of materialism.

1 *Eugène von Guérard's Australian Landscapes*, Hamel and Ferguson,
  Melbourne, 1865, text for plate I.
2 James Smith, *Argus*, Melbourne, 4 December 1857, p. 5, about von
  Guérard's *Mount Wilson, from Mount Dryden*, 1857.

3 *Illustrated Journal of Australasia*, Melbourne, January 1858, pp. 35-6.

4 Marcus Clarke, preface to Adam Lindsay Gordon, *Sea, Spray and Smoke Drift*, Clarson, Messina, Melbourne, 1876, pp. v–vi.

5 *Argus*, Melbourne, 26 October 1866, p. 7.

6 *Argus*, Melbourne, 2 March 1864, p. 5.

7 George Neumayer, *Results of the Magnetic Survey of the Colony of Victoria, Executed During the Years 1858-64*, J. Schneider, Mannheim, 1869, pp. 116–18.

8 Information from Lance Cosgrove who visited Lake St Clair in 1992 with Simon Cuthbert to take photographs of the vistas sketched and painted by Piguenit. See photographs illustrated facing contents page and p. 23, and drawings and paintings illustrated pp. 6, 17, 24, 55, 71 in Christa E. Johannes and Anthony V. Brown, *W.C. Piguenit 1836-1914, Retrospective Exhibition*, Tasmanian Museum and Art Gallery, Hobart, 1992.

9 See Johannes and Brown.

10 *Australasian*, Melbourne, 24 November 1866, p. 1063, col. 1.

11 Alexander von Humbolt, *Cosmos*, introduction to vol. 2, Henry G. Bohm, London, 1849.

URBANITY IN THE BUSH

The Era of the Heidelberg School

Melbourne in the 1880s was 'marvellous Melbourne', rich and prosperous. With its imported opera and theatre and the grand International and Centennial Exhibitions in 1880–81 and 1888–9, the city presented itself to the world as modern and sophisticated, like its rivals Glasgow, Liverpool, Philadelphia and San Francisco. There was a building boom, speculation was rife, land prices soared. All were indicators of an economy out of control, but who bothered when prospects looked so good?

The artists of Melbourne took the style of the times. They walked around town in frock coats, wearing pink cravats and swinging canes. They held open studios, as artists did in Paris and London. Up flights of stairs, in rooms of smart Japanese decor, young men dispensed green tea and biscuits to young women (colleagues and students) and their mothers. The men were bohemians, an 'impressionist' coterie, who camped under canvas at Box Hill and in an old, echoing house at Heidelberg. In later memory that time at Heidelberg in the 1880s was an endless summer of pink skies, yellow hillsides, red wine and Ruby tobacco.

The elegant, older leader of the 'Heidelberg School' was Tom Roberts (1856–1931), fresh from a few years in the aesthetic London of Whistler and Oscar Wilde. In 1889, with the provocative example of Whistler's 1884 exhibition of 9 by 5 impressions in mind, he suggested to his friends in the camp at Heidelberg that they hold an exhibition of small oil sketches. The exhibition, staged light-heartedly as a publicity stunt and never intended as a statement of the artists' total endeavour, nonetheless became for all time the signature of Australian 'impressionism'. The Heidelberg crew made an aesthetic occasion of their exhibition. They found a commercial patron to supply Liberty silks to drape the walls of Buxton's Rooms in the city. They solicited a piano, teacups and furniture to accommodate guests. They went to a timber yard for lengths of kauri wood from which to fashion Whistlerian wide, flat, painted frames. Their tiny impressions were painted on the lids of cigar boxes supplied by Louis Abrahams, a Melbourne tobacconist who, in his spare time, joined the country excursions of Roberts and his companions. Friends among the press publicised the event. From the first whisper in the gossip columns that the 'Impressionist' exhibition was planned until the final auction sale of the leftover sketches, the event was orchestrated to be a total aesthetic experience such as Whistler commanded.

Tom Roberts and his younger companions at Heidelberg, Charles Conder (1868-1909) and Arthur Streeton (1867-1943), were the three main protagonists, supported by a meagre contribution of work by four other artists, Frederick McCubbin, Charles Douglas Richardson, R.E. Falls and Herbert Daly. They called their show of August 1889 'The 9 by 5 Impression Exhibition'. Charles Conder produced a catalogue illustration showing Convention with torch extinguished and her bonds loosened. If that image were not inflammatory enough, the first page of the catalogue carried a teasing message:

> TO THE PUBLIC – An effect is only momentary: so an impressionist tries to find his place. Two half-hours are never alike, and he who tries to paint a sunset on two successive evenings must be more or less painting from memory. So, in these works, it has been the object of the artists to render faithfully, and thus obtain first records of effects widely differing, and often of very fleeting character.

Australian impressionism was never mistaken for the French impressionism of Monet and his contemporaries. A painted impression was understood in Melbourne for what it was: a brief, momentary impression recorded without detail for the sake of a total effect. In interviews with the press in 1889 Tom Roberts and the others explained that mental impressions are rarely purely visual. 'A tram car rushing round a corner . . . a stretch of meadow-land after rain . . . a pair of street urchins at a game of marbles',[1] produced impressions on the mind that were

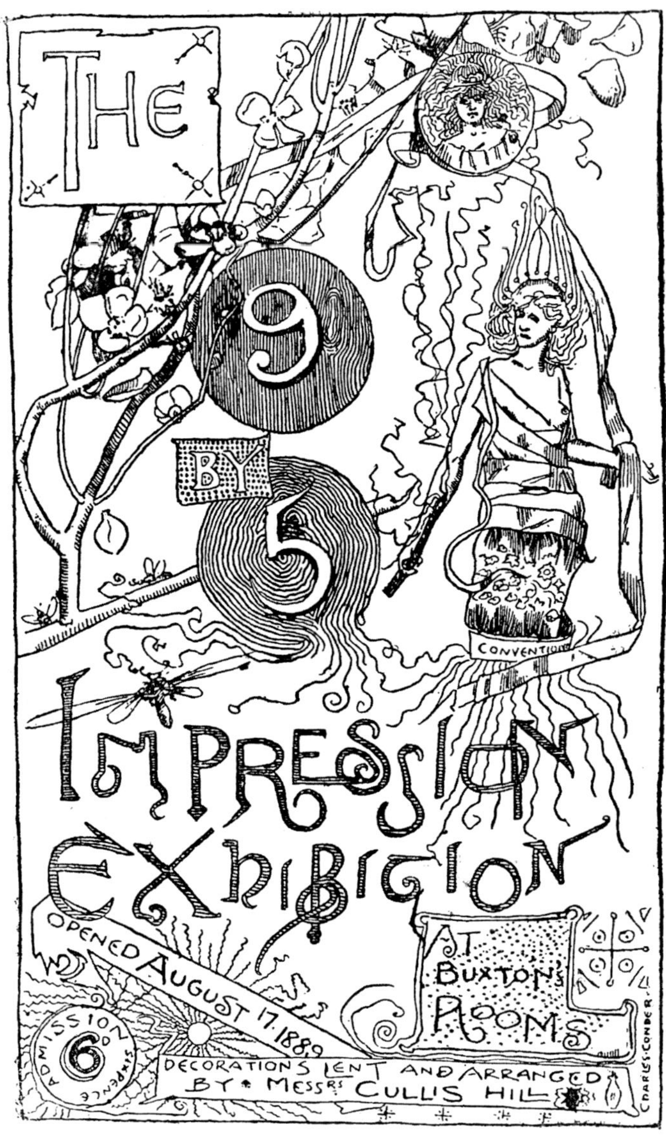

compounded of sight, sound, smell and more elusive moral and emotional associations. Even the absence of something keenly sought could form the major impression. The artists took delight in the idea and to the end of their lives spun out the rich, romantic theme of the senses.

In the winter and early spring months leading to 'The 9 by 5 Impression Exhibition' the three painters lived together, pored over art journals and discussed what it meant to paint a true, personal impression. Their conclusion at the time was that an impression was best

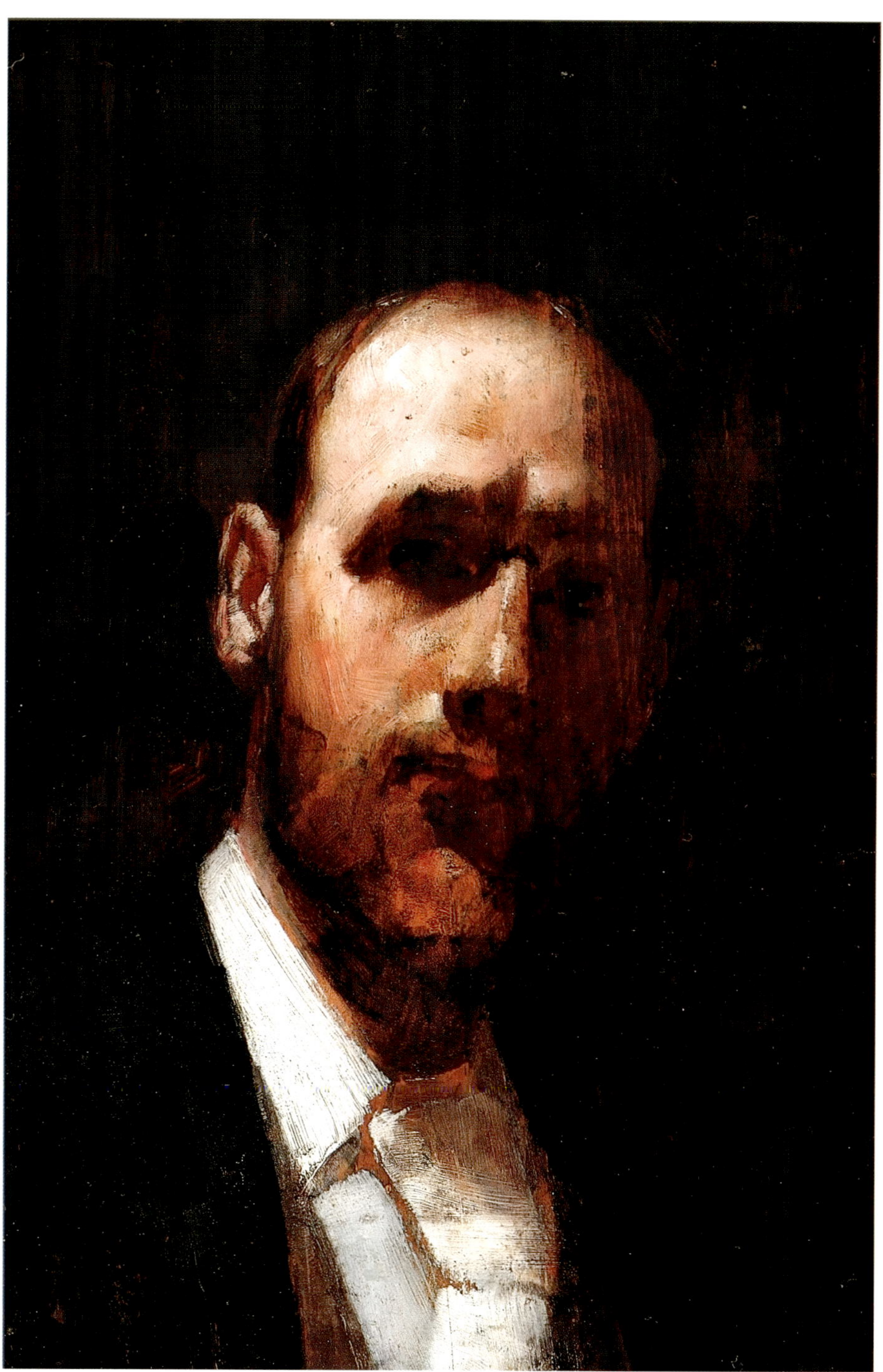

23 Tom Roberts
1856–1931
(*Self portrait*) 1889 from 'The 9 by 5 Impression Exhibition'
oil on wood panel
35.4 × 24.8 cm

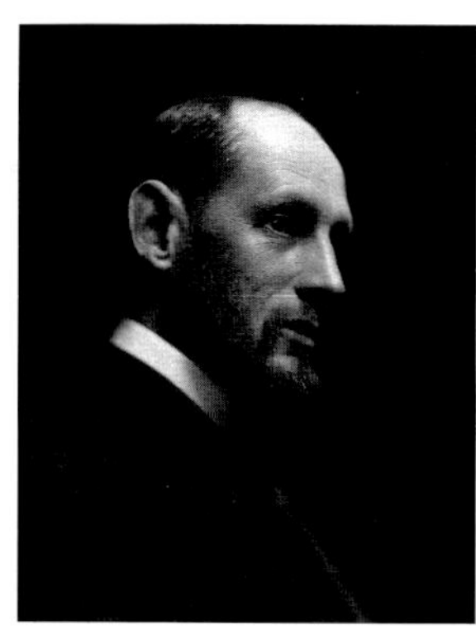

Photograph of Tom
Roberts taken in
London, at least
fourteen years after *Self
portrait* (plate 23).
Photograph by H. Walter Barnett
La Trobe Collection, State Library
of Victoria

expressed by a selective emphasis of one pictorial quality with a vague suggestion of ambience. The 1889 impressions employed a pungent colour, or deep shadow, or blurred forms, or sharp outline, or unexpected viewpoint, or an empty field, to convey the immediacy and selective quality of a first strong impression.

Tom Roberts, who for years had worked with a commercial photographer, painted an impression of himself (plate 23) reflected in a mirror. One sees from the fact that his hair is parted on the other side from the way he combed it that he was not aided by a photograph (which would imply a studied interpretation the opposite of impressionistic). The artist's moment of self-appraisal in the mirror is conveyed emotively by the way the viewer too, has to look searchingly into deep shadow to see the eyes. The image is succinct, the palette confined to cream, brown and black, the image brushed in without detail to form a pattern of light and shade. The self portrait may have been either catalogue no. 23, *Cream and Black*, (lent to 'The 9 by 5 Impression Exhibition') or catalogue no. 86, *Head Study*, (bought by Dr Douglas Stewart from the auction that ended the show).

The Melbourne impressionists were from the first generation to train together in Australia. The society they lived in was, as always, in flux: a migrant society with people coming and going. Melbourne trainees of the 1870s and 1880s included many who had been born in the colonies, among them Frederick McCubbin, Bertram Mackennal, Clara Southern, Arthur Streeton, E. Phillips Fox, Rupert Bunny and David Davies. Up to half of them had been emigrants from Great Britain, for example Tom Roberts, Charles Douglas Richardson, Jane Sutherland, Charles Conder (via Sydney) and Louis Abrahams. And as many artists again had come to the colonies in adulthood, *after* receiving an art training in Europe.

The young artists took their formative artistic influences from their own society, including an immense respect for European art. Reading about and debating art events in Paris and London, studying paintings and prints by Whistler and other notorious members of the avant-garde in exhibitions sent from abroad, the young colonials established a group ethic. There were lasting, practical influences at first hand from artists of their community: the older Swiss painter Louis Buvelot; the German director

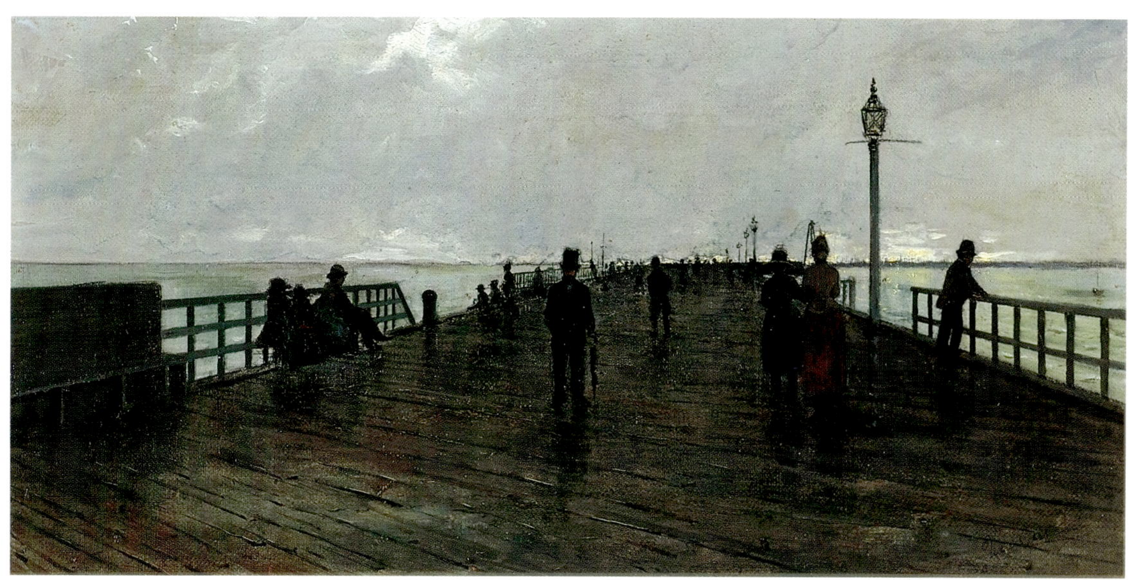

24 Ugo Catani
1861–(19?)
St Kilda Pier 1886
oil on canvas
18.0 × 36.0 cm

of the National Gallery and teacher of painting at the National Gallery School, Eugene von Guérard; the English art teacher Thomas Clarke. More recent European styles were appraised in paintings by new arrivals such as Arturo Loureiro (who was Portuguese) and Carl Kahler (an Austrian). Two Italians, Ugo Catani (born 1861) and Girolamo Nerli (1860–1926) had a direct influence on the local development of impressionism. In fact we can say that impressionism, Italian-style, was an immediate influence, even though French painting in general was afforded the most respect of any art. Colonial artists followed the British in looking to Paris for artistic direction in the 1880s and 1890s. Many went to Paris to acquire artistic finish and returned sporting some Parisian ideas.

The two young Florentines Ugo Catani and Girolamo Nerli disembarked in Melbourne at Cup time in 1885. They set up a studio in Collins Street, took in students, and proceeded to paint and exhibit a range of portraits, imaginative themes, and scenes of Melbourne life. Small oil impressions were included in their exhibitions quite as a matter of course and without the attention-getting tactics of the subsequent '9 by 5ers'. At a studio viewing by Catani in 1893 'one of the best' works was 'a view of St Kilda pier in the gloaming after a rainy day'. A 'bit of Collins-street on a wet night' was likewise 'a very clever study' and Catani also showed 'a very clever . . . most original' sketch of a female performer 'under the limelights, the heads of the orchestra showing in the dull yellow glare of the candles fixed to their music stands'.[2]

Catani's *St Kilda Pier* 1886 (plate 24) was one of a number of wet-weather subjects painted by the Italians which came in for admiring attention in Melbourne and Sydney. This small work has an austerity of colour, composition and drawing very rarely seen before in Australian painting. A grey rectangle of sky above a grey rectangle of sea and pier forms an uncompromisingly basic geometry for the image; and within it the sea each side of the sharply receding St Kilda Pier divides the lower part of the image into three triangles. The stylish composition and an equally succinct division of colours into areas harks back to a group of Florentine painters a generation earlier who were known as the Macchiaioli ('patch'-painters).

Although Catani (and Nerli) had recently studied at the Florentine Accademia under teachers opposed to the

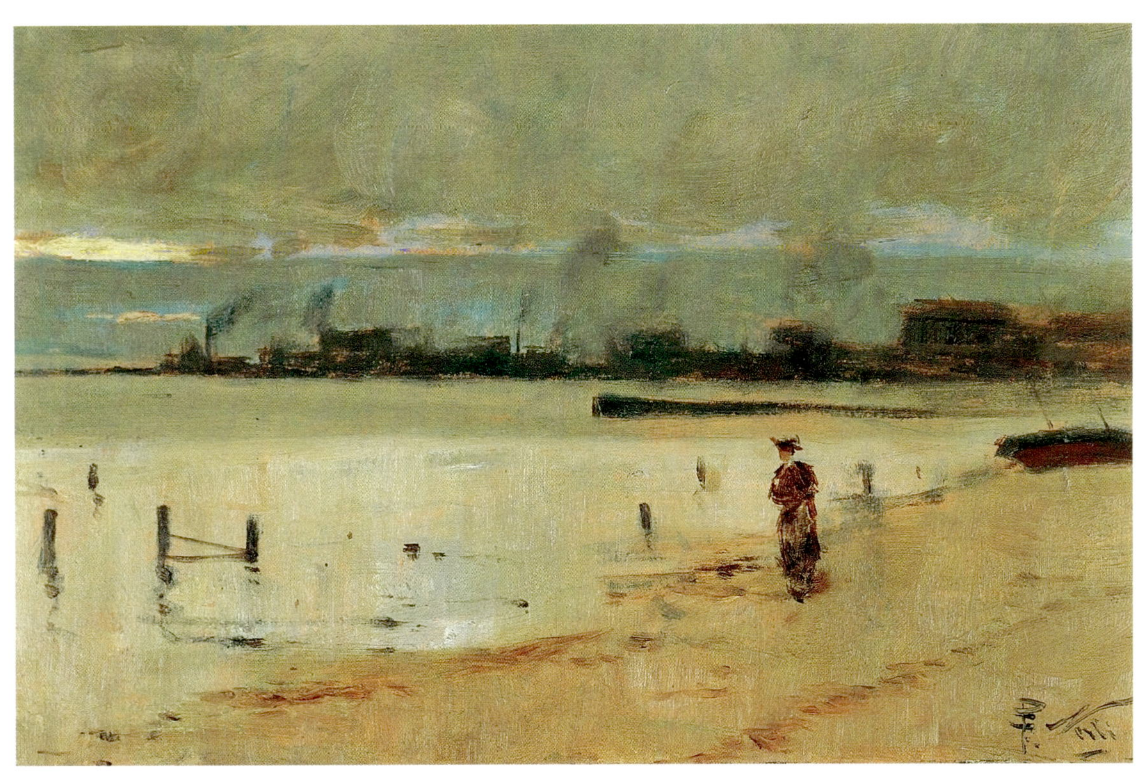

25 Girolamo Nerli
1860–1926
Looking towards Port Melbourne from St Kilda (1890–91)
oil on board
21.5 × 34.0 cm

Macchiaioli, the influence of that local form of impressionism was strong in their work. For example, Nerli was described as practising a 'style of vagueness' which allowed no more than 'suggestions of his subject . . . three splashes of paint to the right and three to the left constituting the picture'.[3] The aptness of that description of Nerli's style is well demonstrated in the horizontal painting *Looking towards Port Melbourne from St Kilda* c. 1890–91 (plate 25).

'St Kilda,' wrote a journalist in 1880, 'is one of the most fashionable and favourably situated suburbs of Melbourne . . . within easy reach of the metropolis by a ten minutes' railway ride'.[4] It was the beach resort most available to the city. During the summer months and on public holidays people went there for recreation. Strolling up and down the beach and esplanade, or promenading on the pier, Melburnians in elaborate clothes enjoyed the latest bourgeois pursuit of leisure. Artists of the 1880s quickly registered the change of social emphasis from the disciplined piety of the 1860s to fun and fashion in the 1880s. During this period art ceased to expound an elevated moral science and began to serve the cult of leisure and consumption.

The images of pleasure painted in the 1880s did not separate scenes of play from signs of labour. Behind Nerli's image of a lone figure on the wet St Kilda sands is a smoky vista of industrial Port Melbourne. Factories and warehouses, piers, breakwaters and steamships signified the industrial progress that was the workaday background to the cultivation of leisure.

One year after coming to Melbourne, Nerli went to Sydney where, at the Art Society's Sketch Club, he met the eighteen-year-old black-and-white illustrator Charles Conder. They became friends. No one in Sydney was especially clever with colour before Nerli arrived. His sunny images, exhibited in December 1887, produced the comment that his colour was worth emulating because the English dimness that had prevailed in Sydney to date was 'quite at variance with our bright sunny scenery'.[5] Soon after meeting Nerli, Conder was noticed for the first time by Sydney artists not for his clever drawing but for poetic colour.[6] The Art Society of New South Wales had a copy of Chevreul's *The Contrast of Colours* (given in 1884) which Conder may have read.[7] He wrote a list of colour complementaries in his May 1887 sketchbook,[8] and from that time introduced complementary hues 'Violet & Yellow, Green & Red, Blue & Orange' as keynotes in his paintings. This structured use of colour was Catani's and Nerli's Italian practice: discreet notes of blue and red in Catani's grey St Kilda picture; red, blue and yellow in Nerli's beach scene.

For the ingenious compositions of his illustrative work Conder had looked to American illustrations and Japanese prints and he built upon those lessons about pictorial structure when looking at paintings by his friend Nerli. Conder's considerable accomplishments in modern design were paraded in the lovely *Fisherman's Bridge, Double Bay* 1888 (plate 26). Below a decorative, high horizon line a top-heavy composition of rectangles and triangle-shaped creases in the sloping land leads down to an empty, grassy foreground. Against the aesthetic greeny-yellow of the grass Conder painted small colour accents of yellow, red, black and cream. The image as a whole was broadly, even blandly, painted. The impressionist vagueness of the image served to emphasise the detailed treatment given to the bridge and foreground figures. Likewise the mannered drawing and dot-headed grasses stood out as modern stylisms.

The informality, selective emphases and odd geometry of 1880s impressionist images were in sharp contrast to the paintings of earlier decades. Whereas art had once striven for an objective representation, the new paintings were avowedly subjective. An all-encompassing outlook had seemed almost necessary to complete a scene in the 1860s. On the other hand paintings of the 1880s and 1890s brought the vista close and took an almost perverse enjoyment in recognising the limits of human vision. The impressionist foreground was typically large, close and empty – the point of view of someone in the landscape. The human bias extended beyond the portrayal of figures in the landscape, going outside the image itself to the viewers of the picture. Not only was an image scaled to the figures in the scene, it was skewed to idiosyncratic individual perception. Pushed into the landscape, the onlooker, for the first time in Australian art, was obliged to feel the effect of his or her subjective presence in the way a scene was presented.

The Heidelberg School is much closer to the present

than its chronological place would suggest. Closer in several respects. The artists have a life in popular imagination outside their art. Having once presented themselves as media personalities they have remained larger-than-life public figures. The art itself is modern, that is, the subjects are urban, scaled to human size; the perceptions are subjective; the style and presentation demand attention in their own right for being consciously artistic. Part of the urbanity of the Heidelberg School painters was their use of fashion. They employed the 1880s-style colours: yellow, salmon pink and blue. A few years later Fox and Tucker introduced the Parisian fashion colours of the late 1880s – bright greens, yellow and lilac.[9] The compositions had a Japanese flatness and mannered decorativeness. The frames around the paintings were patently aesthetic (there was an 'Artistic Framing Company' in Melbourne in the 1880s). The titles of pictures were wittily modern: 'A Scheme in Apple Green and Fawn' called attention to the impressionist aesthetic of colour; 'Collins St., 11 a.m.' declared the very moment of a visual impressionism; the title 'Impressionists' camp' attached to a blurred interior with two lounging male figures represented the bohemian way of life; and 'La Favorita' was a witticism, a title taken from the 'La Favorita' brand of cigars which provided some of the tiny panels on which the impressions were painted.

The exhibition of impressions held in August 1889, a roaring success from the point of view of sales and promotion, was followed closely by the financial crash in which Melbourne suffered far worse than Sydney. The next decade has been summed up in a recent history book as 'the nervous nineties'. Art went to extremes of illustration and artifice, tendencies which, when they were combined in one painting, co-existed uneasily at best. In 1890 came the beginning of an artistic dispersal that pushed the 1880s generation of Australian artists further afield as time went by.

In May 1890 Conder, Emma Minnie Boyd, Arthur Boyd (Snr) and George Walton sailed for England. Tom Roberts had been out of town for some months before then. As far as can be understood from the available evidence, he retreated from town because he felt discouraged. Through the early 1890s Roberts seems not to have realised that the sluggish market for paintings was a result of a general

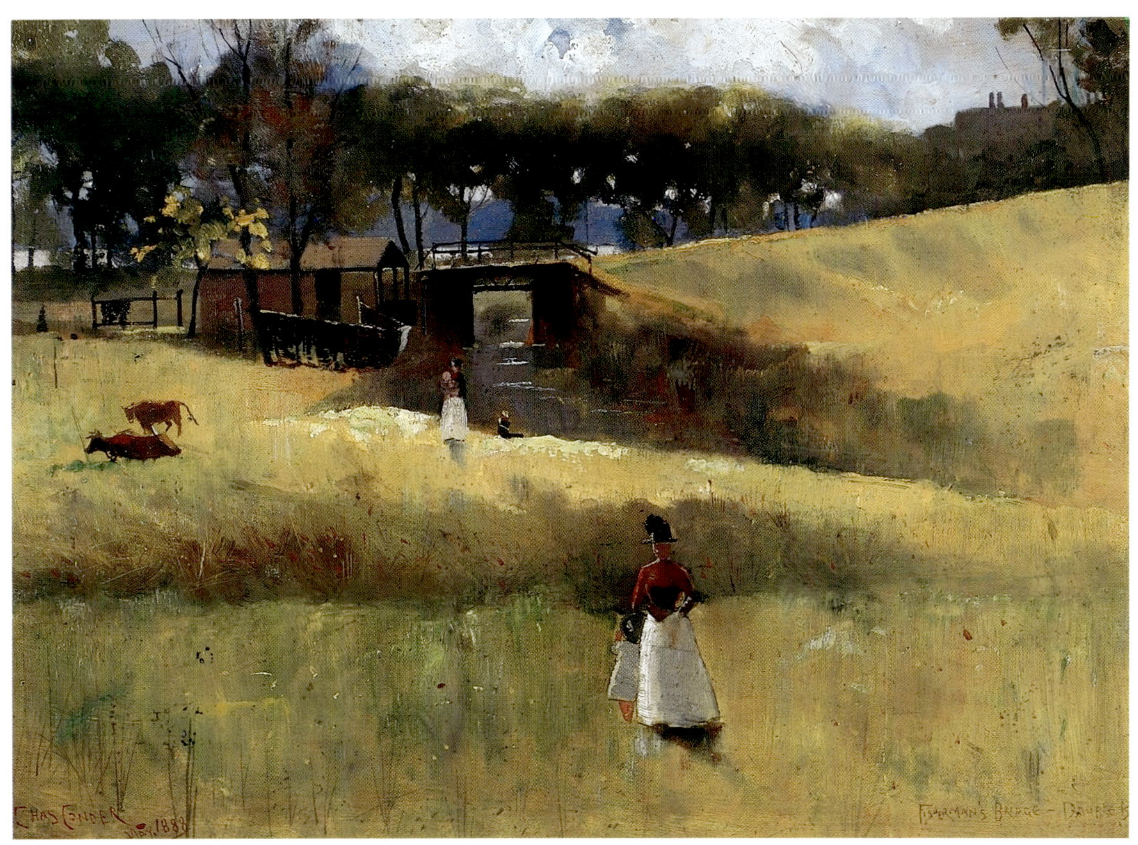

26   Charles Conder
1868–1909
Fisherman's Bridge, Double Bay 1888
oil on wood panel
33.7 × 45.9 cm

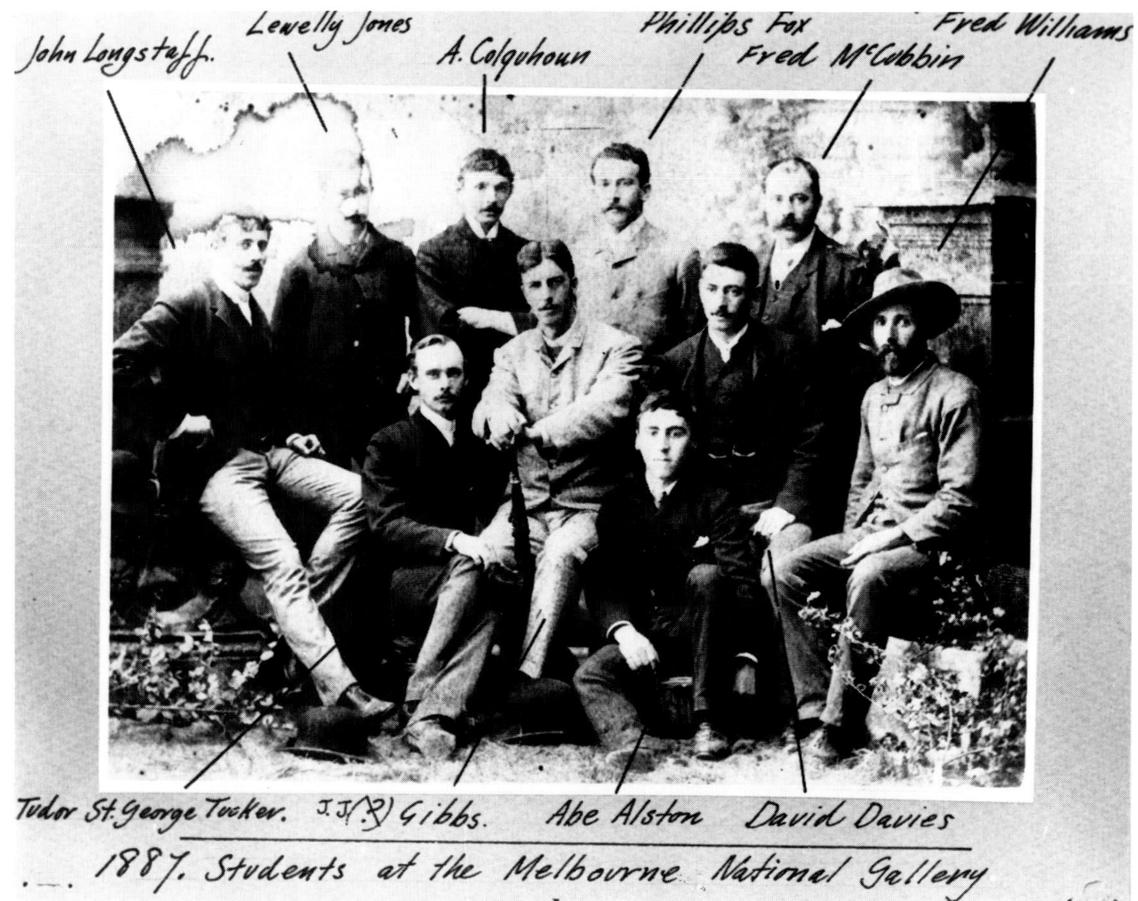

Students at the Melbourne National Gallery in 1887.
With them is their teacher, Frederick McCubbin, who was then Acting Master and Instructor of the School of Design, National Gallery Schools.

La Trobe Collection, State Library of Victoria

economic collapse and not a reflection of personal failure. Disenchanted with city life and professional endeavours, he spent most of the 1890s living and working in the country in northern Victoria and outback New South Wales. He kept his Melbourne studio for some years but spent little time there and eventually settled, restlessly, in Sydney.

Midway through 1890, after Conder's departure, Arthur Streeton visited his married sister in Sydney for a few months, and over the next two years moved between Sydney and Melbourne. His mood, when in Melbourne, was nostalgic for the good old days of one or two years ago. Eventually, like Roberts, Streeton packed his bags to go and live under canvas in the 'Curlew Camp' on Sirius Cove, Sydney. Unhappy at home, artists turned their eyes to Europe, this time not merely travelling to expand their education but hoping to establish a reputation in London. Of the artists represented in this book Streeton – who left Australia in January 1897 – Roberts, David Davies, Tudor St George Tucker and Phillips Fox were all living in London by 1903.

The course of Australian impressionism may have been different in the 1890s if it weren't for the severe economic depression. If the urban and fashionable trend of the 1880s had continued the subjects would have been less rural, nostalgic, masculine and nationalistic than the series of major pictures produced in the depression.

Jane Sutherland (1855–1928) was an artist whose paintings got better and better through the 1890s. She essayed masculine subjects every now and then, but mostly stayed within the domesticated realm, painting the farm and country scenery of the outer suburbs that had been popular in the 1880s, and peopling her rustic scenes with children. Despite Sutherland's achievement in depicting a dry landscape in subdued tones of grey-green and brown that was acknowledged to be 'racy of the Australian soil and climate'[10] and 'most distinctively Australian in atmosphere and out-of-door light and colour',[11] she was hampered by being female. Quite simply she was left behind when her men friends, Roberts and Streeton, left Victoria for New South Wales. As a woman she could not readily make excursions far out of Melbourne to paint typical subjects of Australian rural life. The large, ambitious, nationalistic images were out of her province.

In the 1890s Jane Sutherland experienced the extra loneliness of a woman artist who had stepped out of line and become dependent on a group of male competitors, with nowhere to go when those men retreated into an exclusively masculine realm. She had hung on at the National Gallery School from 1871 to 1886 for the sake of professional company, not for the instruction, which she did not need. Inhibited by convention from mixing socially with male artists on equal terms outside the various art institutions, she found in the National Gallery School, the Buonarotti Club,[12] the Victorian Academy of Art and the Victorian Artists' Society, places where art and intellectual ideas were debated without fear or favour. When Tom Roberts returned from London in 1885 and gathered his old friends together for painting excursions and the establishment of a strictly professional art society,

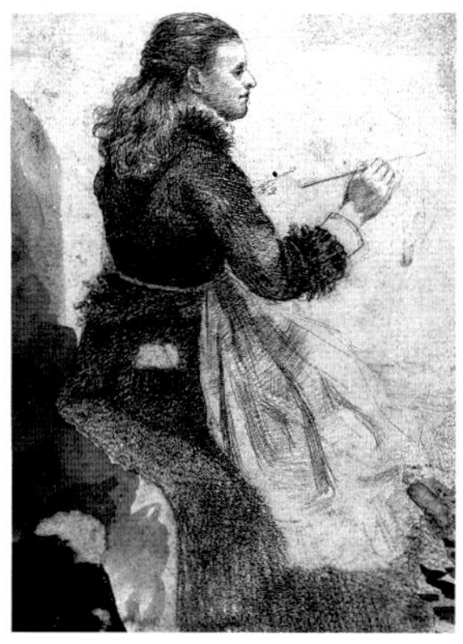

A sketch of Jane Sutherland by her father George, probably drawn in their North Carlton house c. 1880.

La Trobe Collection, State Library of Victoria

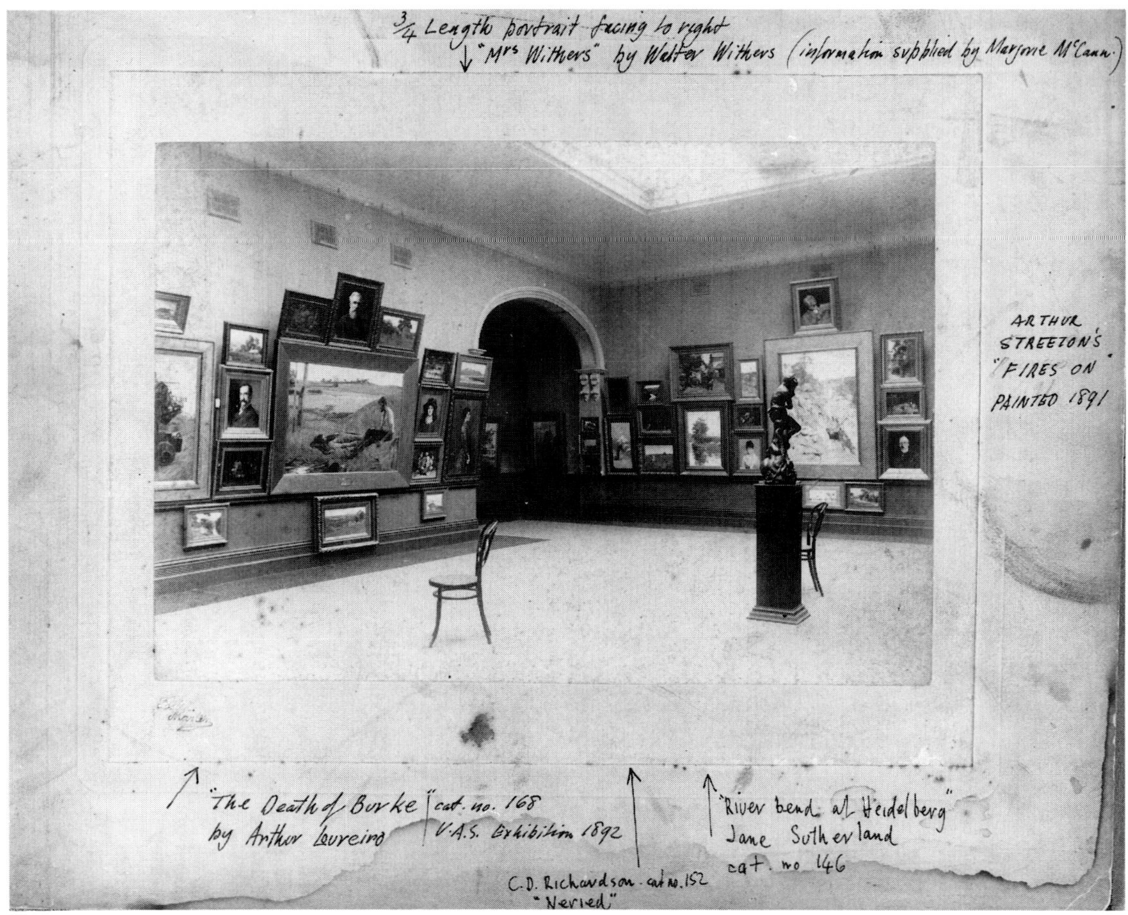

Victorian Artists' Society exhibition held in 1892 at their newly built and fashionable premises in Albert Street, East Melbourne. It remains their home to this day.

La Trobe Collection, State Library of Victoria

Sutherland made a major decision. Rather than stay within the group of women watercolourists of her day, which included Madame Mouchette (under whom she had studied), Emma Minnie Boyd and Mrs Elizabeth Parsons, she threw in her lot with Roberts and the male painters. She did join Mrs Parsons' 'Stray Leaves' club in 1889 along with Roberts and Streeton.[13]

It was no mean feat to achieve a degree of sexual equality without losing social respectability. Sutherland had to work hard at it. She required female companionship (Nellie McCubbin, Nancy Elmhurst-Goode) when going with the men to paint at Box Hill in the years 1885 to 1888. Unlike the men, who relaxed under canvas for the weekend, she had to rush out to Box Hill and back home in a day. She found female companionship mandatory even when moving into the Grosvenor Chambers studios in 1888. The woman she shared with was Clara Southern, and

Jane Price had a tiny studio nearby.

One result of mixing with male artists was that Sutherland became known by local suffragettes as 'the leader amongst the lady artists of Victoria of the open air school,[14] with a reputation for having painted 'practically the first examples of the plein air school attempted and achieved by a lady so far' in Melbourne.[15]

By 1894, left behind in Melbourne, she had found a painting ground in 'solitary and uncultivated country' at Mitcham, beyond Box Hill.[16] At nearby Blackburn she had the companionship of Frederick McCubbin (who had moved there in 1893). And, during the year she was at Mitcham, she shared a studio at Blackburn with other artists she and McCubbin had known well since the 1880s – Tudor St George Tucker, Tom Humphrey and George Pitt Morrison. Morrison had only just returned from France and (like Tucker) was experimenting with a light-filled palette and broken colour, of which McCubbin and Sutherland took note. When McCubbin moved to Brighton in 1896, and Tucker to Hampton in 1895, Sutherland (coincidentally?) went to live with relatives in North Road, Brighton.

In the mid-1890s she was one of the first to experiment with laying on paint with a palette knife (and was reprimanded for it in the press).[17] Her career as an oil painter came to an abrupt halt in 1899. According to one report her illness was a result of overwork. Some said that a vegetarian diet had endangered her health.[18] More likely she suffered from a weak heart, like others in her family. For more than a year Sutherland was unable to work. Afterwards an invalid, she was entirely dependent on others, unable to walk, unable to paint in the country or get about on her own even inside the house. Sickness did not stop her working. She made pastel drawings on paper, pushing onward with her earlier experimentation with colour. We are told that in older age 'Jeanie' Sutherland was 'timorous' and quiet, though she 'never failed to light up and grow animated when she talked of her active painting days. The feeling of painting in a group seemed to have particular significance for there was so much discussion, comparing of notes, and tireless experimentation'.[19] It was an age when different things were expected of men and women, even in art. Having transgressed the social code, discreetly but nonetheless noticeably, Sutherland was on undefined territory artistically and socially. She did not join the suffragette movement in Melbourne. Nor did she identify particularly with the efforts of her fellow women painters, Clara Southern and Jane Price. Those with whom she had identified, her Heidelberg School friends, even Frederick McCubbin, explored masculine themes beyond her reach. Through the 1890s she had much more in common with painters like Tucker who were ten years younger. All in all, Sutherland's career from 1890 onwards was unusually lonely. Perhaps 1970s feminists were not wrong to perceive her enforced immobility from 1899 as an exaggerated, punishing parody of the woman's lot.

Little gossips (plate 27) 'a woodland scene with children',[20] was exhibited in May 1888 at the first exhibition of the Victorian Artists' Society and reproduced in the catalogue. Unlike Sutherland's other paintings in the exhibition, it was not for sale, presumably because it had been acquired already by a friend or patron (perhaps by Nellie McCubbin, a companion on some of the excursions to Box Hill).[21] The similarity of image and style with *Obstruction, Box Hill,* exhibited in 1887, suggests that they were painted at Box Hill around the same time. The white bonnet and pink dress appeared in both works: probably the same child posed for the two images.

Sutherland accompanied Roberts, McCubbin and Louis Abrahams on some of their painting expeditions to Box Hill in 1886, 1887 and 1888. Arthur Streeton joined the later jaunts. They all showed Box Hill pictures at the May 1888 exhibition, earning the comment that there was a 'Box Hill School' who had 'the same feeling, a common thought, and a similar mannerism, while they hunt on the same Box Hill camping ground'.[22]

Tom Roberts inaugurated the Box Hill camp near his aunt's house, in scenery he had enjoyed as a boy of fourteen.[23] His perception of the Box Hill camp was of male camaraderie, even at the time he was painting love scenes there which included women:

> I went down last week about 7 pm. I met the other two at Box Hill. They had come to see if I had brought more provisions to add to theirs. Fortunately I had so we only needed to get some bottled liquid labelled 'Carlton'. The spot we are camped in is so cut off

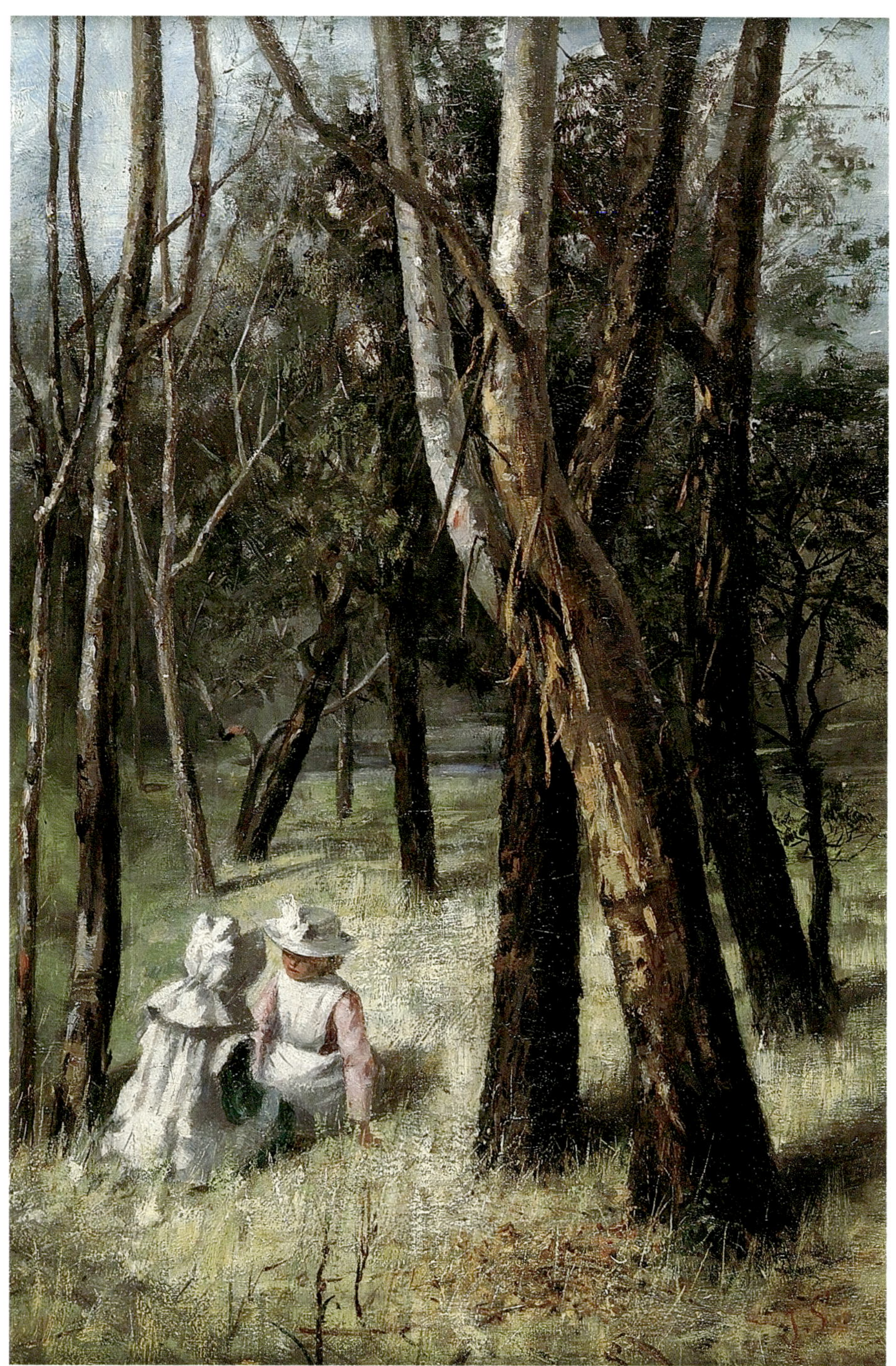

27 Jane Sutherland
1855–1928
Little gossips 1888
oil on canvas
48.5 × 36.0 cm

that when the night is dark it is very difficult to cross the creek at all. We had a candle which A[brahams] lit only when half across the log when it didn't much matter . . . he went in all the same and we had to wrap him up in my plaid while certain portions of him were hung by the fire. It was supper time by this & we explored the tent for some chops but it was all in vain to shake blankets – 3 lbs of pork chops . . . were gone. The bread we never saw again.[24]

Streeton's much later recollection was visual:

I close my eyes. I see again . . . black wattles & ti-tree down by the creek – the Houstons cabin the messmate tree & its mistletoe & horehound patch beneath [and at the end of the day] the run for trains on Sunday night & Prof [McCubbin] far up ahead, mopping his brow near Jack Gange's [place and in the distance the evening] flush over [the] Dandenongs & . . . [the] quiet grey valley beyond White Horse Road toward Macedon.[25]

Streeton cultivated nostalgia even as a youth. Within a year of Conder's and Roberts' departure from Heidelberg he already had a repertoire of honeyed memories of the Box Hill and Heidelberg camps. Judging from the fervent recollections in letters he loved the companionship, the talk of literature, the painters' appraisal of poet Browning's use of visual imagery, their approval of the manly stride of Walt Whitman's verse, their anxious rivalry in finding painterly ways to emulate the novelist Thomas Hardy. As an exemplar of the interdependence of man and nature Hardy was profoundly important for Australian impressionism. He forced his human protagonists into a symbiotic relationship with the landscape:

A Saturday afternoon in November was approaching the time of twilight, and the vast tract of unenclosed wild known as Egdon Heath embrowned itself moment by moment. Overhead the hollow stretch of whitish cloud shutting out the sky was as a tent which had the whole heath for its floor.
The heaven being spread with this pallid screen and the earth with the darkest vegetation, their

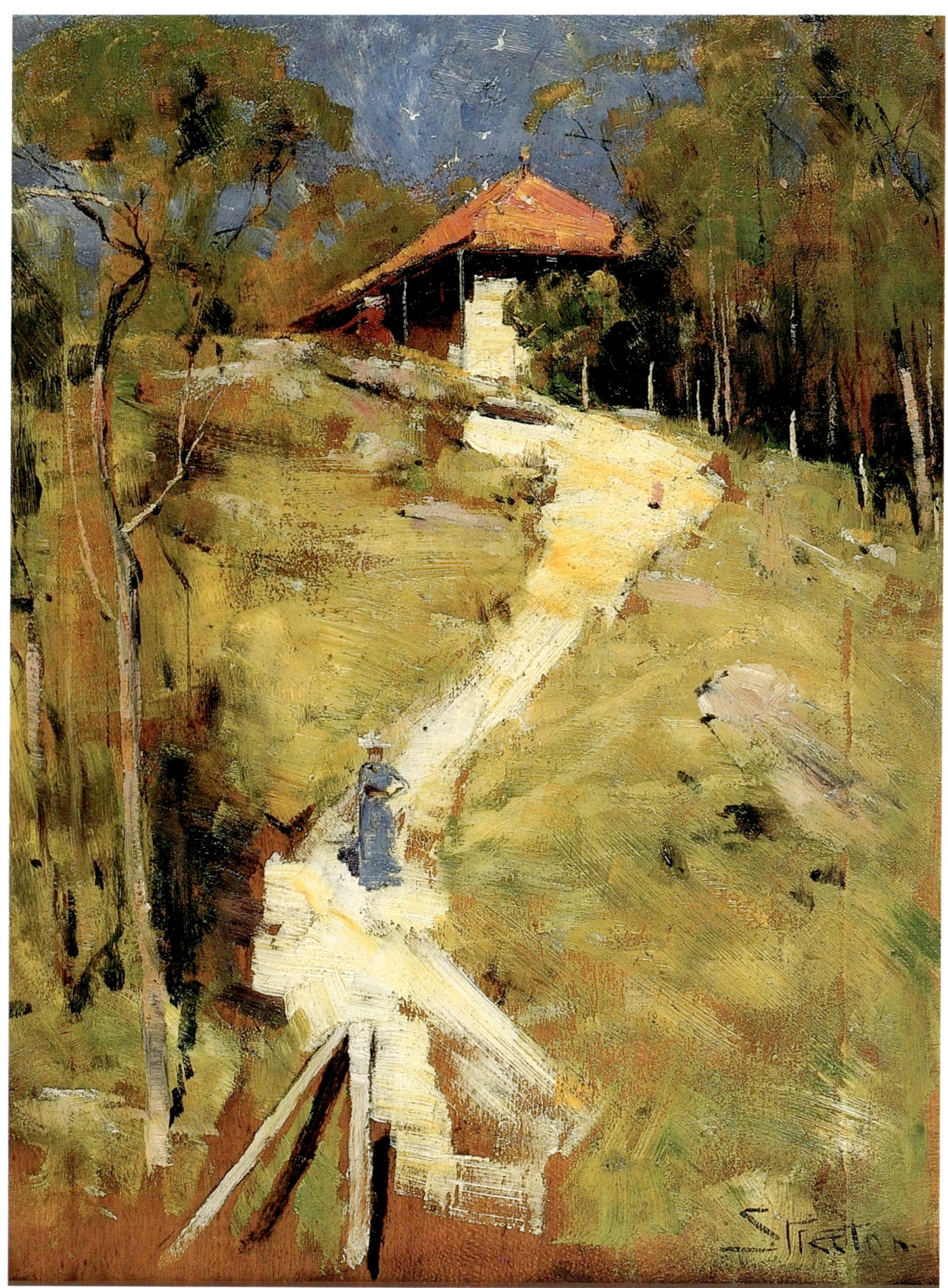

28 Arthur Streeton
1867–1943
(*Sunlight: the path to Podge Newton's*) (1895)
oil on plywood panel
28.2 × 21.5 cm

meeting-line at the horizon was clearly marked . . . Looking upwards, a furze-cutter would have been inclined to continue work; looking down, he would have decided to finish his faggot and go home. The distant rims of the world and of the firmament seemed to be a division in time no less than a division in matter.[26]

Through the 1890s Streeton and Roberts painted and wrote letters that created a Hardyesque marriage of people and landscape. For Streeton in Sydney it was a world of young men and women under the arch of a blue sky in a summer landscape of khaki foliage, blue sea and sunstruck soil. The landscape rises up, the blue sky reaches down in shifting planes of blue to cap the horizon and enclose the human figure. A couple of summers before Streeton painted the woman dressed in blue descending the steep path *Sunlight: the path to Podge Newton's* c. 1895 (plate 28), he was visited by a Melbourne friend, the musician George W.L. Marshall Hall. Together they lazed about at Curlew camp and at a friend's house above Mosman Bay, chatting, painting, writing poetry and composing images and music that were alive to the joys of an Australian summer.[27] 'Here I am in this divine place,' wrote the composer, 'among bronzed gums beaten out against the magnificent blue sky like figures on a vase. All warmth, sunshine and gloriousness. Streeton has been doing grand work – such life and movement and joy & intenseness of living in it.'[28] Robust paintings, such as *Sunlight: the path to Podge Newton's*, like the masculine poems and clamant music produced by Marshall Hall in the 1890s, evoked an image of a sunny, vital Australia that became Streeton's special theme.

Streeton had been preceded at Curlew Camp by Tom Roberts, whose friends, the Braschs, established the camp in 1890. Sydney and its blue harbour held little artistic appeal for Roberts. His romance was outback among pioneering farmers, shearers, drovers and lonely goldminers. He used his city connections to make his way outback. And whereas through the 1890s Streeton developed a painting style of Whitmanesque vigour, Tom Roberts maintained a tender manner of painting, even in subjects of masculine labour. *Towards Millera* 1894 (plate 29) is typically appreciative of the theme of mankind

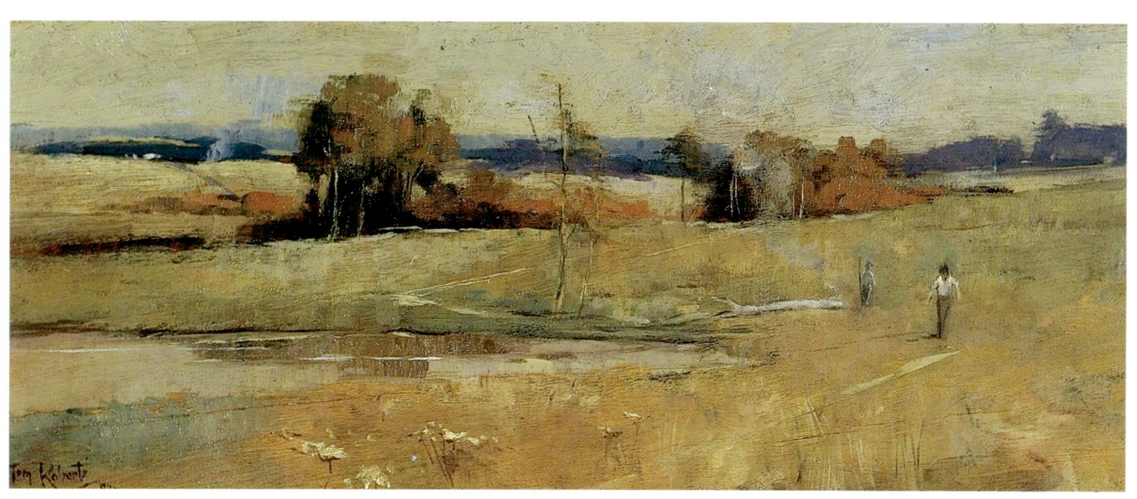

29 Tom Roberts
1856–1931
Towards Millera 1894
oil on plywood panel
15.5 × 37.5 cm

in harmony with nature. The scene is of two figures strolling through pastureland beside water. Blue smoke rises against the purple hills. This remote spot in northern New South Wales, to which Roberts made his way on horseback late in 1894, provided as tranquil and tame a scene as any that were much nearer the cities

Before arriving in this green valley he had been, in quick succession, in Melbourne, Brockelsby, Sydney, Tenterfield and Drake. On 13 October 1894, in Melbourne, he went to Blackburn with the McCubbins and others. They picnicked on 'the green flat by the creek side in a wilderness of young gums & gathered masses of maiden hair . . . & the Prof [McCubbin] sang 'Who is Sylvia?'.[29] From there Roberts went, via Brockelsby Station near Corowa and Sydney, by train to Tenterfield and coach to the township of Drake and on horseback 33 miles over the hills and far away to visit his friend Walter Reeks, who was washing gold at Millera.[30] The last was the important part of the journey. Roberts jotted pencil notes as he rode, tracing his sensations:

> From Drake bridle track, steep country, green grass, apple tree & Jones oak. Track always rough, narrow, dark & it drops, dips steep – with cut stepping places for the horses [on the] stretch below palm fronds in the thick gully. [On] one hand the mountain haze open in afternoon sunlight, opposite the tree tops bright green cut against purple shadow. Track winds along the little creek by stumps of cedar, tall (gum trees), fern covered banks, slender palm, the Tamarind dark rich green, creeper hanging in festoons from the highest trees, staghorn [?] ferns in big clusters . . . soft perfume of cut wood. [T]he whip bird. [T]ill opening of valley & change of timber, on the slope grass trees like London [Guards] with busbies – moving with scarlet blue tailed Lorries & the bell birds . . . [G]rassy flat with horses. [O]ther stream by the hillside with an avenue of more oaks tall & soft against sky as the hair of a beauty. [S]cent of shit, brutes of ants, a dog's bark, station cattle . . . Timbarra creek fringed and islanded with oak or ti tree, the banks sloping back great rounded shoulders, a ring [of] timber along one razor back spur, dip to

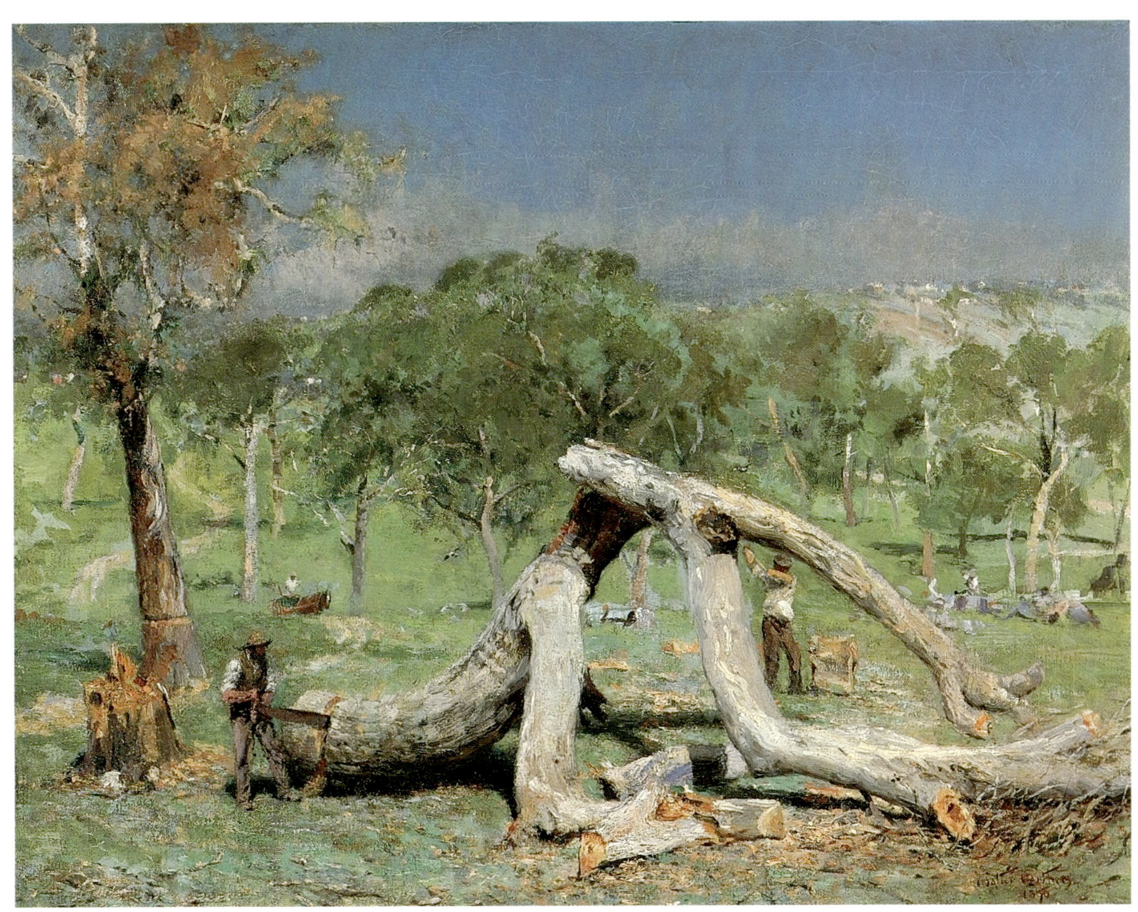

30   Walter Withers
1854–1914
A Fallen Monarch 1890
oil on canvas
76.0 × 99.0 cm

river, dusk, pile of wide & distant mountains a silken
band. . .along belly, cross creek & camp & welcome.[31]

These evocative notes of a journey indicate how much
the artist wanted and actively sought to be alone with
nature. During a few weeks at Millera he painted *Towards
Millera, scene on the Timbarra* (private collection) and the
goldmining subject *On the Timbarra: Reek's and Allen's sluicing
claim* (Art Gallery of South Australia). He rode across to
George Ogilvie's station, 'Yulgibah' on the Clarence River,
for another session of painting. Then, after coming back
to his friends at Millera, he rode 125 miles south-west
to other friends at Newstead, near Inverell. This solitary,
purposeful contact with the landscape was Roberts'
artistic research, from which he gained the knowledge
and the special feeling for place which were to provide
the *expression* of his paintings.

Unlike Streeton (who unselfconsciously preferred
glamour), Roberts was in search of an inconspicuous
natural style. It was a higher ambition which he failed
to achieve. The indecisive, soft, even formless description
of *Towards Millera* corresponds with the receptive mood
but not the precision of the handwritten notes scribbled
during the journey on horseback. In this instance, as in
many, Roberts was a better writer than painter. The image
transcribes some of his impressions: the wide mountains
like a thread across the belly of the landscape and trees
soft as hair against the sky. That it does not have the
same precision as the writing indicates a failure between
Roberts' genuine response and his capacity to realise his
impressions in art. We see in the painting and read in
the notes that Roberts feminised the landscape: trees were
like the hair of a beautiful woman, landscape forms were
like rounded shoulders. His weakness was in relying on
sentimental associations that were impressions by proxy
rather than true perceptions. Sentimentality was a
limitation that beset Roberts throughout his career.

Not every artist rode so bravely into the landscape to
find a style that paid homage to nature. Walter Withers
(1854–1914) stayed at Heidelberg, painting a single subject
of figures in picturesque roadways, painting it over and
over without losing interest, in fact often with conspicuous
success. *A Fallen monarch* 1890 (plate 30) – an unusually
strident image for Withers – is dominated by the broken-

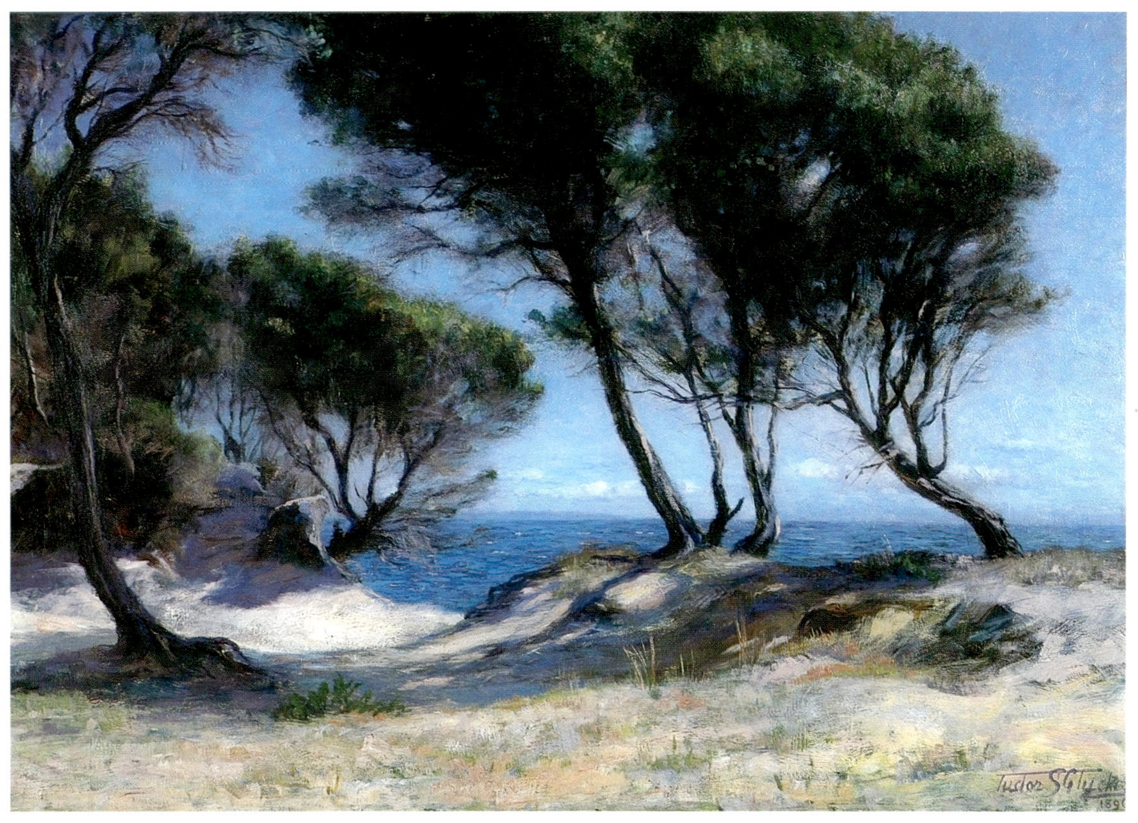

31   Tudor St George Tucker
1862–1906
Ti trees near Sandringham 1896
oil on canvas
70.0 × 100.4 cm

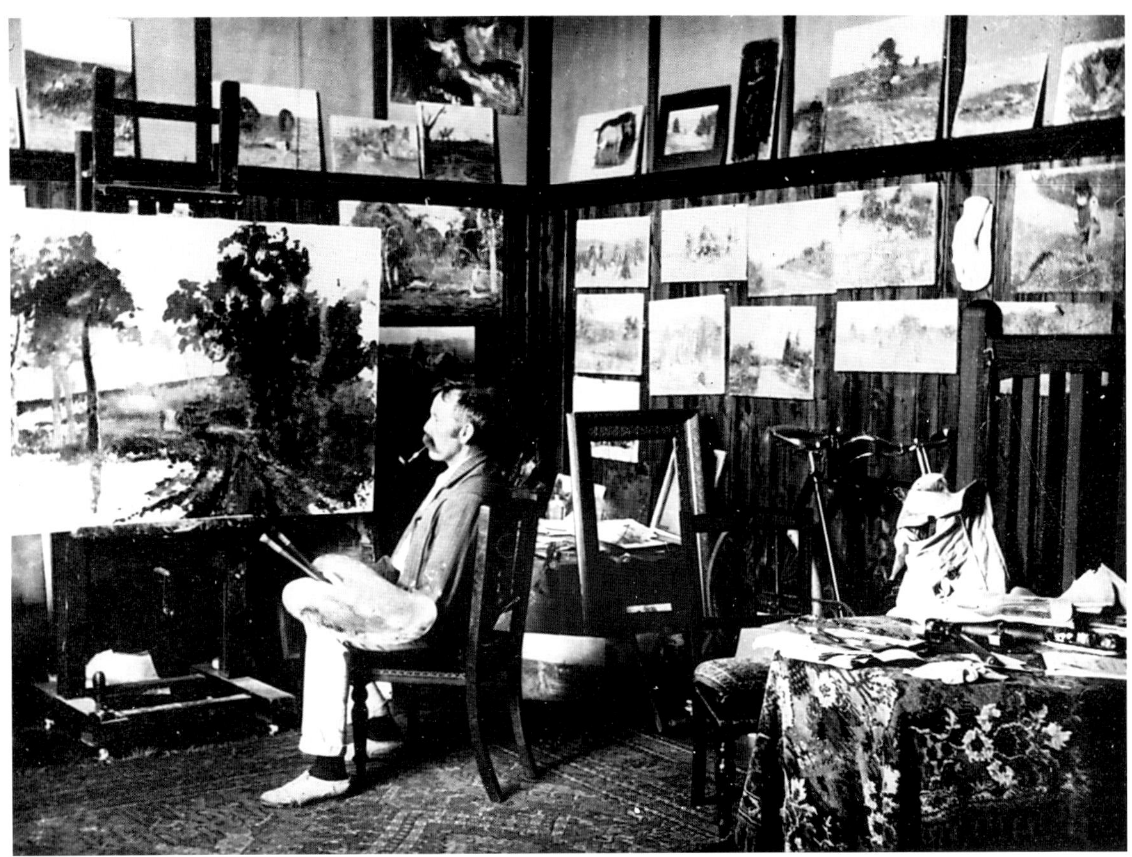

Walter Withers in his studio in Eltham, then the rural outskirts of Melbourne, in 1906.

La Trobe Collection, State Library of Victoria

backed form of a shattered red gum. The suggestion is that the tree which was nurtured by nature has been brought down by the same force. Nature's uncaring power is further demonstrated by the stark light of an approaching storm. Under the clamorous sky and sharply painted upper hillside the timber-getters by the tree appear puny. But this image of a fallen monarch, instead of representing the slack aftermath of failure, has an atmosphere of electric intensity, almost of expectancy, as if the scene, which includes human beings, is essentially a natural drama beyond man's capacity to intervene. Once again we perceive the interpenetrating themes and the moody example of Thomas Hardy.

At the extreme edge of experimentation in Melbourne in the 1890s, Tudor St George Tucker (1862–1906) in *Ti trees near Sandringham* 1896 (plate 31) used divided colours of sapphire and violet, pink, lilac and green, to evoke the light on warm sand above a summer sea. This was as close as Australian painting came to Monet's 1890s impressionism: similar both in its overt symbolism and its blissful coloured light. Tucker had studied in France in the late 1880s, where he and E. Phillips Fox encountered a style of modified impressionism. Missing the first shock of the economic depression in Melbourne, they returned in the early 1890s with a rainbow palette and brush manner that were markedly different from those of the Heidelberg School.

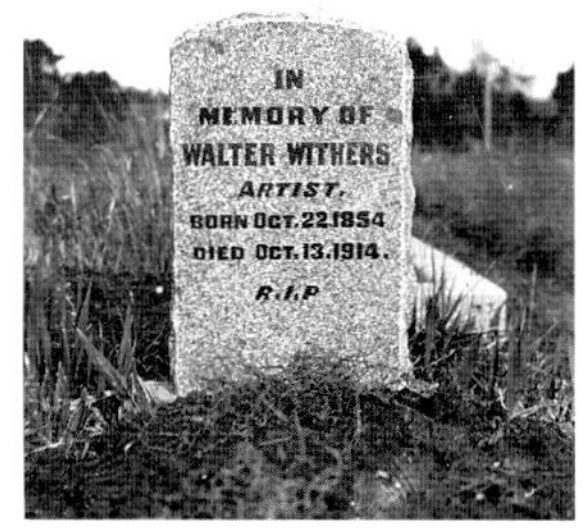

Walter Withers' headstone, St Helena's Cemetery.
Photograph by J.K. Moir
La Trobe Collection, State Library of Victoria

In Paris, according to Conder's report, Tucker had been regarded as the 'strongest' artist among the Australian contingent. He shared the same interests as Conder and Fox in coloured atmosphere and poeticised portraits, landscapes and figure studies. By comparison with Fox, who was myopically involved with his art, Tucker's technique was fastidious and his style a homage to lucidity. In Melbourne, Tucker's paintings evoked praise for qualities of light. In a seascape like *Ti trees near Sandringham* reviewers noted that its theme was 'the perfect harmony of sea and sky'.[32] An image of a young French communicant had an almost visionary 'rippling play of white light'.[33] An Australian landscape was praised for an effect of light on 'the yellow earth' where 'purple and pink permeate the shadows in a curious manner, according to the flickering sunshine'.[34] Since his student days in the 1880s Tucker had a reputation for being an aesthete, a trendsetter who pursued a variety of bizarre new ideas. He was dandified; he was interested in clothes; and he was almost as devoted a musician as artist. In Paris, Tucker was as 'aesthetic as ever'. Living poorly in a cold damp studio, he nevertheless had a piano and a new affectation: playing an African stringed instrument.[35] The exalted quality of his art had been established early. Some years before leaving Melbourne to study in Paris he gave a paper about Ralph Waldo Emerson at the Buonarotti Club.[36] Emerson's transcendental ambition had been to open imagination to nature – to merge the mind into the swimming light. As a sub-theme he encouraged Americans to find creative independence from Europe. Tucker in maturity expounded an Emersonian theme of light; 'All things swim and glitter', 'all forms are fluent', wrote Emerson; equally, the eye observing Tucker's painting receives an Emersonian message of 'evanescence and lubricity'.

Ironically, back in Melbourne, Tucker and Fox settled

in Heidelberg in a house, 'Charterisville', lower down the hill from where Roberts, Conder and Streeton had lived. They opened an art school whose students visited 'Charterisville' regularly for summer schools through the 1890s. There, in vivid colours of grass green, blue, lilac and yellow, and in a broad, painterly style, the same fields, river valley and ranges were painted that the 'Heidelberg School' had rendered in quieter tones during their much shorter time on the hill above 'Charterisville'.

Opalescent light, milky and shot with jewel-like colours became McCubbin's dream at Macedon in the early 1900s. Frederick McCubbin (1855–1917) was the oldest male painter of the Heidelberg School (apart from Withers) and two years younger than Jane Sutherland. He stayed in Melbourne through the 1890s and learnt new lessons about how to see light in divided colours. His painting companions of the 1890s included Pitt Morrison, Tucker, Jane Sutherland and Tom Humphrey. The mysticism of prismatic colour that led Tucker to paint figures floating in a tide of light brought McCubbin to a similar mysticism some years later. His young daughter Kathleen, shown burrowing in the bracken in the 1913 painting *At Macedon* (plate 32), is nearly invisible in a bush landscape where there is no distinction between brushstrokes, colour, tones and the twigs and leaves they describe. All is texture. The medley serves to describe the refraction of light on a multiplicity of small surfaces. As with Tudor St George's seascape the overall image, far from denying an emotive subject, actually underlines the idea of a magical communion with nature. In late paintings such as this small 'gem', McCubbin achieved a stylistic and thematic metamorphosis from his formal beginnings. Whereas in the 1880s he had wanted to achieve the grave power and significance of traditional history painting but lacked the skill to achieve his ambition in older age, he brought to the bush a vision of incandescent light – like Turner's, he thought.

Not one of the painters discussed so far in this chapter was brought up in the country. Streeton was born at Mt Duneed near Geelong. The others were city born. And all were city bred. On the other hand Sidney Long (1871–1955) was born in Goulburn, New South Wales, and had his first art lessons there from a Mrs Miller 'who taught him to copy German oleographs and paint pretty things

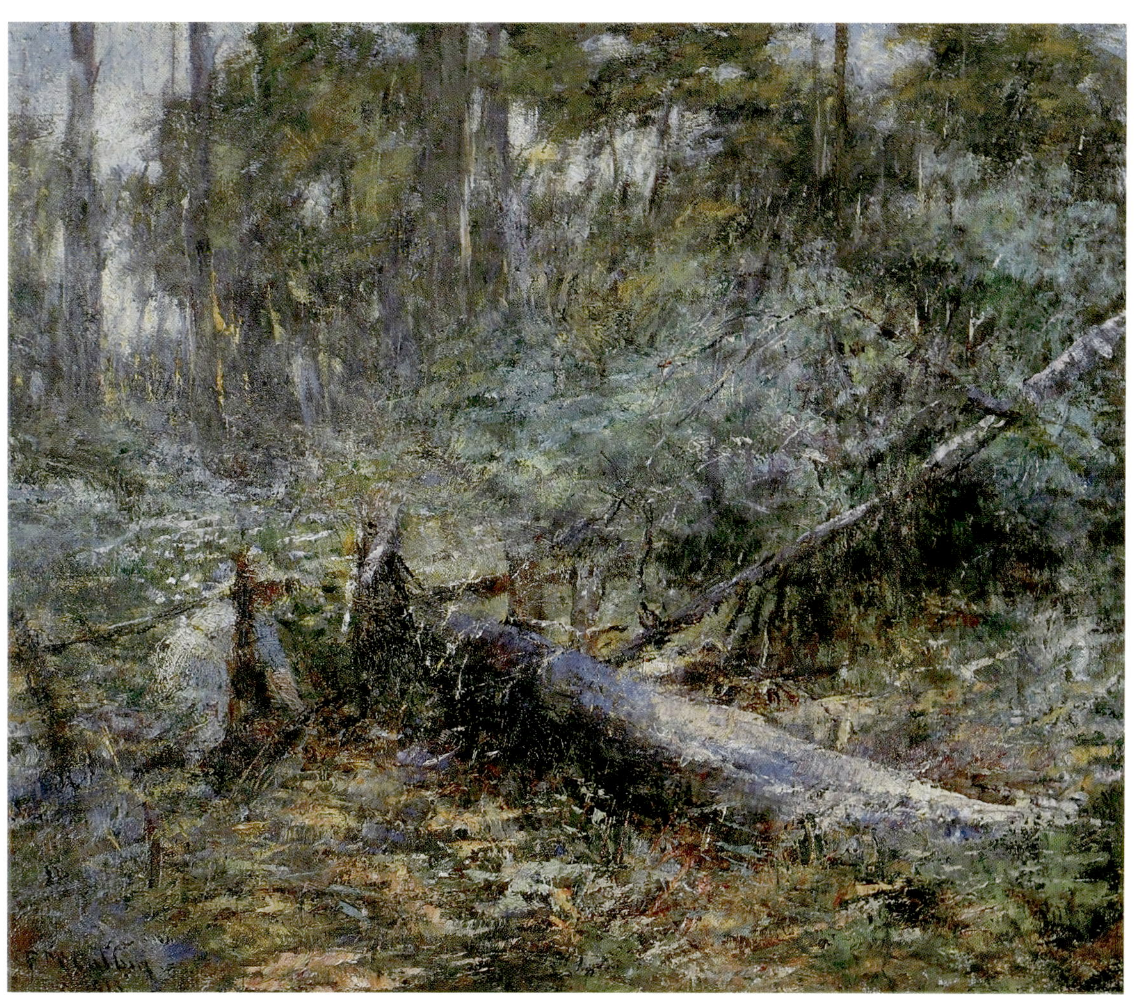

32   Frederick McCubbin
1855–1917
At Macedon 1913
oil on canvas
51.8 x 61.2 cm

on satin'.[37] The country lad escaped to Sydney where, through the 1890s and into the new century, he nurtured a precociously fashionable and colourful style evident in *The sheep pool* 1898 (plate 33). To the end of his days Sid Long maintained the creed of studying the landscape at first hand, taking himself into the country at every opportunity, while on the contrary his paintings and prints did not appear at all like straight reportage. One appreciative critic remarked that 'local topography is, to him, only a peg on which to hang the luminous web of his fancy'.

> The chief feature of his work is its striking originality, and the success with which the painter divides his work into magnificent masses. Occasionally it savours of the theatrical, as when he throws his foreground into deep shadow, while his distance is illuminated by all the brilliancy of an Australian sun. This is noticeable in 'The sheep pool' and to some extent in the more ambitious picture of 'Pan'.[38]

To *The sheep pool and Pan* we might add the other well-known work *The Spirit of the Plains*, painted in 1897, which Long recreated as an aquatint after the Great War.

Long's colours – 'strong, almost garish', his invented fauns and naiades and stylised outlines describing, for instance, 'decorative trees which were quite unlike any ordinary growths of garden or bush', were intended to express a heartfelt vision. The style which to most viewers appeared an idiosyncratic embroidery on ordinary nature was the artist's expression of 'the primitive landscape of the country': one of the first serious attempts to capture the spirit of Australia through imagination rather than imitation.[39] 'It is this difference of environment that will make our Art distinctive,' wrote Long. 'The brilliancy and dryness of the summers and the comparative mildness of the winters give to our landscape a range of hot, warm colours peculiar to ourselves ... the more serious and sombre side of [the landscape] has not been touched yet ... [But] Australian feeling is not to be got by sticking to the gum tree.'[40]

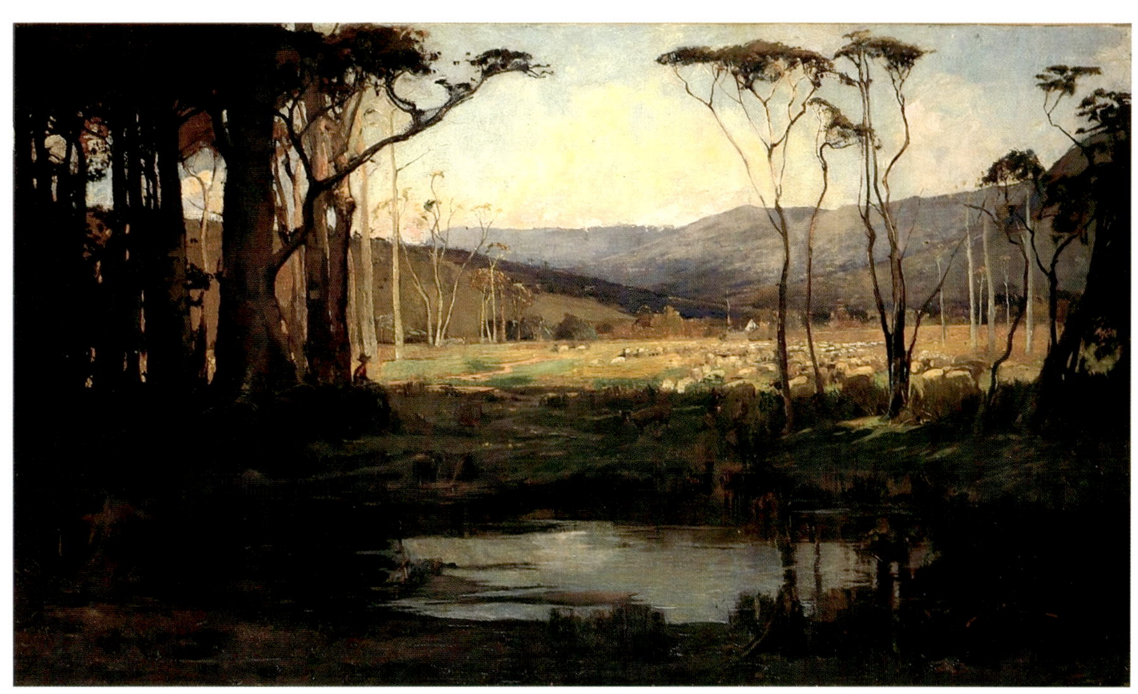

33   Sidney Long
1871–1955
The sheep pool 1898
oil on canvas
82.0 × 140.0 cm

1 *Table Talk*, Melbourne, 19 July 1889, p. 5.
2 *Table Talk*, Melbourne, 3 March 1893, p. 2.
3 *The Press*, Christchurch, New Zealand, 1 June 1896, p. 6.
4 *Australasian Sketcher*, no. 95, vol. VIII, Melbourne, 10 April 1880, p. 54.
5 *Australian Art: A Monthly Magazine*, Sydney, January 1888, p. 5.
6 Amandus Fisher, notes to John Rothenstein, 1936, Tate Gallery Archive 7910/16.
7 Minutes of Art Society's meetings, Royal Art Society papers, Sydney.
8 Conder sketchbook held by the Mitchell Library.
9 'Report from Paris' in *Gossip*, Melbourne, 18 June 1890, p. 22.
10 *Argus*, Melbourne, 29 March 1890, p. 11.
11 *Argus*, Melbourne, 20 April 1893, p. 7.
12 The Buonarotti Club was formed by John Longstaff, Tucker, Alexander Colquhoun, Cyrus Mason and others in May 1883. Sutherland started attending in mid-1884 and belonged until 1887 – the full period of its existence. She was elected a member in July 1884. See Buonarotti Club Papers in State Library of Victoria.
13 *Table Talk*, Melbourne, 28 June 1889, p. 3.
14 *Age*, Melbourne, 19 May 1894, p. 14.
15 *Sun*, Melbourne, 21 April 1893, p. 7. She was not the first woman to paint en plein air.
16 *Age*, Melbourne, 19 May 1894, p. 14.
17 *Table Talk*, Melbourne, 23 October 1896, p. 16; *Argus*, Melbourne, 23 October 1896, p. 6.
18 *Table Talk*, Melbourne, 18 October 1900, p. 5.
19 Margaret Sutherland, 'Young Days in Music', *Overland*, Melbourne, No. 40, December 1968, p. 24.
20 *Age*, Melbourne, 20 April 1888, p. 6.
21 *Little gossips* is inscribed reverse in ink: 'Helen Gray / With love from / Aunt Nellie / Oct. 1914.' The McCubbin grandmother was Jean Gray.
22 *Daily Telegraph*, Melbourne, 1 May 1888, p. 3.
23 Madame Elmhurst Goode reminiscences, this part not published by Croll, in R.H. Croll papers, Mitchell Library; R.H. Croll, *Tom Roberts*, Robertson & Mullens Ltd, Melbourne, 1935, p. 18; William Moore, *The Story of Australian Art*, Angus & Robertson, Sydney & Melbourne, 1934, vol. 1, p. 70.
24 Tom Roberts to Lillie Williamson, 15 April 1886, papers in private possession.
25 Arthur Streeton, letter to McCubbin, 8 April 1901, McCubbin papers, LaTrobe Library, State Library of Victoria.
26 First lines of Thomas Hardy's *The Return of the Native*.
27 Marshall Hall had recently dedicated an Overture to his friend Arthur Streeton, Delmer papers, Mitchell Library. Letter seen while it was still in a private collection.
28 Marshall Hall letter to Frederick Delmer, Mosman, [mid-February 1893].
29 Roberts' letter to S.W. Pring, 14 October 1894. ML Mss 1367/2. He said he was thinking of going to Corowa.
30 Roberts wrote on 22 October from 'Brockelsby', Corowa, to say he was coming to Sydney on Wednesday. Roberts' letter to S.W. Pring, 22 October [189]4, S.W. Pring Papers, ML Mss 1367/2, Mitchell Library.
31 Tom Roberts' notebook [1894], S.W. Pring papers, ML Mss 1367/3. See also Roberts' letter to Pring, 3 November [18]94, same papers, ML Mss 1367/2.
32 *Argus*, Melbourne, 1 June 1896, p. 6.
33 *Sun*, Melbourne, 2 September 1892, p. 6.

34 *Table Talk*, Melbourne, 5 July 1895, p. 7.

35 *Gossip*, Melbourne, 18 June 1890, p. 22.

36 See minutes of meeting 1 October 1884, Buonarotti Club papers,
   LaTrobe Collection, State Library of Victoria.

37 D.H. Souter, 'Sid Long, Landscapist', *Art and Architecture*, Sydney, vol.
   2, 1905, p. 638.

38 ibid.

39 Quotations in order of appearance are: *Sydney Mail* 21 September
   1896, p. 537; *Sun*, Melbourne, 9 January 1924; Sid Long, 'The Trend of
   Australian Art Considered and Discussed', *Art and Architecture*, Sydney,
   vol. 2, 1905, pp. 8–10.

40 Long, *Art and Architecture*, pp. 8–10.

TO EUROPE FOR
THE SAKE OF ART

1900–1920s

Paradoxically, the birth of Australia as a nation coincided with the dispersal of her best-known artists. In 1901, after a debate lasting more than twenty years, the six Australian colonies declared themselves a common nation with a cultural as well as social cause, and at that very time the country's most prominent artists sailed for 'Home'. Arthur Streeton left in January 1897. David Davies, who had recently been praised as 'an Australian of the Australians',[1] sailed a few months later on the same ship as George Coates. The 'father of Australian impressionism' left: Tom Roberts, poised to leave early in 1901, accepted a commission to paint the opening ceremony of the first Commonwealth Parliament and delayed long enough to almost complete his 'big picture' before he too went to London.

Australia in depression offered her artists even fewer financial favours than usual whereas Europe was a challenge at the best of times. In the 1890s and early 1900s many of Australia's most ambitious artists chose to seek their fortunes where it counted, on the other side of the world. Ambrose Patterson left for Paris in 1898. Richard Hayley-Lever left in the following year. Percy Spence tried his luck for a second time in England in the late 1890s. Henry Fullwood sailed in March 1900. The young winner of the first New South Wales travelling scholarship, George Lambert, departed in September 1900 on a ship that also carried one of Victoria's most promising young painters, Hugh Ramsay. Max Meldrum, who was given the Victorian travelling scholarship Ramsay had not won, left around the same time. Of these three, Ramsay was obliged to return to Australia when he contracted tuberculosis, Meldrum stayed until 1911 and Lambert until after the Great War. E. Phillips Fox and John Longstaff left Melbourne in March 1901, both for the second time. George

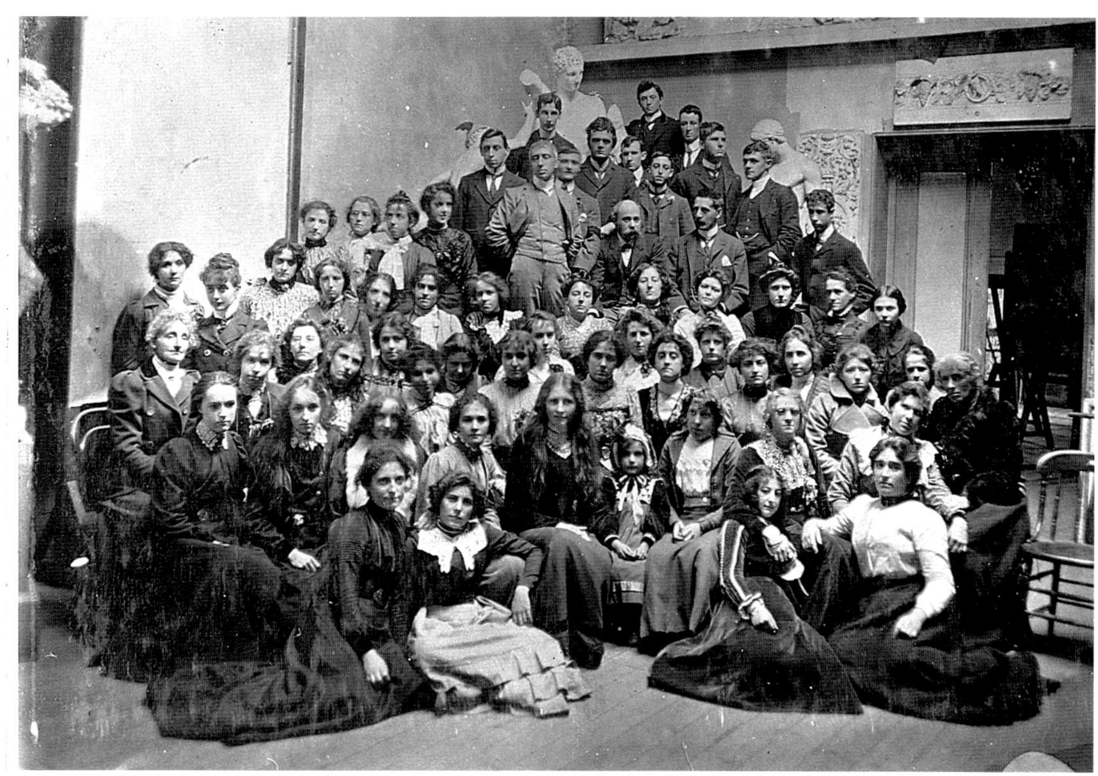

Bell sailed in April 1904. Fred Leist went in 1908, Sid Long left in October 1910 and Blamire Young, who had been in Australia since the early 1880s, returned to his home country in 1912. The artists went singly, each one agonising over whether to go to London or Paris.

Why did so many artists go to England? Why did as many choose Paris? Why not Munich, Rome, Belgium or even America? The reasons were complex. Australians went to Great Britain because it was the mother country. Native-born artists were encouraged from their student years to look to the cultural traditions and monuments of Great Britain and to believe that nothing new and colonial could match that tradition. They were taught to cherish the British heritage as theirs by right. And they were trained in a European tradition. For more than a decade after the establishment of the Melbourne National Gallery School in 1870 its students learnt their trade through making copies: translating in most cases not directly from original works of art but from plaster casts of classical Greek and Roman sculpture, prints and oil-painted copies of great European paintings and

Frederick McCubbin in 1893 surrounded by students from the National Gallery School. McCubbin was the Master and Instructor of the School of Design, National Gallery Schools. The School was housed in the National Gallery of Victoria building that is now the Victorian State Library and Museum.

La Trobe Collection, State Library of Victoria

contemporary works of art (many of them British) purchased for the National Gallery of Victoria. These students – the first generations of art school trainees in the colonies and including in their number Tom Roberts and Frederick McCubbin – thoroughly absorbed a tradition that directed them to Europe.[2] Nowhere but in the museums of Europe could they acquire a first-hand knowledge of great works of art. In the 1880s a Victorian travelling scholarship was mooted for the National Gallery School, to be awarded annually through a painting competition. The first of these scholarships was awarded to John Longstaff in 1887. One of the conditions of the award was that the winner donate to the school a copy painted in Europe from a work by a famous master.

In choosing where to study in Europe colonial students followed the pattern of English artists, who in the early nineteenth century looked beyond their own art centres to Italy and from mid-century to the 1870s looked to Germany. Before the 1880s colonial students who ventured beyond London likewise tried Italy, Munich and Paris as centres of study. By the 1880s Paris was recognised as the centre of art and it attracted students from around the world. London's appeal to colonial artists ebbed, flowed and ebbed again between 1880 and the 1920s. Through the 1880s Tom Roberts, John Russell, Bertram Mackennal, C. D. Richardson, John Longstaff, Rupert Bunny, E. Phillips Fox, Iso and Alison Rae, Alice Chapman, Kate Earle and many others went abroad to study. Most of them went first to England, then crossed to Paris. Students leaving for Europe in the 1890s and 1900s were likely to go to Paris: James Quinn, Alice Muskett, Florence Fuller, Ambrose Patterson, Hugh Ramsay, George Lambert, Kathleen O'Connor, Margaret Preston, Bessie Gibson and Agnes Goodsir are just a few names in a long list of Australian artists who chose to study in France rather than England.

If London's artistic standing was not high compared with Paris, the chances of patronage and reportage were greater, particularly after Edward VII came to the throne in 1901. In the two decades leading to the First World War, London drew colonial artists with the promise of an art reflecting the political splendour of a great Empire at its zenith: the social glamour of the Edwardian period. During those decades London became the home of many

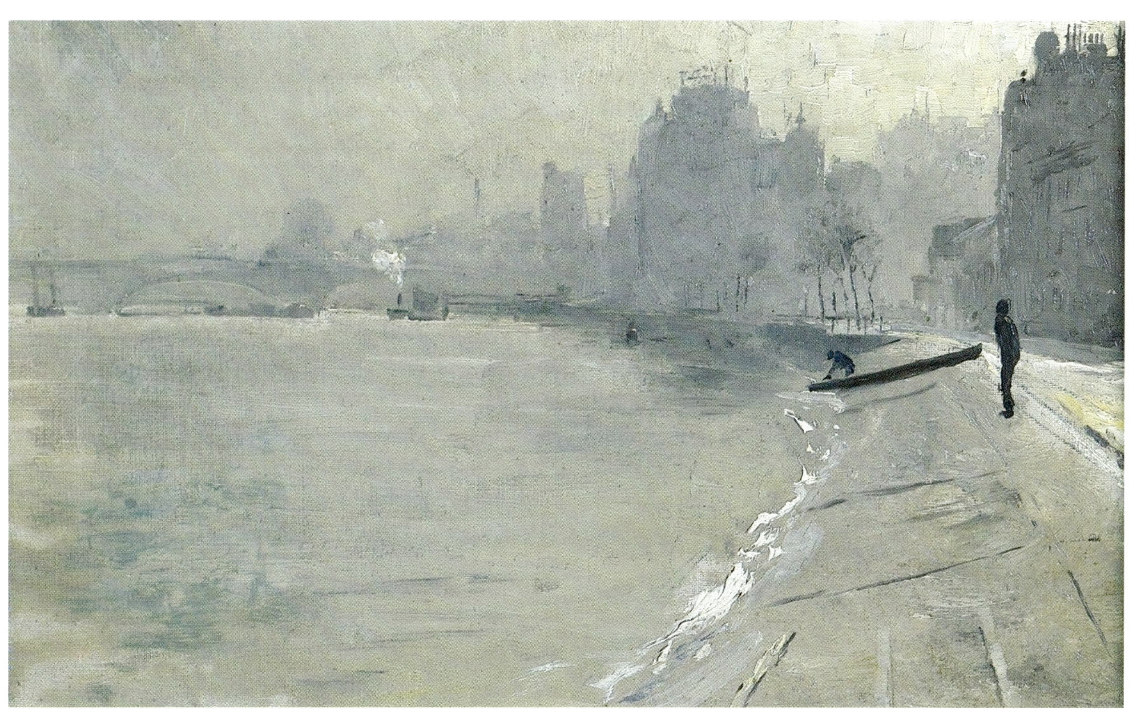

34   Tom Roberts
1856–1931
The towpath, Putney 1904
oil on canvas
25.3 × 40.7 cm

of Australia's foremost artists, both those who had established reputations in Australia, like Roberts and Streeton, and socially ambitious younger painters such as Lambert. Statistically, it attracted more men than women, presumably because the dominant Edwardian image of the artist was a suave and clubbish male. Notably, the centre of art activity for Australians during that period was the Chelsea Arts Club, a male enclave.

At the time of Federation, only a very few Australian artists resident in London – the sculptor Bertram Mackennal and the painter Mortimer Menpes were two – had made a successful and secure career for themselves, and during the next fifteen years George Lambert had a similar success. As a rule, Australians in Great Britain struggled for recognition. Letters home to Australia from Streeton, Davies, A.H. Fullwood, Aby Alston, and within a short while, Roberts, Fox, James Quinn, George Coates, Sid Long and others, told the same story of disappointment. Their paintings for some years were rejected from exhibition after exhibition of the influential New English Art Club, the Royal Society of British Artists, the Institute of Painters in Oil, the Royal Academy, the International Society of Sculptors, Painters and Gravers. Later, having been selected for exhibition, their paintings were frequently ignored by European critics and buyers.

Tom Roberts arrived in London in April 1903. After a short break he went to the spacious studio arranged for him at the Imperial Institute to view his unfinished 'big picture' of the opening of the First Commonwealth Parliament of Australia. Completed, shown at the Royal Academy in May 1904 and approved by the King, this commission marked the zenith of Roberts' career. He was aged forty-eight. Afterwards he went through years of self-doubt, named by him his 'black period', when nothing he painted with ambition succeeded as a work of art. The best paintings were small, quiet in colour and untroubled in mood. The quiet tonal view of *The towpath, Putney* 1904 (plate 34) was painted during a foggy January day from a window of the Roberts' apartment on the embankment just above Putney Bridge.[3] Lillie Roberts was ill and Roberts was at home caring for her.[4] Perhaps because he had things other than art on his mind, he painted without fumbling or correction, using the barest of means. There

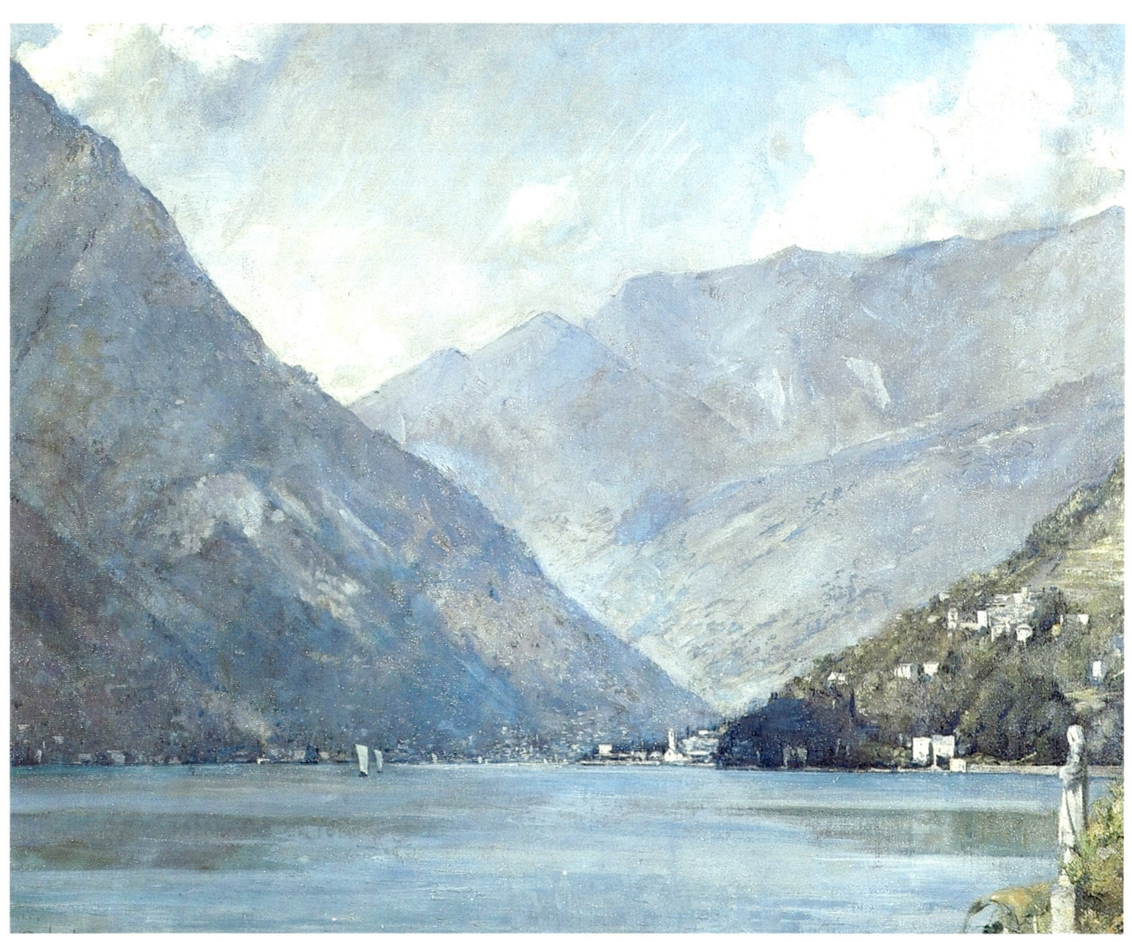

35   Tom Roberts
1856–1931
The first basin, Lake Como 1913
oil on canvas
65.5 × 85.0 cm

is just sufficient description to set the scene, the minimum of tone and even less colour, with the result that each aspect of the image has a precise relation to everything else. Whistler's poetic impressionism had challenged Roberts in his youth when he saw paintings by that artist in London and the influence of Whistler's select colour, fastidious tonality and idiosyncratic compositions may be seen in this work. The subject, a view of the Thames at Putney, was one Whistler himself might have painted. Nonetheless Roberts avoided the touches which made Whistler's images remote and decorative instead of immediate and true-to-life. Roberts had this painting or another of the same group in mind when referring to a 'little thing . . . of the Embankment in fog' the 'innocence' and success of which he wished to match in later paintings.[5]

Roberts' black period lasted until, in 1913, his wife Lillie and his friends decided to act. Roberts was sent off to Lake Como to stay with rich and influential friends, the Nalders. From the grounds of their eighteenth-century villa 'Passalacqua' (now known as Villa Nalder) on the lake shore at Moltrasio, he painted the view of *The first basin, Lake Como* (plate 35). The social life at 'Passalacqua' was agreeable to Roberts. By day he painted views of the lake scenery veiled in radiant mist and at nights he played bridge with his hosts and their guests, going to sleep to the sound of church bells and the tinkle of fishermen's floats which he thought sounded 'very like bullfrogs at times'. During this visit he painted enough works to consider holding an exhibition. Back in London he contemplated his success. 'I did work,' he wrote, 'and am getting ready for a show in February next . . . Now I sit and look at the paintings and they bring back all the pleasure – the sunlight on the faint mist, and pale-azure shadows passing over the great hills.'[6] Orchestrated by Lillie and friends, the exhibition at Walker's Galleries from 3–14 February 1914 was a modest success.

Tom Roberts returned to Australia after the war, building a small house at Sassafras in the Dandenong Ranges. He died in 1931. Homecomings were important for Roberts, whether to his aunt's home at Box Hill near Melbourne in 1885, to the place of his birth in Dorset, England in the 1900s, or to the Dandenong Ranges to the east of Melbourne at the end of his life. They rounded

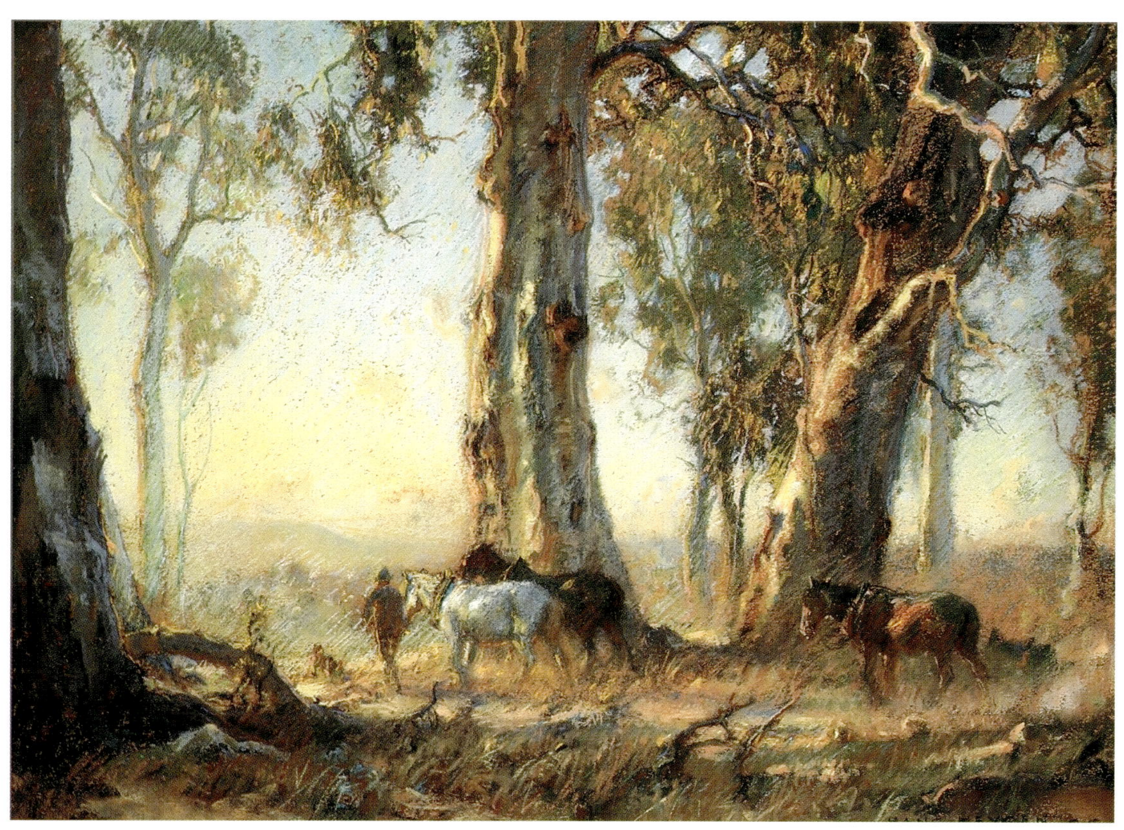

36 Hans Heysen
1877–1968
(*Late afternoon light, Hahndorf*) 1915
pastel on paper
33.0 × 45.0 cm

out his experience as an expatriate of two countries and gave meaning to his rovings. The Dandenongs, scene of his final years, had been on the horizon of many 1880s Heidelberg School paintings.

Expatriatism was an ambitious choice. For many artists it involved considerable hardship yet Australians, then and since, have judged the European works of most of the expatriates – including Roberts and Streeton – to be less significant than their earlier, local productions. In part the judgment has been parochial – its basis the taste for Australian subjects – but all in all the European careers of most artists do seem tame. What would have happened if the artists had stayed in Australia? If Roberts among the older group, or James Quinn among the younger, had painted in Australia during the Edwardian years would they have experienced a flowering like that of Frederick McCubbin and Hans Heysen in the decade before the war?

McCubbin's long-term reputation depends as much (if not more) on the stylistic advances in his post-1900 paintings as on the quieter images of people in the bush painted in the 1880s and 1890s.[7] *At Macedon* 1913 shows bushland transformed from prosaic illustration of individual trees and undergrowth to a vivid painterly surface in which colours have been woven in a complex tapestry. The reputation of the younger painter, Hans Heysen (1877–1968), was made between 1908 and 1914, with images of bushland and farming. In image after image stalwart gum trees and grazing sheep and cattle were lit with such effulgence that the works literally glowed with Australian virtue. Yet the calmly beautiful pastel *Late afternoon light, Hahndorf* 1915 (plate 36), was produced during the Great War, a time of deep trouble for Heysen. During the War, artists and museum personnel reacted to the fact that Heysen had German parentage by refusing to exhibit his paintings, their jingoism reflecting that of Australian society as a whole.[8]

Not all painters travelled with the ambition of becoming famous public figures. David Davies (1864–1939), like Roberts, had been to Europe as a young man; like him he had returned to Australia to earn a considerable reputation in the 1890s, living and working in Heidelberg for longer than most other artists. Whereas Roberts' style was more conventionally illustrative than impressionist,

Davies was a tonal impressionist who painted dusk and moonrise images. Possibly the hard times of the 1890s induced Davies to take his family back to England. From 1896 to 1904 he painted in Cornwall on the coast at St Ives and the nearby villages of Lelant, Newquay and further north at Tintagel. In 1904 he left romantic Tintagel for the home of his Celtic ancestors, Wales.[9] There in the winter of 1905–6 or 1906–7 he painted *Cottages in snow, North Wales* (plate 37).[10]

As in Roberts' two paintings, the colour and light are subdued. Davies' image is evoked by a brusque manipulation of colour and brushmark which indicate snow, stone and sky. The painterliness is in contrast to Roberts' technique in which the underlying drawing is still important. Roberts had studied in the 1870s in Melbourne and in the early 1880s at the Royal Academy Schools, South Kensington, where drawing was thoroughly taught and techniques of painting in oils were hardly taught at all. On the other hand Davies had studied painting under George Folingsby in Melbourne in the 1880s and then had the experience of working with tonal painters at St Ives in 1892. Around the time of painting *Cottages in snow, North Wales*, he explained in exactly what sense he was a colourist:

> I am given credit for being a strong colourist in a quiet way . . . I don't think it is a paradox. You see, colour is more temperamental, more individual. Everyone does not see colour alike. The aim is to see colour intensely, and render it without being unduly vehement. That, I think, would explain what is meant by being a strong colourist in a quiet way. The aim is not to emphasise the local colour, the actual colour of the object itself, but to get the vibrating quality of colour one sees in Nature.[11]

One characteristic of Davies' art is that although the subjects were quaintly picturesque there was no fudging the realities of a scene. In this painting, for example, two telegraph poles are evidence that modern technology had reached the remote Welsh village.

David Davies' choice of village subjects was typical. Before, during and after the Edwardian period, out-of-the-way places in Europe had a special attraction for artists. St Ives on the Cornish coast, where Davies spent a year in 1892, had been visited by Fox the year before (1890–91) and the Australian expatriate Louis Grier was an earlier and long-term resident. Other Australians who painted at St Ives and the neighbouring town of Newlyn in the 1890s and early 1900s were Richard Hayley-Lever, Louis Grier, Will Ashton and J. S. MacDonald. Artist colonies such as St Ives and Newlyn were an increasingly important feature of European culture through the second half of the century. As a matter of course Australians studying in Paris in the late 1880s and early 1890s – Rupert Bunny, Aby Alston, Isabel (Iso) Rae, Fox, George Pitt Morison and two English artists who had spent some years in Australia, Tudor St George Tucker and Charles Conder – visited Brittany and Picardy during the summers. Cornwall in England and Brittany in France were valued for preserving an earlier way of life in a Europe which had changed radically during the industrial age. Villages there had cobbled streets and stone cottages and the people maintained some of the customs of an earlier age such as folk costumes. Brittany, Cornwall and Wales had an extra value in having histories back to the Romance period of King Arthur and his court.

Artist colonies then as now served a romantic notion of refuge from the demands of clients and the pressure of modern urban life. The high-minded artist of popular imagination was virtually the opposite of the period's other role-model, the city-dwelling, sophisticated artist who was skilled in marketing and promotion. The majority of artists had it both ways. Part of the time, or with part of their minds, they believed that art could only be a high calling if the artist was removed from ordinary life, free to pursue art as a vocation without the pressure of material considerations. When in that frame of mind they sought out subjects representing a pre-industrial and non-urban way of life. But most Australians in Europe, and their confrères who painted folk subjects, did not live all year round in country villages. They took a middle course, spending the summer months travelling through picturesque scenery or living at one of the colonies of Pont Aven, Concarneau, Etaples, Newlyn or St Ives. Back in Paris or London during the autumn and winter months, they worked up country subjects for showing in a Spring Salon or Royal Academy exhibition. For example, David

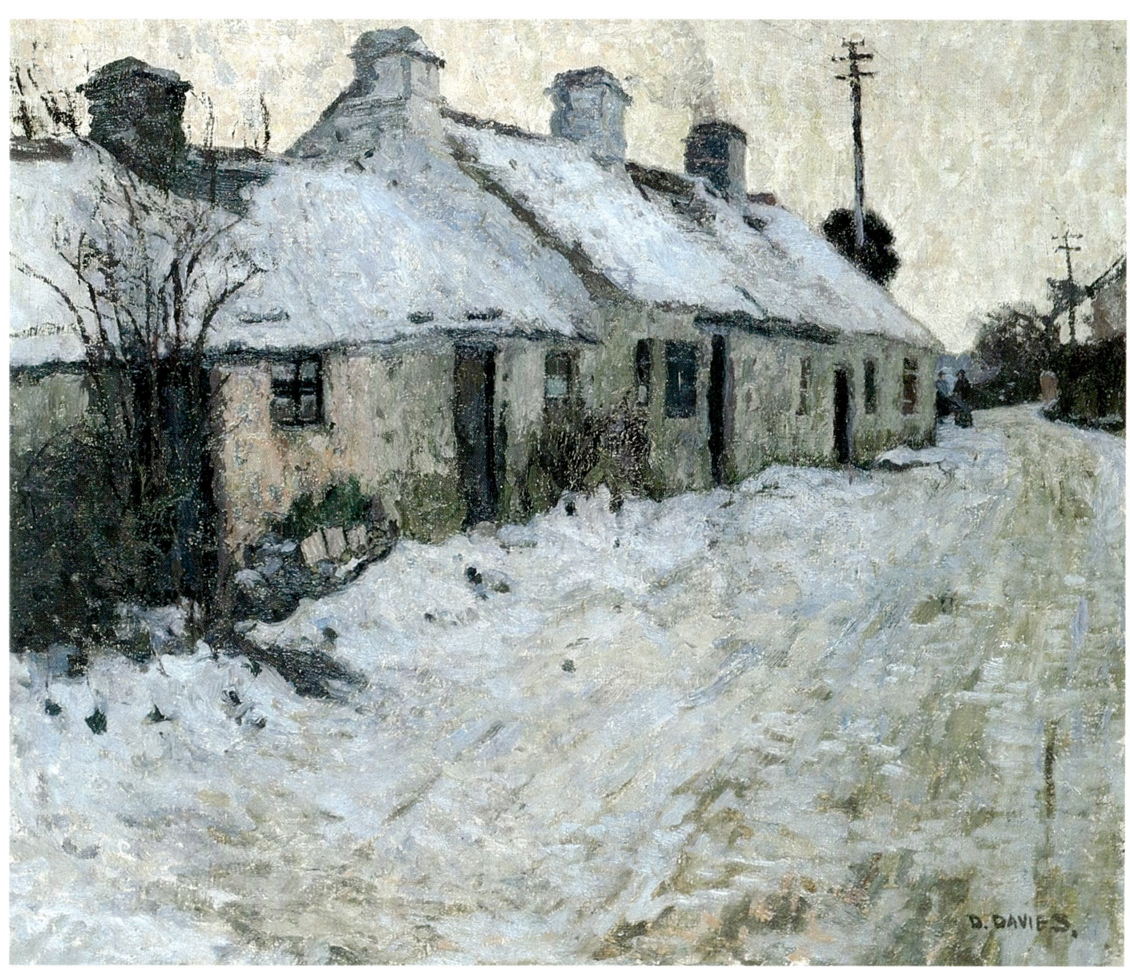

37   David Davies
1864–1939
Cottages in snow, North Wales (1906)
oil on canvas
51.0 × 61.4 cm

Davies maintained a studio in Pimlico through the years he was in England and from 1908, when living in Dieppe (in a flat attached to the school where his wife taught English), he maintained the necessary contacts for exhibiting paintings in Paris, London and the United States. After the war, like other expatriates, Davies planned to return to Australia (which had become symbolic of pastoral peace and plenty by comparison with war-torn Europe) but the years went by, and in the end he settled back in Cornwall where he died at Looe in 1939.

John Russell (1858–1930) was the only male expatriate of this generation who was able to pursue art as a vocation. Independent of sales of pictures, he had an income that was sufficient to support a large family and a number of hobbies – including the expensive sport of yachting. There was no need to sell paintings. His painting career lacks much of the documentation through exhibitions and reviews which outline the progress of other artists. But although without a career in the marketing sense, Russell was able to pursue an impressionist style with all the more rigour because for many years he kept aloof from considerations of a career.

The watercolour of *Races at Saint Tropez* c. 1910 (plate 38), was painted after his wife, Marianna, died in March 1908. Her death altered Russell's way of life dramatically. The home on Belle-Ile, the scene of Russell's married life, was sold and the apartment in Paris became his headquarters. For months at a time Russell travelled (probably on his sea-going yacht) along the coast of France and the Ligurian coast of Italy, painting at Salso-Maggiore, Paraggio, Spezia and Portofino (where he lived on and off for a number of years)[12] or inland at Lake Orta. He painted in the Apennine mountains of Italy and at Uber Saanan and Schonreid near Berne in Switzerland. During the war he lived in England, like the majority of expatriates who had been in France. Another sign that Marianna's death was a major disturbance in Russell's life was that he stepped up the rate of production of paintings, now working mostly in watercolours.

As we see from this watercolour the medium suited Russell's style. Colours were put down in bright strokes separated from one another on the white paper. The speckle of colour patches gives an effect of animation appropriate to the marine subject, telling a yachtsman's

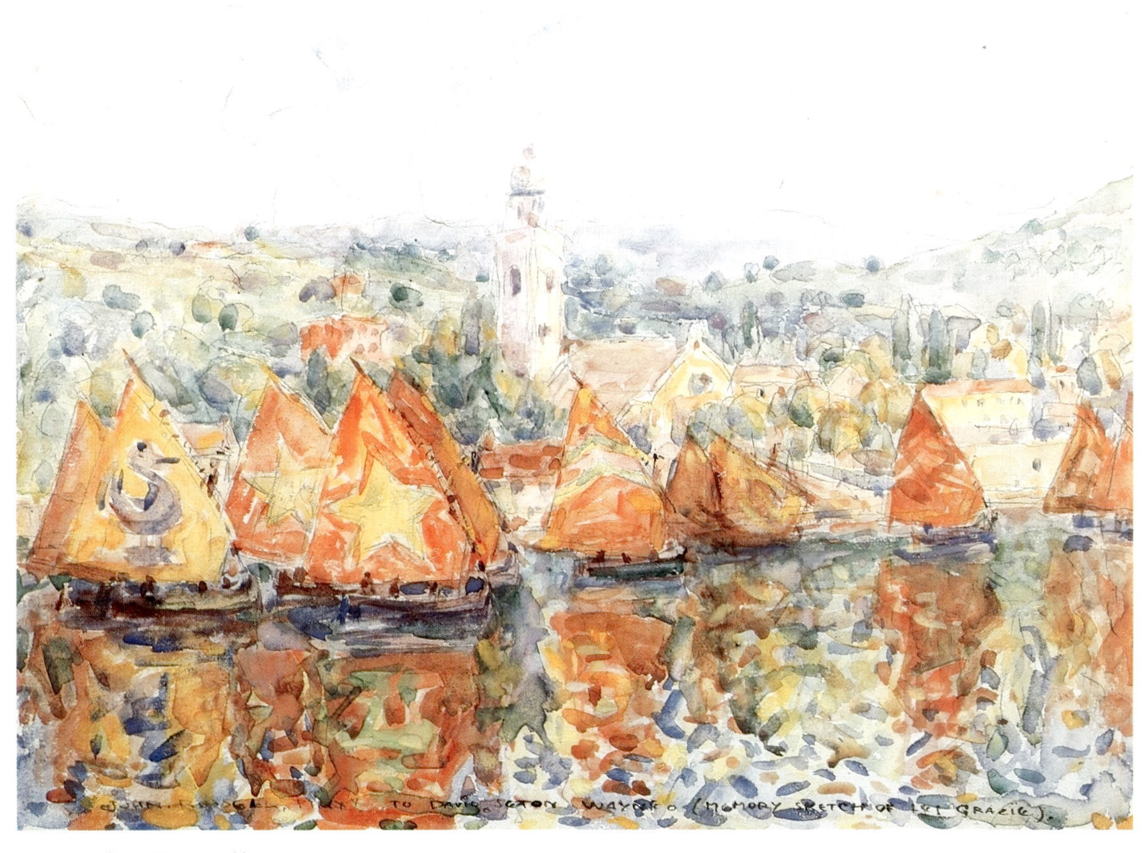

38   John Russell
1858–1930
Races at Saint Tropez (1910)
watercolour on paper
25.8 × 35.8 cm

story about a breeze that bends the sails of yachts in the centre of the image while leaving other boats on the left completely becalmed. It is worth speculating that the Saint Tropez watercolour included Russell's own yacht.[13] When he returned to Australia after the war he brought the yacht to harbour at Watson's Bay in Sydney.

For women artists who lived overseas the professional challenge was the same as for their male colleagues, though they had other incentives as well. Most were unmarried and had independent incomes. Whereas in Australia they struggled to have their professional status recognised, living on the other side of the world from Australia widened their social horizons, put them in the company of other artists, allowed greater social freedom than they would have had at home, and freed them from the unattached woman's traditional responsibility of caring for aged parents and needy relatives. Accordingly the number of women artist expatriates was high.

The sisters Iso (1860–c. 1940) and Alison Rae were among the earliest Australians to settle in Etaples, an estuary village on the north coast of France which attracted many artists. The Raes went from Melbourne to Paris as students in 1887, and by the early 1890s were painting and living for long periods in Etaples. Conscious of needing professional support for their work, in 1898 they were among the first members of the Paris Club of International Women Artists. The idea of forming the club arose out of conversations about 'the extreme difficulty of getting "a fair start" ' if one were a woman artist in France. The aim of the club was the same as for similar clubs in Australia and elsewhere: 'firstly, to unite together women artists for mutual help in exhibiting in different countries and, by means of centres, to lessen the cost of sending pictures; secondly, to create club-rooms for the use of members; and, lastly, to help forward the cause of international women artists in every way.' For membership two things were required: each member had to have studied in Paris and must have produced 'strong work'.[14]

Iso Rae chose the subject of *Roasted chestnuts, Etaples* 1917 (plate 39) and simplified the description to include, within a web of grey tones, only the essential motif and colours that established the appropriate mood. The subject is all the more moving for being simple, merely a group of Allied soldiers sampling roasted chestnuts in a French village.

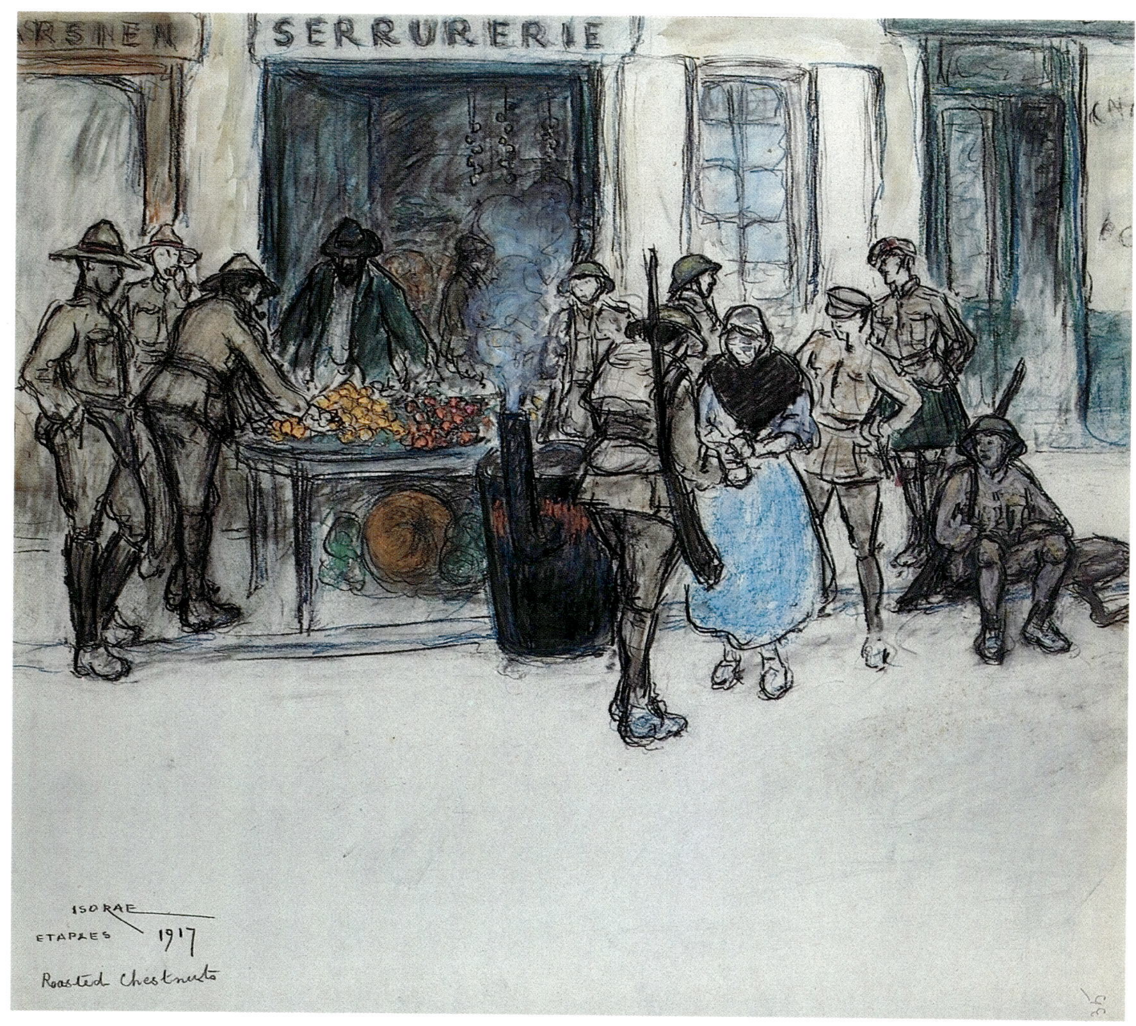

39   Iso Rae
1860–c. 1940
Roasted chestnuts, Etaples 1917
pastel and gouache on paper
46.0 × 53.0 cm

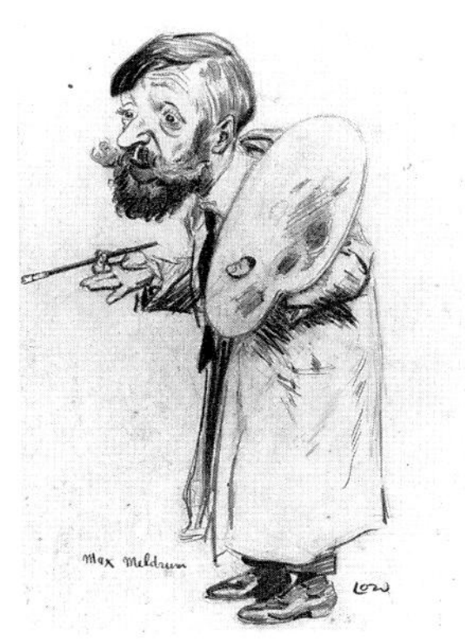

David Low's cartoon
depicting Max
Meldrum in the early
years of this century.

La Trobe Collection, State Libary of Victoria

The 1917 date tells viewers that the scene is set in the most devastating year of the Great War. Imperial casualties by the end of that year totalled over two million and French casualties (with a smaller population) totalled over three million: 1917 was the year the Allies and the Germans faced the dismaying possibility of a very long war. Rae was known for the poetry of her work. Out of the many Australians who painted at Etaples – Iso and Alison Rae, Rupert Bunny, Edward Officer, Alice Muskett, James Quinn, Arthur Baker-Clack, Marie Tuck and Hilda Rix Nicholas – it was Iso Rae, the one who stayed the longest, who in the 1890s set the style associated with that colony. Her mature style was linear and characterised by 'large' effects, with 'colour broad and simple' and an 'execution powerful and unaffected'.[15]

Rae was not only an artist of conviction but strong-minded about other things as well. She and her sister were among a small group of artists to remain in Etaples throughout the entire war. Iso worked at a YMCA hut, her sister at the war hospital. The town was virtually a military encampment and, between bouts of war work, Iso made sketches of soldiers in the streets, among them the pastel drawing of soldiers buying roasted chestnuts. Living on in Etaples after the war, reportedly 'so rooted to the place that only another war can shift them', the sisters remembered three weeks when Etaples was the target of twenty-six air raids: parts of the town were in ruins, people were dead and dying, there was a constant state of emergency and the intrepid sisters slept in their clothes.[16]

Younger Australian artists shared the ambition that had sent their elders to study and to prove their abilities in European art centres. Max Meldrum (1875–1955) was a generation younger than Russell, Rae, Roberts and Davies. He studied in Paris from 1900, copying eighteenth-century paintings in the Louvre and pursuing a tonalist style like that of the seventeenth-century Spanish painter Velasquez. A tonal style had become fashionable but nevertheless Meldrum was unusual in finally scorning the recent impressionist and post-impressionist phases of French painting. Always contradictory, he was intensely curious about the merits and failures of these modern styles and, for example, translated an article by Emile Bernard – a post-impressionist – about the failure

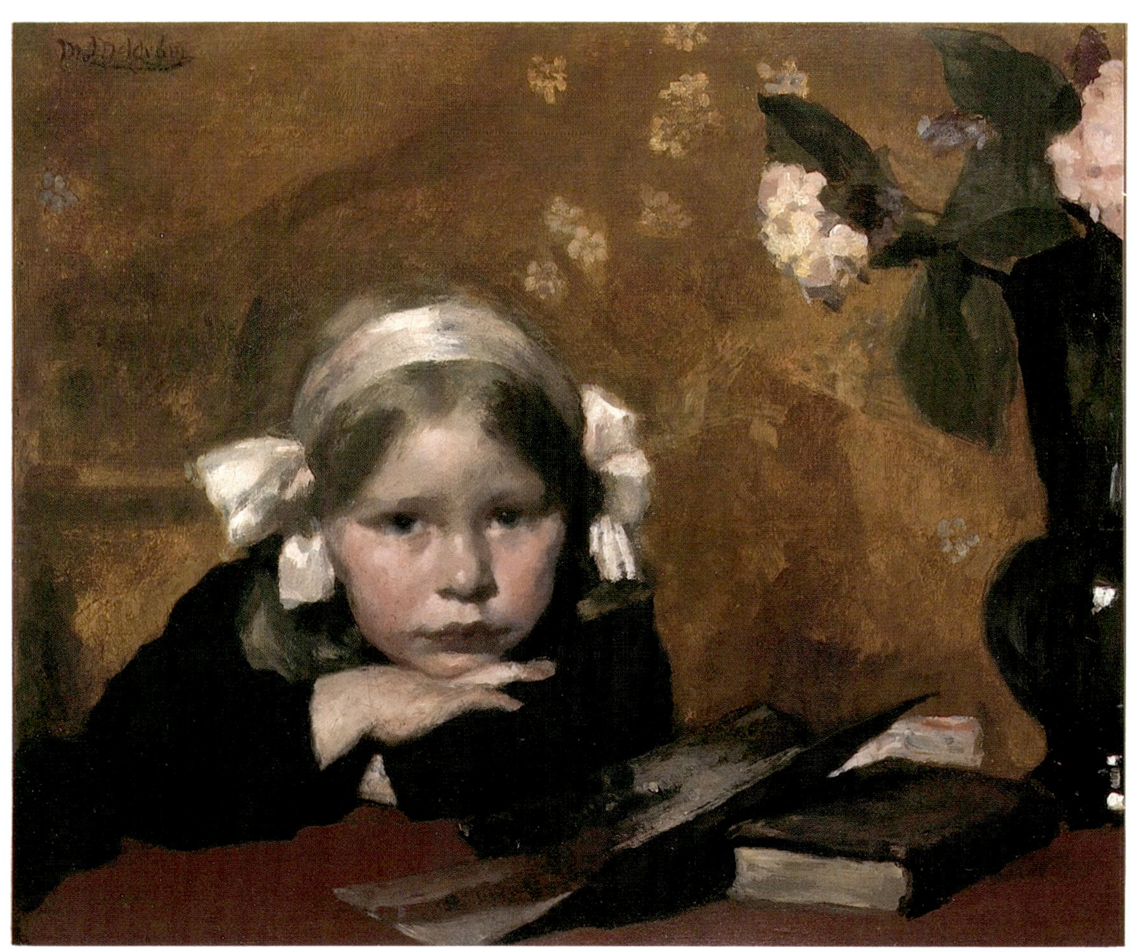

40   Max Meldrum
1875–1955
Portrait 1910
oil on canvas
49.0 × 59.0 cm

of impressionism, for publication in Australia.[17] Whereas most English-speaking students in Paris mixed with students who spoke their language, Meldrum moved in a circle of French artists. Two of his friends were a young sculptor from Rennes, Norbert Nitsch (1884–1902), and his painter brother Charles (1882–1972). Through the Nitsch brothers he met and married their sister Jeanne who was in Paris to study singing. From 1903 Max regularly visited his wife's family at Rennes, settling there in 1907 or 1908.

The painting of the artist's four-year-old daughter Ida, first titled *Portrait* (plate 40), was painted in 1910 when the Meldrums, with Charles Nitsch, were living at 'Le Logis' in the village of Pacé near Rennes. For a number of years the brothers-in-law painted the same or similar subjects. Each produced scenes of Picherit's farm on the other side of the courtyard from the Lodge. Their canvases showed the long, low farm building under brilliant snow and, again, in summer shadow. They painted the straight avenue of trees leading to the lodge. There were portraits by Charles and Max of members of the family. And each artist posed interior scenes with figures, spinning-wheel, Chinese screen, books and table arranged to tell some story. Charles' style tended to be more colourful, post-impressionist and decorative than Meldrum's, however the gold tonalities and discreetly patterned background of *Portrait* – a pattern and colours abstracted from the Nitschs' Chinese screen – show that Meldrum too could paint decoratively.

At some stage before 1919 Meldrum folded back the canvas of *Portrait* to cut off the vase on the right and some of the upper image. Cropped of its decorative elements in this way, the image focused squarely on the child. The artist had a didactic reason for the change.

Back in Australia since December 1911, he had shown his French paintings at exhibitions in Melbourne and Sydney and begun to formulate a theory of tonal painting. An ardent and argumentative individualist, he may have hoped to escape the influence of provincial Melbourne by articulating and teaching his own theory. *Portrait* was reproduced, cropped, under a new title, *Ida*, in a book expounding his theory published in 1919.[18] The next few decades were stormy, as Meldrum's teaching of a tonal style first divided local painters against each other and later was challenged by other, modern, schools of opinion.

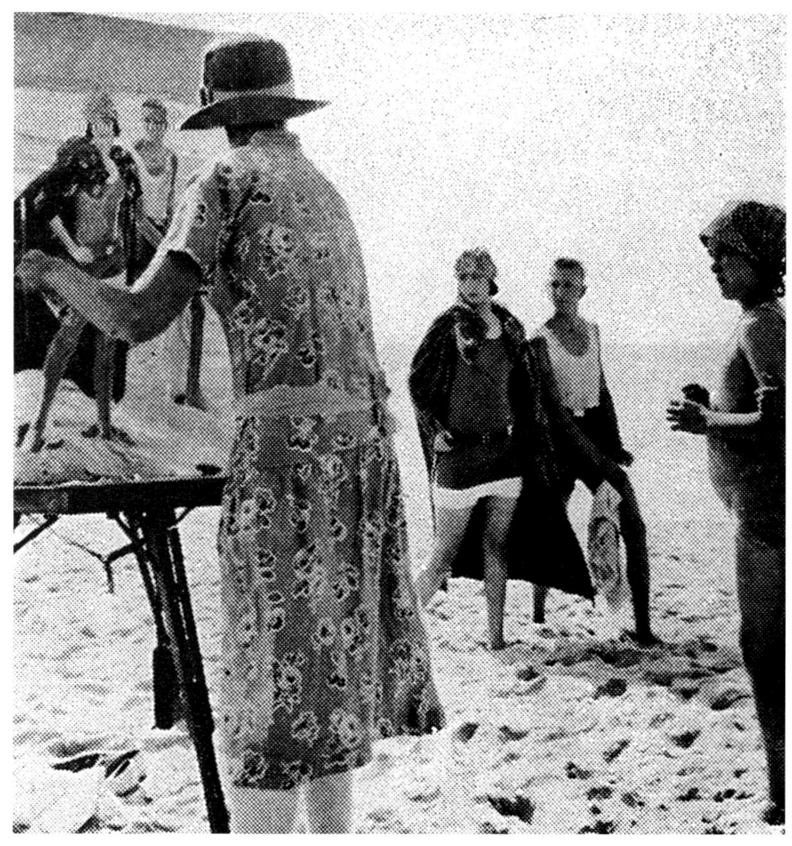

Hilda Rix Nicholas painting on Bondi Beach in the summer of 1926-7. The work she is painting was titled *Sur une Plage, Sydney* and was shown at the New Salon Paris in 1927. The photograph is from *The Home* April 1927, page 24. *The Home* was a popular Australian glossy social magazine of the period and was published in Sydney.
Janine Burke Collection

Hilda Rix Nicholas (1884-1961), with Meldrum's student Clarice Beckett, was the best woman artist to emerge from the artistic milieu of Melbourne in the decade of the First World War. She was born in Ballarat. Her father, Henry Rix (author of the nationalistic poem *Advance Australia*), was employed in the Education Department. Her mother, a talented painter, was a member of the Sutton family who ran a well-known Melbourne music store. Hilda was brought up in South Yarra and educated at Merton Hall, a few classes ahead of Clarice Beckett. They were, however, to follow very different paths.

After studying under Frederick McCubbin at the National Gallery School from 1902 to 1905, Hilda waited to go to Europe with her family. Mrs Rix and her two daughters finally left for London in March 1907. After a brief summer course in France with John Hassall,[19] Hilda went to Paris to the Academie Delecluse. Auguste Delecluse, whose teaching she later described as 'dull coloured and conscientious', whose colour was 'too drab to carry one far', was the teacher who 'set her palette', which is to say that she started to paint in oils under his direction.[20] The young Australian was inspired more by the varied nationalities of her student companions than by Delecluse. 'Here were students of every type, shape and nationality ... Neatly dressed Americans, fiery-looking Russians, dainty or picturesque French and well-tubbed English.' She moved from teacher to teacher, studying for a while with the American Richard Miller (whose crisp brushwork, light palette and carefully judged subjects had a lasting influence) and at the Grande Chaumière where she took advice about bright colour from the Spanish painter Claudio Castelucho and about drawing from Theophile Alexandre Steinlen: Steinlen's stylish line drawings of scenes of modern life had an immediate effect on her own work.

Rix Nicholas was the Australian who made the clearest connection with the various journalistic genres in contemporary European art. During this period France, like Britain, was in a fervour of empire. The romance of empire had in the 1890s led Paul Gauguin from the folk subjects of Brittany to exotic images of the Marquesas Islands in the South Pacific. Rix Nicholas used the experience of painting in picturesque Picardy as the springboard for a trip to the French colony of Morocco to sketch tourist subjects. Her drawings were in a characterful style that owed something to Steinlen and a debt to fellow Australian, Iso Rae, whom she met during several summers in Etaples. An exhibition of the Morocco pictures held at Galerie Chaine et Simonson in Paris in November 1912 brought an appreciative response from the press:

> Miss Rix devoted her whole time to wanderings among the people, watching their mode of life in the market places and elsewhere . . . bringing away some marvellous trophies as the fruit of her observations. All Miss Rix's work shows her as unusually observant, with a keen eye for colour, and an intense sense of correctness in line. No one can see her work without realising her sensitive sympathetic nature, which is reflected in the live people, full of their own little subtleties of personality.[21]

The French State bought a drawing from the exhibition.

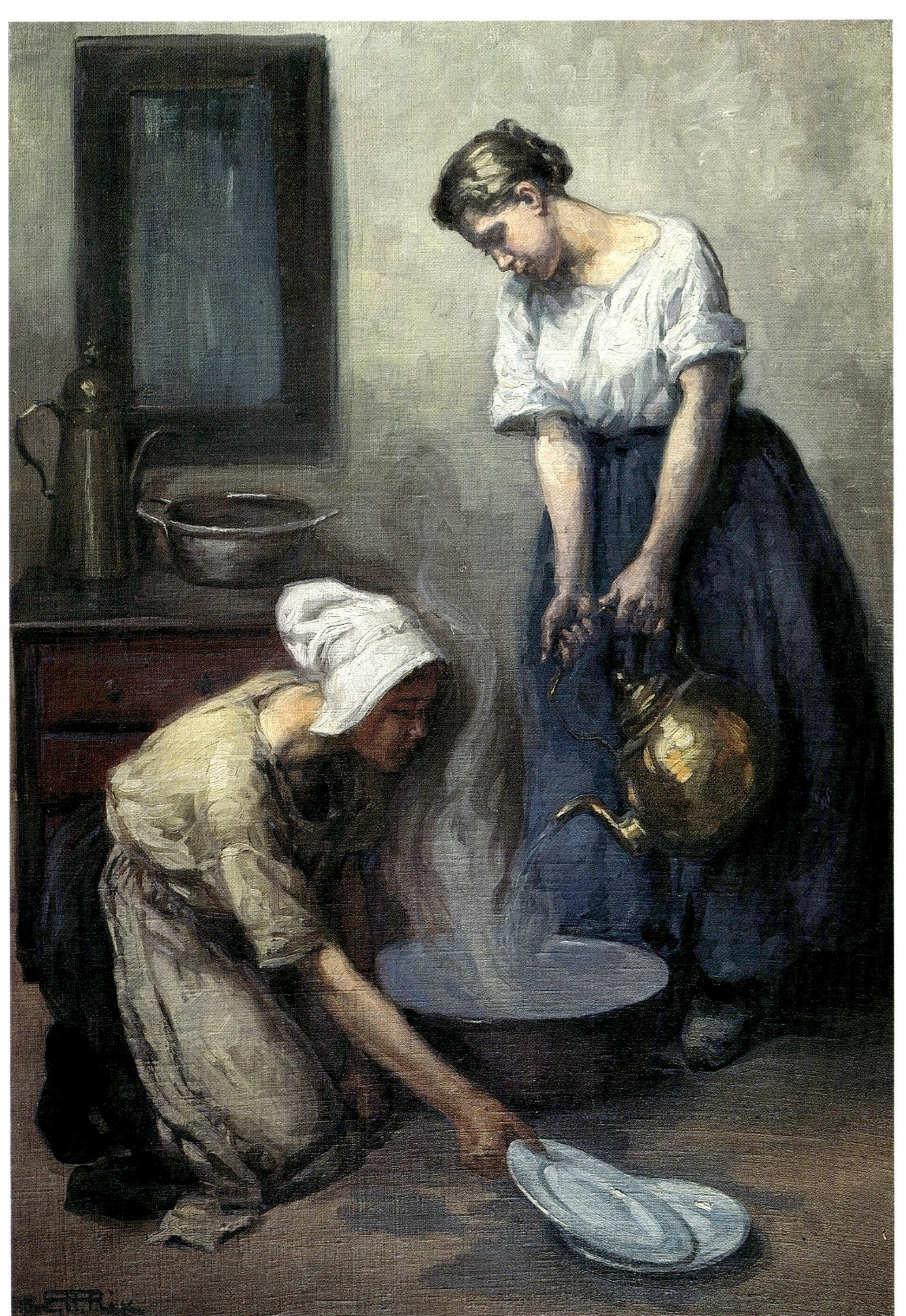

41   Hilda Rix Nicholas
1884–1961
Work (1909)
oil on canvas
162.0 × 130.0 cm

After the war Rix Nicholas applied the lessons in exotic subject matter back in Australia, choosing subjects that expressed the 'breeziness, breadth, and freedom of our Australia'.[22]

Work c. 1909 (plate 41) shows Rix Nicholas' early promise as a painter of storytelling images. The subject was probably posed and painted in Paris at the Grande Chaumière's afternoon costume classes rather than at Etaples. Despite the bare interior, white bonnet, steam, brass and pewter – all of which were typical of Etaples subjects – the actions and appearance of the two young women do not resemble the brawny fisherfolk of most Etaples images by Rix Nicholas and other artists. A major strength of the work is its sober, controlled colour. Evidently Delecluse still ruled the painter's palette, or possibly, as well as emulating Iso Rae's selective style of drawing Rix Nicholas also admired her subtle use of greys.

E. Phillips Fox (1865–1915) had worked in France from 1887 to 1891 and for months at a time between 1903 and 1905 before marrying the English painter Ethel Carrick (1872–1952) and going to live in Paris in 1905. Although he was very much the senior and more influential partner for some years, his wife had a keen sense of what subjects might appeal to a contemporary audience and she possessed a style of considerable verve with which to express herself. When other Parisians of the Australian–American circle – Rupert Bunny, Frederick Frieseke, Kathleen O'Connor – were painting scenes in the Luxembourg Gardens, so did she. Street markets – especially flower markets – were popular subjects. She painted them. The same went for beaches (perennial favourites in French painting since impressionist times), old bridges, and Gothic churches. She visited, in turn, Venice and Spain, Northern Africa and later Switzerland, Kashmir and India in search of travel subjects. When gardens and flower subjects were popular, during the 1930s depression and later war years, she painted them in great quantities. Carrick's subjects and her style were those of a practical woman, a good manager.

The subject of her ICI collection painting *Rue Mouffetard, Paris* c. 1910 (plate 42), in Montparnasse, was a couple of blocks north of Boulevard Arago where the Foxes had a studio apartment. Carrick probably visited the market

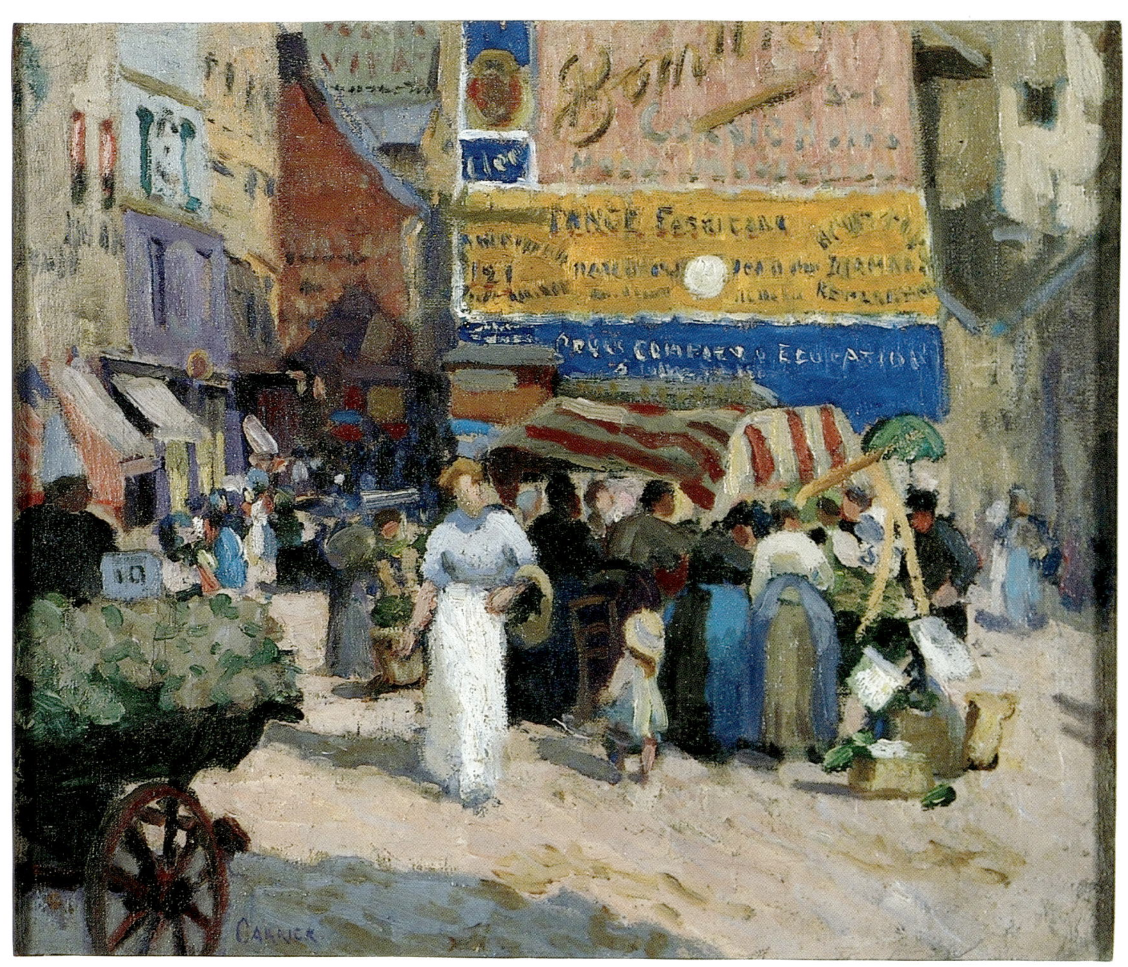

42 Ethel Carrick
1872–1952
Rue Mouffetard, Paris (1910)
oil on canvas
38.1 × 45.6 cm

regularly to buy her fruit and vegetables. It is within the bounds of possibility that she imagined herself – a red-haired woman in a white dress and with a basket over one arm – in the centre of her own picture. As often with paintings by Carrick, the composition is effective as an arrangement of rectangular shapes and as a combination of unusual colours. The patterning of solid colour, stripes, splashes, dots and slurries of paint, shows her remarkably sophisticated style. In some respects Carrick was a more accomplished artist than her husband. He admitted the greater modernity of her style after she became a member of the 'avant-garde' Autumn Salon.[23]

The chief difference between these two painters was that Fox loved the act of painting for itself and out of sheer involvement in the practice of painting wasted a lot of time pursuing effects which a more practical, design-conscious artist would avoid as being unprofitable. He distrusted 'the Society business' of art. 'I think the Society business is bad for the English painter . . . the French ones are more bohemian . . . live more simply and put their whole effort into their work'.[24] In the summers of 1909 to 1912, as well as painting other subjects, Fox and his American friend Frederick Frieseke painted a series of nudes in sunlight.[25] Both artists responded to the freedom Paris offered for treating a subject that was regarded back home in Australia and America as slightly risque. The female nude was popular in French art – a trend reflected in the work of Bonnard and Matisse – but it was not the popularity of the subject that inspired Fox so much as the problem of painting flesh in sunlight. The majority of Frieseke's nudes were painted in the garden of his house at Giverny, outside Paris. Fox painted his in the centre of Paris in the garden outside his and Ethel's studio apartment at 65 Boulevard Arago. He rigged up screens for privacy: 'we have fixed things up so that no-one can see, & we are not disturbed'. Painting flesh in sunlight was 'very interesting work, but mighty difficult – I try to complete a [size] 25 canvas at one go – for better or worse – I find I get better results – coming back when one is not in the same attitude generally busts up the show'.[26]

Fox's nude of 1911 (plate 43), shown from above, flattened against the grass and splotched with vivid patches of sunlight, does not have great appeal as a nude or

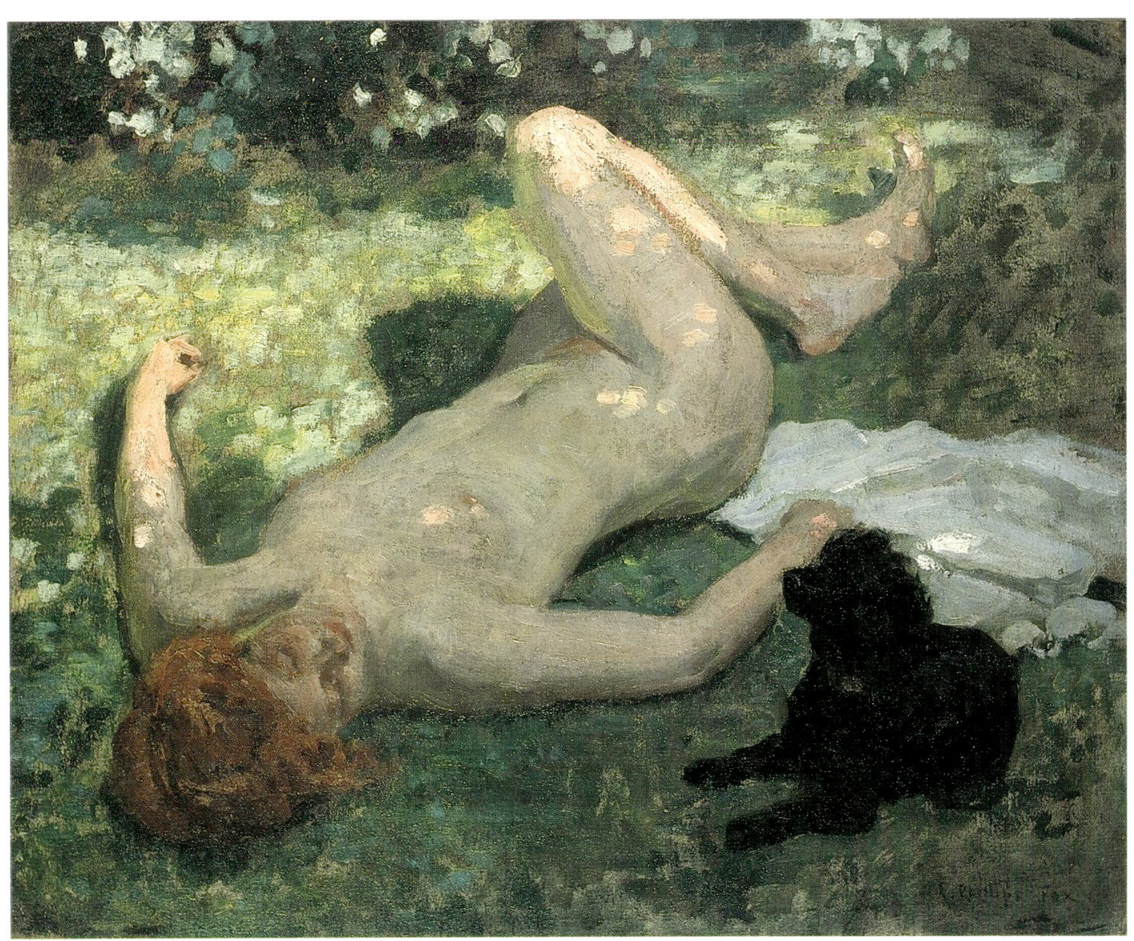

43   E. Phillips Fox
1865–1915
(*Nude*) 1911
oil on canvas
65.0 × 81.2 cm

as a composition and perhaps not even as a colour scheme but it does tackle a challenging technical problem. A contemporary appreciation of a nude by Frieseke fits this work equally well, painted for the 'sheer beauty of flesh painting . . . the dazzling sheen of flesh, seen in sunlight, and all against a cool, green background, relieved on the grass by a shawl'.[27]

Paris offered the challenge of what was thought to be the best, most advanced art then being produced in the western world. For most of Fox's lifetime the aesthetic of the avant-garde had not been used to judge all artists or at least had not divided his generation of artists. The crunch came in the decade before the First World War. Measured by the standard of modernity an artist either identified with the new or took a conservative stance. In 1911 Fox was able to declare without much rancour that Ethel had achieved success as a modern painter in Paris whereas his art was regarded as conservative. 'There is a lot of talk here about the post impressionists – I am sure you would not like them nor would you feel any interest in the Autumn Salon which claims to be the coming art – God help us if it turns out so.'[28] In the same letter he observed with some disapproval that Rupert Bunny (who was his contemporary in age) had been bitten by post-impressionism.

Bunny (1864–1947) demonstrated the truth of Fox's diagnosis in 1913 when he exhibited a group of energetic, brilliantly coloured paintings in the Autumn Salon. These marked a definite departure from the images touched with a gentle symbolism which he had shown in the New Salon for some years. Those had been images of women relaxing on balconies, shaded from the sun by striped blinds or, in the evening, listening to distant music or to the sound of the sea on a faraway shore: images of dreaming and reflection rather than scenes of action. By contrast, Bunny used the new, garish style for mythological subjects of violent action and lawless emotions. One such work is *Potiphar's wife* 1920 (plate 44), a monotype or, in other words, a painting on metal or glass which was transferred by pressing it on a sheet of paper. The medium of monotype, spontaneous and fresh, suited Bunny's new style. The uninhibited subject of *Potiphar's wife* was offset to some extent by the sheer decorativeness of pattern and colour.

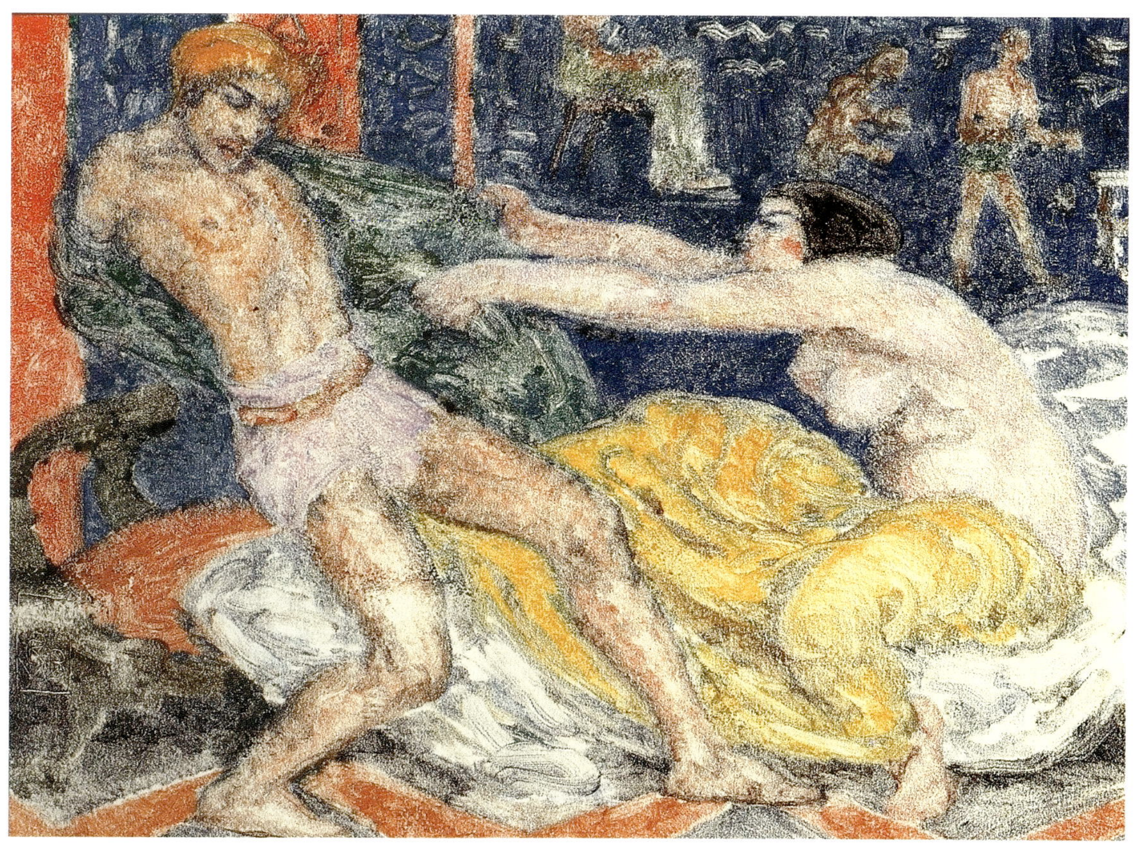

44   Rupert Bunny
1864–1947
Potiphar's wife 1920
colour monotype on paper
27.5 × 37.5 cm

There was no decision to break from his earlier style. Bunny painted in both styles before and during the war years, in his pictures of women slipping slowly towards a modern notion of a busy woman's life, as she sewed, worked in the garden, or chatted to a friend. The war had brought women into the work force. They did manly jobs, wore manly clothes and asserted a greater independence. Bunny modified his imagery just sufficiently to hint at the change. His women were still softly pretty, still enclosed within room or garden, but their clothes were less hampering and their expressions slightly more alert. His most summery and light-filled pictures ever were painted between 1912 and 1917, among them *The letter* c. 1914–16 (plate 45). All in all, however, what was happening to women did not please Bunny. The romance was gone. After the war, when skirts grew short and bodies boyish – and his favourite model Jeanne grew older – he stopped painting women.

For different reasons, Bunny stopped painting energetic mythological subjects after holding a final exhibition of these images in 1922. Perhaps he saw in the crude colours and savage subjects a reflection of the disturbances of war. If so, he was not alone in reacting against the aggressive aspects of pre-war modern art. A rash of art writing in the years after the war speculated that there was a connection between the war and the energetic, anti-humanist bias of avant-garde art just before it. Through the 1920s Bunny painted landscapes in a style which alternated in emphasis between strong pattern and colour and an interest in naturalistic effects of light and weather. Each winter he deserted Paris for the south of France, painting the hill farms, orchards, villas and seaside towns in the region of Ceret, Sanary, St Paul du Var, de Lavandou, Avignon, Toulon, Cassis and the Pyrénées (plate 46 a, b and c). Of the landscapes the small preliminary oil sketches, complete in colour and form, were as a rule more satisfying than the larger canvases. Bunny kept the sketches for himself. They were painted in the open air and used as studies for larger oil paintings which he produced back in his studio for exhibition and sale.

Modernity challenged the older artist Rupert Bunny, and was an issue for the next generation in Paris. Bessie Davidson (1879–1965), a friend of Margaret Preston, may yet be judged as good an artist as Preston. Because her

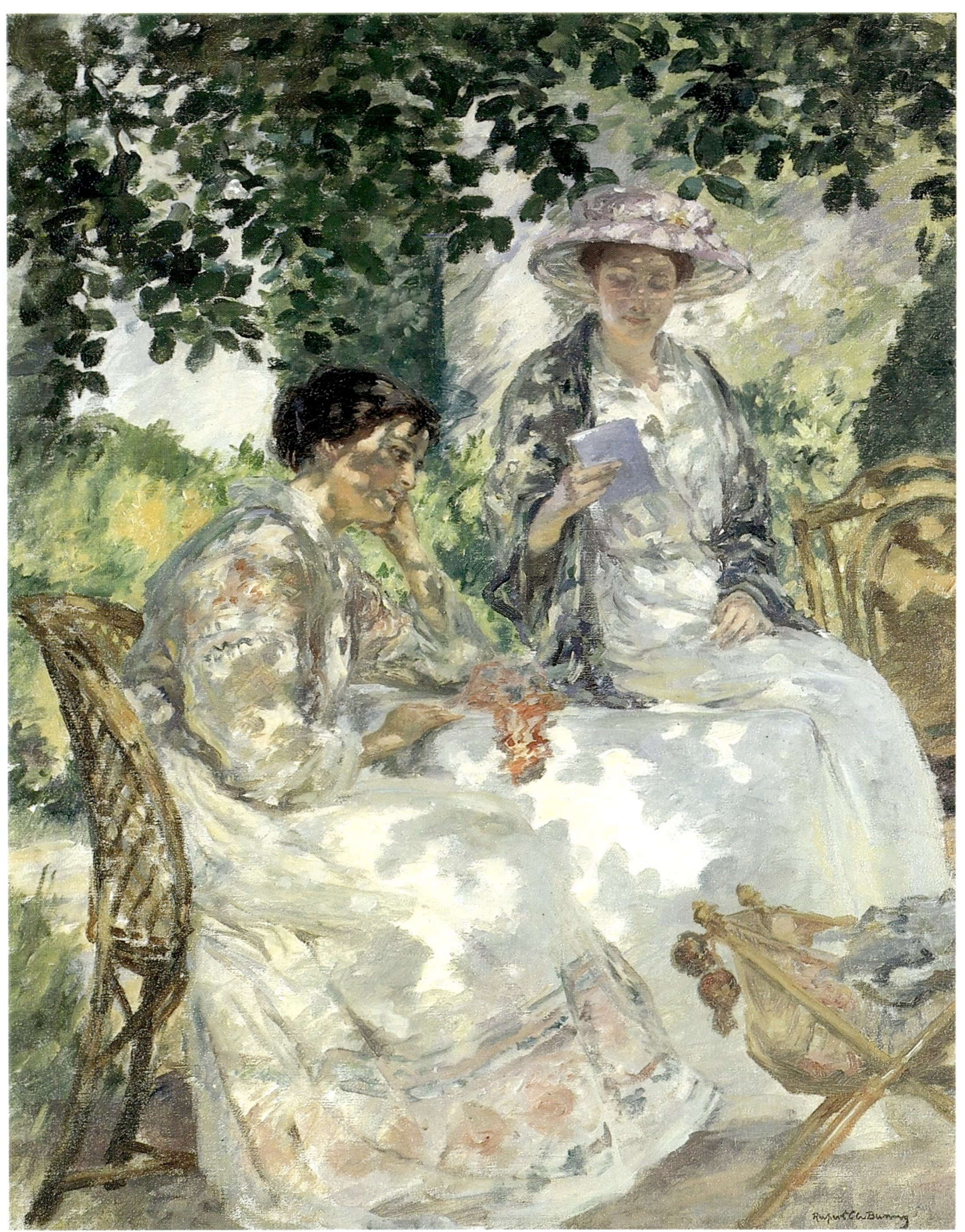

45 Rupert Bunny
1864–1947
The letter (1914–16)
oil on canvas
73.3 × 60.2 cm

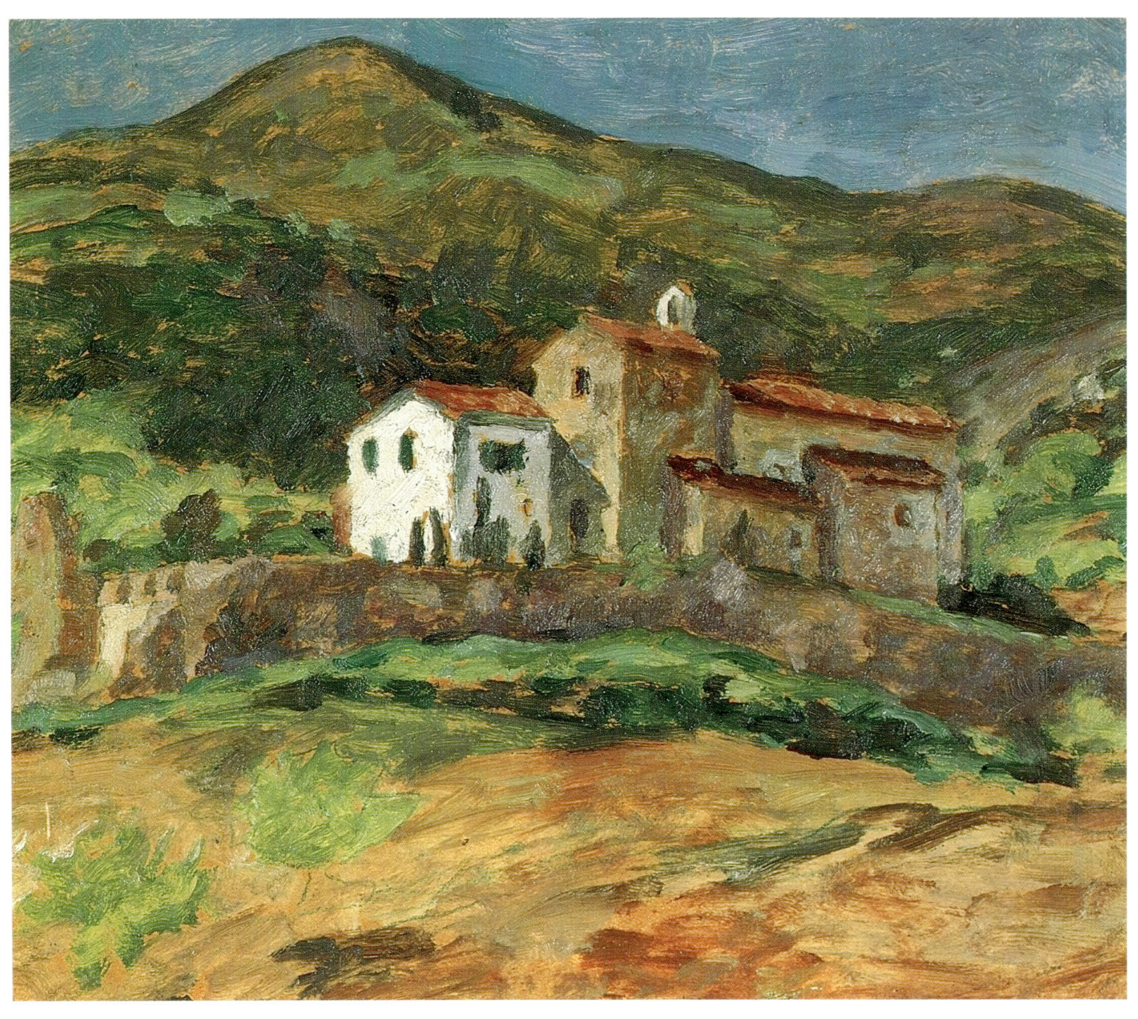

46   Rupert Bunny
1864–1947
A group of three south of France landscapes
a   *The Capucin Monastery of St Feréol, Ceret* (1926)
oil on paper mounted on plywood
21.0 × 24.0 cm

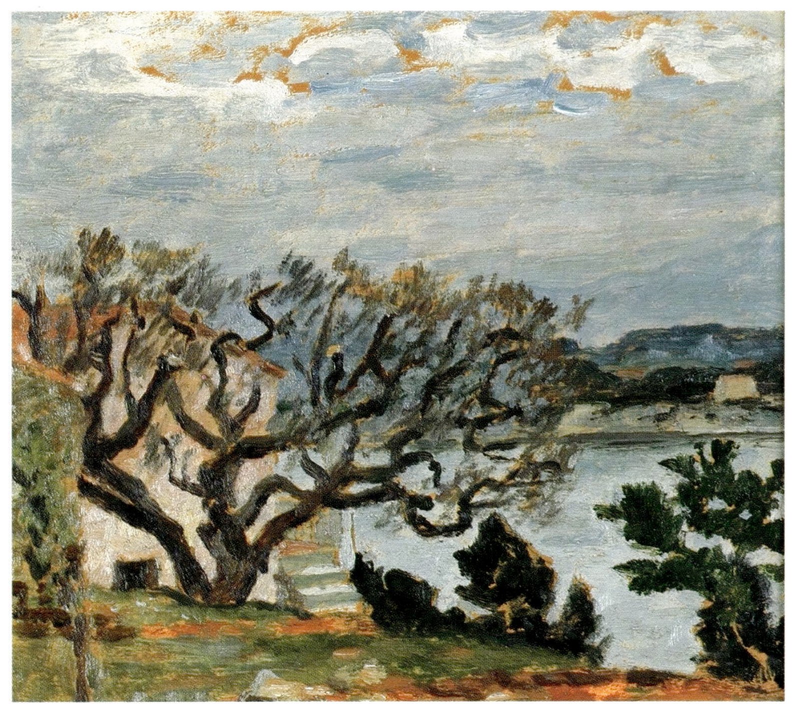

b   (*St Paul du Var*)
(1923)
oil on paper
mounted on
plywood
21.0 × 23.5 cm

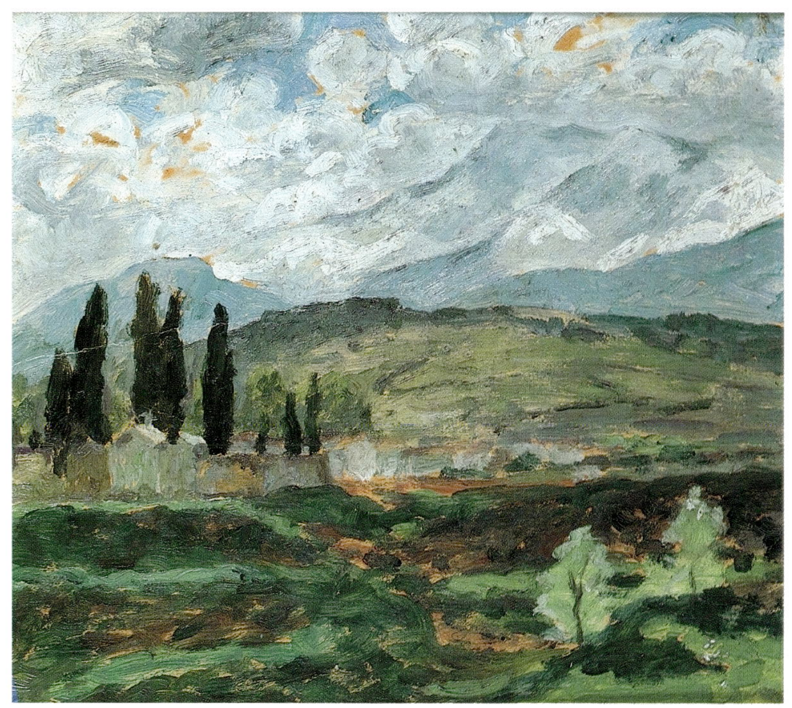

c   (*Near Sanary*)
(1925)
oil on paper
mounted on
plywood
21.0 × 23.7 cm

career was spent mainly in France it has not yet been thoroughly appraised, hence the extent of her achievement remains unknown. She went to Paris first with Margaret Preston in 1904 and they were there until December 1906 when they returned to Adelaide. In mid-1910 Davidson settled in Paris for good, though she made occasional trips back home to Adelaide. *Still life* c. 1913 (plate 47) was possibly painted while Preston (then still Macpherson) and another Adelaide painter, Gladys Reynell, were staying with Davidson in her flat at 64 Rue Madame. The manner of painting cloth with a rough hatching of dark over light is similar to a 1914 *Mother and child* by Davidson in the Art Gallery of South Australia. It was the style adopted by Reynell between 1912 and 1915, and the painting of china in this painting – in fact the china itself – resembles Preston's style in still lifes of around 1910–17.[29] The stylistic mixture of solidly realistic drawing and modelling and a modern approximation of these things in *Still life* also suggests a date pre-war. Its half-way modernism is apparent by comparison with the fluent, all-over style of Kathleen O'Connor's *Still life with white tulips* c. 1935 (plate 48). Kate O'Connor (1876–1968), resident in France for most of the period between 1905 and 1955, had a keen interest in haute couture. She wrote about fashion and was a designer with a fashion house and painter of fabrics and ceramics as well as a traditional painter of pictures. The palette and style of her oil and tempera paintings benefited considerably from her practice as a fashionable designer.

It would seem that Davidson had an influence on her Adelaide friends as they embarked on a modern style of painting in Paris in 1912–13. With her, they visited the American Club, where Rupert Bunny, Richard Miller and George Oberteuffer were members. Bunny was already known to Preston. They took lessons from the two Americans and through Bunny met the Scottish painter John Duncan Fergusson, who was yet another model for Preston's modern style.

Once the artists of Paris had divided themselves into modern and conservative camps, the rhetoric of modernity was bound to affect Australian art communities in turn. When Preston returned to Australia after the war she found the battle lines already drawn up.

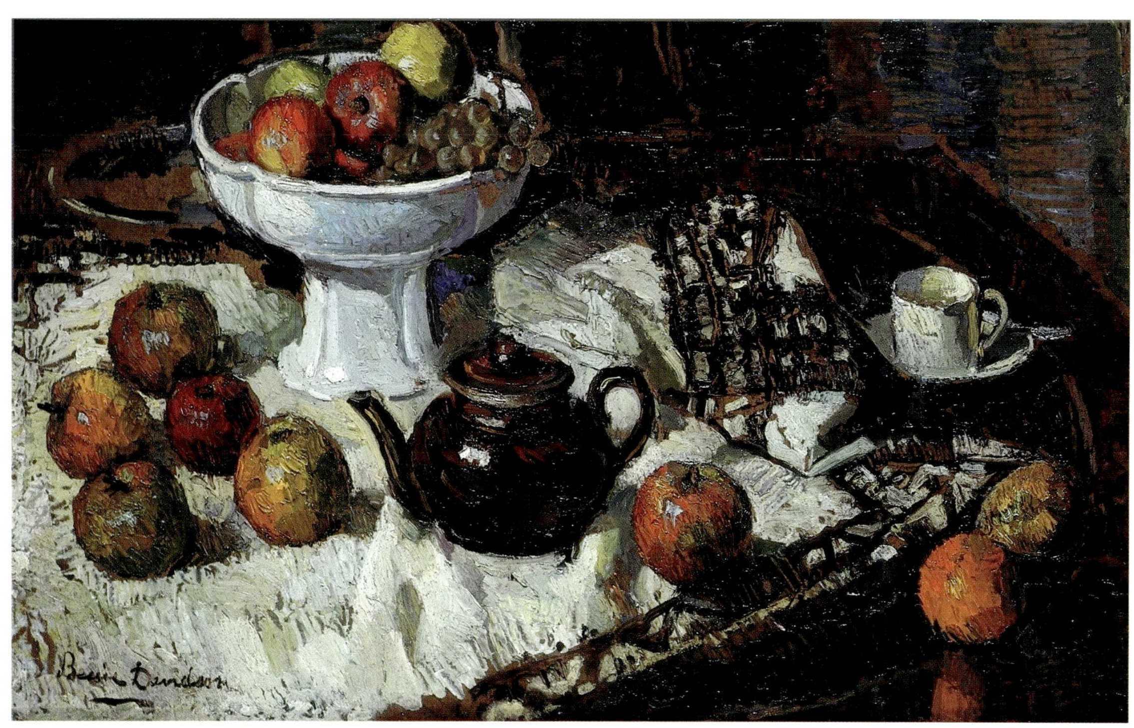

47   Bessie Davidson
1879–1965
Still life (1913)
oil on board
44.8 × 72.8 cm

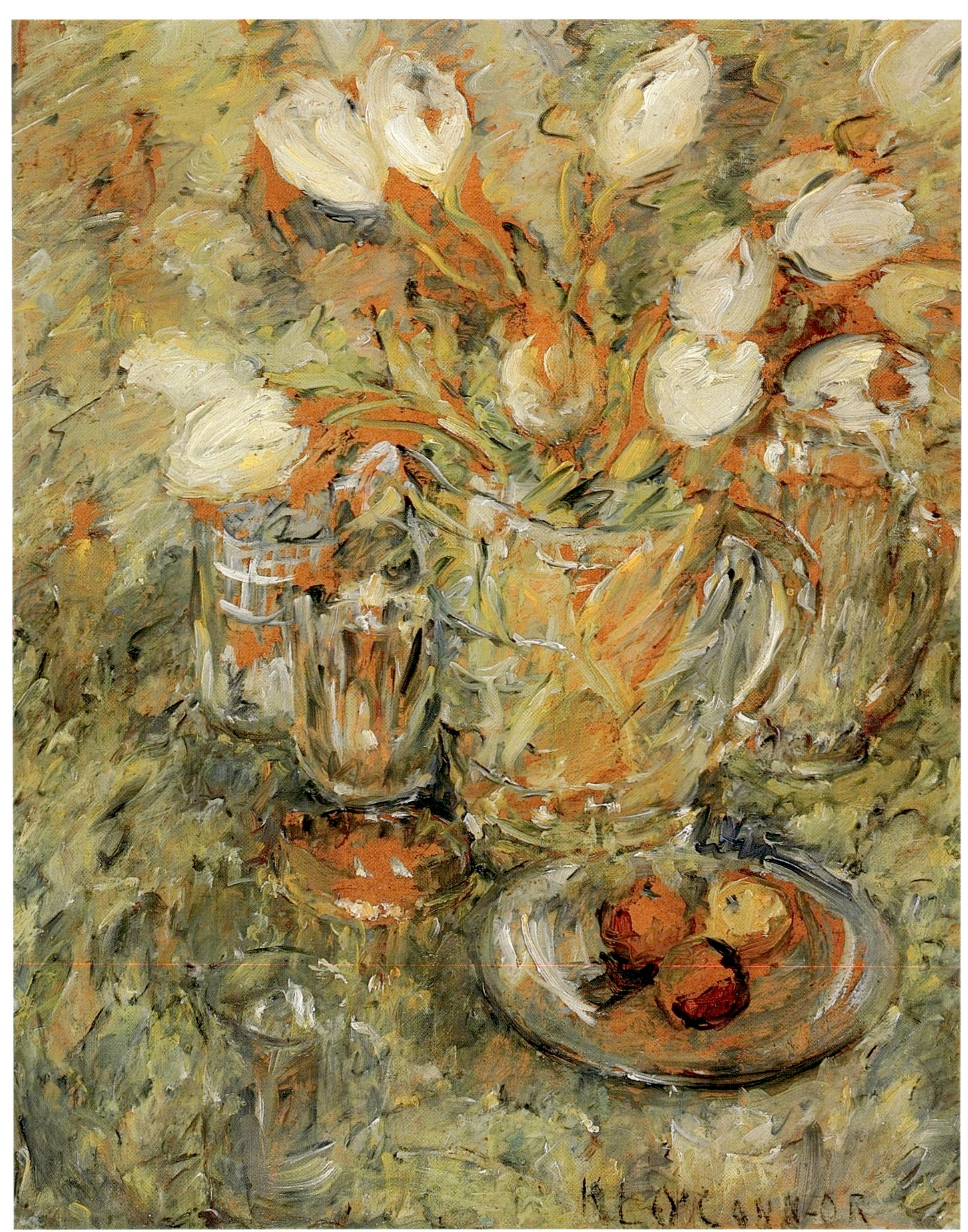

48   Kathleen O'Connor
1876–1968
Still life with white tulips (1935)
oil on board
76.0 × 63.0 cm

1 *Sydney Mail*, 26 December 1896, p. 1336.
2 Earlier there had been private classes, and a number of artists who took lessons in the colonies went to study in Europe. In 1992 Alison Inglis gave a paper on the subject of copying by Melbourne art students in the later 19th century, the Articulate Surface conference, Humanities Research Centre, Australian National University, and National Gallery of Australia, Canberra (papers to be published). See also Alison Inglis 'A Mania for Copies' in Ann Galbally and Alison Inglis, *The First Collections: The Public Library and the National Gallery of Victoria in the 1850s and 1860s*, University of Melbourne Museum of Art, 1992.
3 *British Australasian*, London, 28 April 1904, p. 543. Roberts in a 1903 letter gave his home address (44 Kenilworth Court) as 'Putney Bridge'.
4 *British Australasian*, London, 14 January 1904, p. 61.
5 Tom Roberts' letter to S.W. Pring, 11 February 1909, S.W. Pring papers, Mitchell Library.
6 Tom Roberts' letter to Miss Bessie Fraser in Melbourne, 31 October 1913, published in R.H. Croll, *Tom Roberts, Father of Australian Landscape Painting*, Robertson & Mullens, Melbourne, 1935, pp. 175-6.
7 McCubbin visited England and Paris (with two days in Normandy on the way back to London) for a short time in 1907.
8 For example, in Melbourne in 1915 the Australian Art Association asked Heysen to declare his allegiance in view of 'many rumours of your lack of sympathy with the British cause'. In Sydney in 1917 the National Art Gallery of New South Wales excluded Heysen's work from their loan exhibition of Australian art. See Mary Eagle, *Australian Modern Painting between the Wars 1914-1939*, Bay Books, Sydney, 1990, p. 26, and Heather Johnson, 'Art Patronage in Sydney 1890-1940', a thesis submitted in fulfilment of the requirements for the degree of Master of Arts, University of Sydney, May 1988, pp. 48-9.
9 See *Sydney Morning Herald*, 31 December 1904, p. 7.
10 He continued to visit Wales after settling near Dieppe in 1908.
11 *British Australasian*, London, 29 November 1906, p. 20.
12 I have not yet established whether Russell found moorings for his sea-going yacht at Portofino after selling his house at Belle-Ile. It seems likely.
13 Saint Tropez is on the coast of the south of France. The title of the watercolour was supplied by the family who owned the work. Ann Galbally's catalogue does not record any Saint Tropez subject.
14 Quotations are from C. Gasquoine Hartley, 'The Paris Club of International Women Artists', *Art Journal*, London, 1900, pp. 282-4.
15 Review of one of I. Rae's works published in the *Art Journal*, London, March 1899, p. 95.
16 *Daily Telegraph*, Sydney, 20 March 1925, p. 9.
17 'The Failure of Impressionism' by Emile Bernard, extract from *Mercure de France*, translated by Max Meldrum, *V.A.S.*, Melbourne, May 1913, pp. 1-2.
18 Colin Colahan (ed.), *Max Meldrum, His Art and Views*, Alexander McCubbin, Melbourne, 1919, p. 15.
19 See John Hassall's advertisements in *Studio*, London, April, May and June 1907. Rix arrived in London in May 1907.
20 Hilda Rix Nicholas, 'An Artist's Life in Paris', *Home*, Sydney, March 1922, pp. 24, 25, 88, 90, 93.
21 *British Australasian*, London, 19 December 1912, p. 21. For the French press see quotations published in Rix Nicholas' exhibition catalogue,

Horderns, Sydney, 11 June 1919. See also 'Sketching Morocco: A Letter from Miss Hilda Rix', *International Studio*, New York, vol. LIV, no. 213, November 1914, pp. 35–41.

22 Hilda Rix Nicholas characterised the style of Australian musician Daisy Kennedy with these words. Mrs H. Rix Nicholas, 'Australian Artists Abroad', *Art in Australia*, Sydney, February 1922, p. 69.

23 Fox letter to Hans Heysen, 13 September 1911, Heysen papers, National Library of Australia.

24 Fox letter to Norman Carter, 10 September 1909, Carter papers, Mitchell Library. See also Fox quoted in *Bulletin*, Sydney, 21 May 1908, Red Page.

25 Frieseke began his series of nudes in 1907 and painted them till 1914.

26 Fox letter to Hans Heysen, 13 September 1911, Heysen papers, National Library of Australia.

27 Clara MacChesney, 'Frieseke Tells Some of the Secrets of His Art', *New York Times*, 7 June 1914, section 6, 7, quoted in the catalogue *American Paintings from the Manoogian Collection*, Detroit Institute of Arts and the National Gallery of Art, Washington, 1989, p. 166.

28 Fox letter to Hans Heysen, 13 September 1911.

29 See Gladys Reynell's *Old [Irish] Woman* 1915, Art Gallery of South Australia, and Margaret Preston's *Summer* 1915, Art Gallery of New South Wales, and *Still life with teapot and daisies* c. 1915, Art Gallery of New South Wales. Davidson was painting colour schemes, for example, *Blue and orange*, exhibited Société Nationale des Beaux Arts 1914, such as Preston began to paint within a year or so. Early in 1913 Davidson moved from Rue Madame to Rue Boissonade.

THE SEARCH FOR ORDER BETWEEN WARS

1920s–1930s

Blamire Young (1862–1935) was modern decades before it was an issue. He came to Australia in 1884, a new graduate of Cambridge University, to teach mathematics at Katoomba College in the Blue Mountains. Pursuing an interest in art, he built himself a studio, became a close friend of black and white artist Phil May, and in 1893 followed his example of going back to England to pursue art seriously. There (advised by Phil May) he studied with two of May's friends, the leading poster artists James Pryde and William Nicholson (the Beggarstaff brothers), returning to Melbourne in the mid-1890s the possessor of an exemplary modern style. Young told artists in Melbourne that decoration was fundamental to good art. By decoration he meant the controlled use of colour, drawing and composition for the clearest expression of an idea. He deplored the materialism of Australia, whose artists were obsessed with capturing exact qualities of light on natural forms but could not care less about ideas or emotions. 'I seek to paint the soul through the body,' wrote Young, 'I must paint so that he who sees my picture and looks into it may surprise some new thoughts among the shadows – thoughts that I have hidden there for him to find.'[1]

The large watercolour in the ICI collection (plate 49) of a young woman looking through parted curtains shows Blamire Young c. 1910 using colour and composition imaginatively to evoke mood. The original title of the work is not known, though there are clues within the image that suggest the subject might be Alfred Tennyson's poem *Mariana*. Some years earlier Young had painted a gathering of eminent Victorians, *Alfred Tennyson reads 'Maud' to his friends* c. 1905 (National Gallery of Australia), in which that poet figured. In the later image, which is half-medieval and half-contemporary (which is to say Edwardian),

Thea Proctor as she appeared in *The Home* magazine of 1 October 1927, page 29. This magazine played a large role in popularising Thea Proctor's modernist colours and designs, as her work often depicted a sensual world of elegant figures which fitted in with the magazine's middle-class aesthetic.

Photograph by Bernice Agar
La Trobe Collection, State Library of Victoria

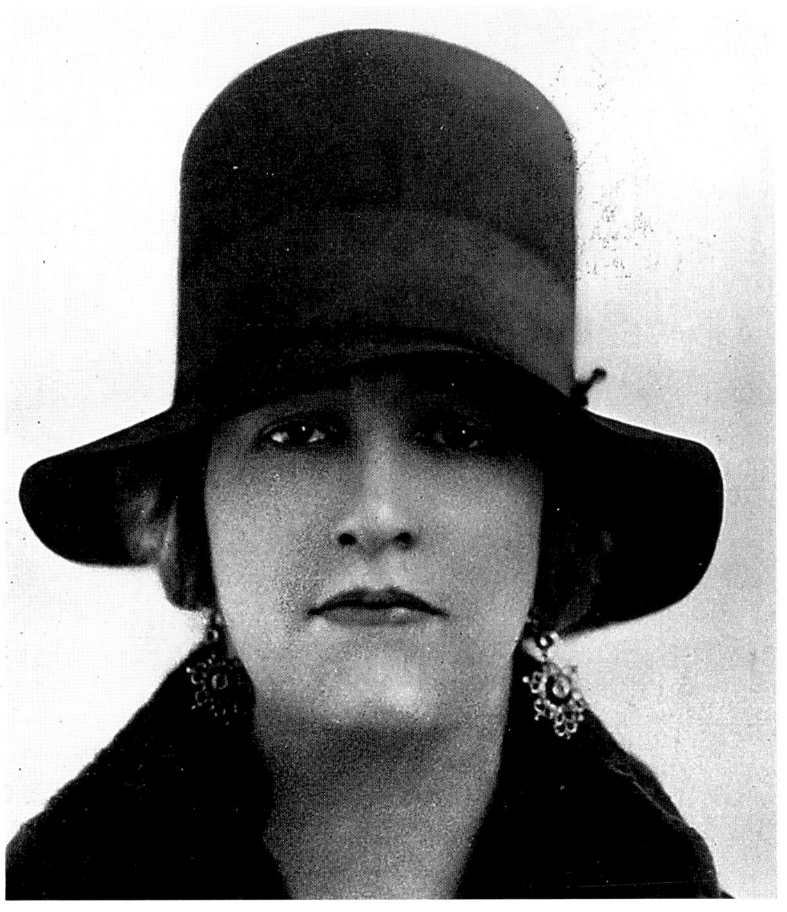

Young visualised the central motif of the poem 'Mariana'.

Mariana

> drew her casement-curtain by,
> And glanced athwart the glooming flats.
> She only said, 'The night is dreary,
> He cometh not', she said;
> She said, 'I am aweary, aweary,
> I would that I were dead'.

The dominant colour is a rich, sad blue shading into mauve. Within the vertical image a great deal is made of the exact positioning of the woman's head against the evening sky. Mariana is perched high on the window ledge, holding apart the curtains to look out. Below her head the lower two-thirds of the image is filled with an expanse of drapery that descends in a measured rhythm,

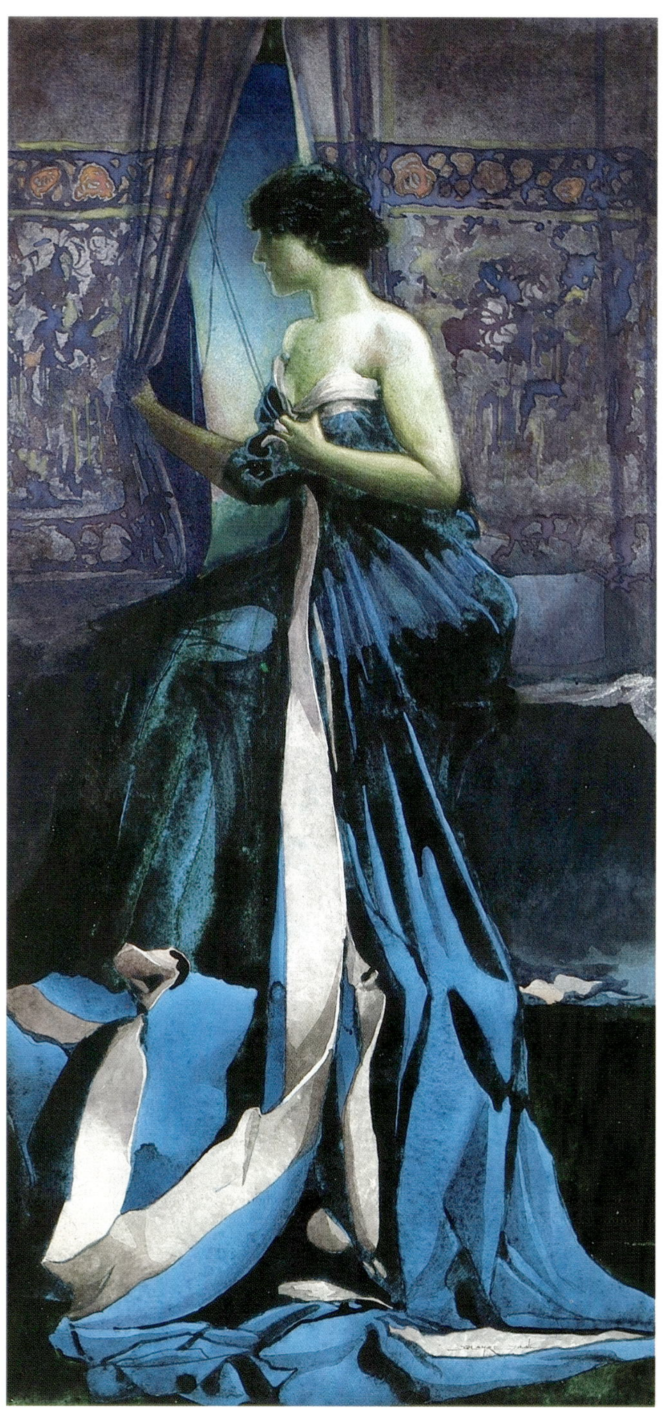

49   Blamire Young
1862–1935
(*Mariana*) (1910)
watercolour on paper
81.5 × 41.0 cm

from ledge to seat to floor, a graceful tempo that echoes the cadences of Tennyson's poem. Blamire Young may have had in mind John Everett Millais' 1851 painting *Mariana* which has the same storytelling elements: a young woman in a dramatically blue dress looking through a curtain in a setting suggestively medieval.

The swing 1925 (plate 50), a colour woodcut by Thea Proctor (1879–1966), also tells a story. Like Blamire Young's work it is modern in style but has nostalgic overtones in the story – modernity in fancy dress. The artists knew each other, both were interested in the theatre and, choosing to tell stories in their art, developed styles of colourful clarity that were the hallmark of the advertising art of their times rather than of *high* art. Proctor, like Young, defended imaginative art against what she felt was a conspicuous lack of storytelling imagination in Australian culture.[2] Young's and Proctor's lives and their reported thoughts suggest that they lived out their fantasies to some extent. As well as creating images of the 1870s Proctor dressed in clothes that were subtly suggestive of the period when her mother had been a young woman. Blamire Young pursued ways of creating images subjectively, for example drawing faces, figures and objects suggested to him by 'accidents' of paint staining.[3] The interplay between subjective feelings and the study of 'objective' external appearance or process has been typical of imaginative Australian artists. Norman Lindsay's bacchanalian fantasies were woven around a scientific theory of light. George Lambert and his younger follower, Arthur Murch, put people and objects in unexpected relationships and heightened the tension by describing them with painstaking accuracy. In the late 1930s Sidney Nolan and James Gleeson had a creative habit similar to that of Blamire Young, dreamily spinning out their subjects through a semi-automatic process of staining, drawing, painting and assembling. Australia's imaginative artists and writers generally have had mannered styles, they have told stories from the past, and their interest has been in illusion and large philosophical issues rather than a psychologically penetrating humanism.

Proctor's and Young's Edwardian brand of modernism preceded the Great War which drastically altered the terms for modern art. It was widely said at the time that the war brought Australia maturity, and with maturity the

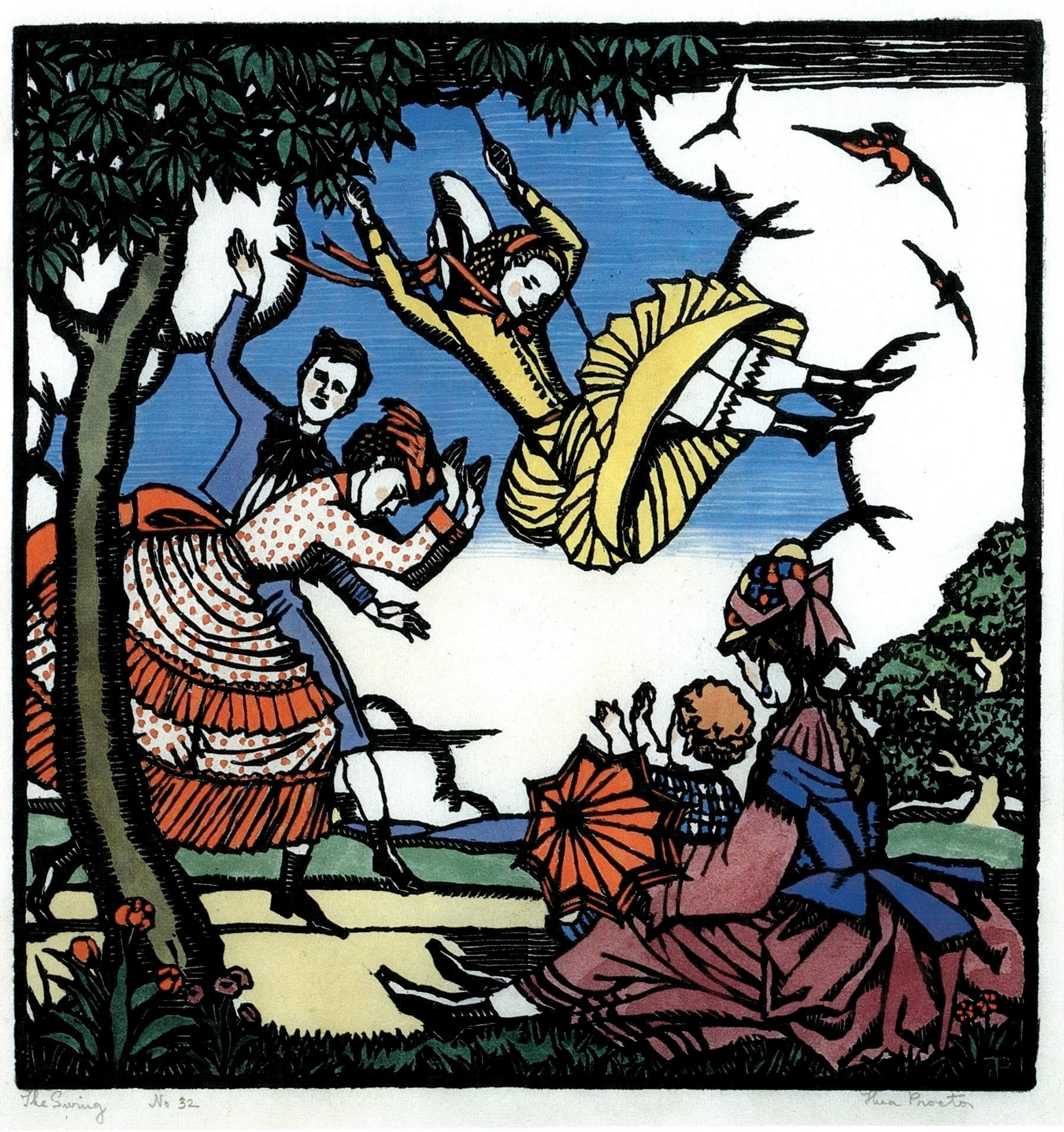

50 Thea Proctor
1879–1966
The swing 1925
hand-coloured woodcut on paper
22.5 × 24.9 cm

question of national identity was revived. What was Australia to the world outside? What was typical of Australians as a people? How was the country to be characterised? Did Australia even possess a distinctive culture?

National feeling was strong around the world in the twenty years between the First and Second World Wars. It is symptomatic that its universality went unrecognised. In places as far apart as Australia and Austria, in countries as disparate as England, America and the newly united Soviet Union, battle lines were drawn up between national and modern expression and, moreover, the same arguments were used to separate conflicting directions in social life. To observe how nationalism was posed against modernism is to gain some insight into why they were placed in opposition to each other.

Modernism did not seem a true reflection of national ways of life, partly because modern technology had introduced sweeping changes that altered life considerably. The war in Europe, which resulted in ten million deaths, broke the fabric of society in a drastic and terrible way. Afterwards, the discontinuity with the past was recognised and not relished. The post-war nostalgia for an earlier way of life ran counter to the forces for change through modern technology. Fear of change, fear of disruption, the need for reassurance were strong emotional factors in deciding attitudes to modern art. Modernism nonetheless represented a contemporary reality. Even before the war, like every other western country, Australia was committed to modernity through its acceptance of electricity, radio, the aeroplane and functional design. Modernity was the way the world was going. Its victory was assured.

France was the only country in a position to endorse modern art as national expression. Nineteen-twenties cubism with earlier post-impressionism acquired the name 'School of Paris', which echoed the great Raphael's famous homage to the Greek 'School of Athens' and claimed a respected tradition for the new style. In other countries modern styles were disparaged as foreign and futuristic. In Germany in 1937 Adolf Hitler defined 'modern' art by opposition to ethnic art. Modern art, he said was defined by its proponents:

as nothing but an international communal experience, thus . . . killing altogether any understanding of its integral relationship with an ethnic group. On the other hand its relationship to time was stressed . . . There was no longer any art of peoples or even of races but only an art of the times . . . According to such a theory . . . art and art activities are lumped together with the handiwork of our modern tailor shops and fashion industries . . . [with the maxim:] every year something new . . . National-Socialist Germany, however, wants again a 'German Art' . . . of eternal value . . .

Hitler recognised the multiracial tradition of German culture though he saw its diversity as given final character by one group, the Aryan:

We desire for ourselves an art which takes into account within itself the continually growing unification of this race pattern and, thus, emerges with a unified, well-rounded total character.[4]

Both America and the Soviet Union consciously pursued earthy identities. Despite being far apart in almost every respect – technologically, socially, economically, politically and culturally – these countries promoted an image of themselves as homely folk. They advocated salt-of-the-earth folksiness as a true self-image in contrast to the sophisticated foreign import, abstraction, which was pervasive nevertheless. Italy and Germany proposed an ideal humanism as their national styles, Germany looking to the Aryan ideal and Italy to the classical. Here, as elsewhere, national identity was a preoccupation of official culture. Australia alone virtually ignored the human motif (apart from the work of Napier Waller and Rayner Hoff), finding her national identity in the landscape and specifically in the light that gave colour and atmosphere.

In human terms the war was a disaster from which society recovered only very slowly. For some years afterwards Australian painters expressed themselves most feelingly when portraying the landscape. And so the war contributed to an already existing tradition whereby the landscape rather than the people was used to express human emotions as well as national aspirations. Penleigh

Boyd (1890–1923) was invalided out of the army in 1918 after being badly gassed at Ypres. Between 1919 and 1922 he painted convalescent landscapes such as the serene and peaceful *Portsea Pier* c. 1920 (plate 51). The blue in this post-war seascape expressed infinite summer warmth; a gentle breeze promised continuity. Boyd's romanticism was recognised by Australian audiences. One fulsome reviewer wrote:

> One has only to look at his series of Portsea canvases to observe that the beauty of that sacred place has come to him as a vision to be disclosed [and] in revelation of which he, glorious youth, is only Providence's proud instrument.
>
> Painters will applaud his quality and the depth of his feeling when he engages the sun as a spotlight . . . The flood of colour and the dexterity with which he handles tea-tree scrubs, giving it a poetry and consequence that is unnerving to philistines who have picnicked with the flies in its stifling shade, show that he is an incurable romanticist who is almost ready to dye scenery to suit his whim.[5]

Boyd emulated the style and subjects of the most famous Australian artist of all, Arthur Streeton. Streeton's paintings were romantic as well as being among the most briskly masculine produced by the earlier generation of landscape artists. The difference between Boyd and his mentor was that the interpretations of the 'Cherub' – as young Boyd was known by his old National Gallery School fellows – were so typical and so 'near to prettiness' that they trembled on the edge of banality.[6]

In 1918, around the time Boyd was invalided out of the army, Streeton accepted an appointment as an official war artist. Sent to France to record the scenes of famous battles, he portrayed the devastated landscapes in a chastened, almost delicate style. By contrast his vision of the Australian landscape on returning home was more optimistic than ever. He bought land and built a home at Olinda in the Dandenong Ranges near Melbourne, and in painting near his home rendered the distant vista in a blue no less magisterial than Boyd's heavenly azure. Despite knowing the landscape well and possessively, Streeton did not indulge in an overtly sentimental

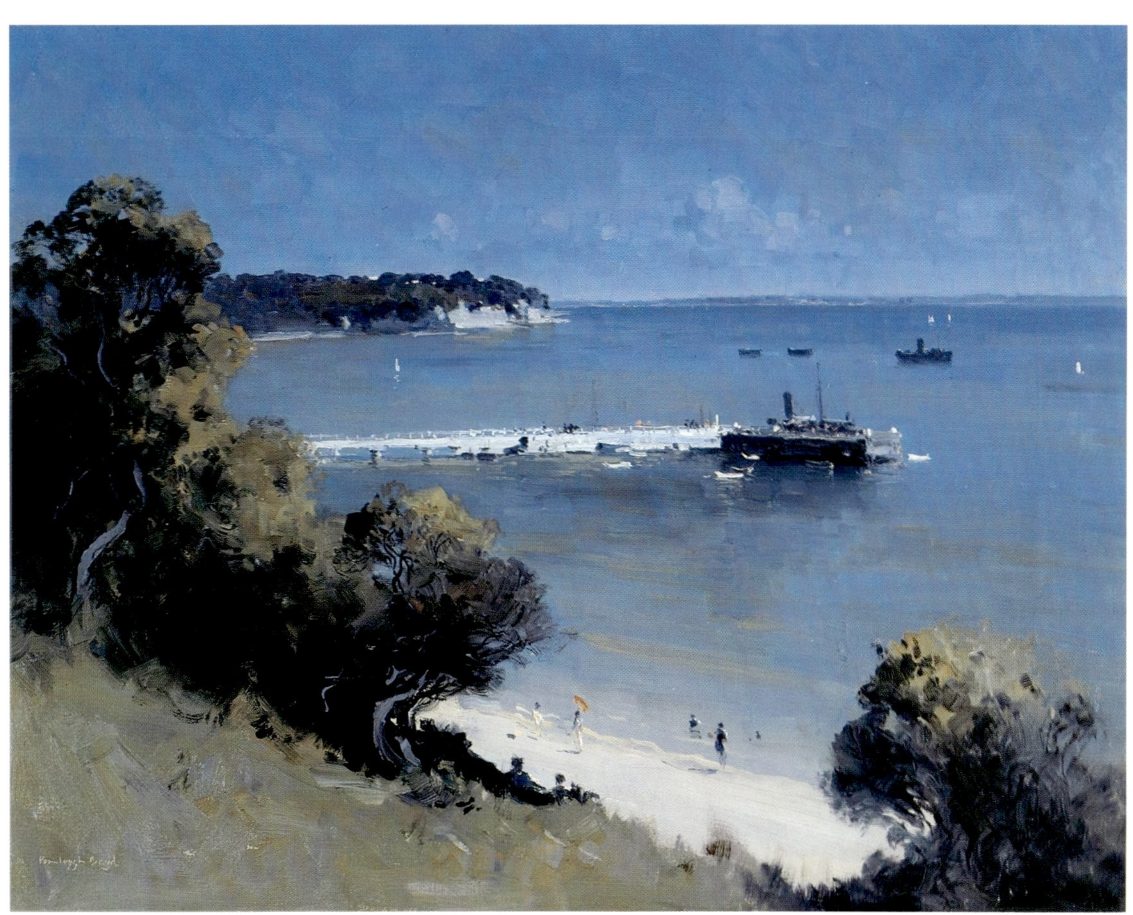

51   Penleigh Boyd
1890–1923
Portsea Pier (1920)
oil on canvas
66.0 × 87.1 cm

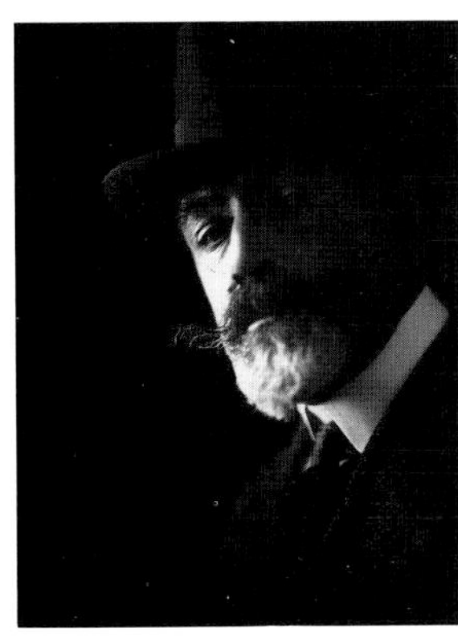

Arthur Streeton in mid-life.

Photograph by Mina and Max Moore
La Trobe Collection, State Library of Victoria

interpretation. The scene of *Blue and Gold, Olinda* 1926 (plate 52) was disciplined into broad horizontal bands of khaki bush, blue hills and paler sky. Paint was applied in brusque strokes of nearly uniform shape and size. There were no fussy details which would distract attention from the unity of his interpretation. One look at the painting tells everything: partly cleared bushland, new settlement, new undergrowth glinting brightly in the sun, a summer haze faintly blurring the hills, and only one small cloud on the horizon. This vision after war showed Australia as a brave new world.

Whether the assertive confidence of Streeton's 1920s paintings was in reaction to the mangled landscapes of France or in summation of his own previous vision, it suited the needs of his post-war audience. Australians, individually and collectively, suffered from the war. There was scarcely a family untouched, either by the death of a son, husband or brother or by the responsibility of caring for those returned servicemen who had difficulty in adapting to civilian life. The code of the times did not allow people to acknowledge the social problems that arose in the aftermath of war because strong national sentiment had developed around the concept of sacrifice. Australia claimed its birth as a nation among other nations as a reward for valour. Motifs of official remembrance were youth and death, bravery and success: the obverse of how returned servicemen actually appeared in Australia post-war. The dead could be mourned but Australians who worshipped the ANZACs of heroic memorial could not understand and could hardly admire those who lived on, maimed and embittered. As a group, the returned servicemen were at odds with society, an unwelcome reminder of suppressed realities. Their ills were first aired in the early 1930s when they became a Depression-period symbol of injustice. Later in the decade, when Australia faced another major world conflict they, rather than the mythical ANZACS, represented the realities of war.

Three artists dominated landscape painting after the war: Streeton (1867–1943) of Melbourne, Hans Heysen (1877–1968) of Adelaide and Elioth Gruner (1882–1939) of Sydney. Hans Heysen's sales soared to match Streeton's. In fact, in an exhibition in Adelaide at the height of the depression in 1931, his paintings fetched £4000, which was an Australian record.[7] Heysen was known for imposing

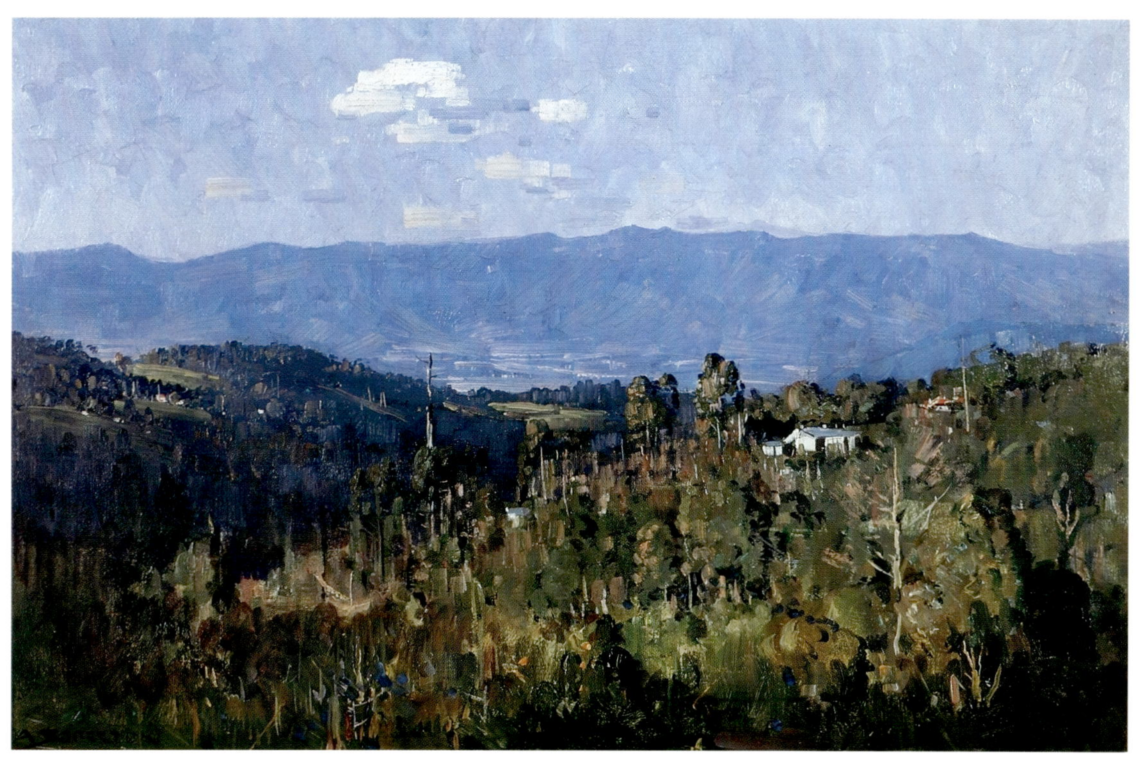

52 Arthur Streeton
1867–1943
Blue and Gold, Olinda 1926
oil on canvas laid down on board
51.7 × 77.6 cm

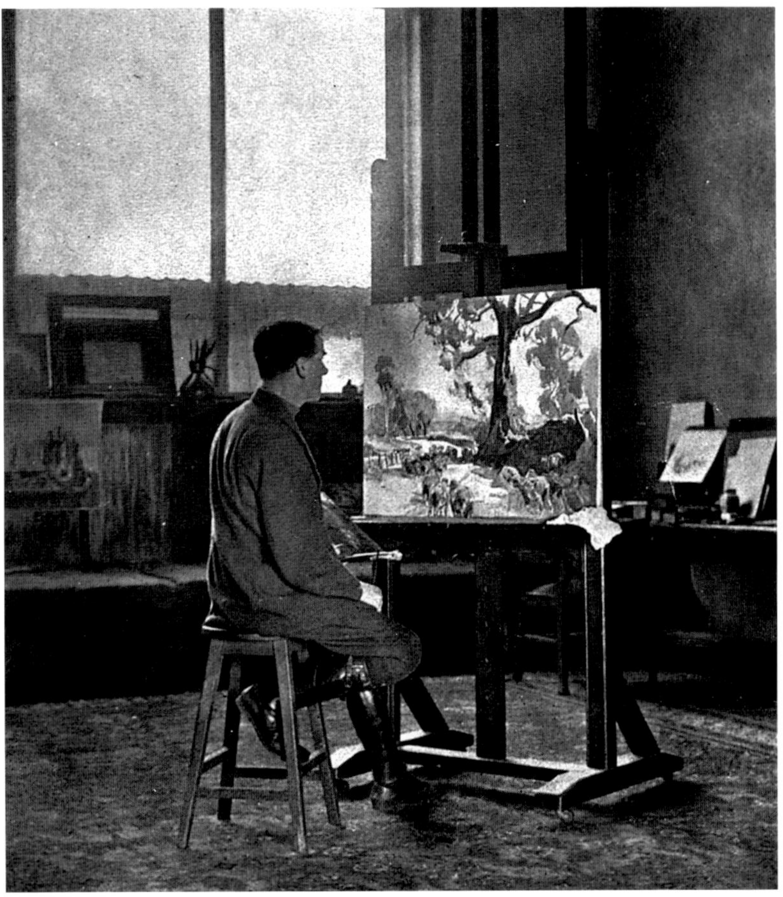

Hans Heysen in his studio in Adelaide's Mt Lofty Ranges. His sunny landscapes of gum trees became immensely popular and inspired a generation of imitators. The photograph is from *The Home*, 1 December 1921, page 16.

Photograph by A. Wilkinson
La Trobe Collection, State Library of Victoria

gum trees and spectacular effects of light. Year by year the art societies of Adelaide, Melbourne, Sydney and elsewhere showed his impressive efforts to tackle 'this most absorbing problem – light through everything – in the deepest shadows as in the most dazzling sky'. According to the reviewer just quoted the 'large, light-barked gums [in the region of Hahndorf], painted against a flood of sunlight, are peculiarly adapted to his exposition of the painting of light'.[8]

Gruner's contribution was summed up in 1929 when Basil Burdett compared the artist's earlier 'lyrical' interpretation – 'personal, rather than national or general' – with the simple formality he later achieved. Burdett concluded that Gruner 'had essayed to impose a classic restraint upon the earlier, emotional romanticism which, for all its qualities of spontaneity and freshness, was liable to lose control'.[9] Through the twenties and early thirties Gruner made several visits to the Monaro plains

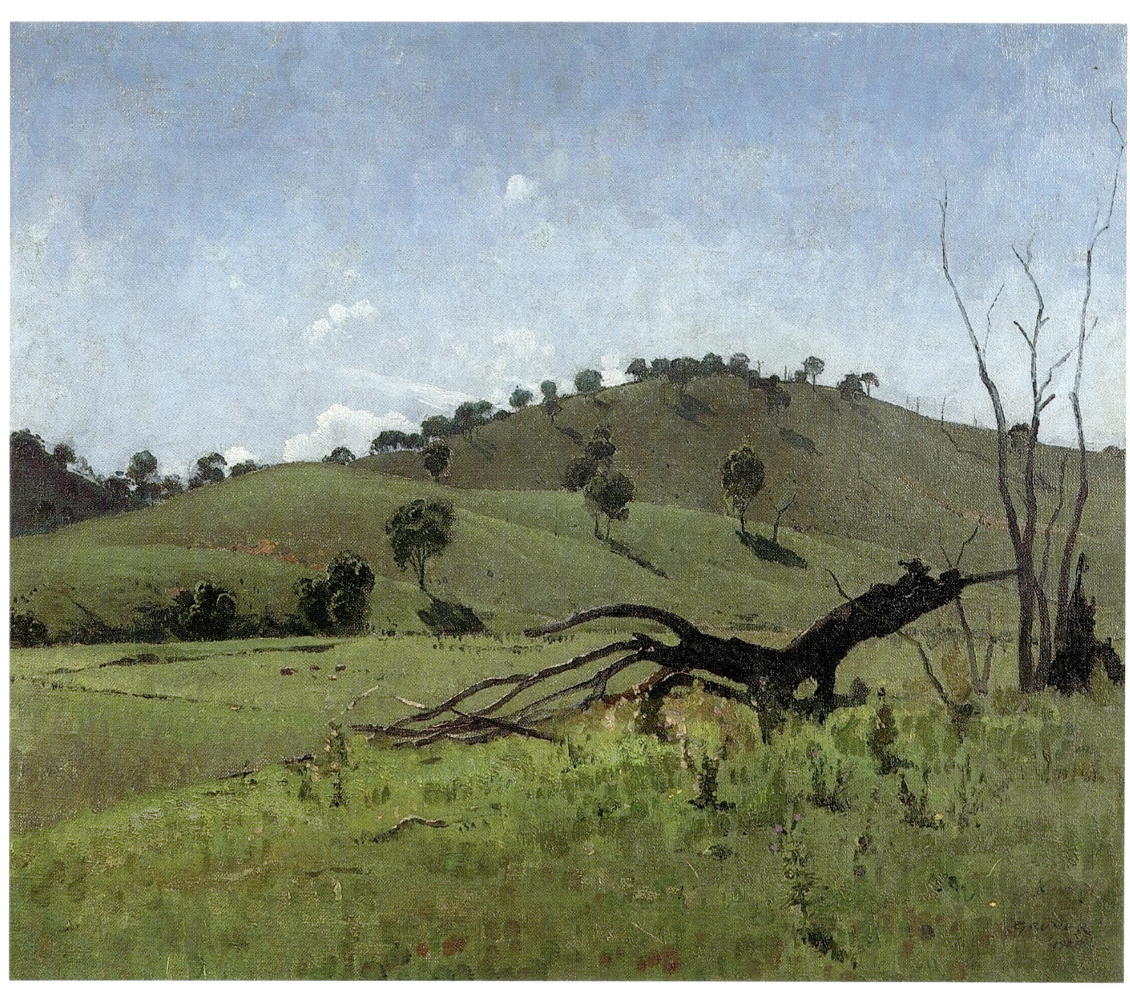

53 Elioth Gruner
1882–1939
Yass landscape 1928
oil on canvas
50.5 × 60.5 cm

and the district lower down around Canberra and Yass. He saw the rolling hills thinly covered with grass and accented with narrow lines of roads, trees, fences, and overwhelmed by huge skies, a landscape of unthreatening elegance which permitted a modification towards a more streamlined style. Gruner's earlier views, with their emphatic ruffs of paint silhouetting forms against the light, had described a time of day but no particular place – the scenes could have been anywhere in the world almost – whereas the later paintings successfully characterised specific places. By the same token the later landscapes were modern in their simplicity of form and colour. Among other artists Hans Heysen, from the mid-1920s, followed Gruner in finding landscapes which in form and colour offered a compromise between national expression and modernism.

Gruner's *Yass landscape* 1928 (plate 53) was used to illustrate Burdett's 1929 article about the painter's altered style. As an image it is unpretentious, merely a few acres of cleared pasture land rising up a small hill. The artist looked into the light (his usual practice) and up the hill to find a viewpoint which flattened the scene into a sequence of planes and made a spidery, unexpectedly dark silhouette of the fallen tree in the foreground. *Early morning, Cooma, New South Wales* 1927 (plate 54) is an even simpler image of the Monaro plains flowing to the mountains of the Great Dividing Range. Gruner's motif was the undulant rhythm of the receding landscape and, in keeping with the understatement, the colours were quiet blues and greens.

In reaction to the popular supposition that modern art reflected the chaos and violence of war, Australian modern art between the wars became identified with an objective approach to art and its subjects. Endorsing order and reason, the artists looked for systems rather than exceptions. The search produced a fundamental similarity of style between artists of very different types. Rigorous analysis was as vital for the poetic yet highly disciplined art of Clarice Beckett as it was for the cubist paintings of Roy de Maistre.

De Maistre (1894–1968) painted *The organist* c. 1943 (plate 55) in his maturity, many years after the last years of the First World War when he discovered his direction in art. He was later to say that the single most creative

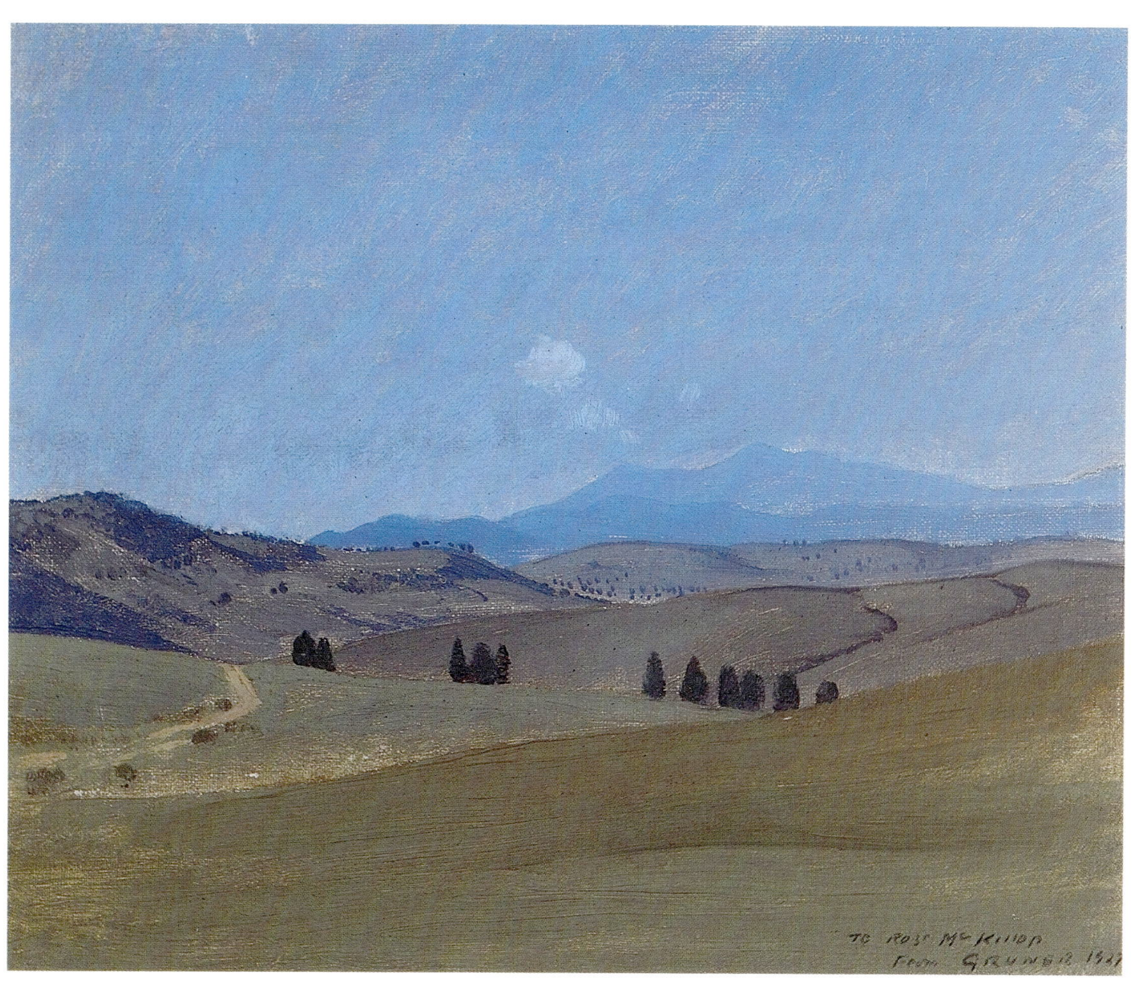

54   Elioth Gruner
1882–1939
Early morning, Cooma, New South Wales 1927
oil on canvas
32.5 × 39.0 cm

period in his career was 1918–19 in Sydney when he was formulating scales of colour to marry visual art with music.[10] De Maistre's first colour music paintings were landscapes and when in the mid-1930s, now living in London, he again painted images of colour music, their form was abstract. None of the mid-1930s paintings were as successful as *The organist* 1943, a direct, elegiac representation of his subject. In one way it is a literal representation. The organ keys, detached from the organ itself, have spread throughout the image in an array of larger and smaller rectangular forms. Their narrow shape informs even the shadowy planes of half light at the side and across the centre of the image. There, within an area of bright light, the staccato theme of the keyboard is offset by the theme of the organist. The image as a whole is ceremonial and moody. Shapes are irregular and dynamic, oblique and therefore active, a dynamism at its most forceful in the centre of the canvas. There deep space and surface pattern compete for attention and an alternating movement is set up, a stepping in and out from bright light into deep shadow. The rhythm is focussed in a musically appropriate way by the controlled sway of the organist's gently moving torso and legs, and the piston-like rise and fall of his arms.

Taxi rank c. 1927 (plate 56) by Clarice Beckett (1887–1935) is a view of Collins Street on a damp winter's evening. In an expanse of smurry grey a row of taxis, the silhouettes of a street lamp and some hurrying figures appear as darker blobs. The only colour is the commercial pink of light globes outlining the facade and foyer of a theatre. Japanese in its selectivity, Whistlerian in atmospherics, *Taxi rank* holds the balance between East and West. There is a Whistlerian spotting and stroking of pink colour; and a flurry of colour on the wet pavement is like the ideogram stamped on a favourite painting by a Chinese connoisseur.

This artist disconcerted her Melbourne audience because her art fitted no known category. The stylistic balancing act extended dangerously further than East and West, pleasing neither the Meldrumites or those of the modern camp in Melbourne. The playwright Louis Esson privately observed:

> Clarice Beckett's work is the most delicate thing possible, little fresh studies from nature, but most

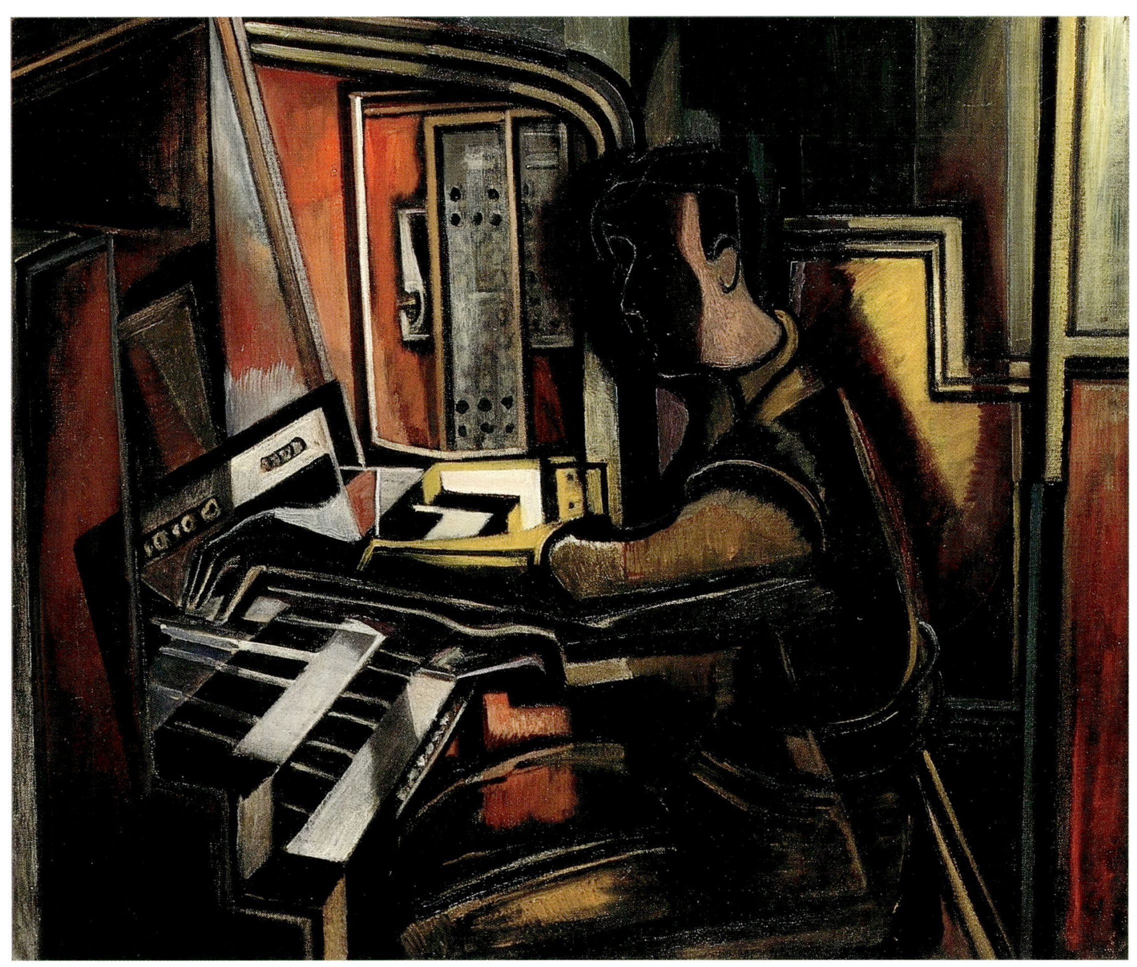

55   Roy de Maistre
1894–1968
The organist (1943)
oil on canvas
51.0 × 61.0 cm

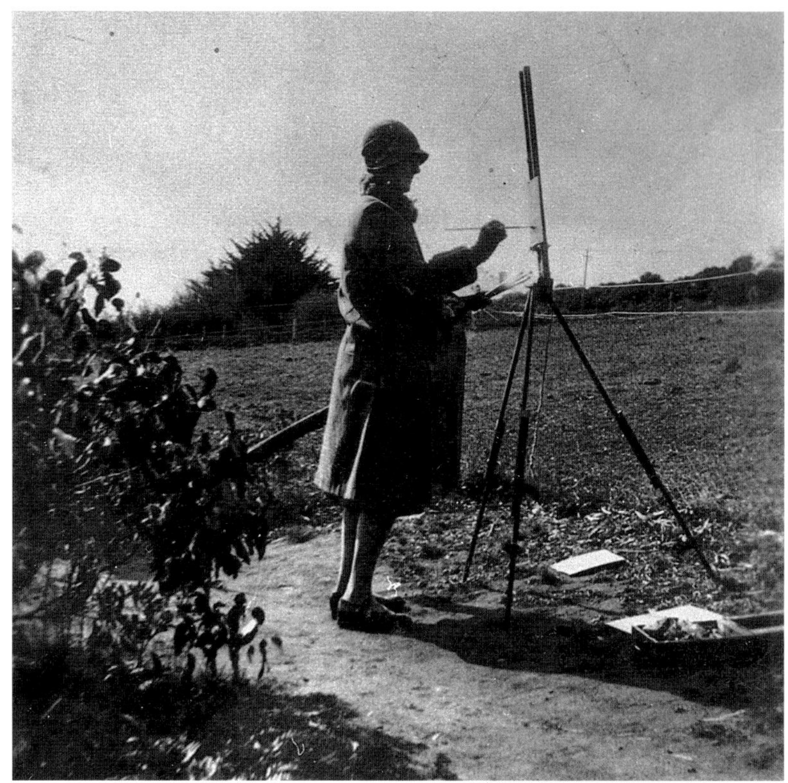

critics are angry because they are not obvious pot-boilers. I could understand her being neglected but it is strange how anything so gentle should get such abuse.[11]

The fact is that Beckett managed to challenge nearly everyone of all artistic camps in Melbourne, simply by her persistence in going her own way regardless of how things were done and how lines were drawn up in the Melbourne art world. The mixture that proved explosive was a remarkably prosaic subject matter (taxis, telegraph poles, bitumen roadways); an austere style that derived from the tonal theory of Melbourne's most irritating artist, Max Meldrum; a vision that made poetry of unregarded things; and sheer determination to show her art annually and in cool disregard for the kindly advice given by the critics of previous years. Her professionalism was practically the only trait to earn Beckett wholesale respect. Wrote 'Salamander' in the *Sun*:

To set up an easel and to transmit to canvas the majesty of Collins Street glittering under spring

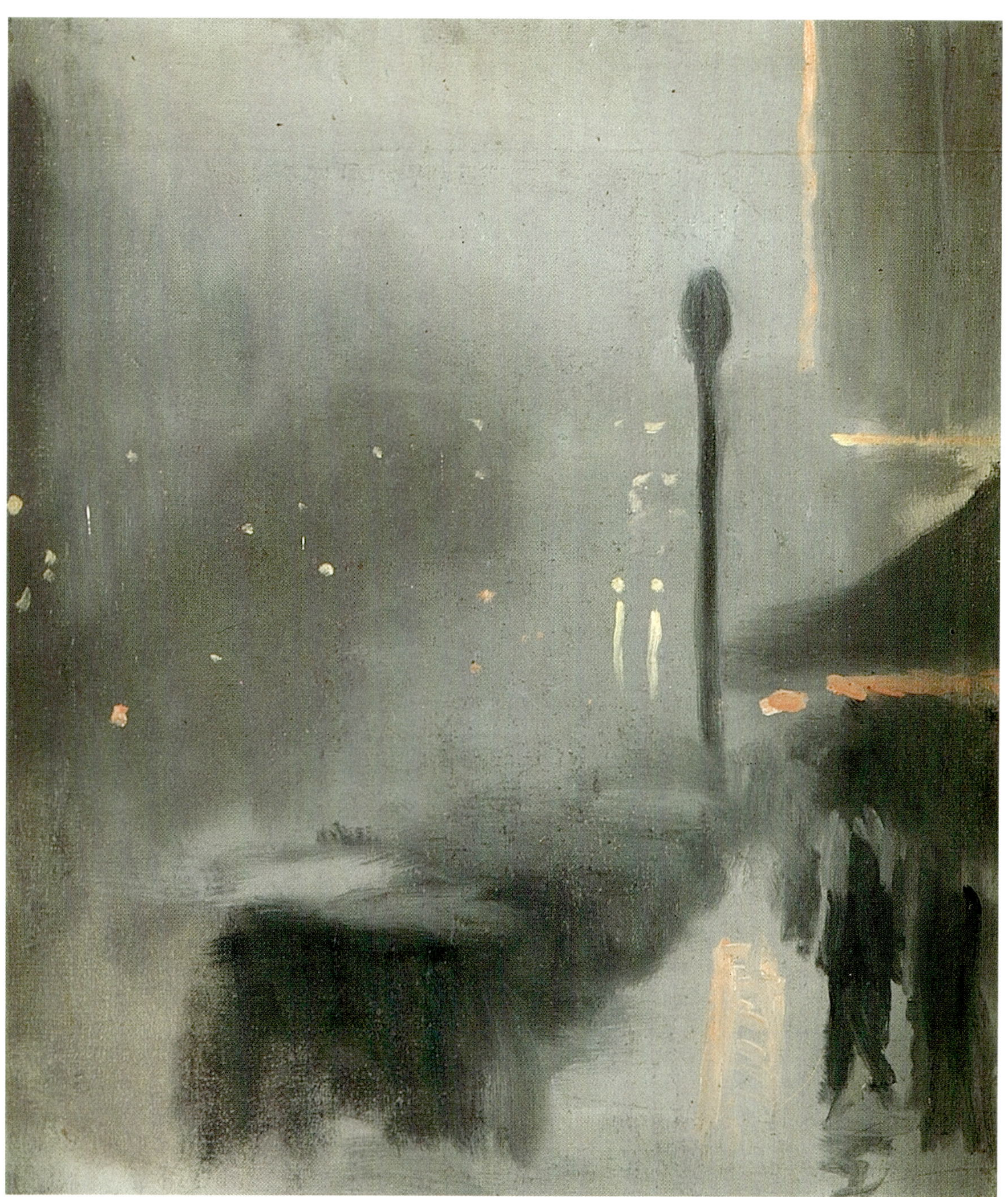

56 Clarice Beckett
1887–1935
Taxi rank (1927)
oil on canvas on board
58.5 × 51.0 cm

sunshine or brooding in curtains of rain on a winter's
eve needs concentration and a steady nerve.[12]

It was left for later generations to admire the restraint
of Beckett's style. Her disciplined yet characteristically
fuzzy tone and colour concentrates attention on one or
two economical shifts in a register, and she used it to
express an image of nature as precise and fleeting as an
image in a Japanese *haiku*.

The works of the modern painters Margaret Preston,
Roy de Maistre, Grace Cossington Smith, Ralph Balson,
Frank Hinder and Godfrey Miller are alike in being
rhythmically patterned. When it came to a choice most
modernists were uninterested in individual appearances
and subjective responses which seemed too superficial
and random, too nihilistic, to be a true description. While
their paintings could be feelingly expressed and carry
subjective messages, in essence they described stable
systems and universal truths. Even when the modernists
took the opportunity for emotional expression offered by
landscape painting, their landscapes, for example those
of Grace Cossington Smith (plate 58) and Horace Trenerry
(plate 57), were generalised and analytical by comparison
with the landscapes by Elioth Gruner (plates 53 and 54)
or Penleigh Boyd (plate 51) which were soft, evocative
and romantic. The modern approach to landscape
implicitly criticised as shallow the Australian tradition of
watching and recording fleeting impressions of light.

The road to Maslins c. 1940 (plate 57) by South Australian
artist Horace Trenerry (1899–1958) is as unadorned as
Gruner's pastoral landscapes of the 1920s, but completely
without his quiet optimism. The road cuts deep into the
land like a scalpel into flesh and the colours, far from
suggesting the green promise of winter pasture, are those
of veined flesh and bare earth. An open quarry and a
cutting on the side of the road underline the sculptural
aspect of Trenerry's landscape. It is unlikely that he meant
to show the landscape as raw, carved earth, although that
is one implication of the imagery. Painters of the
generation between the wars were (mostly) unaware or
at least careless of psychological overtones in their
expression. The Maslins region of South Australia looks
like this image. Trenerry made no verbal claims to
anatomise an inner landscape and there was no suggestion

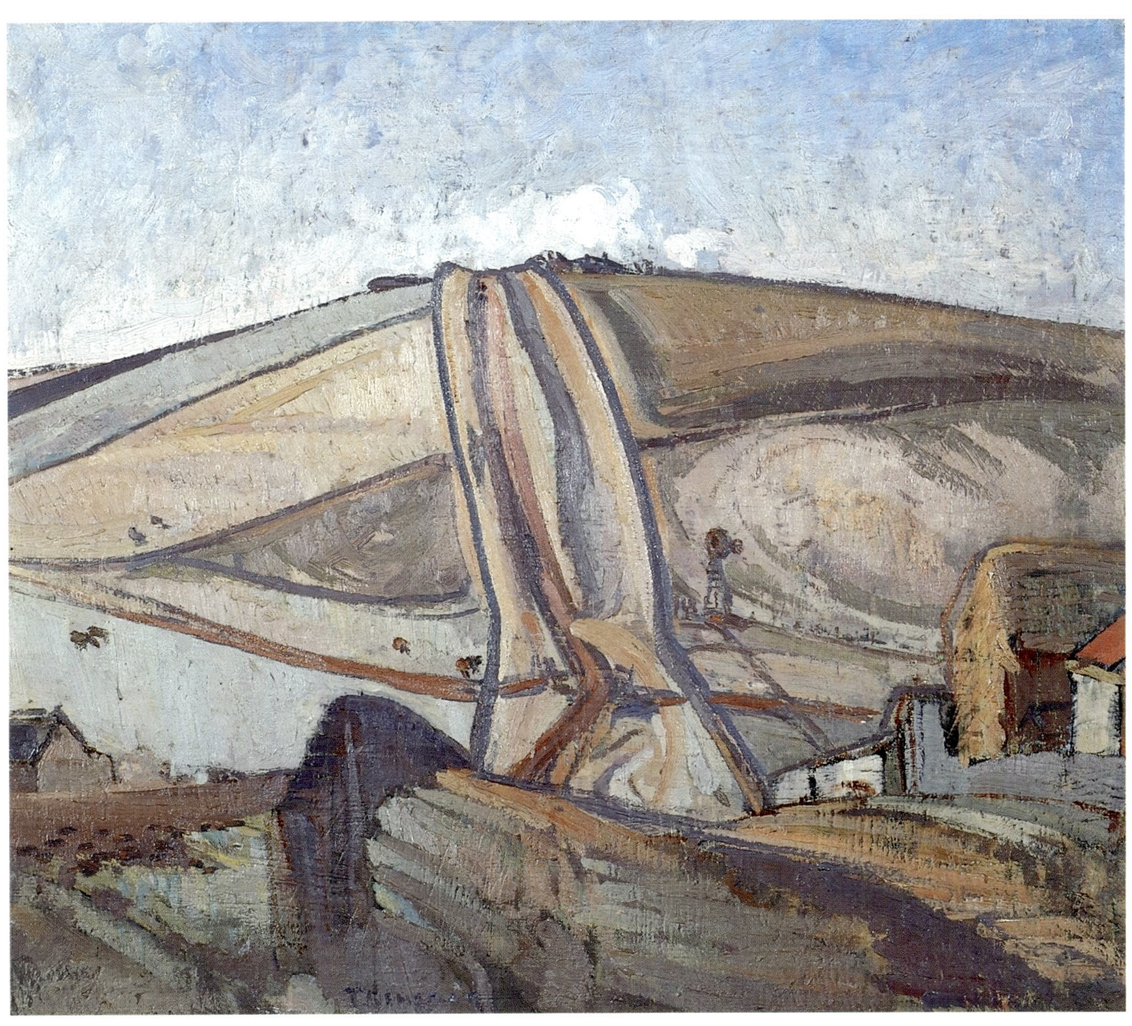

57   Horace Trenerry
1899–1958
The road to Maslins (1940)
oil on board
48.5 × 57.0 cm

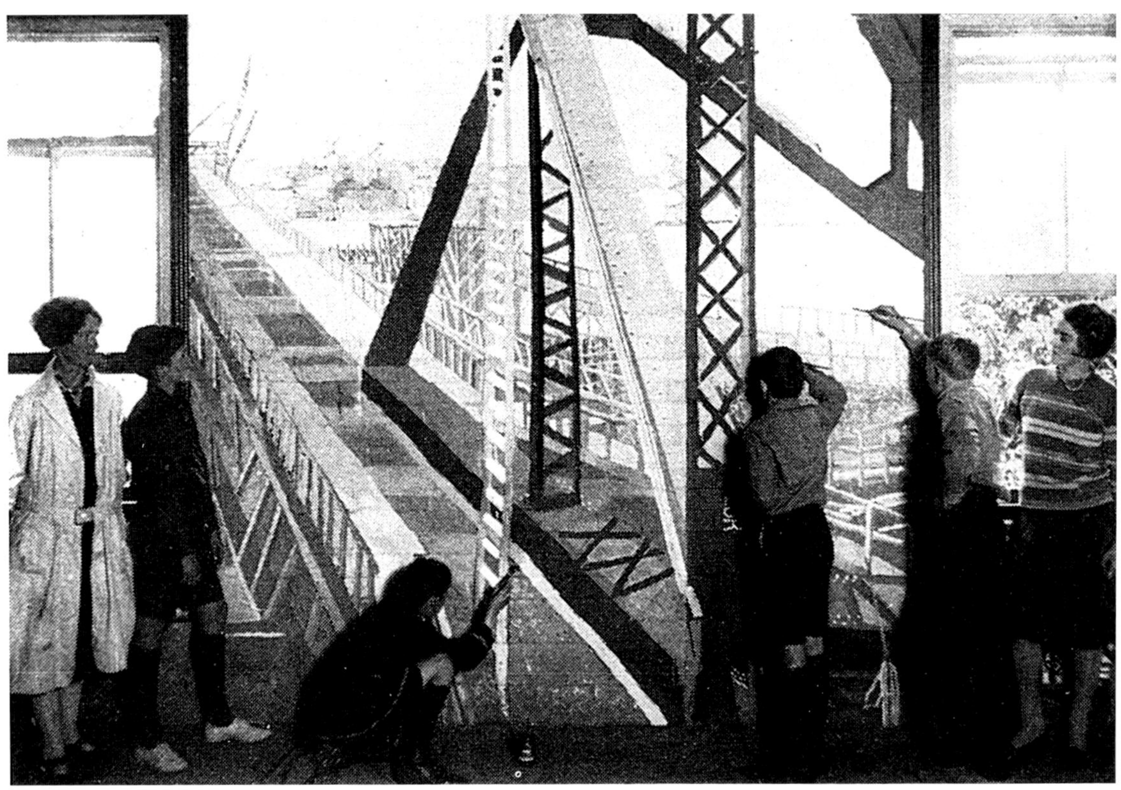

Grace Cossington Smith (far left) and Jean Ramsay instruct the boys of the Turramurra Grammar School in the painting of a mural of the North Shore Bridge, Sydney, 1927. This photograph appeared in *The Home* in November 1927, page 23.

Janine Burke Collection

that he was interested in the geological age of the country, however one should not discount the fact that by 1940 the interpretation of Australia as the world's most ancient, now infertile, continent was emerging as a theme of painting and literature.

The gully 1928 (plate 58) by Grace Cossington Smith (1892–1984) is ambiguous in expression in another way, despite its modern uncluttered line and confident, whippy pattern of interlocking curves and step-by-step colour. An image of Lovers' Leap Creek near the artist's home on Sydney's north shore, the fertile gully is so choked and tangled as to suggest a metaphysical reading. Trees sprout and sprawl, some lie white and dead, others straddle the picture. We look down into the gully, we look up from the depths. Green ellipses of vegetation could be the leaves of young eucalypts so close they tickle the nose, or they could be tree tops and branches at a distance. Whichever way, our place in this scene of crowding fecundity is unresolved. Grace Cossington Smith painted *The gully* on a slightly larger scale than usual, intending

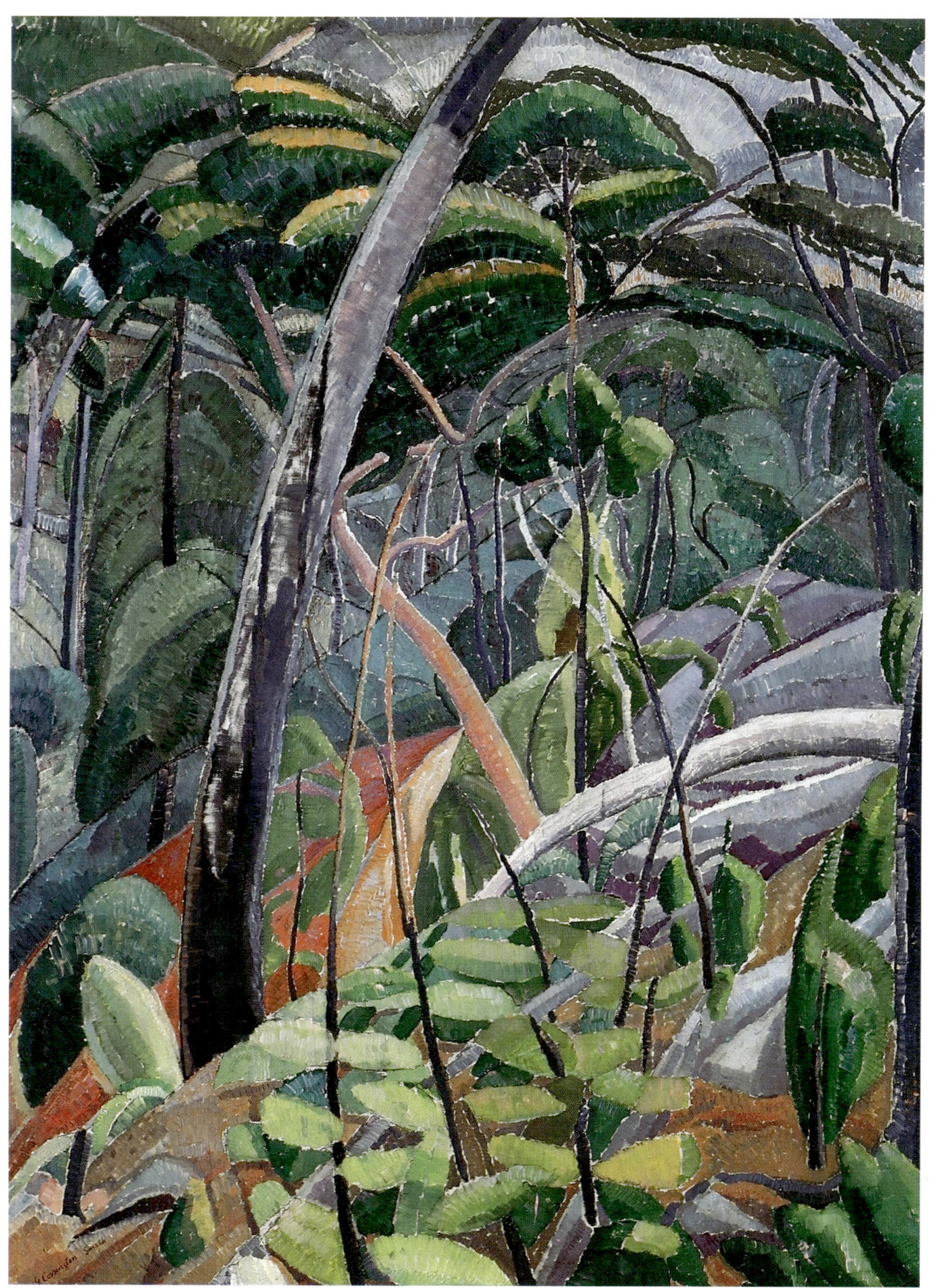

58 Grace Cossington Smith
1892–1984
The gully 1928
oil on board
110.5 × 82.5 cm

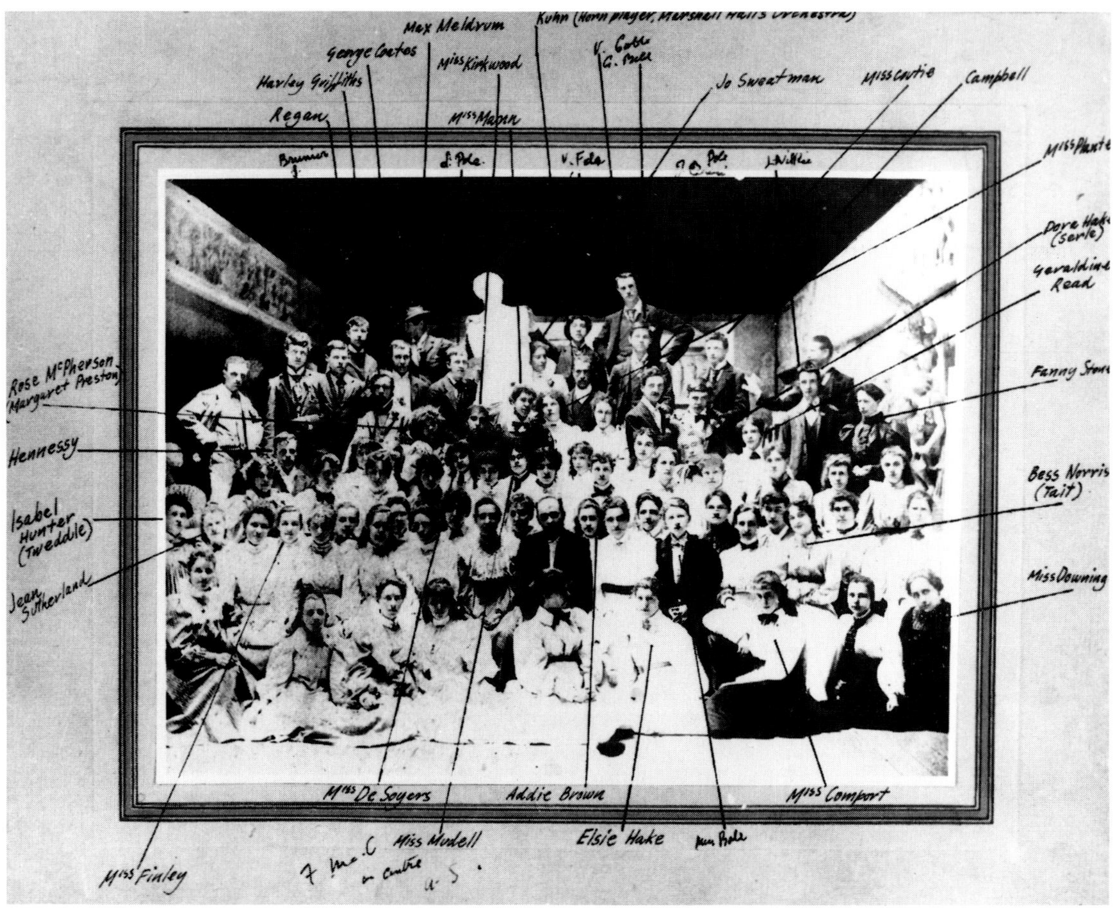

Students of the National Gallery School photographed in 1896-7, including Max Meldrum and Margaret Preston, who were then in their early twenties. The photograph was annotated in the 1960s by George Bell.

La Trobe Collection, State Library of Victoria

it to be the major work in her first solo exhibition in Sydney. One wonders whether, approaching her subject with anxiety, she perceived her own state of mind in the landscape?[13]

The analytical mode of art between the wars is well represented by the colourful and well-designed art of Margaret Preston (1875–1963). Her flower paintings and woodcuts were designed for form and colour, with the artist first studying the flowers to find the shape, pattern and colour that seemed inherent in nature and then using these to construct the composition and colour of her painting. The titles of Preston's works often announce the artistic problem she addressed: *Hibiscus* 1925 (plate 59) and *Bottlebrush and angophora* 1944 (plate 60) were named for her flower subjects; and the cloth became part of the title of *Native flowers on striped cloth* 1932 (plate 61) because its solid stripe served as a foil to the fluffiness of the flowers. Preston has not been interested in suggesting the flowers'

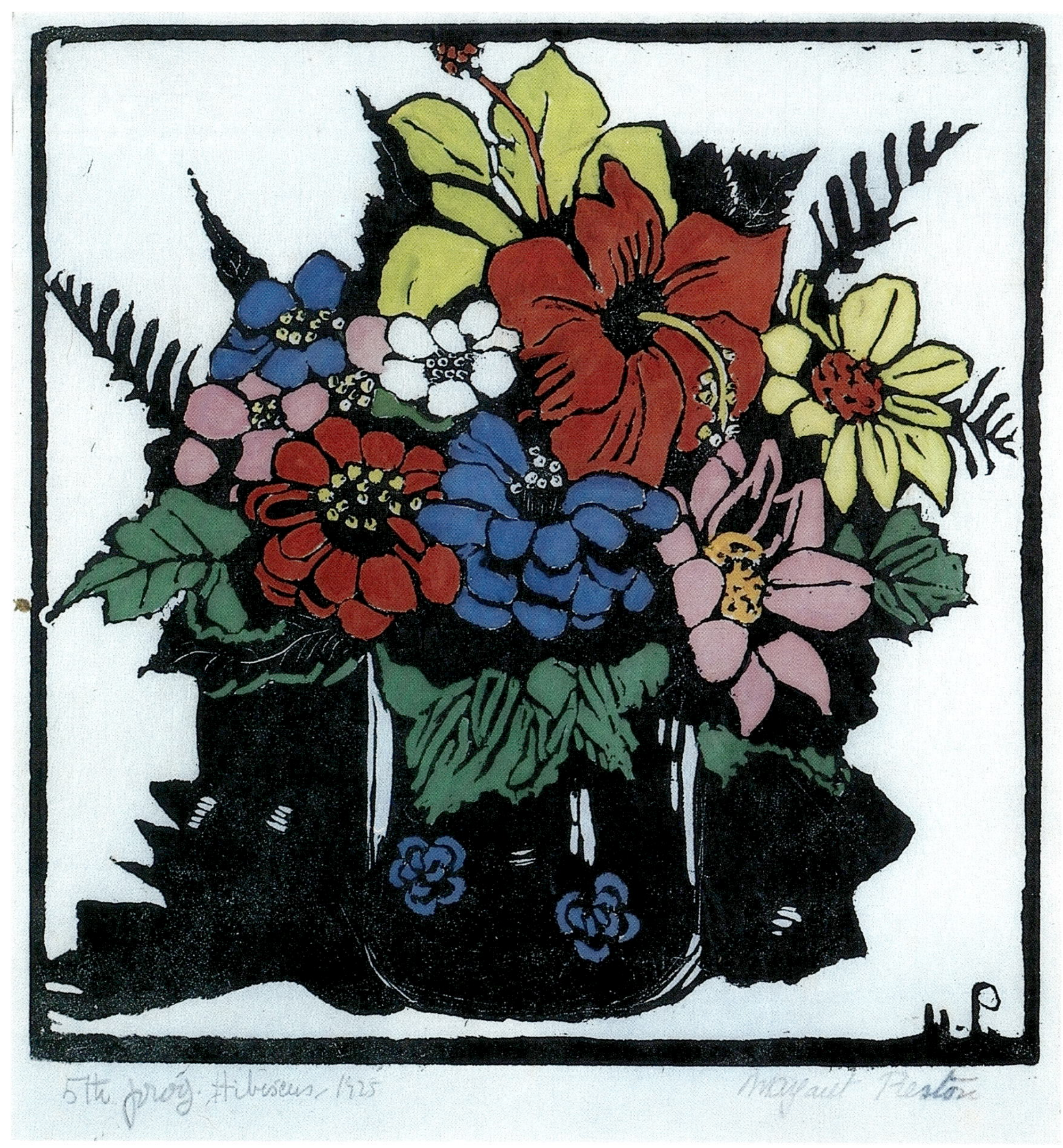

59   Margaret Preston
1875–1963
Hibiscus 1925
hand-coloured woodcut on paper
24.4 × 24.9 cm

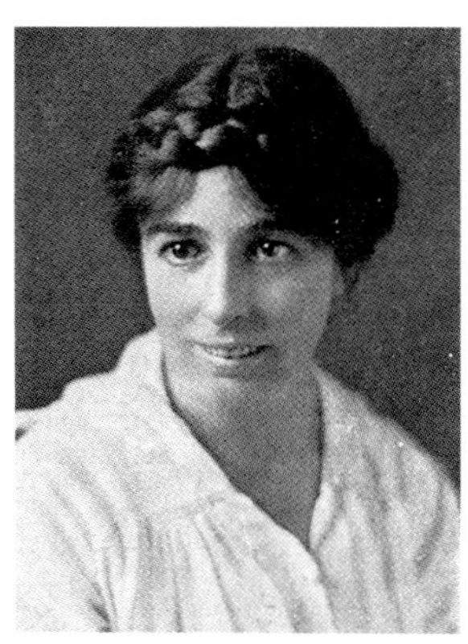

Dorrit Black in 1921.
This photograph
appeared in *The Home*
on 1 December 1921,
page 108.
Photograph by Judith Fletcher
La Trobe Collection, Victorian
State Library

imminent decay. This was in marked contrast to painters, say, of the seventeenth century, a period when flowers were an equally popular subject, though less for their essential form than as poignant reminders that beauty is in essence ephemeral. If anything the modern painters' generalising approach to flower painting stressed eternity. In the life of the species one bloom would replace another, endlessly.

Margaret Preston was pleased to compare herself with a scientist working in a laboratory and observing the workings of nature. Scientific analysis is suggested by the repetitive linear abstractions of Godfrey Miller (plate 98), the schematic form of Frank Hinder's *Flight E.M. 513* (plate 96), and Ralph Balson's 'constructive' and 'non-objective' paintings (plates 94 and 95). These four paintings evidently subscribe to laws of organisation and dynamics – in fact take their style from such laws. Even the stylistically more conservative, cool and careful realism of Charles Meere's *Still life* 1958 and *Landscape* 1959 (plates 71 and 72) and the nude paintings by Dorrit Black (plate 62) and Eric Wilson (plate 64) reflect an attitude of detachment and hint at invariable truths of nature. The artists, stylistically dissimilar, were alike in generalising their subjects, dispassionately articulating the dominant forms and extracting inherent patterns both of form and colour.

Dorrit Black (1891-1951) painted *Nude with cigarette* c. 1930 (plate 62) in Sydney shortly before she opened the Modern Art Centre and introduced modern, post-cubist art teaching to Sydney. In the circumstances, her image of a nude woman smoking was challenging. Not only was the subject casually real rather than ideal, the style was nonchalant. All in all, the pose, minimal drawing and sketchy technique were declarations of independence in the face of a longstanding teaching tradition. *Nude with cigarette* could be a prospectus for Black's life classes. It threw off the protective covering of classical tradition. Naked not nude, smoking therefore modern, young rather than mature, the woman with her cigarette was allowed to represent her own life and personality rather than asked to play one of the standard roles of the traditional nude. Even so, this modern woman was radically altered from life. Bleached of colour, the tenderness of her flesh ignored, rendered flat, within a summarily drawn outline, she was deprived of the texture and warmth of flesh and of bodily

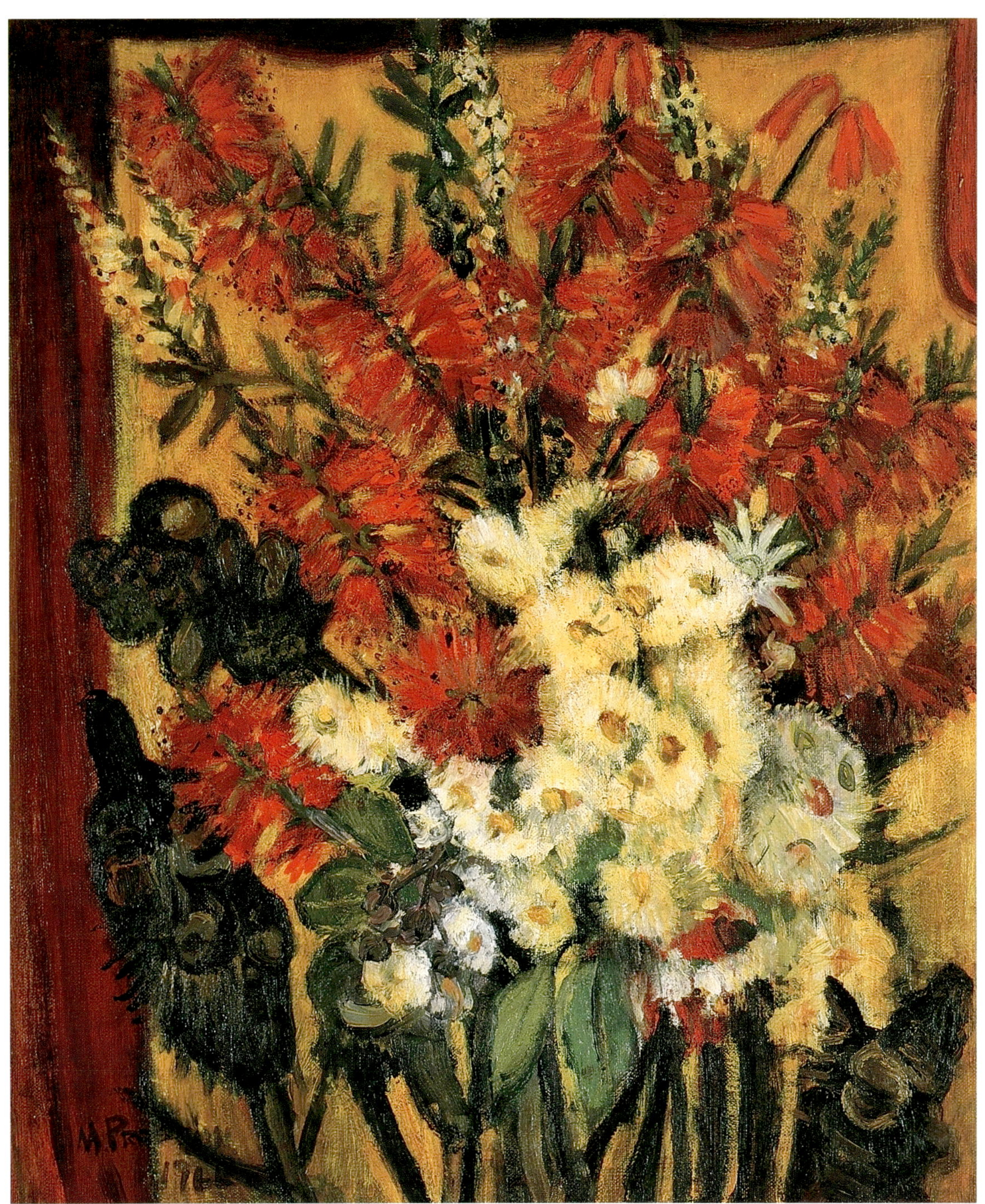

60   Margaret Preston
1875–1963
Bottlebrush and angophora 1944
oil on canvas
54.5 × 45.5 cm

weight and substance. The modern style, which permitted contemporaneity in the pose, had taken away the presence and physicality of the real body – 'abstracted' them.

Art training revolved around the study of the naked human body. In a still rather prudish society everyone from the aspiring student to the suburban philistine was titillated by the idea of unclothed bodies, hence one of the first lessons of the student was to aestheticise the naked body into the formal nude. In December of the year Black painted *Nude with cigarette*, Dumont Dunn's booklet *The Nude in Contemporary Art* was published in Melbourne, crammed with advice for artist and philistine alike:

> Leaving aside the psycho-analytical theory that aesthetics and eroticism are allied, the nude is not only flesh that calls to flesh, it is colour, curve and design. Throughout the vast cycle of change which prosaically we call 'time' painters have endeavoured to express in pigment the sublime symmetry and exquisite grace of the human form. Those to whom the nude represents merely an undressed figure are often mystified by the artist's interest. But to pose a model amid draperies whose colours contrast and yet harmonize with the delicate and subtle reflections upon the flesh, and to use brushes and pigments for rendering the texture of inanimate materials and the vibrant quality of warm skin – here is the problem that evokes the enthusiasm, skill, and mettle of the painter.[14]

In academia and in abstract modern art too, the moral conflict and sexual tension of the nude subject were rigorously sublimated.

Outside the art school, nude paintings had a small but significant place in Australian art. Naked women were drawn and painted in abundance by the bohemian Norman Lindsay whose erotica, sanctioned by classical mythology, sold well and was displayed in smoking rooms, studies and bedrooms, nominally out of the sight of females. The few paintings of nudes exhibited by George Lambert, Bernard Hall, Napier Waller, George Bell, Max Meldrum and others were invariably noticed. The public sometimes failed to see the aesthetic nude as anything

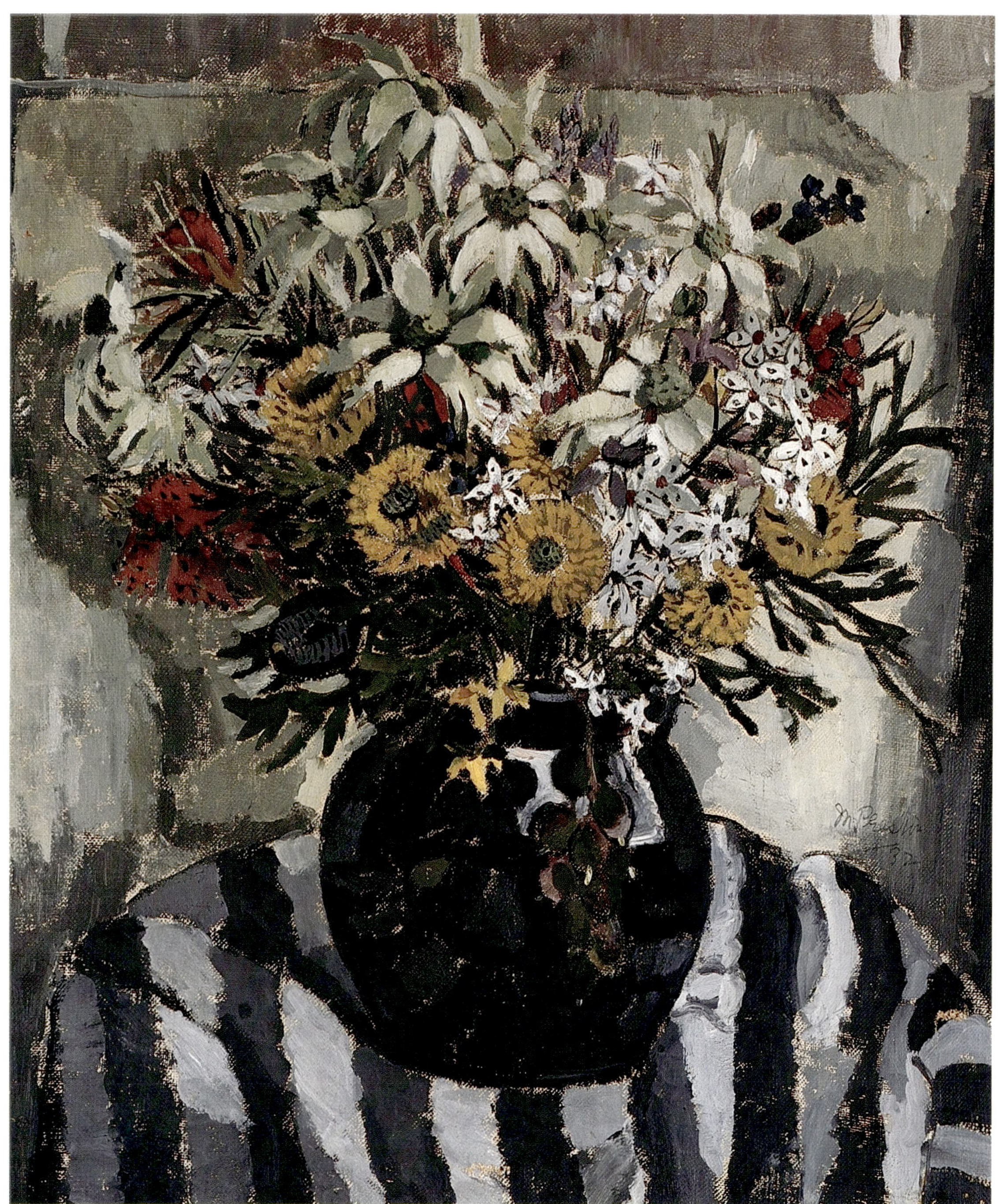

61 Margaret Preston
1875–1963
Native flowers on striped cloth 1932
oil on canvas
45.4 × 38.2 cm

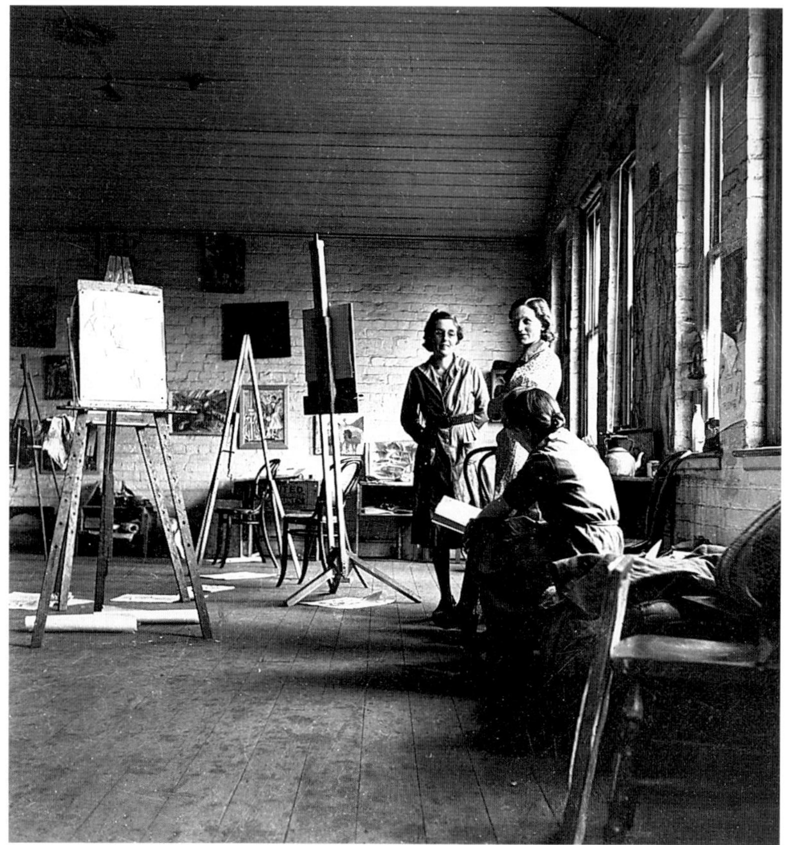

but naked. As, for instance, in December 1907 when *The Lone Hand* was prosecuted in New Zealand for reproducing a nude painting by Bernard Hall.[15] Or in 1914 in Adelaide when a newly acquired painting by the English artist William Orpen was damaged by a visitor to the Art Gallery of South Australia; not the only representative of the city of churches to object to the inclusion of a naked woman in a painting named (some thought provocatively) *Sowing new seed*. Museum nudes, representing as they did the highest of high art, were generally exempt from such expressions of feeling, but the nude that was best known and most closely examined, Jules Lefebvre's *Chloe*, was famed because it hung in a hotel in Melbourne.

The nude subject was central to 1930s modernism in Sydney. In 1932 Dorrit Black's Modern Art Centre was joined by the teaching venture of two other modernists, Grace Crowley and Rah Fizelle. Over the decade the human body became the major theme of Crowley, Fizelle and Ralph Balson who used it to progressively abstract

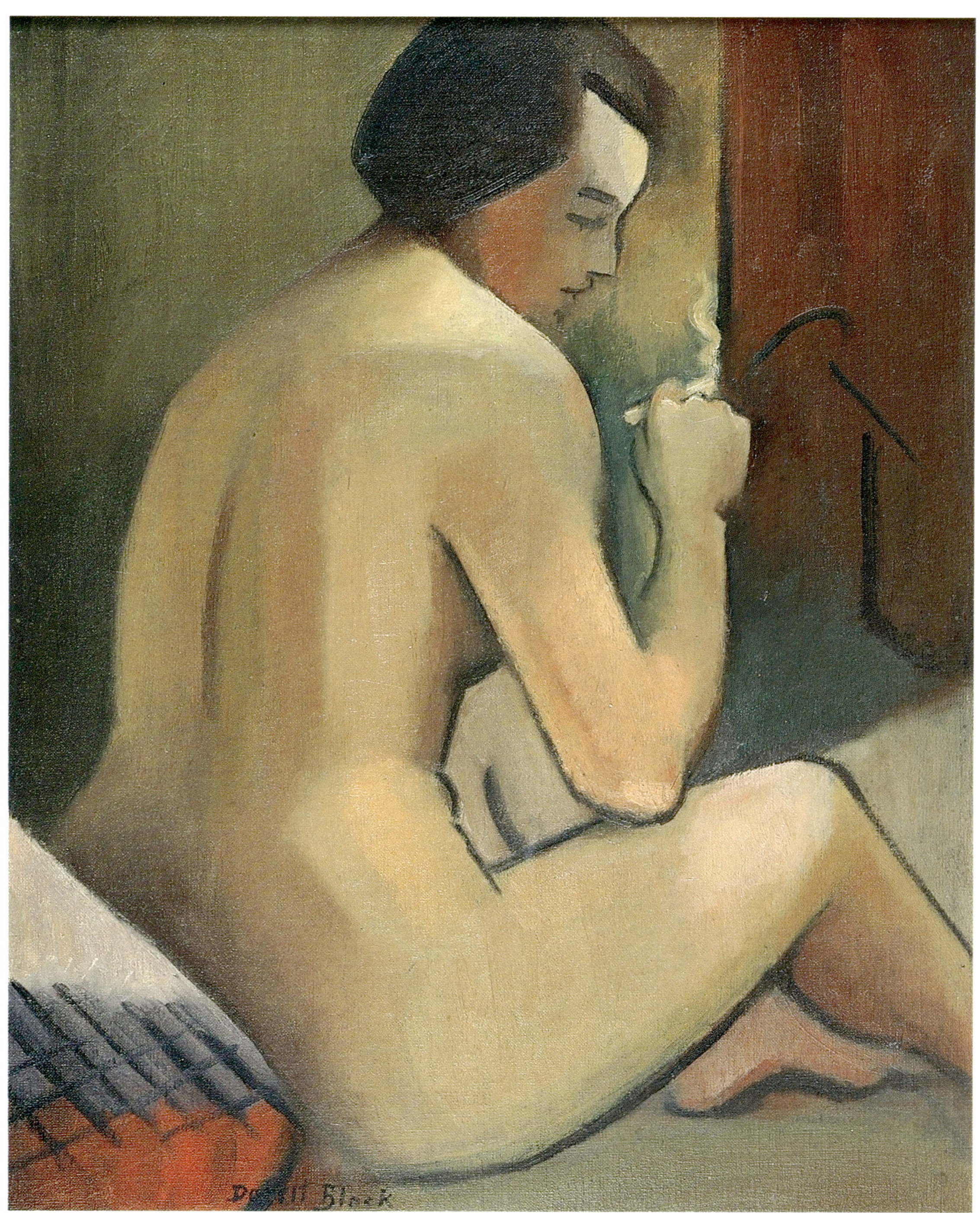

62   Dorrit Black
1891–1951
(*Nude with cigarette*) (1930)
oil on canvas laid down on board
46.0 × 37.7 cm

Ian Fairweather in 1962
painting in his
primitive hut on Bribie
Island where, for many
years, he lived a
hermit-like existence. It
was here, in his
seventies, that he
produced his most
notable works.

from Ian Fairweather *by*
Murray Bail

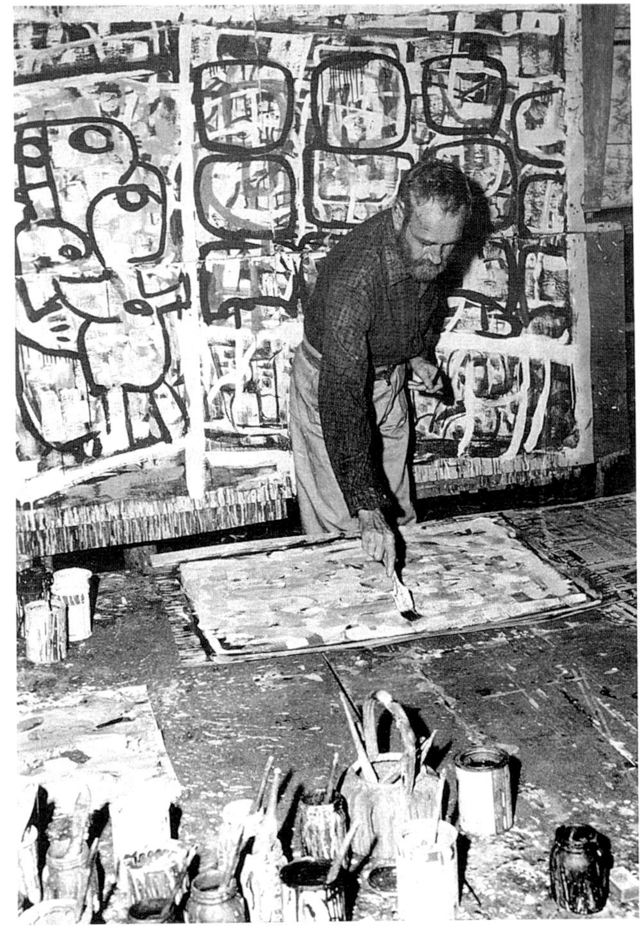

from the subject all the human inessentials until they were able to create satisfying images from the pure geometry of form and the structure of light.

Ian Fairweather (1891–1974), whose style was completely different from the painters just named, may have invoked the human body in an effort to transcend its loaded meanings. Whatever other human needs drove the art of the decades between wars, one need was to deny physical vulnerability and temporality.

Bathers c. 1935 (plate 63), like a lot of Fairweather's paintings, looks as if it was born out of fumblings and suggestions rather than firm decisions. There has been no planning, no motif even. The colour blue, put in once, was endorsed strongly on another part of the cardboard but the placement was isolated, fragmentary, like the half-stated drawing. Cezanne and Picasso were remembered

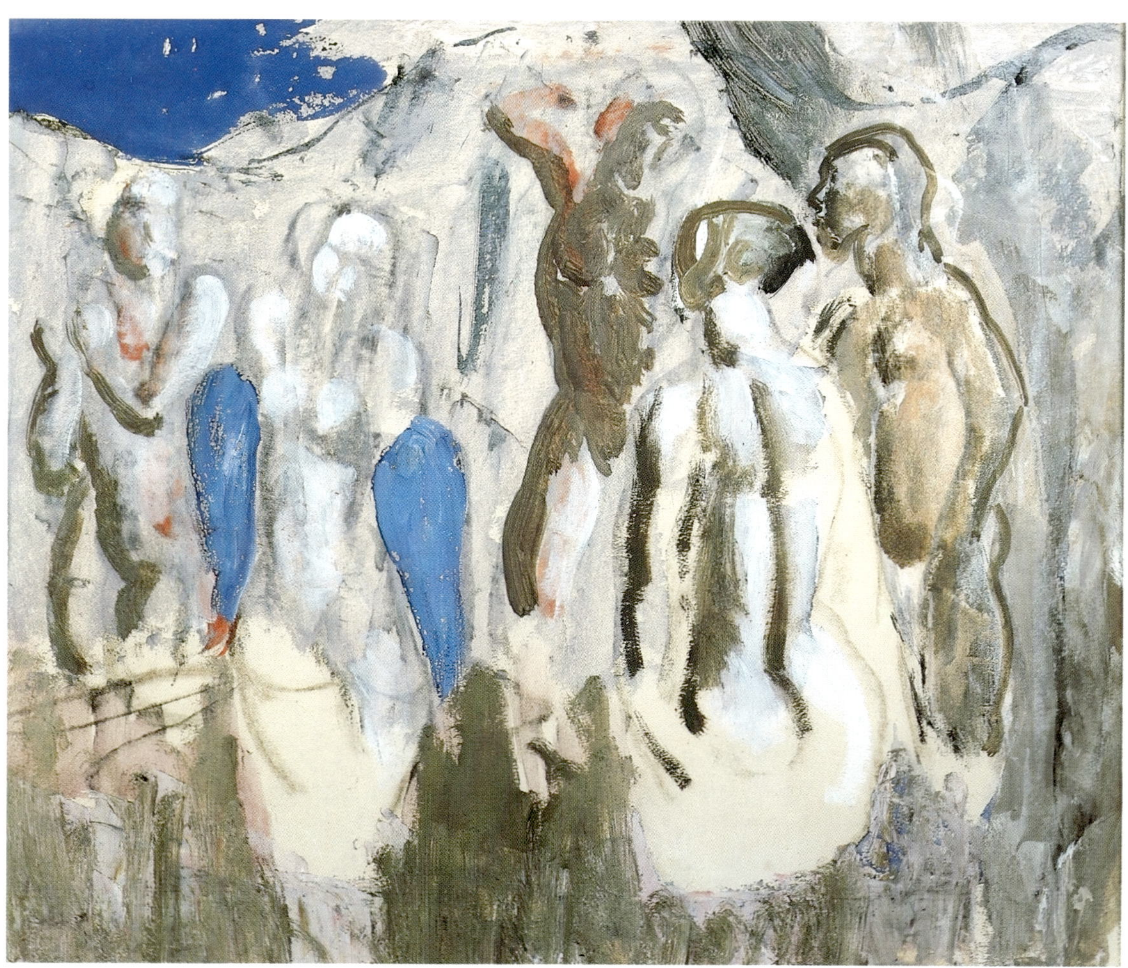

63   Ian Fairweather
1891–1974
(*Bathers*) (1935)
oil and gouache on paper
35.5 × 43.0 cm

along the way: Cezanne in the linking of a nude and the trunk of a tree (for these Fairweather may also have remembered bathers by fellow Slade student Leon Underwood), Picasso in the dark androgynous woman in the centre, and the French modern tradition generally in the shapes of bodies and the way they come and go in shallow depth. There may be a specific remembrance of Picasso's *Les Demoiselles d'Avignon* 1907,[16] in the lifting arm – a formal success which led Fairweather to accentuate the action in a swathe of red paint. Covertly, Fairweather acknowledges the sexuality of the women. Their naked bodies have been modelled along the fleshy inner body, the backbone, muscles of the buttocks and breasts rather than along the edges of forms. These bulging evocations of femaleness confronting the painter/viewer with a display distantly reminiscent of Picasso's jeering prostitutes presumably record the women of Fairweather's experience: the classical nudes of art, 'primitive' nudes, the women bathers of Bali, the housewife with gown hitched above her buttocks across the yard from Fairweather's room in Peking, and the big sisters who crowded his childhood.

One result of the concentration on landscape in Australian art is that landscape became much more loaded with meanings than the human body. Perhaps this was why the human body, rather than landscape and still life, was the culminating vehicle for abstraction in the late 1930s. Ironically, by the time a transcendent abstract art was finally achieved in the 1940s, a new generation had arrived on the scene which was attempting the opposite, focusing on subjective feelings through the emotive treatment of human faces and bodies.

Eric Wilson (1911–46), who painted the resplendent *Nude* (plate 64) in 1939 in London, was a faithful Seventh Day Adventist and a serious, career-minded artist, but even he succumbed to his generation's need to express the living, breathing reality of flesh and blood. He had not attended the Crowley–Fizelle school back in Sydney. Instead, he had been careful to plan a conservative programme of study that would lead to winning the New South Wales Travelling Scholarship.[17] He won in 1937 and for the next few years turned his energies to assessing the art standards of London.[18] As Wilson explained, London brought an escape from 'stagnation' – 'the old hidebound slavery to naturalism' – to the enlightenment

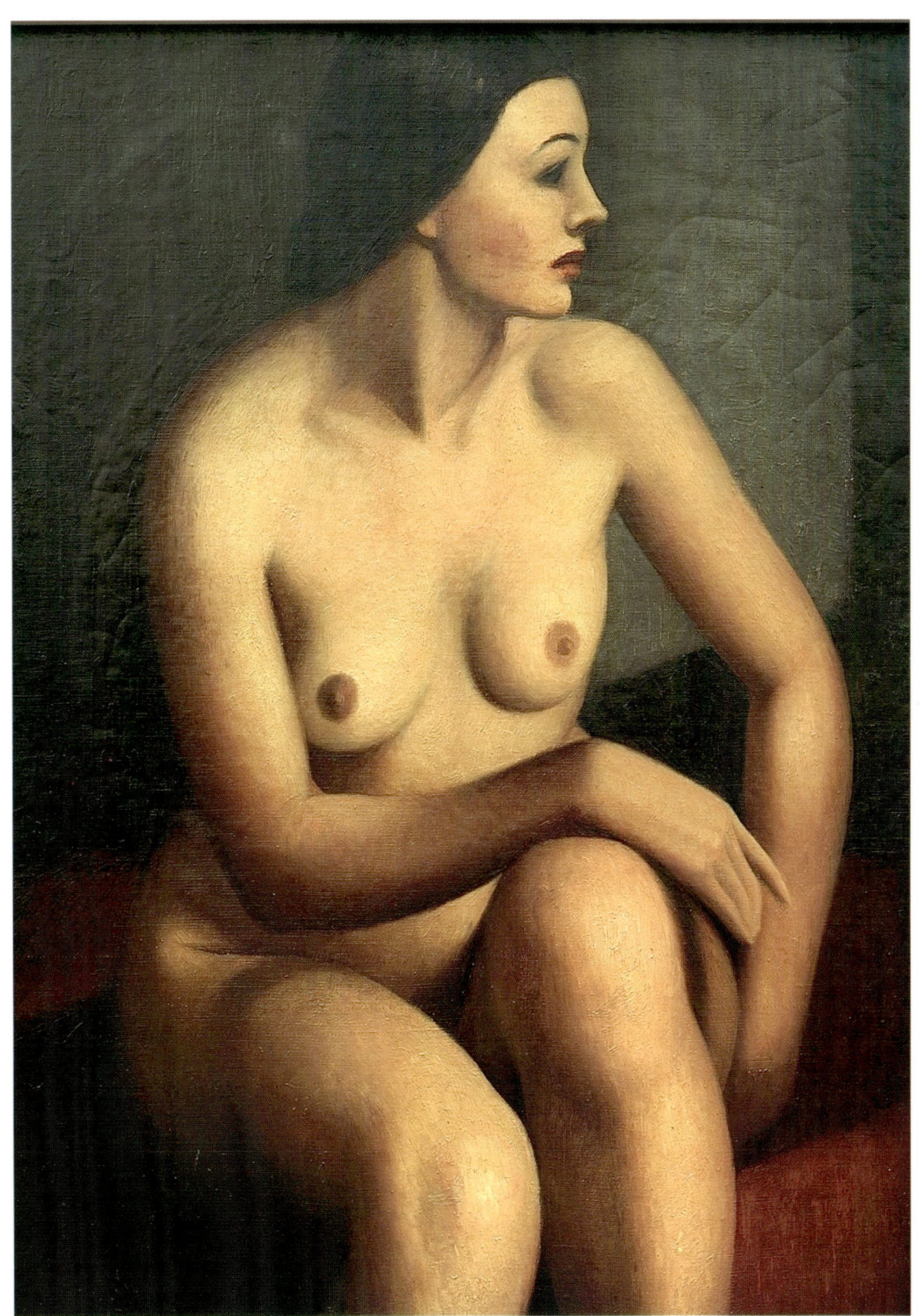

64   Eric Wilson
1911–46
Nude 1939
oil on canvas
76.0 × 56.0 cm

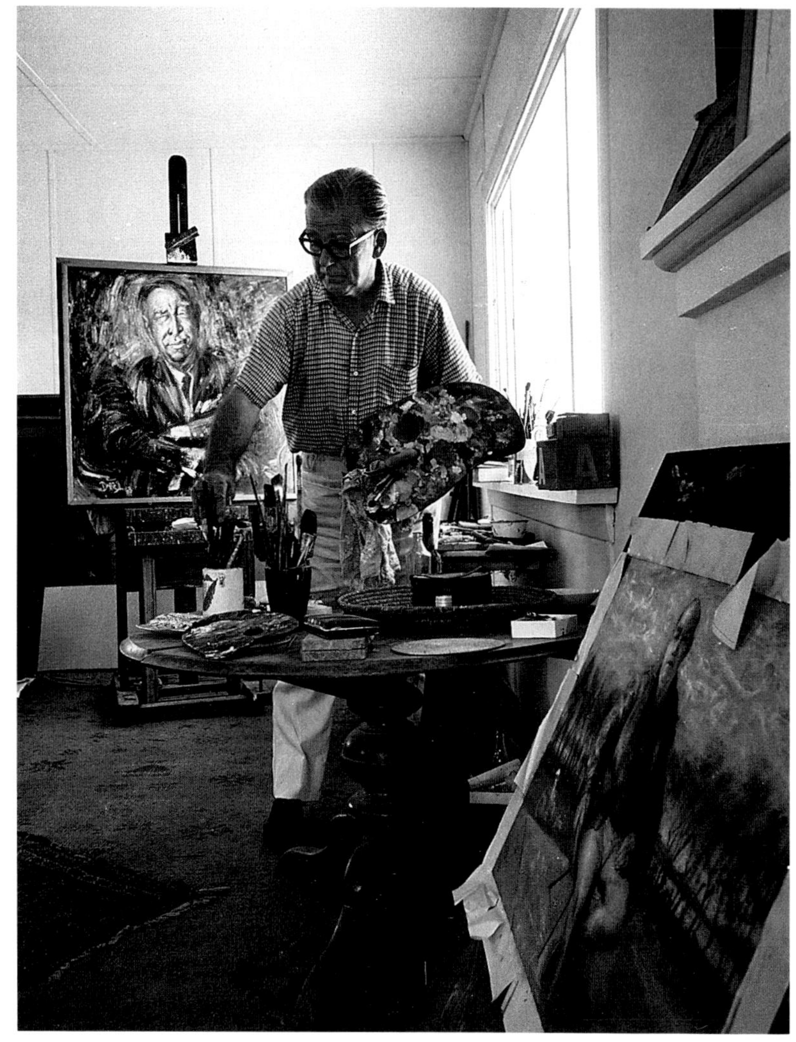

of being 'up to my neck in abstract design and doing tubular nudes'. It did not bring him wealth, however, as *Still Life* 1939 (plate 65) was painted on the reverse of *Nude* to save the cost of new canvas.

The paintings Wilson had been doing included nudes 'in the manner of Modigliani and certain abstract painters'.[19] He painted *Nude* for volume and solidity, posing the model in a perspectival cone of overlapping limbs and jutting knees. Warm-coloured flesh has the firm texture of carved wood and is nonetheless sensuous. '[Amadée] Ozenfant said one's shapes should be so beautiful that [one] continually derived pleasure from coming back to view [them].'[20] To achieve this unusual beauty of form Wilson practised drawing one part of the

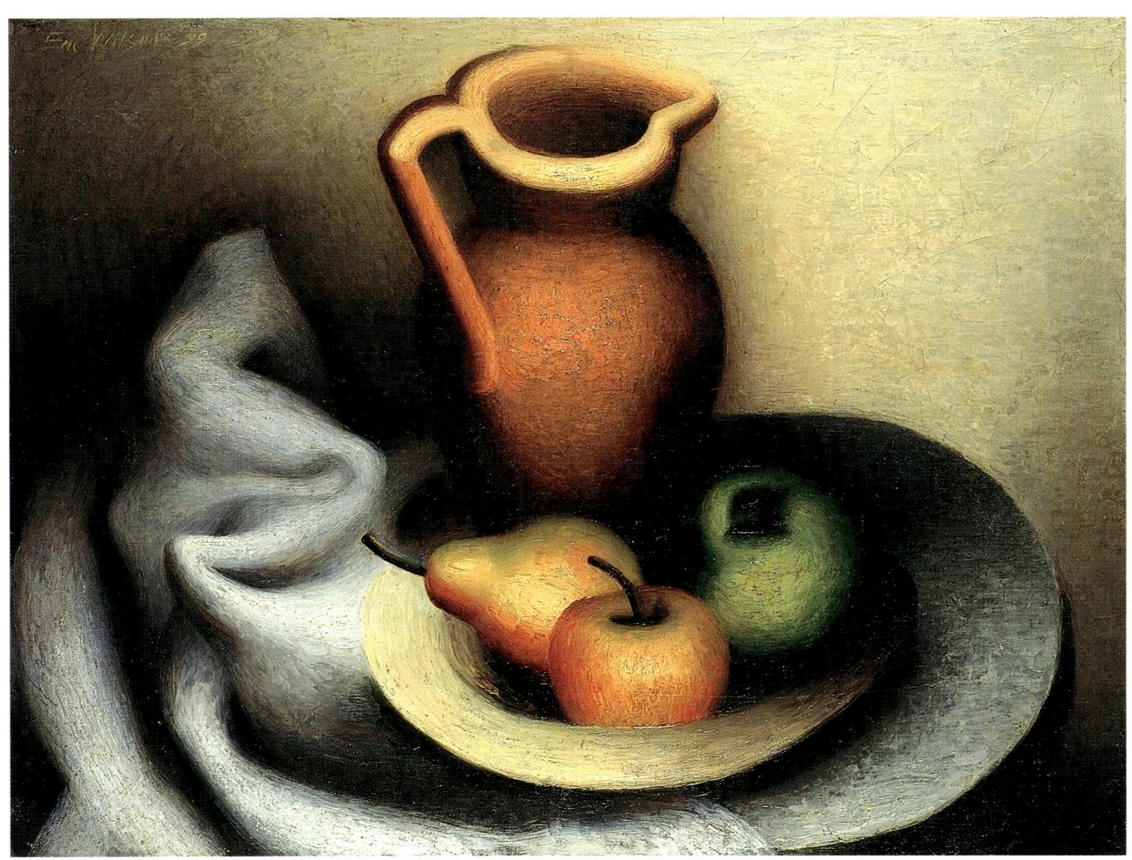

65 Eric Wilson
1911–46
Still life 1939
oil on canvas
54.5 × 75.0 cm

body at a time: leg, neck, shoulder – those parts of the body are powerfully realised in *Nude*. The image spirals into the body rather than extends up and down and, in keeping with the sculptural idea, a lot is made of the modelling and the shadowy hollows between arm, knees and stomach. Henry Moore, at Ozenfant's classes on 22 May 1939, had advised Wilson to try 'more sculpturesque certainty of projection and recession of forms'. Altogether, this painting is wonderfully certain and concentrated in form and the artist has been surprisingly unselfconscious about expressing his pleasure in the female body. 'I am astounded at the prudery we have at home. Here the nude is set on every pillar and no one has cheap or nasty thoughts,' he wrote.

But how were paintings like *Nude* to be received at home? 'Heaven preserve me when I get back to Australia. It's going to be terrible,' thought Wilson. He had to send a painting back to Sydney but was 'sure the trustees of the scholarship won't fall in love with what I've been doing. Everyone says I should have brought something over with me to send back to them.'[21] His fears about standards at home were shared by William Dobell (1899–1970). Talking together they were of the opinion that the best thing for Sydney would be to cause a disturbance:

> thunder at the students to 'kick up' till they acquire the courage to be barbaric rather than safe . . . tell 'em to stick prints of Vlaminck and Derain for example up on their walls and gather courage to paint strongly what they feel and all – and to Gehenna with Lambert and Gruner ideals.

Beforehand, in Sydney, Eric Wilson had been so little interested in what the modernists were doing that now, in London, he had no concept that an Australian modern movement existed that was in advance of his own continental experience. As so often in the history of Australian art, the new convert and his fellows abroad believed themselves to be pioneers: 'I feel terribly humbled and realise like Dobell that to go back with the courage of our convictions will raise the cackles and sneers of the artistically dead.'[22]

This discussion of art between the wars has emphasised

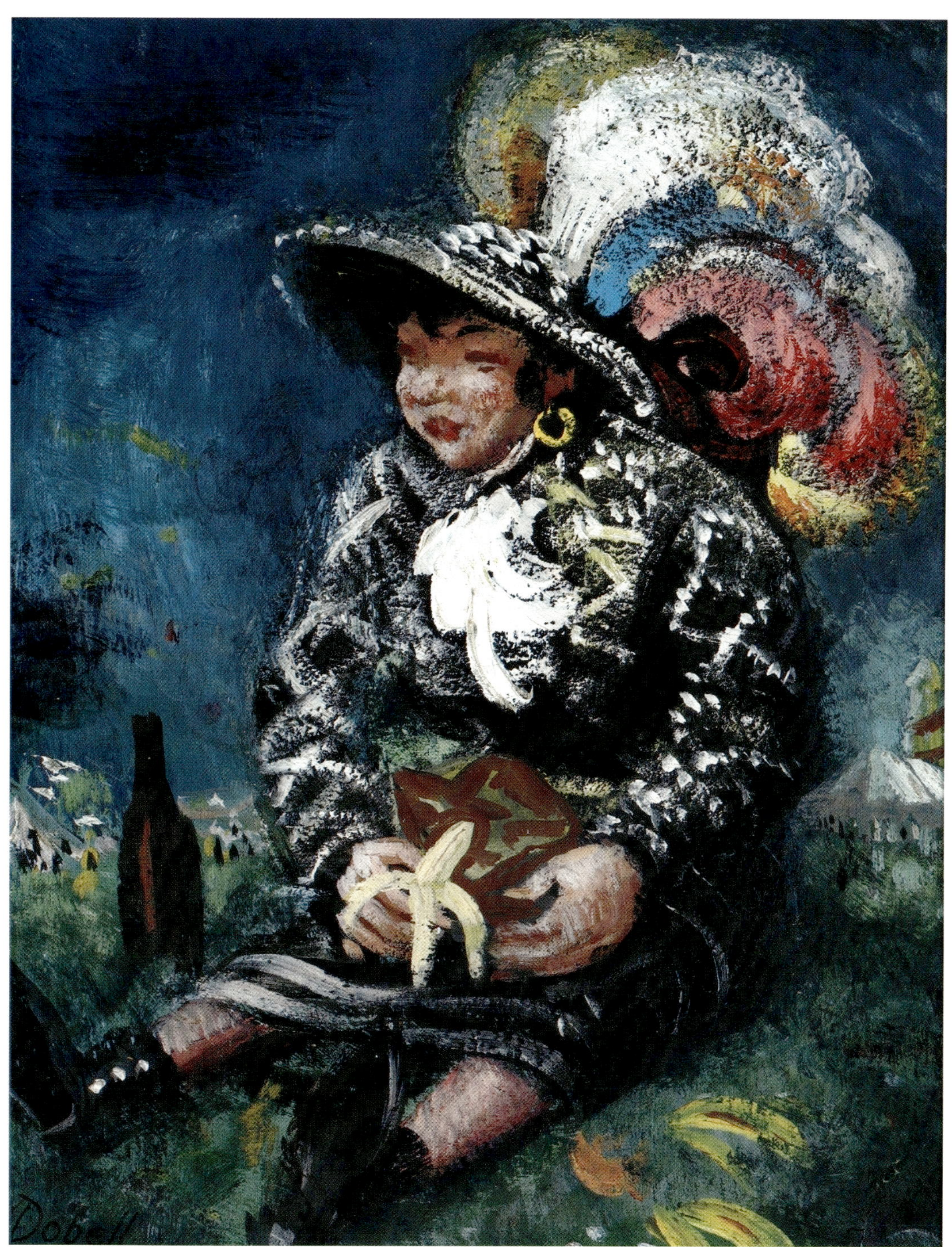

66   William Dobell
1899–1970
Derby Day (1938)
oil on paper on board
19.5 × 16.5 cm

the artists' systematic approach. We have argued that the poetry, imagination and feeling apparent in many paintings was harnessed within orderly styles. It would even be possible to extend that generalisation to Ian Fairweather and to the later art of Albert Tucker, Sidney Nolan, John Perceval and James Gleeson. These artists, too, pursued selective problems of style. So what is the difference which everyone sees between the generation of classical modernists and the surreal and expressionist generation following? Simply this: the first pursued a transcendent goal beyond each subject (and beyond each and every work of art) whereas the later artists – many of them – discovered their ends in each singular and vivid perception. The younger painters would be more extreme yet more naturalistic than their elders because they were seeing individualistically and emphasising perception rather than structure.

So, for example, Dobell in painting *Derby Day* c. 1938 (plate 66) saw the young racegoer eating a banana on the grass, saw the total, comical shape she made, within which the peeled banana was an accent of similar ridiculous form, and painted his small image as a record of a true, odd, stimulating perception. He hated and refused to paint in public, explaining, 'I am scared of people looking over my shoulder'.[23] Many of his best character studies, like *Derby Day*, were of people he saw in public places and recorded in very rough sketches when he was sure they were not looking.

None of Dobell's images were studied generalisations of face and body in the way of earlier modern art. The artist's portrait of fellow painter *James Cook* 1942 (plate 67) expressed an idea of his friend as both urbane and loftily unworldly. He painted on a canvas that was already framed, creating a top-heavy composition with sweet curves, sombre colours and floating, insubstantial light and shade to express the idea.[24] Cook had a close circle of appreciative artist friends who enjoyed the rapid fire of his ideas, his impish humour and love of fun: one verbal image is of him 'playing a little pipe, sitting like a faun'.[25] He was, according to Dobell, 'the most exasperatingly likeable person I have known'.[26] But when Dobell was painting, the presence of another person, even unassuming Jimmy Cook, would make him self-conscious. *If there were token sittings for this portrait, when Cook adopted*

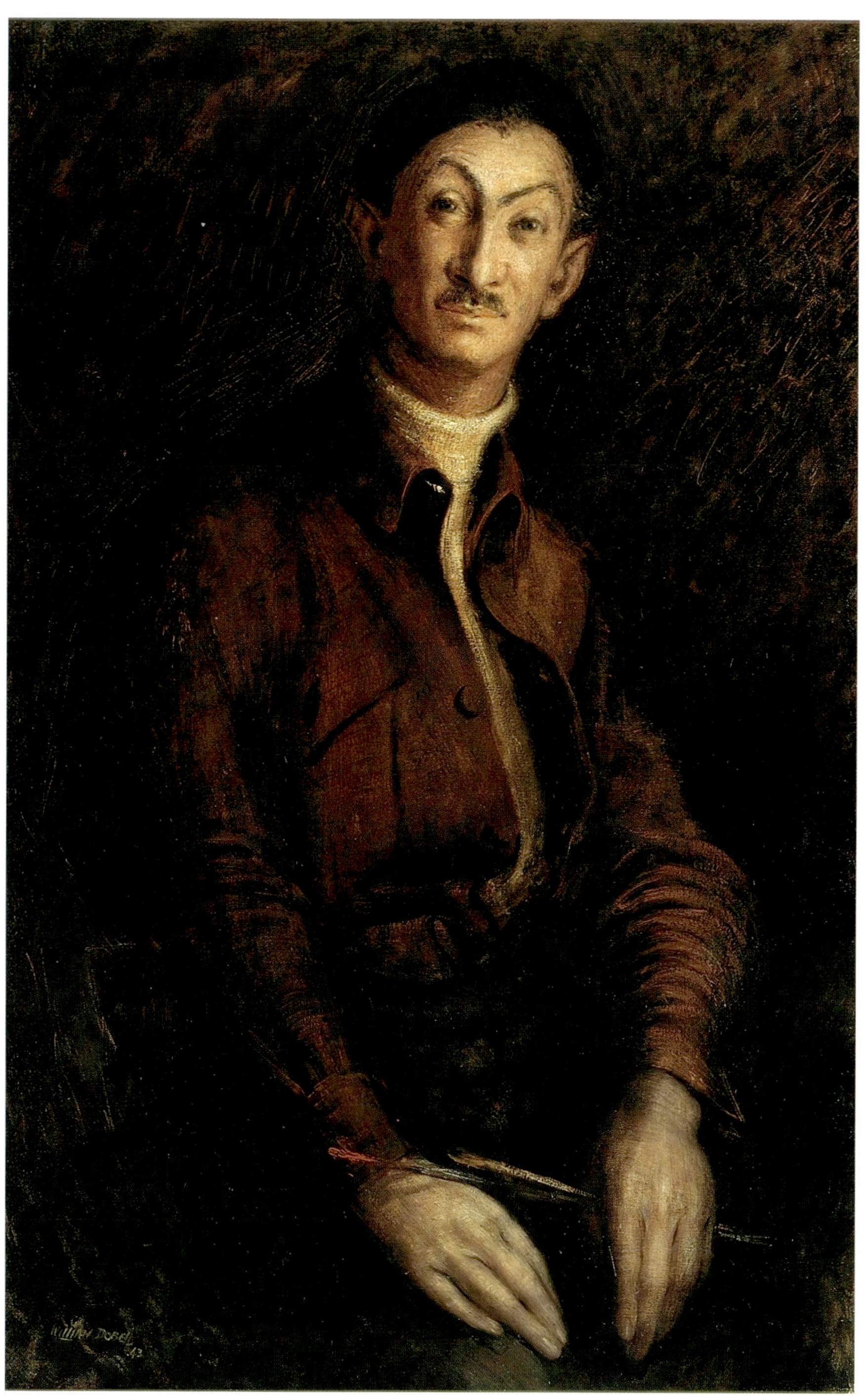

67   William Dobell
1899–1970
James Cook 1942
oil on canvas
90.5 × 70.4 cm

a pose and Dobell assumed the attitude of a portraitist studying his subject, the real work of thinking and painting would have been done when Cook was not present. As a painter and as a person Dobell insisted on privacy. His images were the production of memory and, like most visual memories, described an essence.

One of the very significant incidents in the development of Australian art was the legal dispute in 1944 concerning the award of the Archibald Prize to Dobell's portrait of *Joshua Smith*. The portrait of *James Cook* had been submitted for the prize of 1942 without success. Failure to recognise its quality at that time was to some extent a reflection of the conservative approach to portraiture which underlay the emotional reaction to *Joshua Smith* two years later. The 1944 court hearing arose when two of the unsuccessful artists, Mary Edwards and Joseph Wolinski, took legal action to overturn the award, claiming that *Joshua Smith* 'is not a portrait but a caricature'. J.S. MacDonald, an artist, critic and one-time director of the Art Gallery of New South Wales (1928–36) and National Gallery of Victoria (1936–41), was their main witness, arguing that a portrait was a specific genre bound to rules and, like a sonnet, for example, had a correct form – 'it has to be a balanced likeness of an actual person'. It was understood, he said, that not all images of the human face were portraits – a picture of 'a man drinking a pewter pot of beer is a token; that is not a portrait'. The artist, 'if he wants to paint a portrait' would say, 'Put that pot down beside you and I will paint you as you are not as you are at an instantaneous moment.' The painting *Joshua Smith* was not a portrait, it was 'very unbalanced, a caricature'. MacDonald pointed out that the word caricature came from 'caricare: to overload'.

Dobell's defence was that he was an artist of sound training, whose experience overseas had been supported by winning the New South Wales Travelling Scholarship. He knew Joshua Smith reasonably well, and had a considered concept of his character and body language: Joshua did have long arms, habitually held his hands clasped, he 'naturally sits in a chair that [upright] way' when 'very determined to gain his point'. The artist was prepared to 'admit a slight exaggeration' of physical features for the sake of constructing his meaning: 'I think I succeeded in sticking to my guns as a draughtsman

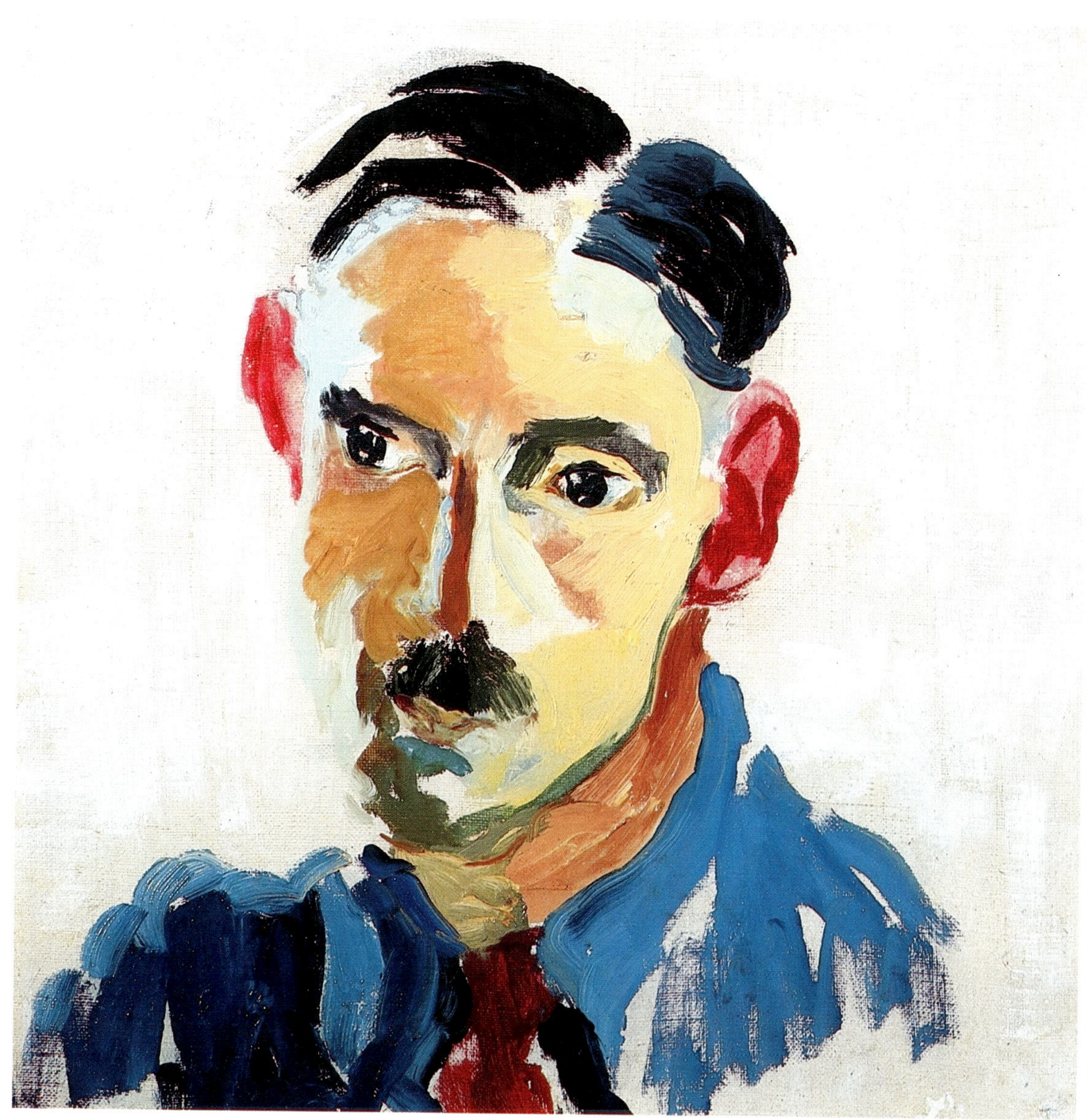

68   Lina Bryans
born 1909
Alan McCulloch (1942)
oil on canvas on plywood panel
38.4 x 37.4 cm

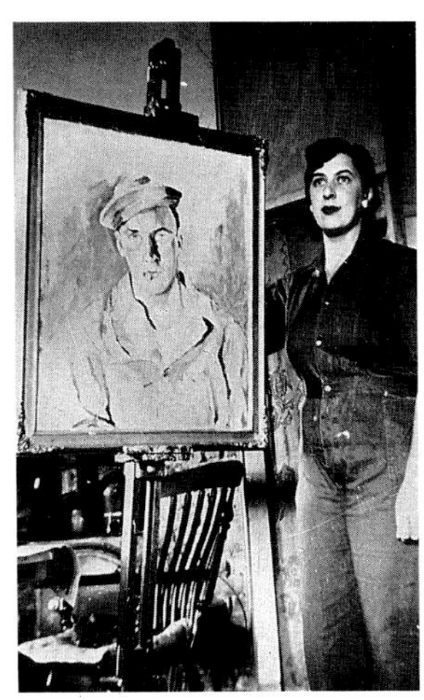

Lina Bryans in the
kitchen of her home in
Darebin Bridge,
Melbourne c. 1943.
Janine Burke Collection

and constructing a picture worthy of the name of a work of art, and I don't think I have distorted to the extent that other witnesses have suggested.'

Dobell was not 'modern' in the way Sydney had been accustomed to think of modernity. Neither were the young Melbourne painters – Arthur Boyd (born 1920), John Perceval (born 1923), Russell Drysdale (1912–81), Joy Hester (1920–60) or Albert Tucker (born 1914) – modern in the old way. In some respects this passionate new generation was ultra-traditional, turning to the old masters for techniques and endorsing certain old-masterish 'natural' effects. Like most students Dobell had been taught 'an orthodox way of painting. For oils, he [had] used hog-hair brushes, small ones for the details, big ones to paint the large areas.' But this was an orthodoxy against which Dobell rebelled. Said Bernard Hesling:

> After seeing the paintings of Rembrandt, Bellini, and countless other masters, he figures he can get at what he wants much better with other tools. Usually he uses small, soft, sable brushes with which he strokes the paint on, one colour over another, achieving a wonderful depth and transparency.[27]

In the 1940s many Australian 'contemporary' painters tried old-master techniques.

Lina Bryans (born 1909) painted as if the act of painting was perception itself. Her portrait, *Alan McCulloch* c. 1942 (plate 68), was shaped by the spontaneous passage of her brush, and the vivid, unreal colours also expressed her immediate reaction to her sitter. 'I always let the subject dictate,' said Lina Bryans. 'I never know how I'm going to do it before I get going. I start by putting down whatever it is that made me want to paint the subject, . . . with portraits . . . the facial expression or a mouth or posture.'[28] Alan McCulloch (who achieved fame as an art writer) was then art critic for the *Argus* newspaper and a young painter who sometimes visited and painted at Darebin Bridge House where Bryans and a number of artists lived and worked between 1942 and 1948.[29] Bryans' image of young McCulloch records only her positive responses, showing what she has seen and felt. She allowed herself absolutely no passive picture-making through filling in the background, modelling the forms and drawing the details.

She did not merely ignore conventional finish, she outlawed it. The artist had a philosophy: 'If it is a good painting, gaps are important because then your eye carries on with what your brain has been suggesting.' In other words, she wanted 'to keep the painting fresh so it looked as if life had been breathed into it'.[30]

By the late 1930s the wheel had turned full circle. Younger painters dealt as obsessively with subjective perceptions as the earlier generation of modernists had with objective generalisations. Their paintings were as focused in a particular time as those of the previous decade had been classically changeless.

The eventual marriage of modern styles and meaningful narrative in figurative images of the late 1930s and 1940s, touched on here, is the subject of the next chapter. From the late 1930s the opposition that had been cultivated between nature and culture came together in a hybrid art that was at once expressive, figurative, narrative, national *and* modern.

1 Blamire Young, 'The Painter and the Model', *V.A.S.*, Melbourne, 1 June 1908, p. 5. See also Gladys Hain, 'Blamire Young and Emotion in Australian Art', *Illustrated Tasmanian Mail*, Hobart, 20 June 1928, p. 9.

2 'The great weakness of Australian art in the past has been its lack of imagination and inventive design,' Thea Proctor, catalogue introduction to exhibition, *Women Artists of Australia*, 1934, (Art Gallery of New South Wales Library).

3 Blamire Young gave a paper about 'The Value of Accidental Effects' to a general meeting of the Royal Victorian Institute of Architects in April 1904.

4 Adolf Hitler, speech inaugurating the 'Great Exhibition of German Art', Munich, 1937, published in Herschel B. Chipp, *Theories of Modern Art*, University of California Press, Berkeley, 1968, pp. 474–83.

5 *Triad*, Sydney, 11 July 1921, cutting in Art Gallery of New South Wales Library scrapbooks.

6 ibid.

7 *Home*, Sydney, 2 August 1937, p. 39.

8 *The Lone Hand*, Sydney, 1 April 1910, p. 674.

9 Basil Burdett, 'The later work of Elioth Gruner', *Art in Australia*, Sydney, March 1929.

10 John Rothenstein, *Time's Thievish Progress*, vol. 3 of autobiography, Cassell, London, 1970. p. 93.

11 Louis Esson letter to Vance and Nettie Palmer, 14 August 1926, quoted in Margaret McGuire, 'The Singular Career of Clarice Beckett: Painting and Society in Melbourne 1916–1936', thesis submitted for Master of Arts, University of Melbourne, 1984, p. 66.

12 *Sun*, Melbourne, 28 September 1927.

13 See discussion of the painting in Bruce James, *Grace Cossington Smith*, Craftsman House, Sydney, 1990, p. 75.

14 Dumont Dunn, *The Nude in Contemporary Art (1918-1930)*, Beaux-Arts, Melbourne, December 1930, p. 11.

15 See *Gadfly*, Adelaide, 22 January 1908, p. 1614; *The Lone Hand*, Sydney, 2 March 1908, pp. 465-6.

16 Reproduced in *La Révolution Surrealiste*, Paris, 15 July 1925.

17 Beginning in 1929, when William Dobell won, Wilson kept a scrapbook pasted with news items and photographs of Travelling Scholarship winners. Obedient to the circumstances of success he went to the Sydney Art School where previous winners had studied, took lessons and advice from Arthur Murch (who had won the prize in 1925), had private lessons from Adelaide Perry, whose style was appropriately realistic and analytical, and so established the style and the subjects that would give him the best chance of winning the scholarship.

18 By his own lights he moved far and fast, deserting the Royal Academy Schools for the Westminster School under the tuition of Gertler and taking extra classes with European refugee Amadée Ozenfant.

19 Eric Wilson, Paris sketchbook [1937], Australian National Gallery.

20 Eric Wilson, diary entry 24 January 1939, Wilson Papers, Australian National Gallery.

21 All quotations from a letter from Eric Wilson to Howard Totenhofer, August 1938, photocopies Australian National Gallery.

22 Eric Wilson, Paris sketchbook [1937], Australian National Gallery.

23 Bernard Hesling, 'Dobell: Daring Artist; Conventional Man', *Daily Telegraph*, Sydney, 13 January 1945, pp. 10-11.

24 Dobell painted a number of portraits on ready-framed canvases, which could indicate that he thought of the framed portrait as a single artistic statement in which composition and edge were highly significant.

25 ibid., and Ben Gascoigne (who first met Cook in Sydney in the early 1940s) in conversation with Mary Eagle.

26 Douglas Dundas', William Dobell's and others' notes on James Cook published in exhibition catalogue, *James Cook 1904-1960*, Arts Council of Australia, 1960.

27 Hesling, *Daily Telegraph*, pp. 10-11.

28 Quotes are from Lina Bryans in interviews with Mary Eagle 1980-83, notes and tapes of interviews in M. Eagle's possession. See also Mary Eagle, 'Lina Bryans', *Art and Australia*, Sydney, vol. 21, no. 2, Summer, 1983, pp. 231-9.

29 Information from Lina Bryans and Sue McCulloch. Alan McCulloch, one year older than Lina Bryans, may have met her through his brother Wilfred who shared or used Bryans' studio in Melbourne in the late 1930s.

30 ibid.

VITALITY

The 1940s

The modern movement, exemplified in the work of its perceived classics: Grace Cossington Smith, Margaret Preston, Dorrit Black and Roy de Maistre, was a crafted, inward sort of art. Like its subject matter – still life constructions and arrangements, streetscapes, domestic and studio interiors, occasionally landscapes – it seemed bound to formal questions, ordered, contained within and addressing itself. This could also be said of the work of the three most distinctive artists of the period: Clarice Beckett, Horace Trennery and Max Meldrum.

To some, modernism seemed incapable of responding substantially to a wider experience or to a literary or expressive narrative which, along with a new landscape interpretation, was universally held to be the achievement of the young Australian painters of the late 1880s and 1890s.

If any work of the 1920s and 1930s could call on a sense of national art it was the Heidelberg School's lingering and sorely tested residue – the blue and gold landscape vision – created by Streeton around 1889 and nationalised by Hans Heysen in 1913 and, for our purposes, exemplified in such Commonwealth works as the former's Dandenong Ranges subject – *Blue and Gold, Olinda* 1926 (plate 52) and, to a degree, in Elioth Gruner's dreamy Southern Tablelands painting, *Yass landscape* 1928 (plate 53).

Both the modern movement and the conservative landscape school failed, rightly or wrongly, in the eyes of the critic Basil Burdett, to address a contemporary, indigenous and predominantly urban Australia, with the urgencies of social change and dislocation of the times.

Towards the end of the 1930s and into the war years however, particularly in Melbourne, a number of artists were working in a not necessarily modern style but one that was resolved to narrative (either personal or public),

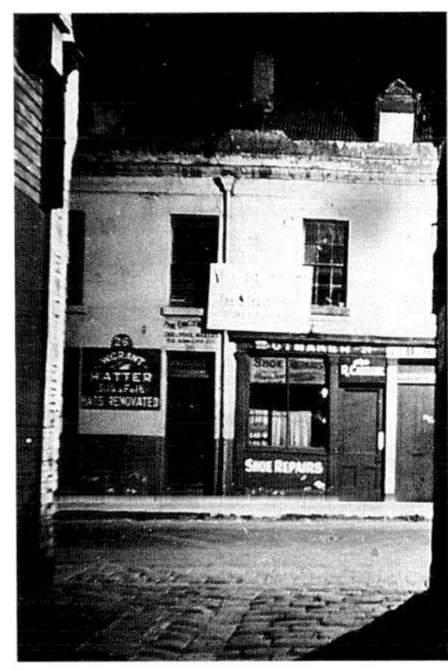

Albert Tucker's loft studio at 26 Little Collins Street. Joy Hester lived here with Albert Tucker until late 1941.

Photograph by Albert Tucker

resonant of locale and stridently directed to contemporary society and social issues. They were energetic, assertive and mostly youthful.

This vitalistic artistic moment was part of, and took place against, a background of new-found intensity in Australian intellectual life and a rich local literary achievement.

When looking at this period however, one must be cautious in drawing generalisations from the actual nature of its painting. A certain freer handling of paint and a concern for texture or vividness of colour can be found in the work of such disparate artists as William Frater (1890–1974) (plate 69), Arnold Shore (1897–1963) (plate 70), Charles Meere (1890–1961) (plates 71 and 72) and Peter Purves Smith (1912–49) (plate 73); but this belies a wide diversity of perception, attitude, artistic background and ambition.

It was a time of fluidity and constant intellectual debate in which the younger artists pursued often very individual goals – though from time to time they were drawn together and at others very much apart, most pertinently in the surrealist/expressive/realist options of the early 1940s.

In a period of relative artistic isolation (though there was less than one might expect) the effect of exposure to art reproductions, books, magazines and films has still to be fully evaluated. Artists arriving from overseas or local artists returning home also provided refreshing exemplars.

The tenor of the times, as the world drew near to universal war, was echoed in the art scene's instability. There was no constant except intense determination and energy. The period's more obvious polarisations, the art schools with their bland old-fashioned modern style, the all important Contemporary Art Society with its complex surrealist/social realist/expressionist interests and the faltering Australian Academy – which really never knew what it stood for – provided no real basis for artistic demarcation.

What was of paramount importance was the emergence of 'the Melbourne school', a group of artists who, in various (and sometimes un-modern) ways, welded their own perceptions of being contemporary and modern to an expressive, vernacular, Australian humanism. They seemed an answer to Burdett's plea.

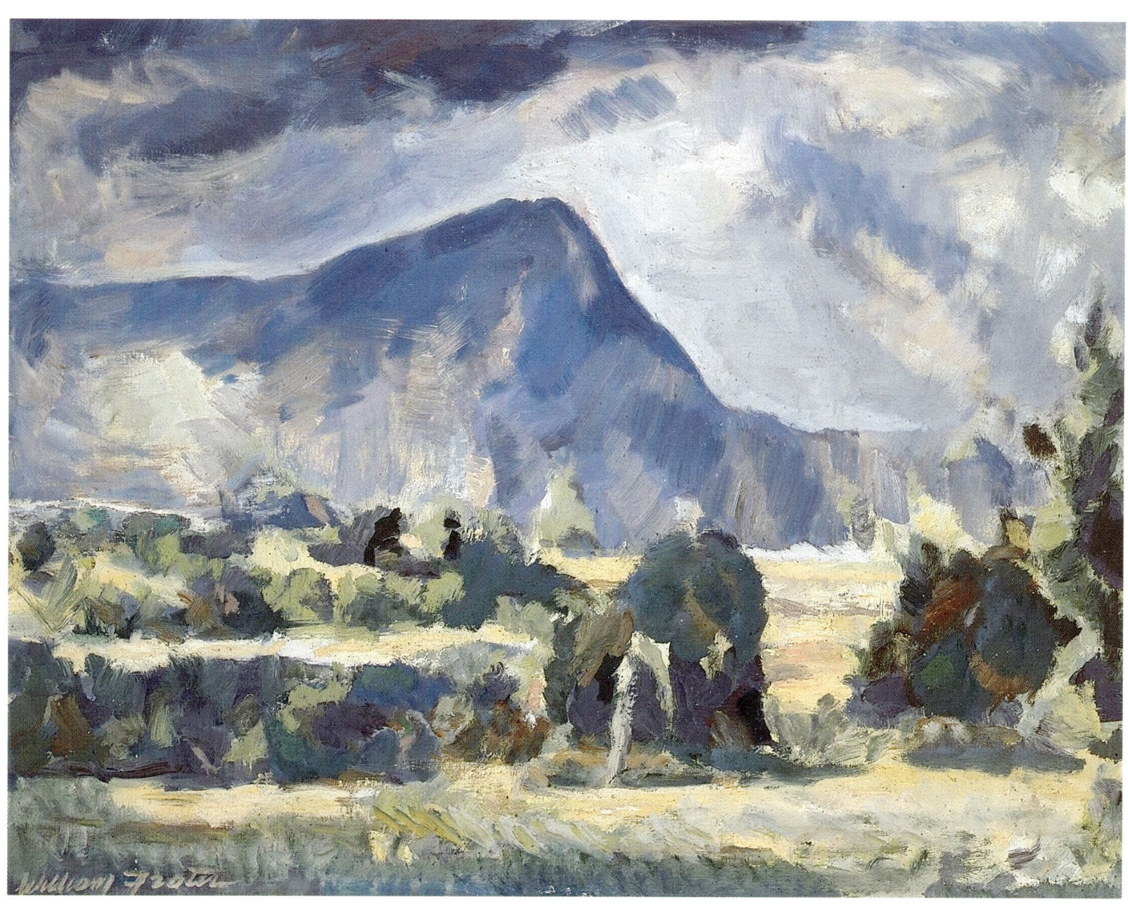

69 William Frater
1890–1974
Sugarloaf, Plenty Ranges (1950)
oil on board
68.0 × 89.0 cm

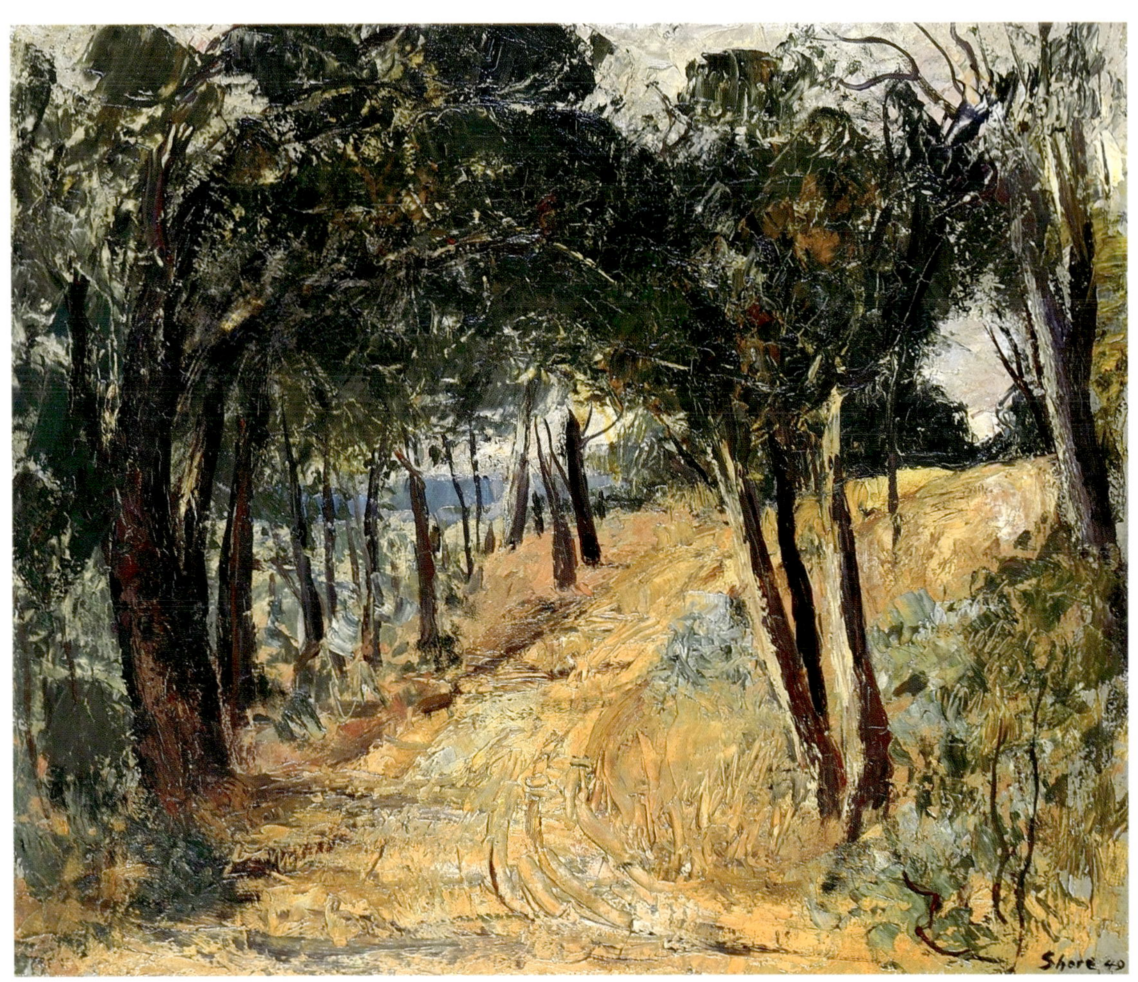

70   Arnold Shore
1897–1963
Arthur's Creek 1949
oil on canvas
51.0 × 61.0 cm

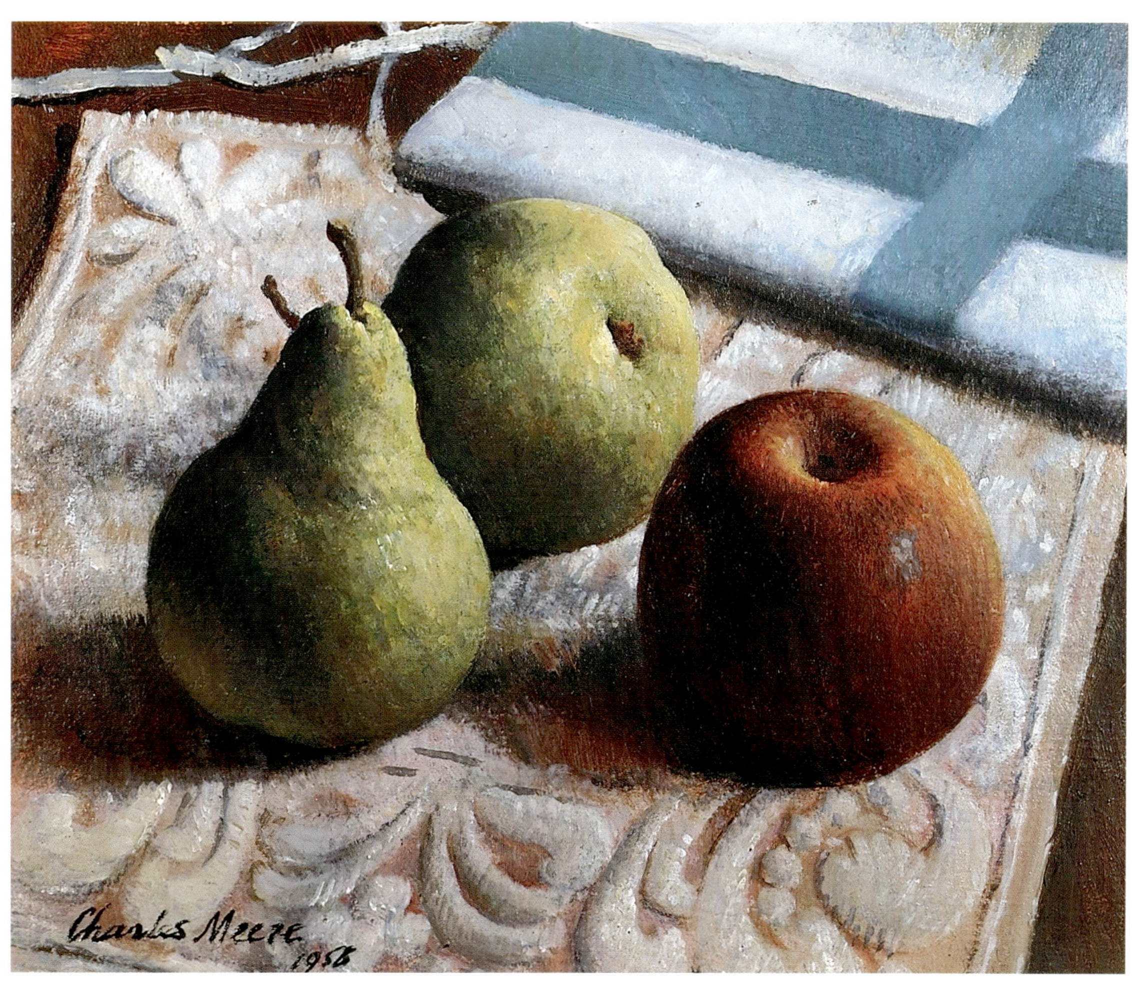

71   Charles Meere
1890–1961
Still life 1958
oil on board
24.5 × 29.5 cm

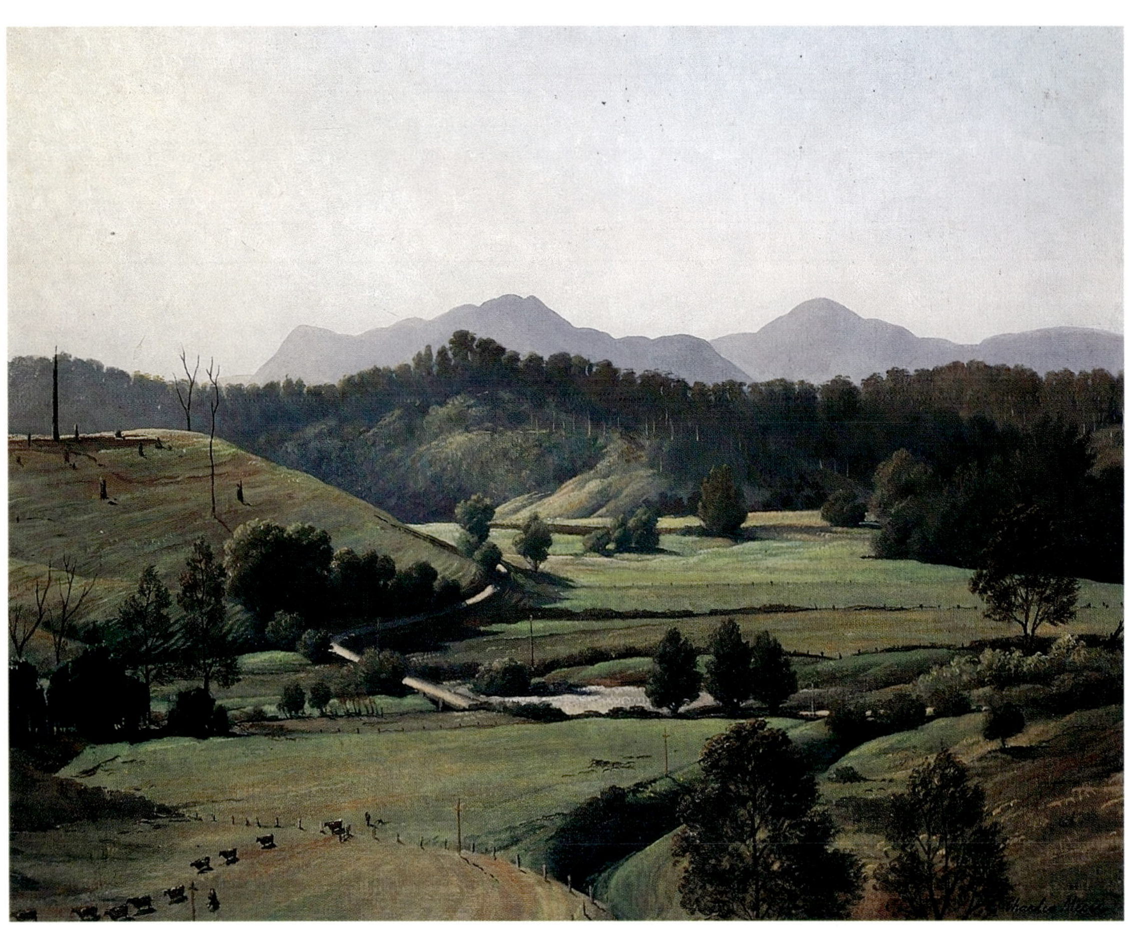

72 Charles Meere
1890–1961
(*Landscape*) (1959)
oil on canvas on board
61.0 × 76.3 cm

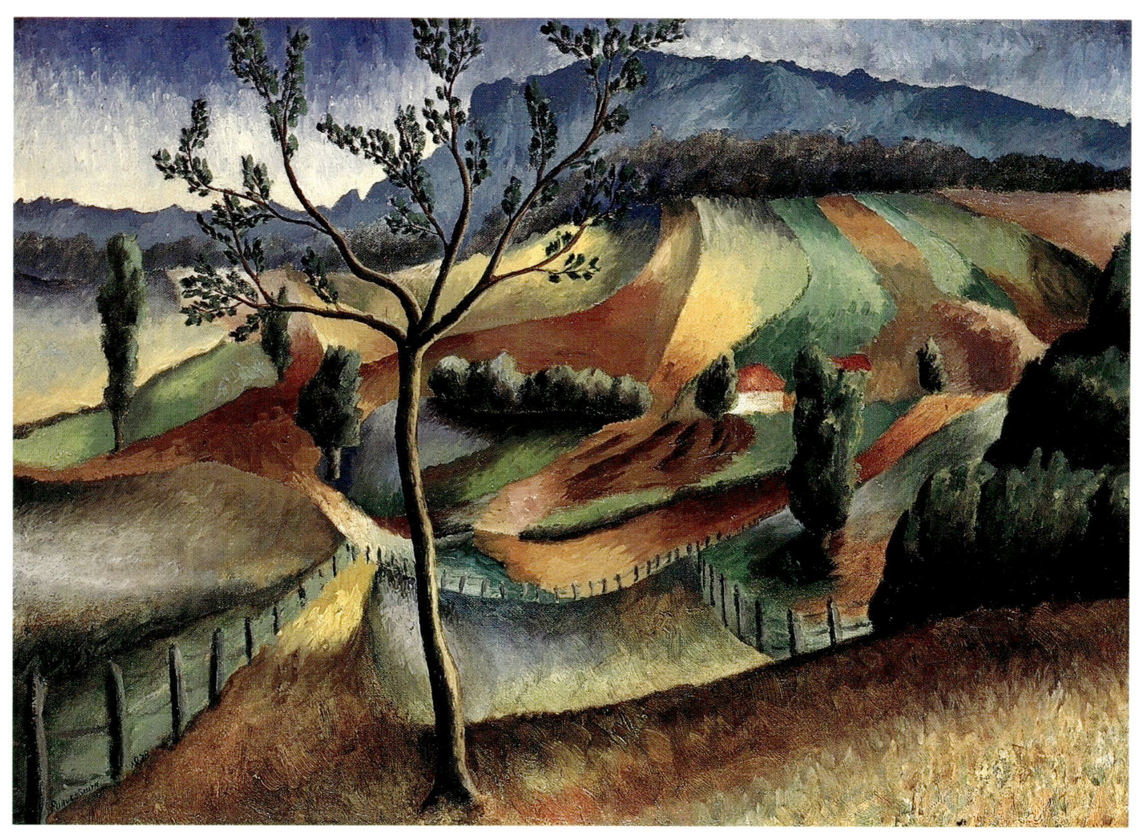

73 Peter Purves Smith
1912–49
(*Landscape near Cassis*) 1933
oil on canvas
46.0 × 60.0 cm

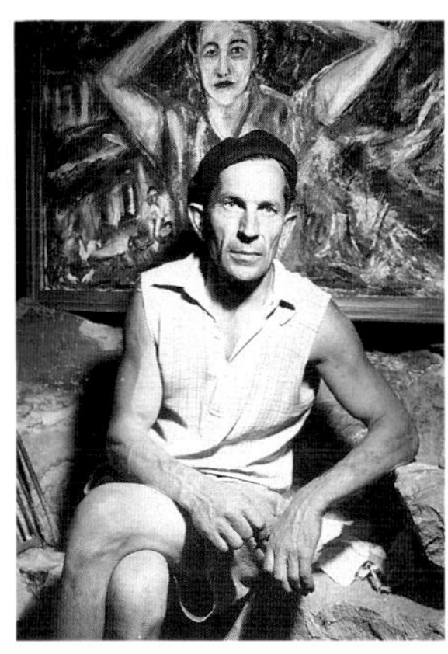

Russian expatriate
artist Danila Vassilieff
at home in 'Stonygrad'
in front of a portrait of
Lottie Schumacher in
1944.

Photograph by Edward Cranstone
Albert Tucker Collection

They were also influenced by new artists coming to Australia, amongst them the nomadic, Russian-born Danila Vassilieff (1897–1958). He moved down from Sydney in 1937 at the same time as a young Viennese Jew, Josl Bergner (born 1920), arrived in Melbourne.

Their subsequent works (with those of the Norwegian artist, Harald Vike, painting at that time in Western Australia) were the first raw, expressive images of urban Australian life. Danila Vassilieff, in particular, profoundly influenced a number of young Australian artists – not only those responsive to social issues and involved politically with the left.

How fresh Vassilieff's work must have seemed when first shown in Melbourne! *A street in Fitzroy* (plate 74) was probably included in his exhibition of September 1937 at Riddells Gallery. This painting was purchased by the most important advocate of contemporary art at that time, John Reed. Like Burdett, Reed was to become a close friend of the artist and a champion of his work.

They were engaged by the chaotic, immediate, untutored spontaneity. The subject – poor children playing with a car tyre and 'billy cart' – was drawn from the inner city slum streets around him and achieved with a directness and energy not seen in Australian art before. Basil Burdett reviewed the exhibition enthusiastically:

> There is a refreshing humanity about his exhibition
> at Riddells Gallery . . . Mr. Vassilieff is interested in
> life first of all, and that refreshing interest is reflected
> in the dynamic character of his work . . . in contrast
> to the static nature of most Australian painting.[1]

Unlike the painting of the British late nineteenth-century social realists, the life and struggles of the working class, apart from the rural hardship/disaster rhetoric of the National Gallery of Victoria Travelling Scholarships, had not really engaged the imagination of Australian artists at any time. Towards the end of the 1930s, in the face of a pressing reality, potent images of public post-Depression city squalor offered to young artists a local exemplar of expressive, contemporary humanism. Josl Bergner, himself a refugee, depicted Australia's own refugees – the urban Aborigines. One of these paintings (which could be of rural Aborigines at Tocumwal),

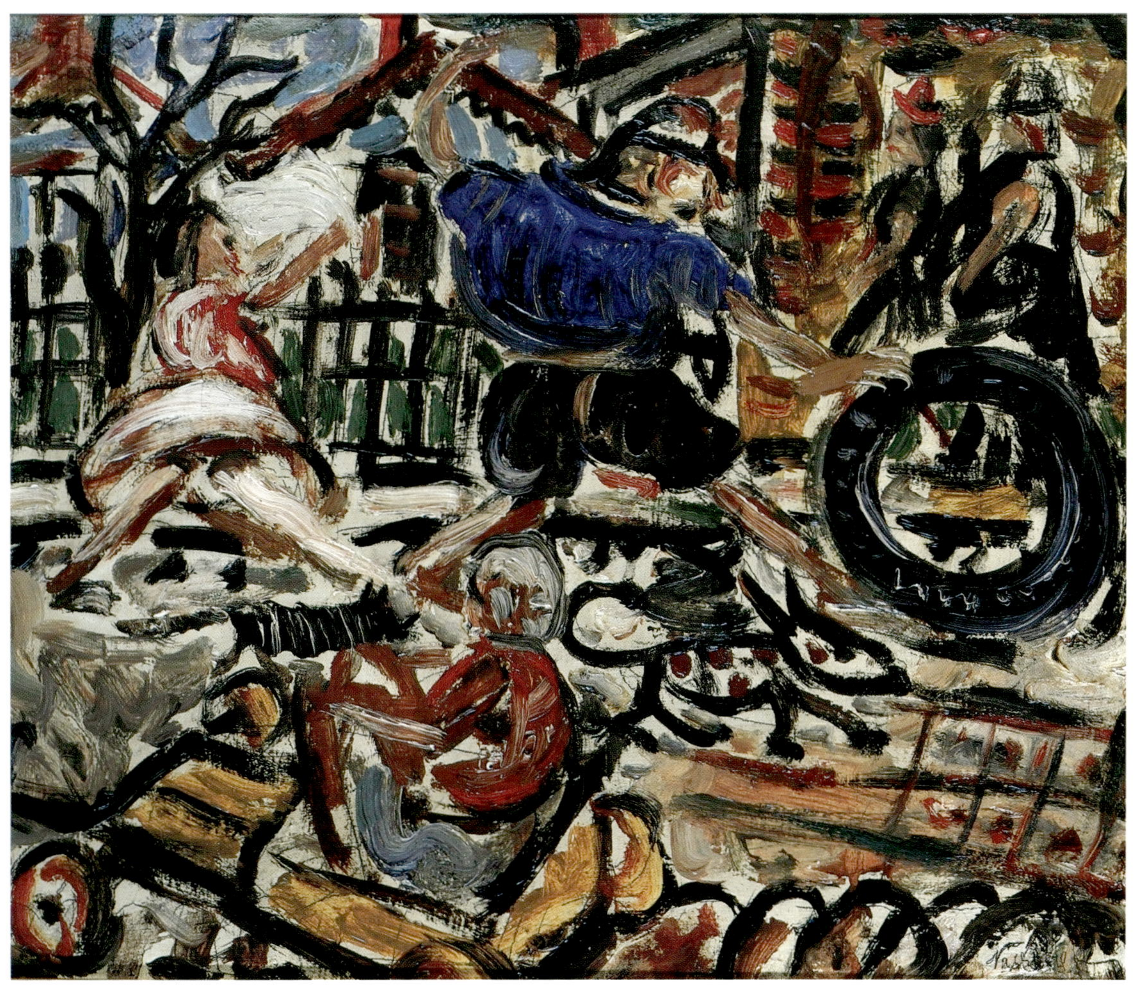

74 Danila Vassilieff
1897–1958
A street in Fitzroy (1937)
oil on plywood panel
37.8 × 44.9 cm

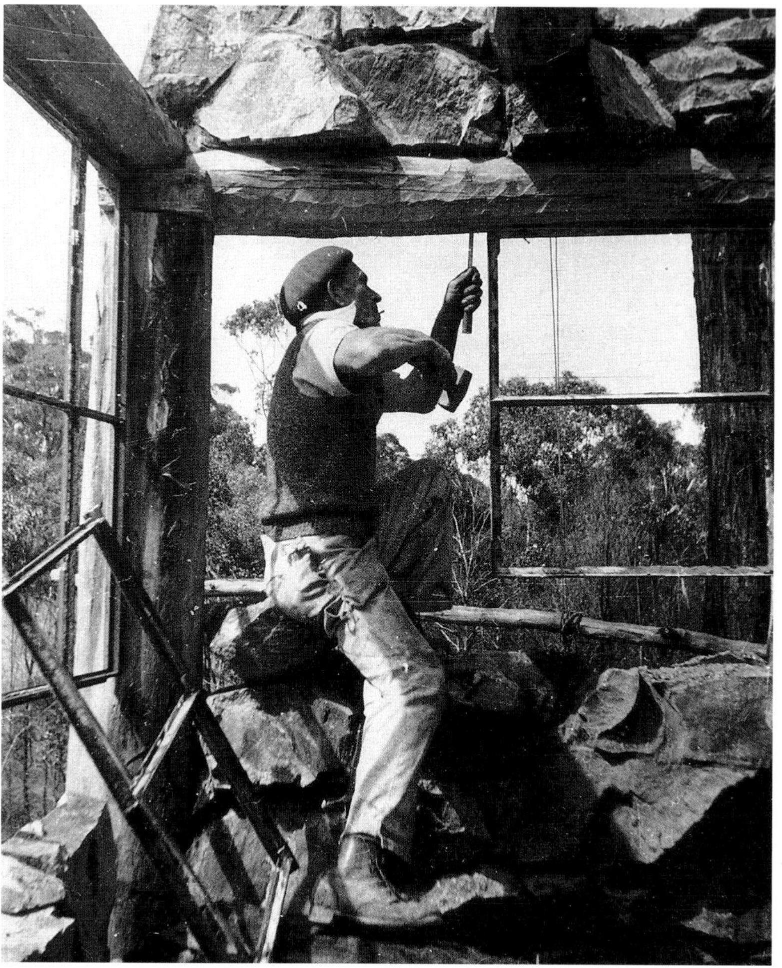

Aboriginal family c. 1943 (plate 75), is a mordant work, intense in feeling, stark, oppressive and crudely finished.

The subject is an Aboriginal mother holding a young child tenderly to herself while the father completes a miserable meal. It is a scene of Australian poverty, futility and utter wretchedness. Along with Bergner's images of the blight of European fascism, these profoundly moving paintings of local injustice were seen to be entering an area of social experience which committed artists should be exploring.

By the 1940s, particularly for those radical artists and intellectuals in the ambience of the Contemporary Art Society in Melbourne, involvement in politics (of the left) and a concern for issues of social justice had become essential – for some, correct art and correct politics were inseparable.

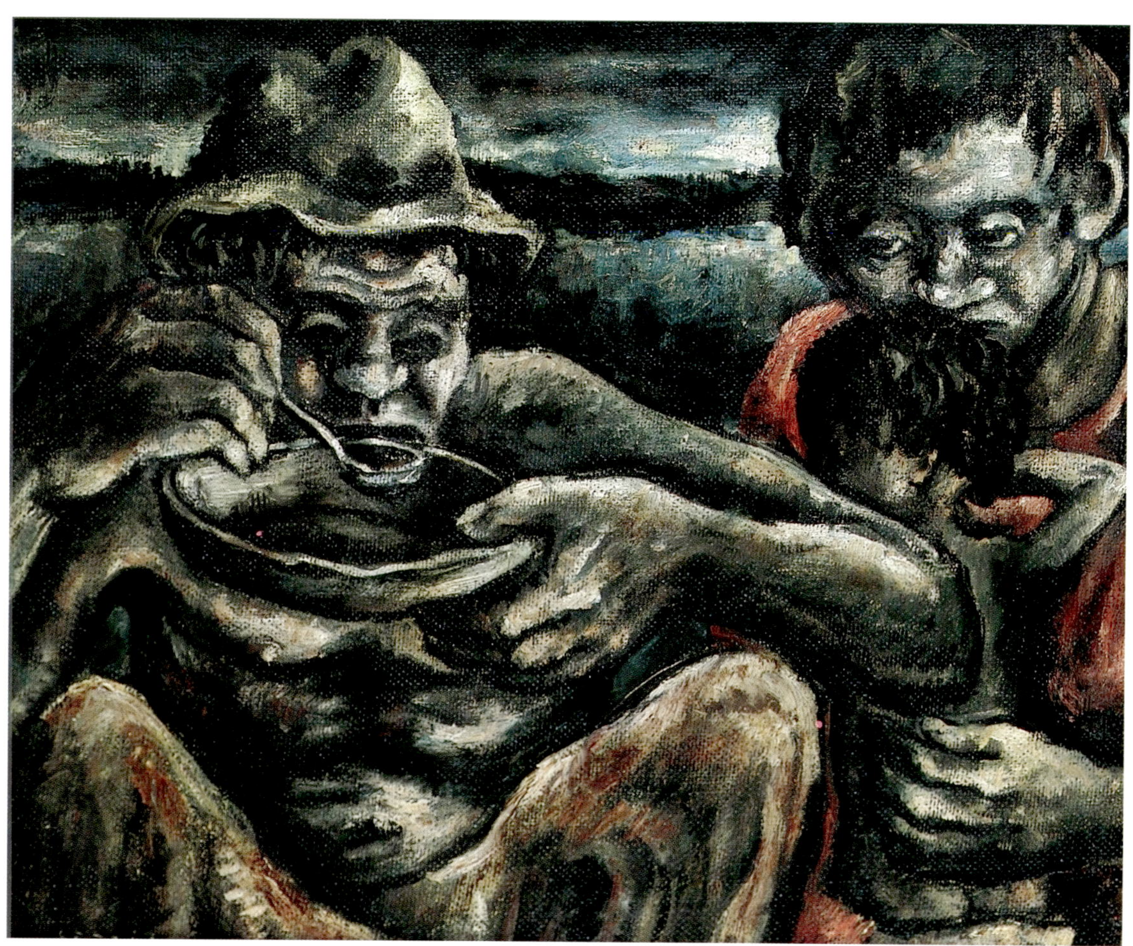

75 Josl Bergner
born 1920
(*Aboriginal family*) (1943)
oil on board
37.0 × 42.0 cm

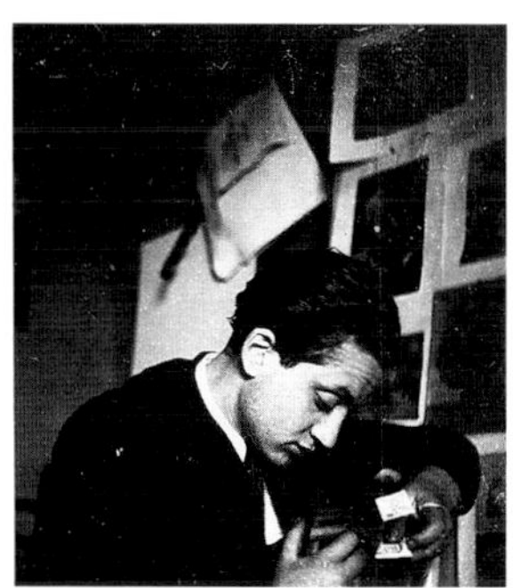

Yosl Bergner in 1939.
Photograph by Albert Tucker

The tone of Bergner's social realism was to be found in the wartime work of the Society's artists, particularly in the most politicised members, Noel Counihan and Vic O'Connor (born 1918). Within two or three years this pair of social realists, with Bergner and championed by Bernard Smith, were presenting a united front. Their joint statement in the catalogue introduction for the Contemporary Art Society exhibition of September 1944 stated:

> We in fact work together as a group. Each seeks to create a democratic art combining beauty of treatment with a realistic statement of man in his contemporary environment. We three painters believe in a human, democratic art with its roots in the life and struggles of the ordinary people, devoid of all obscure cliches and mannerisms . . . an art intelligible and popular, expressing the deepest emotions and aspirations of the people.[2]

Vic O'Connor's *North Melbourne* 1947–8 (plate 76), was painted about the time Bergner left Australia and the social realist group was dissolving. Its subject, like Vassilieff's painting of Fitzroy street children, lacks the overt political message of Bergner's dispossessed peoples and Counihan's images of proletariat labour, but in its melancholic mood and brooding tonal values shares their concern for the urban poor. Painted near the Queen Victoria Market, O'Connor's work charges those streets with human drama. In contrast, the decorative treatment by Sali Herman (1898–1993) of inner city Sydney streets, *Paddington back street corner* 1947 (plate 77), of the same date, has no more a message than old slum charm.

Other Contemporary Art Society artists, particularly those involved with John Reed and the sort of artistic salon he and his wife Sunday had established at Heide, were less definable. Although aligned with the left and absorbing at times the concerns of the social realists, they found it increasingly difficult, from diverse positions, to subscribe to the rigid, united political front demanded by them. It was never a cohesive group and sometimes bitter divisions appeared in the Contemporary Art Society's ranks which were eventually to contribute to its demise.

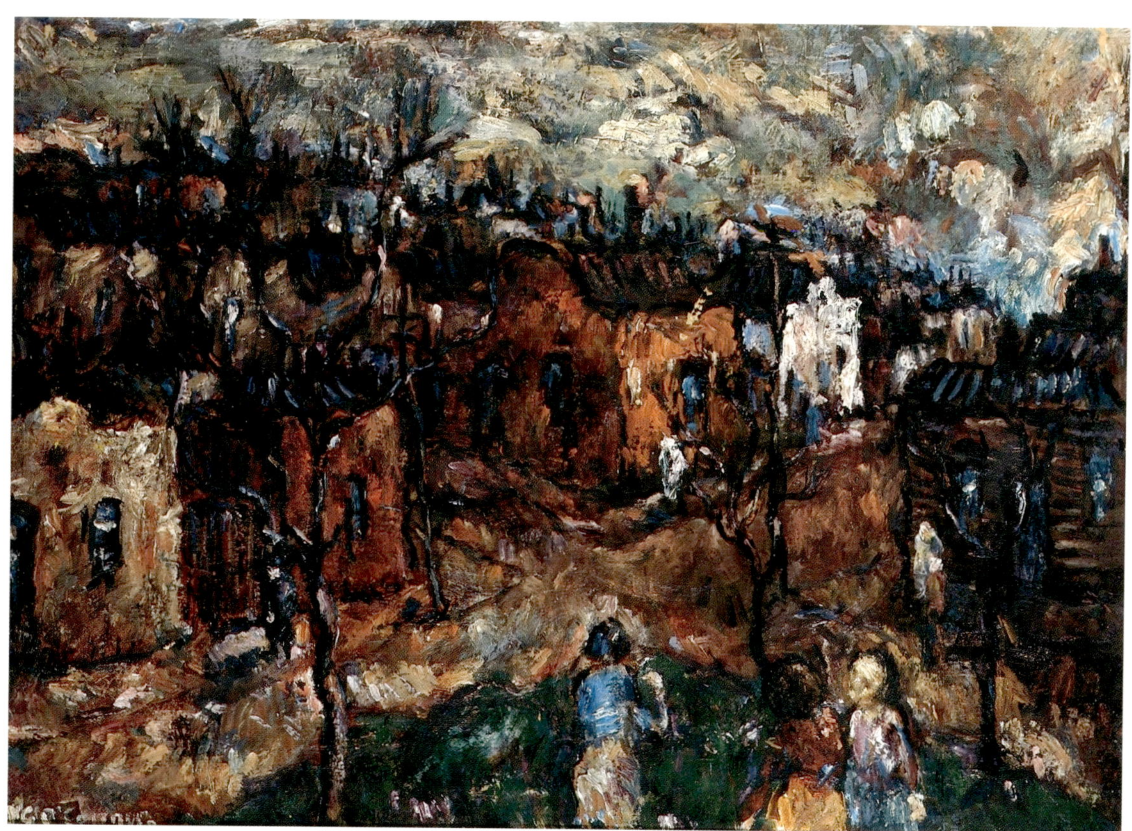

76   Vic O'Connor
born 1918
(*North Melbourne*) 1947–8
oil on board
37.5 × 53.3 cm

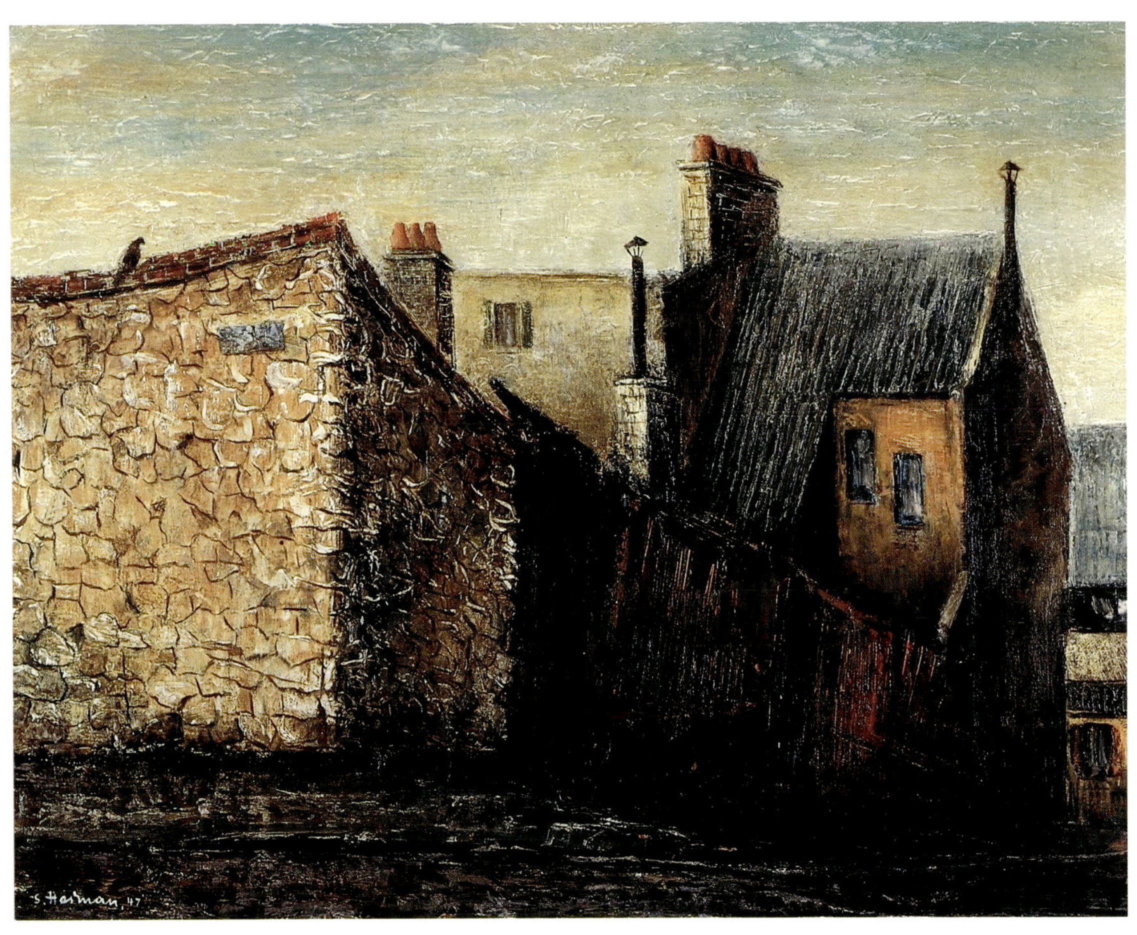

77   Sali Herman
1898–1993
(*Paddington back street corner*) 1947
oil on canvas
30.9 × 41.0 cm

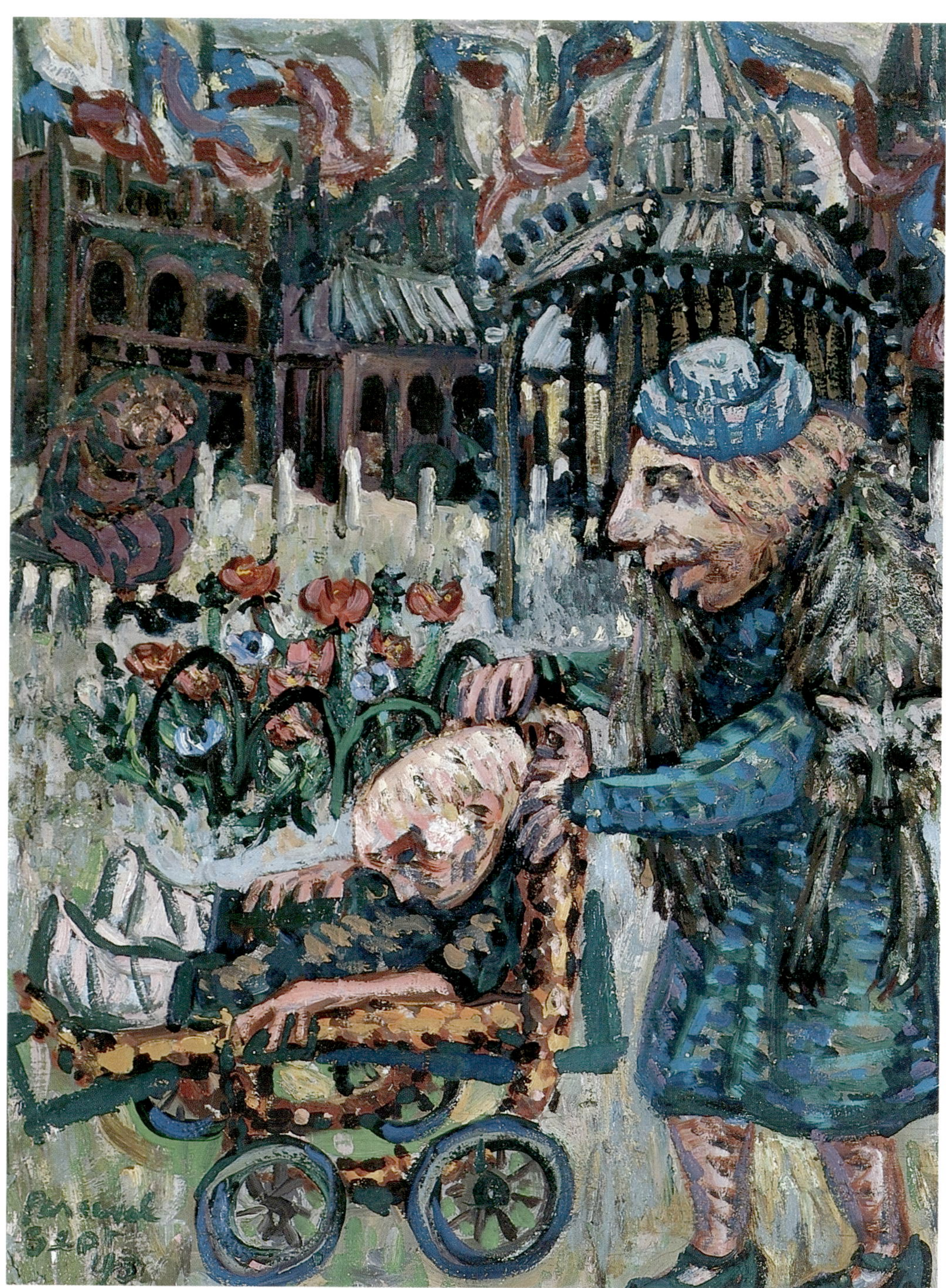

78   John Perceval
born 1923
(*Woman pushing a crippled boy*) 1943
oil on board
65.0 × 49.0 cm

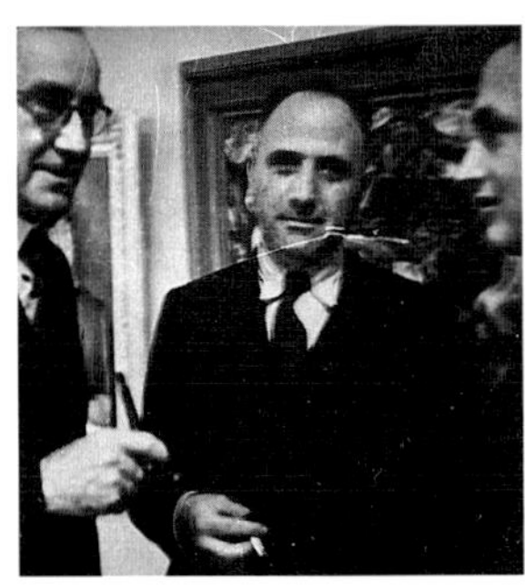

Sali Herman, centre, with Francis Lymburner (in profile on the right) at the Contemporary Arts Exhibition in Sydney, 1940. The man on the left is unknown.

Photograph by Albert Tucker

For the Reed circle creative freedom could never be politically circumscribed. Their individual concerns and perceptions were paramount. With the support of John Reed and Max Harris and their influential literary journal *Angry Penguins*, these artists – Albert Tucker, Arthur Boyd, Sidney Nolan and John Perceval in particular – the so-called 'Angry Penguins', became increasingly the authoritative voice in the Contemporary Art Society exhibitions.

The editorial of the 1943 September edition of *Angry Penguins* argued for an Australian art 'whose growth would inevitably mature into a form of expression which will be unique and in the truest sense of the word indigenous'.[3] Echoing Burdett's earlier call, it came alongside others, demanding the rejection of what they saw as the stifling strident nationalism of other literary journals such as *Meanjin Papers*, and social realist demands for a united political propriety.

In the early 1940s John Perceval, (born 1923) painted some extraordinary expressionist war images which in vitality and untutored power may owe more to his exposure (in reproduction) to the violent art of the German Expressionists than to any immediate references. These contend in boldness with Albert Tucker's comparable images of Melbourne which, if not occupied, was certainly radically changed by the presence of Allied war personnel.

Alongside these paintings of wartime dislocation there are other autobiographical childhood subjects, often from the world of dreams and close in feeling to the work of Arthur Boyd, whom Perceval had met at the Australian Army Headquarters Cartographic Company and whose sister Mary he married in 1944.

Perceval's *Woman pushing a crippled boy* 1943 (plate 78) is perhaps less threatening than others from this world of fantasies. A fairground or park, a flag-decked rotunda and a row of terrace houses create a festive mood which is quite ambiguous, given the central subject. A well-dressed woman with a hat and wearing a stonemartin fur choker, fashionable at the time, is pushing a crippled boy in an improvised wheelchair. Both are observed across a flowerbed by a strange figure seated on a bench. It is a puzzling subject but one with reference to the artist himself. Some years earlier, in 1937, while holidaying with friends on the Mornington Peninsula Perceval contracted

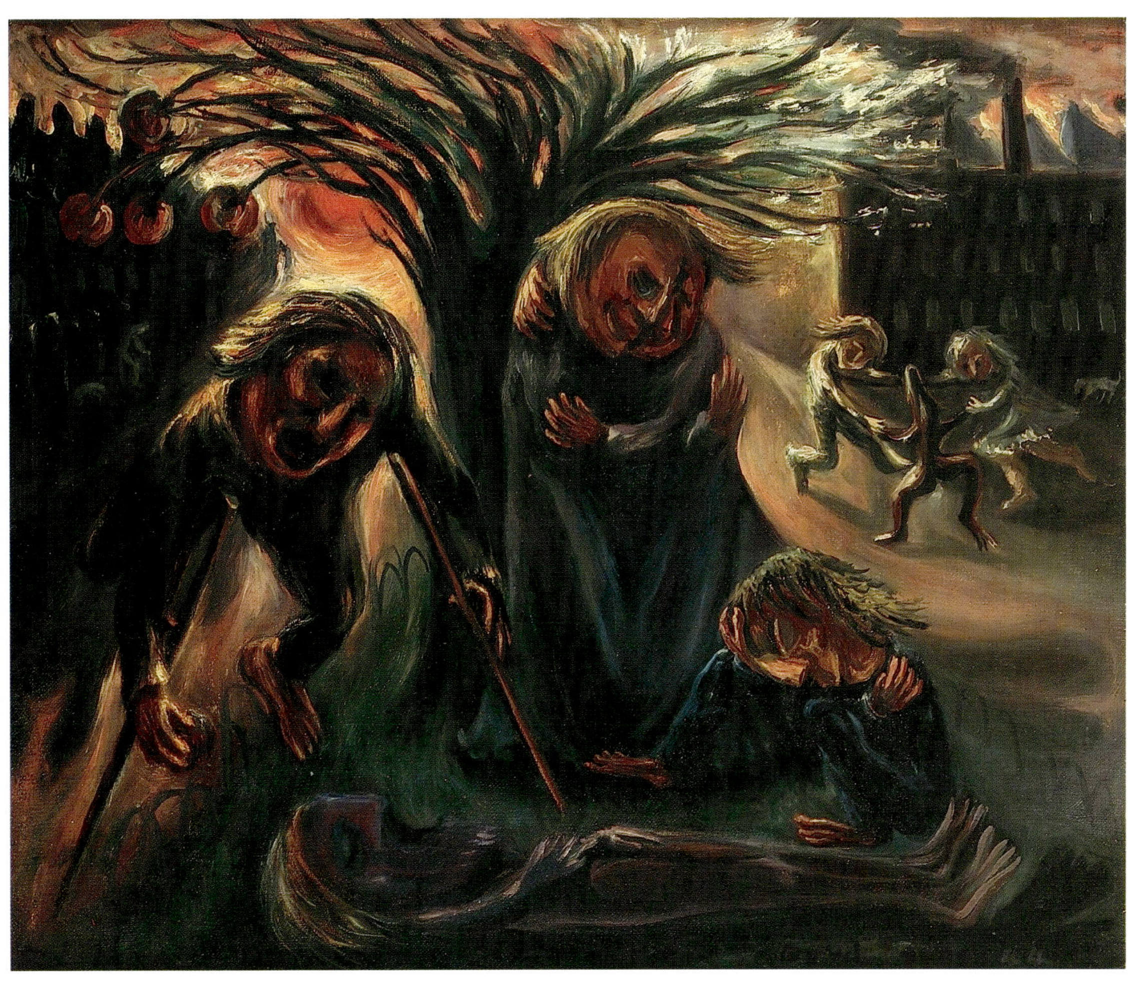

79   Arthur Boyd
born 1920
The Seasons 1944
oil on muslin laid down on board
63.5 × 76.2 cm

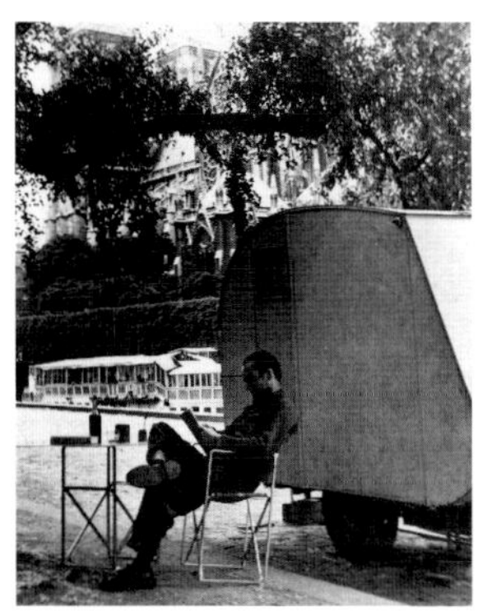

Albert Tucker relaxing
by his caravan parked
next to the Seine.
Photograph by Albert Tucker

poliomyelitis and recovered to be left with a deformed leg supported by irons.[4]

A disabled figure, possibly Perceval, appears on crutches in Arthur Boyd's equally ambiguous but effortlessly artless painting of 1944, *The Seasons* (plate 79).[5] The literate, private vision of this work relates to a number of other so-called South Melbourne paintings by the young Boyd (born 1920) which incorporate images of the grotesque and the maimed, figures of the dead, cemeteries, coffins, kites, tents, anthropomorphic terrace houses, seaside esplanades, fountains and trees. *The Seasons*, with its burning sun, smoking factories, row of houses, concurrently barren, flowering, and fruitful tree, corpse (his grandfather, Arthur Merric Boyd?), cripple, mourner, lovers and children playing has often been read as a metaphor for the cycle of life: youth, maturity, old age, death. Beneath the ancient symbol of the tree of life, figures of joy and sorrow, desire and beauty mingle in a place of the imagination.

Max Harris, who had moved to Melbourne in 1943, recalled some forty-five years later:

> Arthur realised best, and with the most wide-ranging
> originality, the . . . path to an indigenous modernism.
> That is we should eschew the self-indulgent private
> surrealist image, and project such private imagery
> relevantly on to a common visible world.[6]

The Bell-School-trained Albert Tucker (born 1914) was the most complex and, apart from his revealing self-portraits, the least autobiographical of the group. Like Boyd he pursued the world of the imagination, but with wrath. *Image of Modern Evil* 1946 (plate 80) is one of the larger paintings of a series of wartime street imagery – 'Night Images' he called them in 1945 – which the artist worked on from 1943 to 1947 in East Melbourne and then St Kilda.

Previously, Tucker had experimented with surrealist literary imagery and then moved, on the outbreak of war, to a starker social realism in the manner of Bergner. As the conflict continued and came closer to home, his work became decidedly expressionistic, bearing comparison in its savagery to the work of the German painters of human horror, Max Beckmann, George Grosz and Otto Dix.

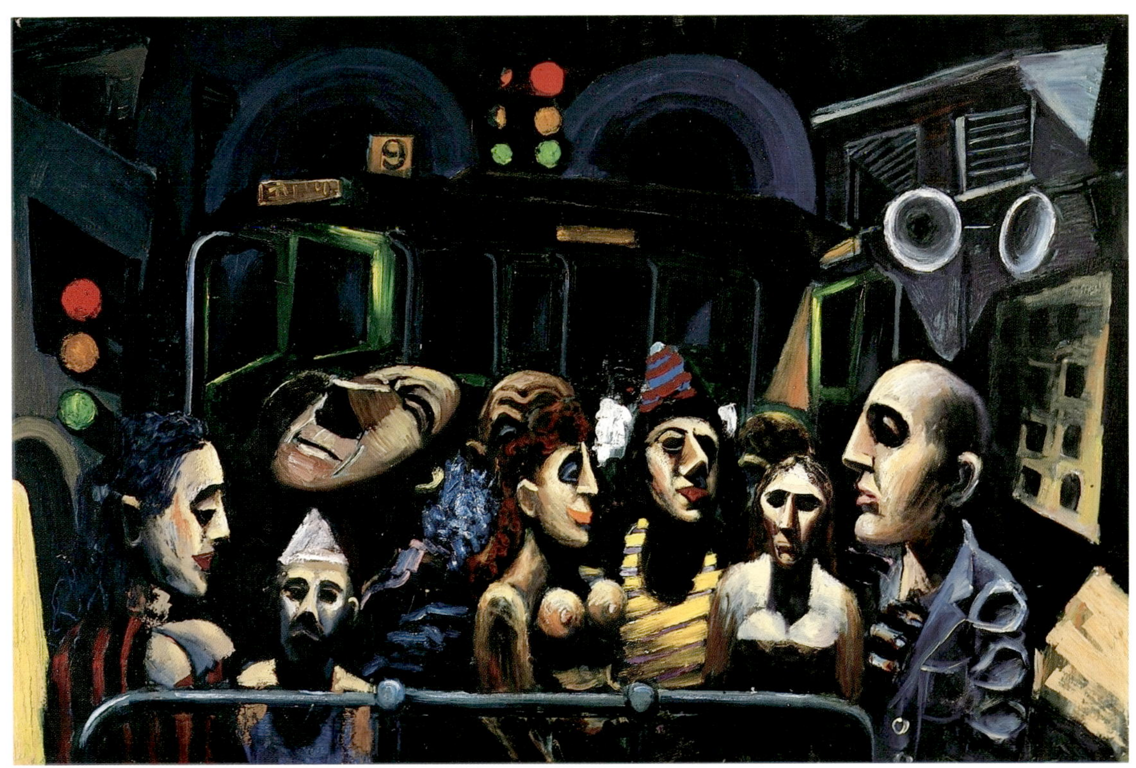

80   Albert Tucker
born 1914
Image of Modern Evil 1946
oil on board
80.0 × 120.0 cm

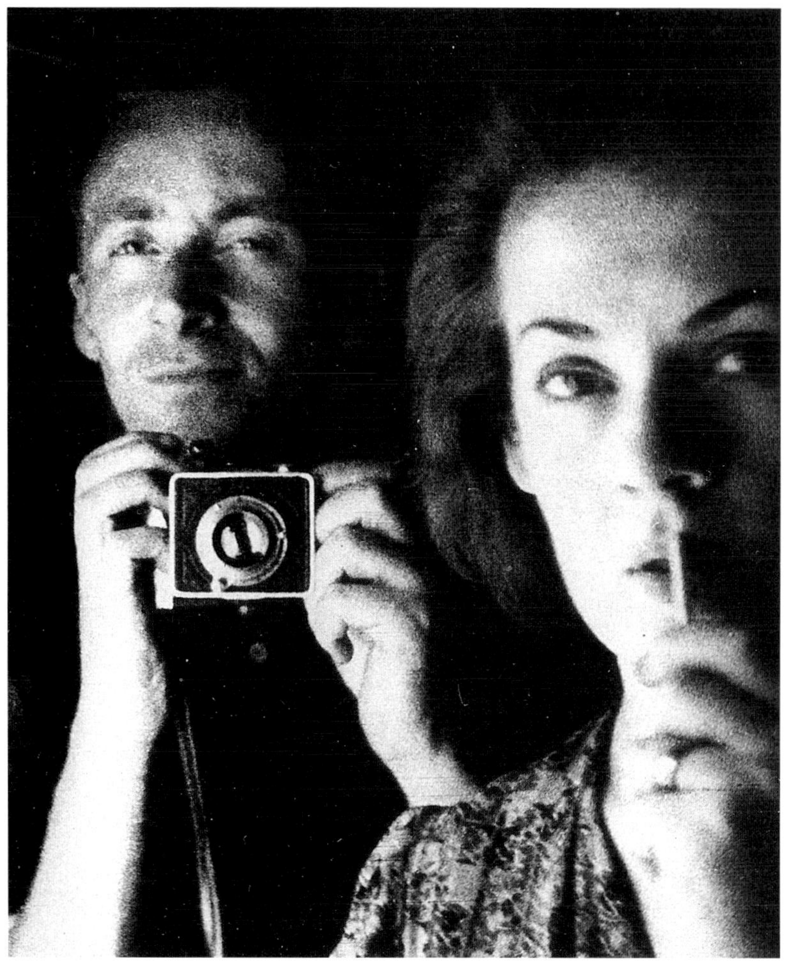

Albert Tucker and Joy
Hester in 1941. This
mirror image was taken
with Tucker's first
camera, a Foth Derby.
Photograph by Albert Tucker

Elements of surrealism still surface in these paintings
from 1943 but their biting critique of contemporary sexual
immorality and moral decay, aggravated by war, goes
much further. Tucker paints a Melbourne of blackouts,
American servicemen on leave, local street girls,
prostitution, drunkenness, violence and murder. They are
in stark comparison to the easy, illustrative style of Herbert
Badham (1899–1961) who created such Sydney wartime
images as *Bar scene* 1940 (plate 81).

Like the Old Testament prophets, Amos or Hosea, raging
against the people of Israel, Albert Tucker saw his role
as a prophetic mission of protest against the vice around
him. *Image of Modern Evil* 1946 is a nightmarish construction.
We look across an iron bed-end (are we dreaming?) to
where an American GI and other strange figures mingle
with prostitutes and bathers. There are dislocated traffic

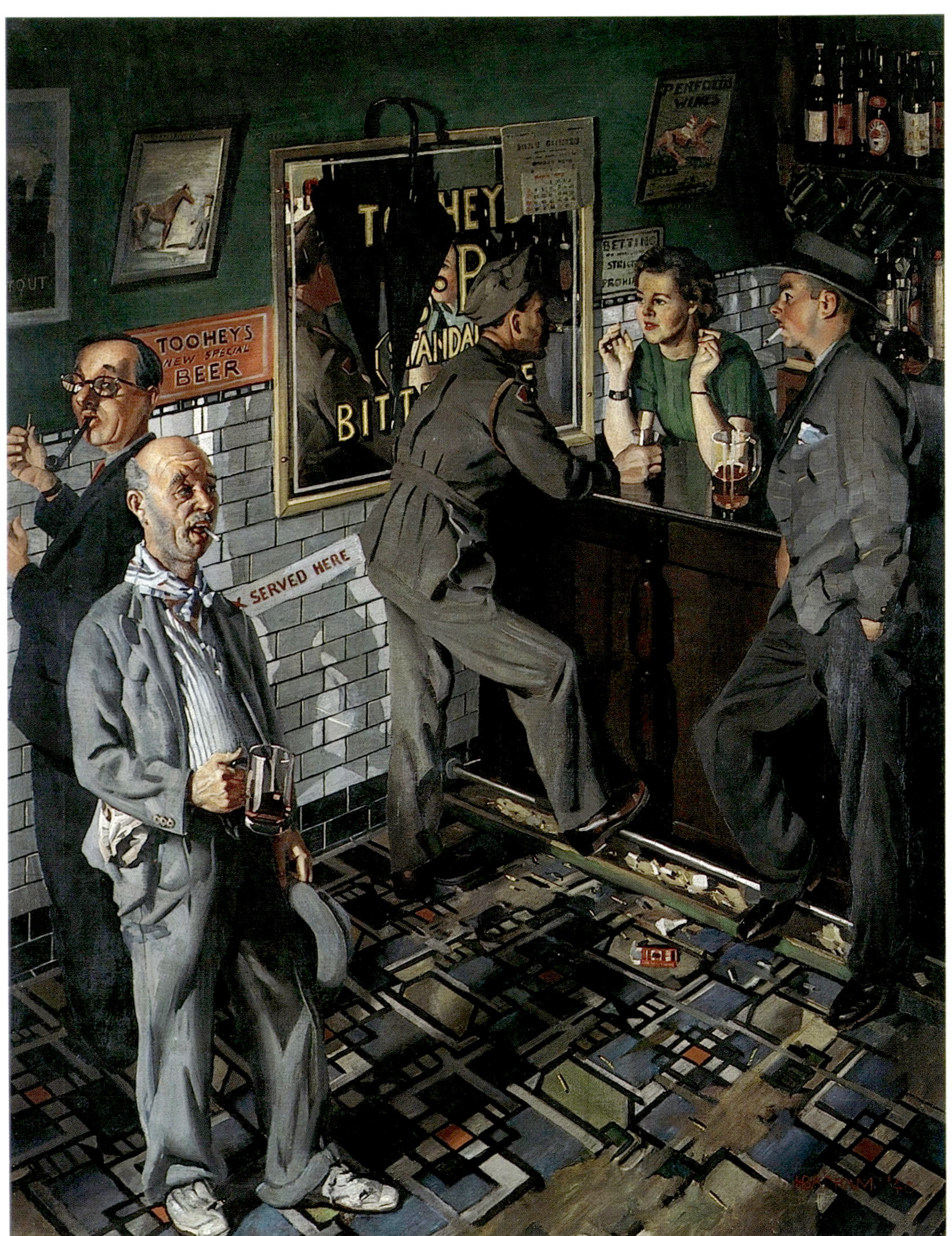

81   Herbert Badham
1899–1961
(*Bar scene*) 1940
oil on canvas
102.0 × 81.0 cm

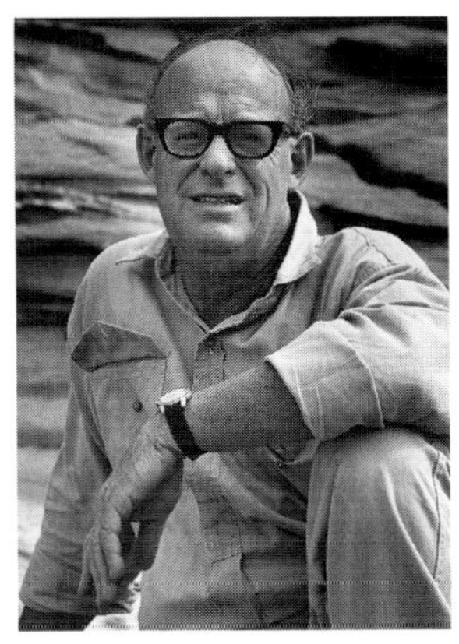

Russell Drysdale at
Tallow Beach in 1969.
Photograph by David Moore

lights, a tram, loud speakers (from a prison camp?) and fantastic buildings and perspectives. The black night is pierced by a pool of light illuminating the figures, grouped together but with no obvious communication or narrative. The painting seems to deal with the psychological state and the inner consciousness. More than others of the series it shows the syncretic nature of Tucker's art at this time, his debt to the ideas of André Breton and the surrealists and the complexity of a vocabulary drawn from the painters of the *Neue Sachlichkeit*, from the cubism of Picasso and others, but submerged into his own private notion of hell.

Tucker's wife Joy Hester (1920–60) shared his fascination with the inner life and psychological states. Her work has a softer, feminine perspective and, unlike his, deals with the personal rather than social. In her drawings during the war and afterwards we see its consequences and other dislocating experiences affecting people, with all their individual vulnerabilities, anxieties and fears. This poetic imagery, implicit in *Girl with hat* 1955 (plate 82), was central to her work up until her death in 1960.

Softer too, and angst-less, is the painting of another Bell School student, Russell Drysdale: *Ticket office, Albury* 1943 (plate 83). Drysdale (1912–81) spent most of 1942 at his family's property, 'Boxwood Park' near Albury. He had been profoundly influenced by the British War Artists' Advisory Committee Exhibition of official war art, which toured Australia in 1943 and included works by Henry Moore, Graham Sutherland, John Piper and Paul Nash. This recording of Australian soldiers on Albury Station is tinged with their sense of brooding and melancholy expectancy.

A similar mood invades his Riverina District paintings of that time. A son of the land, Drysdale, more than any other artist of the period, was to turn away from the predominantly urban images of his contemporaries and pursue a new Australian romantic genre of the figure in the landscape.

Arthur Boyd had also begun to paint complex figures or crowds in landscape settings inspired by the old masters from around 1945. These were mainly drawn from Classical or Old Testament sources but set into the Australian landscape. At 'The Grange', Berwick, painting a series of religious murals for his uncle, he also produced

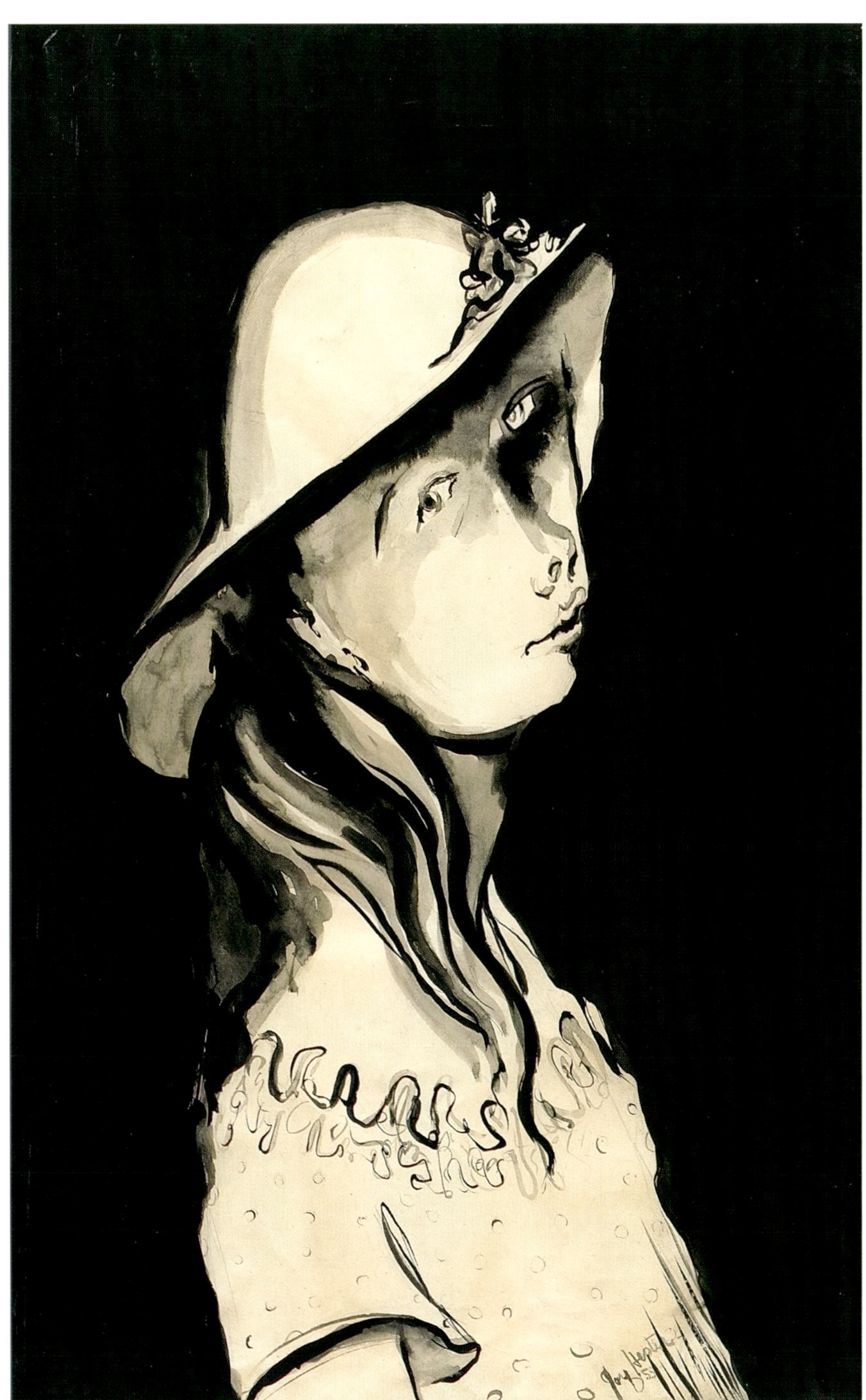

82   Joy Hester
1920–60
(*Girl with hat*) 1955
ink on paper
73.5 × 48.5 cm

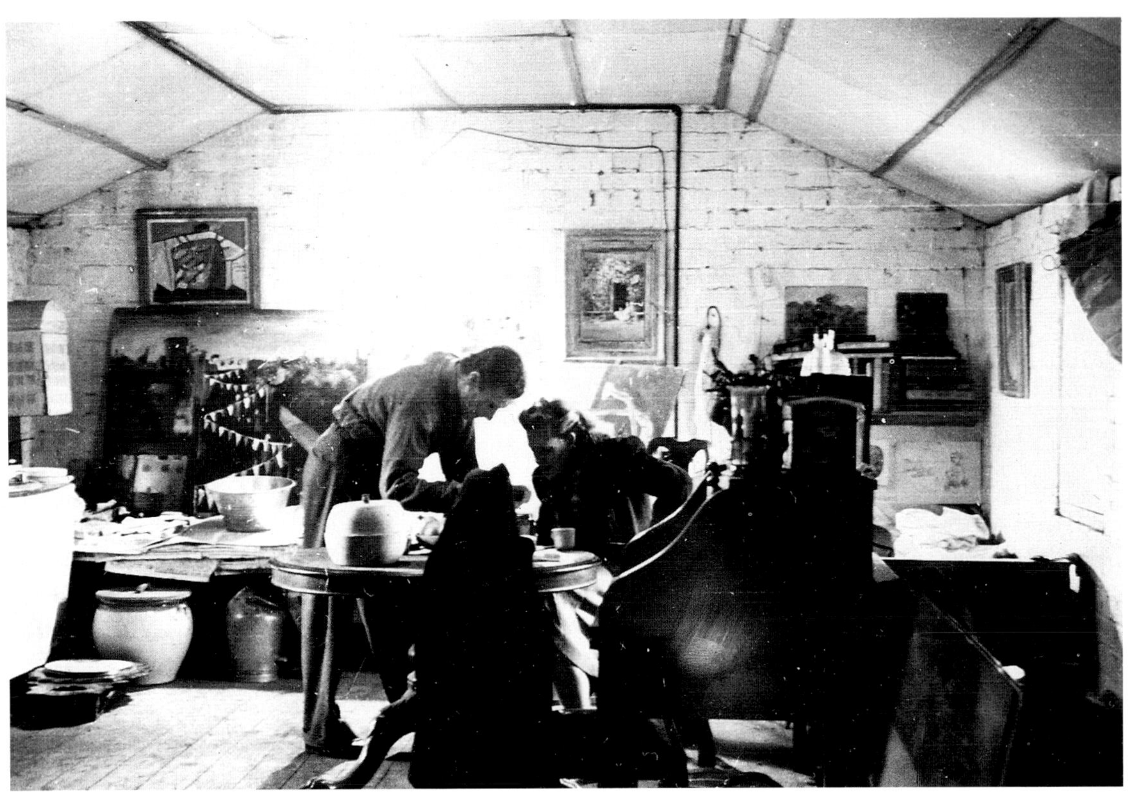

Joy Hester visiting
Sidney Nolan in his loft
studio in Melbourne's
inner suburban
Parkville in 1945.
Photograph by Albert Tucker

straightforward old masterly treatments of the surrounding verdant countryside, often in tempera. *Wheatfield, Berwick* 1948 (plate 84) is a robust Breugelian summer exercise. The next year he was to paint landscapes in the Wimmera, the flat dry wheatbelt of Victoria.

Sidney Nolan (1917–92) also turned to figures in landscape subjects during his earlier wartime stint in that part of the country. Later he extended the dimension of these in the 1946–7 Glenrowan paintings. He explained:

> I find that a desire to paint the landscape involves a wish to hear more of the stories which take place within the landscape. Stories which may or may not only be heard in country towns and read in the journals of explorers, but which also persist in the memory.[7]

He did just that in his series of works illustrating the life of the nineteenth-century Australian bushranger, Ned Kelly. It is the stuff of legend, as the series itself has become legendary. The paintings are full of wry irony, human

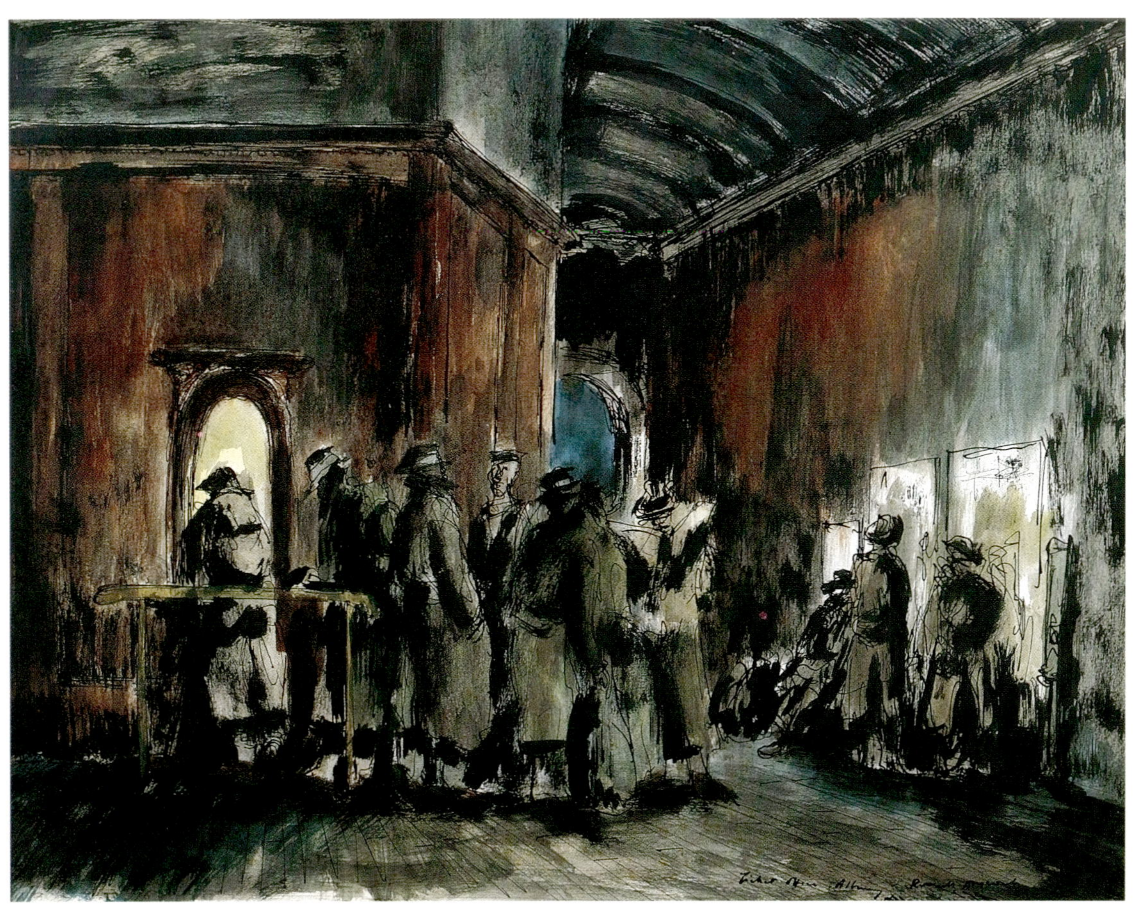

83   Russell Drysdale
1912–81
Ticket office, Albury 1943
gouache on paper
31.5 × 41.0 cm

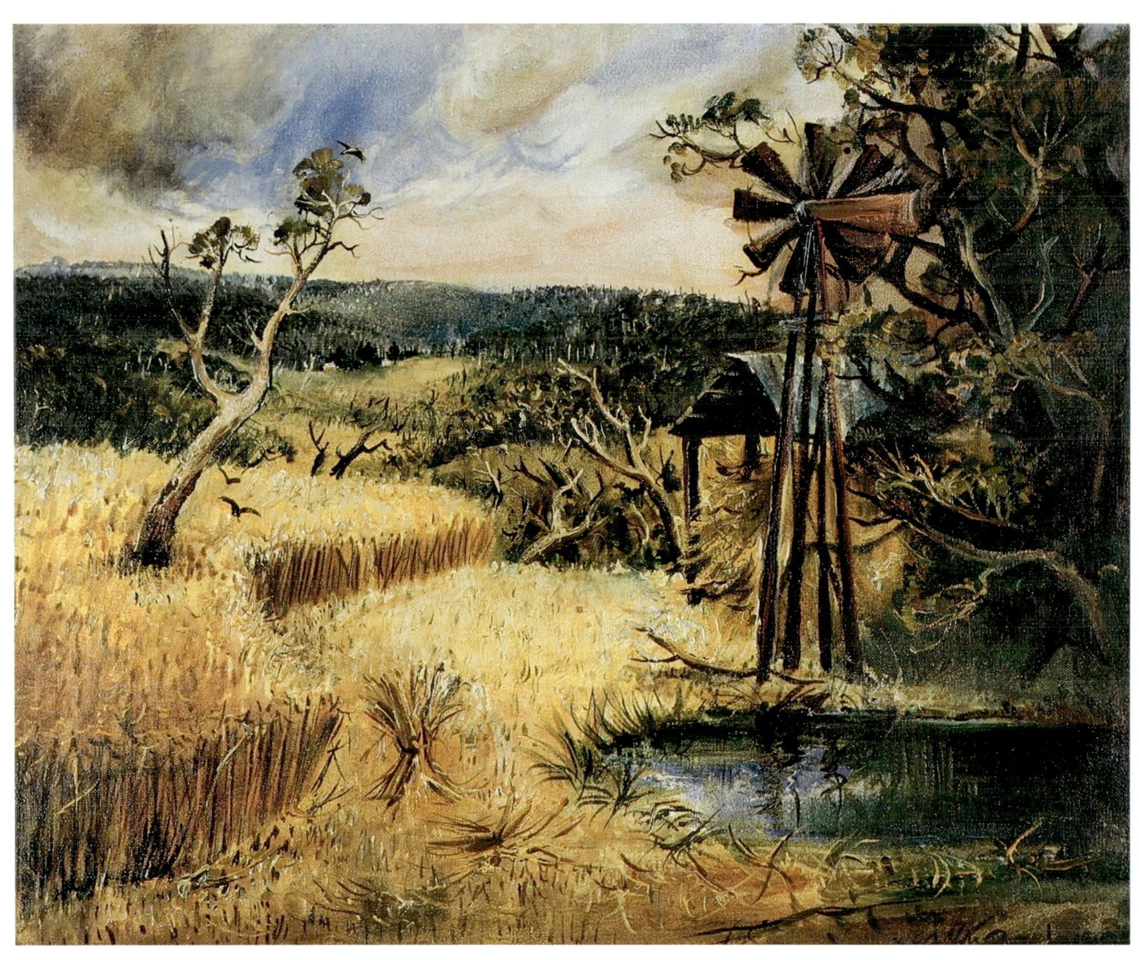

84   Arthur Boyd
born 1920
Wheatfield, Berwick 1948
oil on canvas on board
54.0 × 65.0 cm

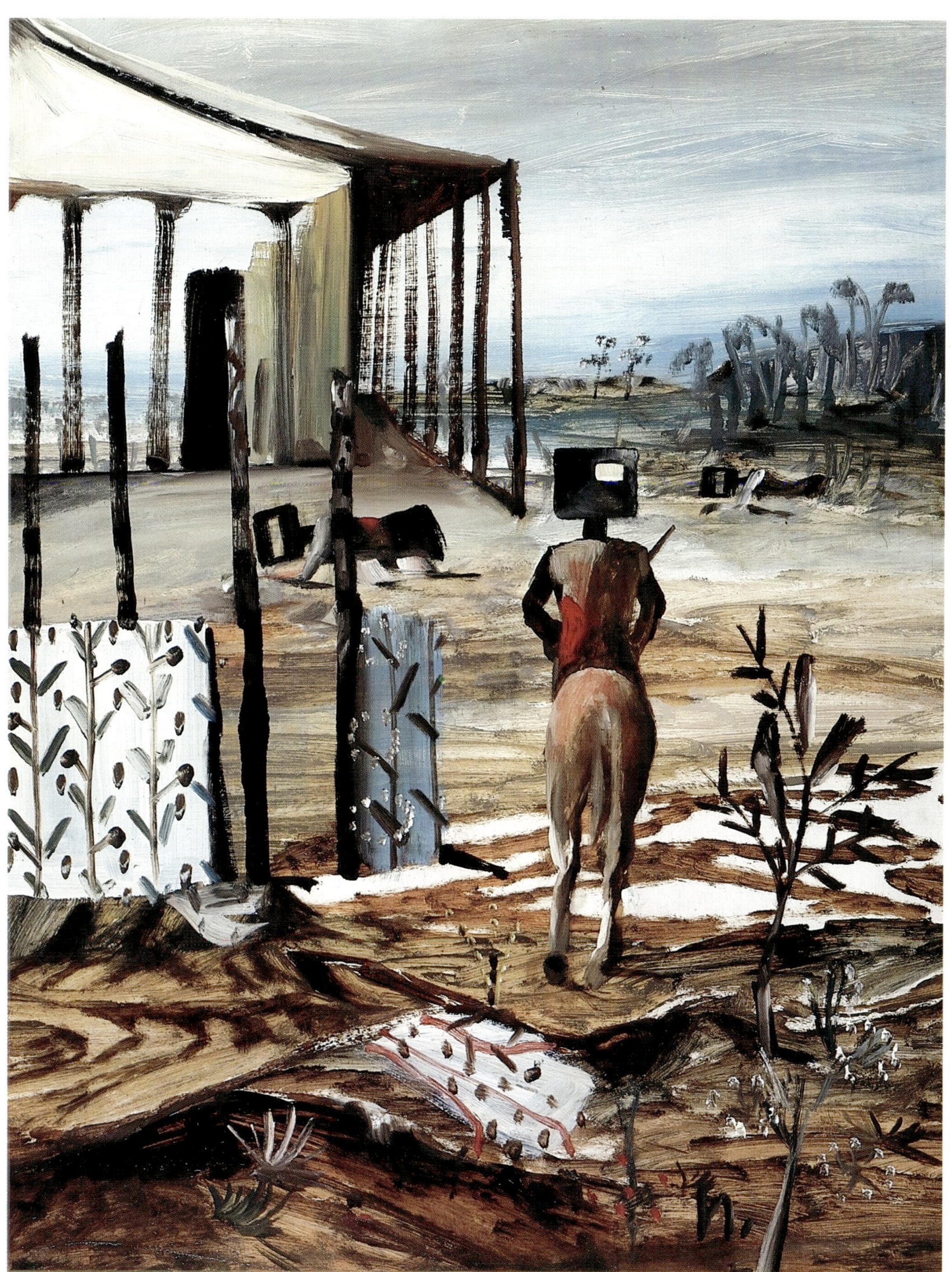

85   Sidney Nolan
1917–92
The Glenrowan siege 1955
synthetic polymer paint on board
91.5 × 71.0 cm

tragedy and violence. In landscapes of great beauty the human drama is played out with a direct, apparently untutored naivety comparable to Perceval's. This is made more distinctive by the use of the medium: ripolin-enamel paint.

Nolan's combination of narrative and symbol was exceptional. He continued to paint this mythical imagery after leaving Australia in the mid-1950s, extending it in another series to which *The Glenrowan siege* 1955 (plate 85) belongs. This work, painted in England, is a subdued re-interpretation of two paintings of 1946, *Glenrowan siege* and *Burning at Glenrowan* where, phoenix-like, a resurrected bushranger returns to survey the scene of his companions' bloody death at Mrs Jones' Glenrowan Hotel, the place of his own capture and arrest.

The 1946–7 Glenrowan paintings, although not recognised at the time of their creation, were of real importance to a sense of Australian culture, history and identity. Some, like John Reed, who was intimately connected with their making at Heide (in classic nineteenth-century Heidelberg School territory), appropriately saw them to be an 'authentic national vision'.[8]

Painting in Sydney and country New South Wales at the same time, Drysdale did not populate his landscapes with the mythic Burkes, Wills, Eliza Frasers, Scalons and Kellys of the past. Like Roberts and McCubbin some sixty years before, his subjects were stoic stockmen, station-hands and townsfolk – the 'outback' people of his own experience.

Maria 1950 (plate 86) belongs to this body of post-war genre which, unlike Nolan's Kelly paintings, was popularly and instantly acknowledged. It specifically harks back to a number of images, *The drover's wife* 1945, *The country woman* 1946, and *Woman in a landscape* 1949, in its character delineation of country types – in *Maria's* case, the outback cafe owner's wife. Drysdale was attempting to define a quintessential Australianness. Skating over the thin ice of sentimentality and theatricality, the best of these works show the means by which Drysdale achieved this – his indebtedness to the romanticism of the English artists Paul Nash and John Piper for mood making, Henry Moore for statuesque form and the surrealists for void. His closest Australian counterpart, Donald Friend, worked closely

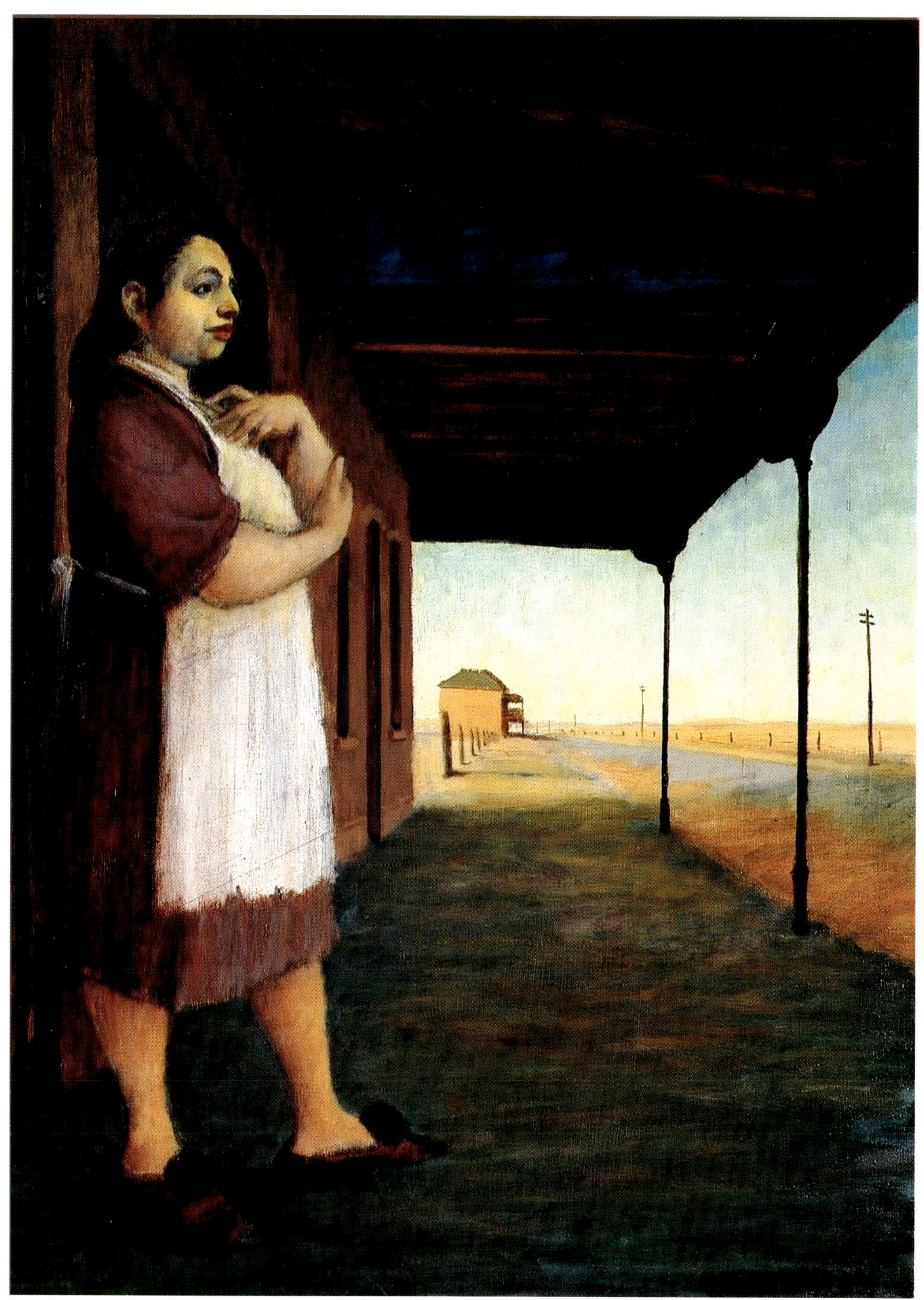

86   Russell Drysdale
1912–81
Maria 1950
oil on canvas
99.0 × 76.0 cm

with him at this time, sometimes painting the same neo-romantic subjects and with the same regard for traditional ways of drawing and painting.

Drysdale's work in this period, more so than Nolan's, manages to revive the notion of Australian subject painting in the tradition of McCubbin's *Down on his luck* 1889 and Roberts' *Shearing the rams* 1888–9. In 1890 Roberts wrote in defence of the latter: 'It seemed to me that I had there the best expression of my subject, a subject [expressing] the meaning and spirit of strong masculine [Australian] labour.'[9] Both artists seem to be after the same goal but where Nolan challenges our understanding of the past Drysdale confirms it. That is, Australianness is defined in relation to man's heroic struggle with the unyielding land.

Sir Keith Murdoch, an enthusiastic patron, had purchased *Maria* in 1951 after its return to Australia from the 1950 London exhibition. In a 1962 letter to Sir Keith, Drysdale described this painting, one of his 'Portraits in a landscape', in this way:

> It's a curious fact that the alien Greek cafekeeper has become a symbol of the Australian country town – whenever one goes out west there is always 'the dagoe's' to eat in. . . people with courage to work and save and give their children a better way of life in a new land. I've tried to express something of . . . that . . . in Maria . . . I wanted to give her strength and a quality of endurance, qualities which make it possible to overcome hardship, heat and loneliness . . . Perhaps there is a beauty in that . . . they are part of the future.[10]

The social realists and expressionist painters offered images of Australia as it was then, and the neo-romantic myth painters offered images as it was then – but also where it had been. The artists working consistently in any sort of mainstream surrealist manner: James Cant, Eric Thake, Herbert McClintock, and, most of all, James Gleeson, seem almost peripheral to this quest for vital indigenous Australian expression in the 1940s. They were seemingly detached from the period's search for an authentic national idiom in painting.

What the surrealist/symbolist tradition certainly

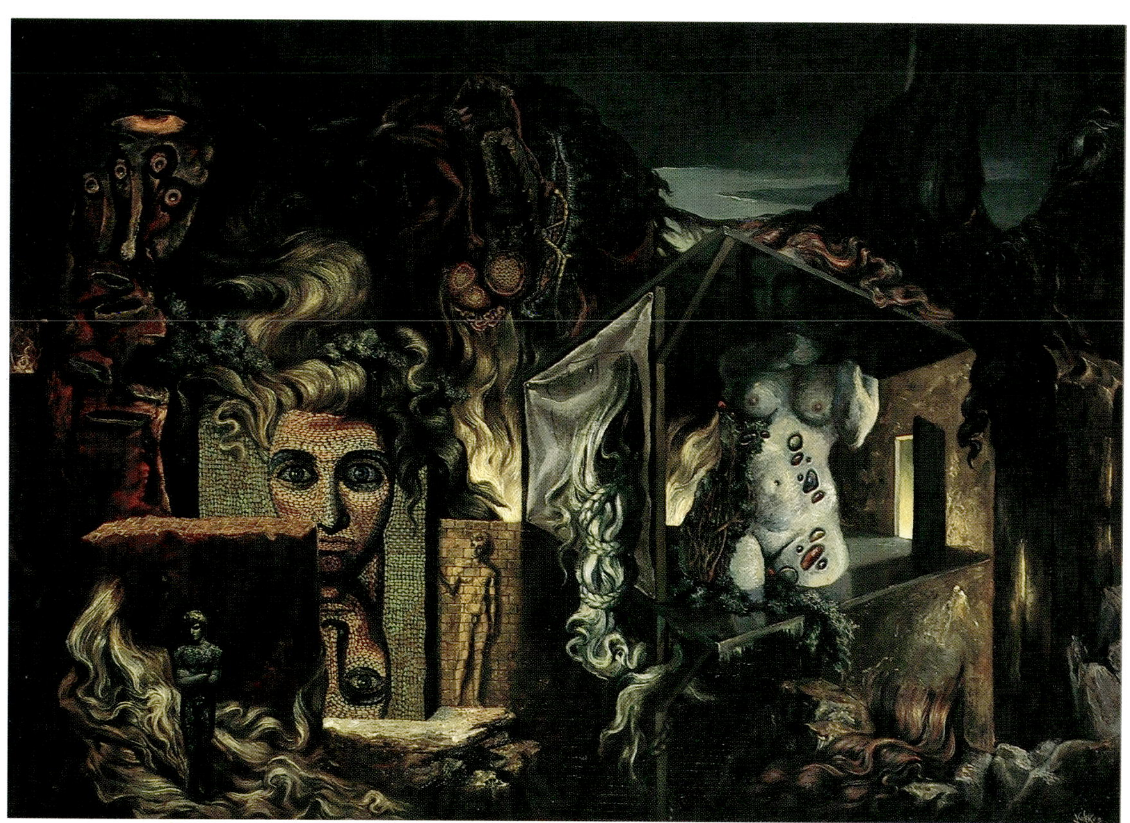

87 James Gleeson
born 1915
Gardens of the Night 1947
oil on canvas
72.0 × 102.0 cm

provided for Australian artistic life was a powerful intellectual, poetic, literary vocabulary. The ideas of Arthur Rimbaud, Henri Rousseau, André Breton and Viktor Lowenfeld were important here, as elsewhere, for their liberating effect on the imaginative processes.

Surrealist painting itself was seductive and exciting to Australian artists and although it was strongly represented in Sir Keith Murdoch's 1939 exhibition (arranged by Basil Burdett and entitled 'French and British Modern Art') it was, in practice, explored only by a few. Australian surrealism can mainly be seen addressing contemporary Australian life in terms of reflecting the inward and private responses of individuals to international fascism and the horror of global conflict.

That 1939 exhibition of contemporary European art included Salvador Dali's *L'homme Fleur*, a painting that antagonised the general public but which gave emphasis to surrealists Eric Thake and James Gleeson, who shared the prize in the Contemporary Art Society exhibition of that year. Its strong presence perhaps also gave local weight to the surrealist paintings of Ivor Francis, Herbert McClintock, James Cant and the faint-hearted surrealist exercises of Albert Tucker and Peter Purves Smith, as well as influencing Russell Drysdale and others.

Recent exhibitions re-evaluating the Australian experience of surrealism have been revealing of its quality and diversity.[11] One artist who made major statements at that time and who has continued to work in the idiom since, is James Gleeson (born 1915). His private response to the destructiveness and chaos of the Second World War was shrill horror. Gleeson's inspired paintings of apocalyptic madness, *The Sower* 1944 and *The Citadel* 1945, are testaments of humanity turned against itself. They are the most significant anti-war statements by an Australian artist.

In 1947 the Contemporary Art Society was in cessation. After the peace of 1945 and into the early 1950s the lifting of wartime restrictions created a wholesale dispersal of Australian artists. Many made for overseas, amongst them Josl Bergner, James Wigley, James Cant, Noel Counihan, Albert Tucker, Sidney Nolan, Donald Friend, David Strahan, Russell Drysdale and James Gleeson.

Gleeson's *Gardens of the Night* 1947 (plate 87), the year of the important Paris surrealist exhibition, was painted

at William Ohley's country place, 'The Abbey',
Hertfordshire. It was exhibited the following year in
London in a group show with a fellow Australian, the
sculptor Robert Klippel, and the British artist Lucien
Freud.

Gardens of the Night is a crowded, sensual and erotic
constructed dream. Potent references to classical antiquity
mingle with metaphors of sexuality in a jewel-like theatre
set. Images reflect themselves, become dissected and
fragmented. Doors open into chambers of the mind. There
are states of metamorphosis, portents of menace. It is a
vivid exploration of another reality at work and of the
human subconscious that owes as much to Hieronymous
Bosch as to Salvador Dali.

The late 1940s and on into the 1950s saw the perennial
testing by Australian artists of themselves on the European
scene. But the relationship had changed. Drysdale and
Nolan (and subsequently Arthur Boyd) in particular were
exhibiting their Australian imagery and achievement on
the international stage and, for better or for worse, not
without success. For others, not so stridently identifiable
in their Australianness, this was not always the case.

1 Basil Burdett, 'Painter finds Urban Life Rich in Colour', *Herald*,
   Melbourne, 16 September 1937, p. 10.
2 *Contemporary Art Society of Australia: Sixth Annual Exhibition Catalogue*,
   September 1944, 3, 'Personal Statements'.
3 *Angry Penguins*, Melbourne, September, 1943, editorial, 'On the Subject
   of Policy'.
4 Max Harris, *Angry Penguins*, (exhibition catalogue), London, Hayward
   Gallery, 1988, introduction, p. 21.
5 Ursula Hoff, *The Art of Arthur Boyd*, London, André Deutsch, 1986,
   part 1, p. 3. Hoff suggests that a similar blond-haired figure in *The
   gargoyles* 1944 is Perceval.
6 Harris, *Angry Penguins*, pp. 23–4.
7 Sidney Nolan in *The Australian Artist*, Victorian Artists' Society, vol. 1,
   part 4, winter, 1948, p. 20.
8 John Reed, 'Nolan's Kelly Paintings', *Art and Australia*, Sydney, vol. 5,
   no. 2, September 1964, p. 443.
9 Tom Roberts, Letter to the Editor, *Argus*, Melbourne, 4 July 1890, p. 10,
   col. 4.
10 Letter from Rose Bay 10 January 1962 to Sir Keith Murdoch, in the
   possession of ICI Australia Ltd.
11 In particular Christopher Chapman's 1993 exhibition, *Surrealism in
   Australia*, National Gallery of Australia, 1993.

THE CULTURE OF CITIES

The 1950s and Beyond

Melbourne art of the 1940s had been subjective, autobiographical and spontaneous. That of the 1950s and 1960s was to be cooler and more objective again. The generation following the Angry Penguins in Melbourne continued to paint stories about human existence – with a significant difference. The individual states of mind expressed in much of the art were no longer those of the artist uniquely but of man (and woman) at large. French existentialism and Zen were favoured philosophies, many studios having a thumbed copy of Eugen Herigel's *Zen and the Art of Archery*. In art the persona of the lonely or alienated city-dweller of French existentialism and the serenely receptive exponent of Zen superseded the 1940s artist–creator who had possessed a haptic sensibility and been engulfed by life.

Through the fifties Australia continued to take its direction from Europe but at the same time discovered cultural affiliations with the United States. Whereas, well into the fifties, Europe struggled to overcome rationing and shortages of all consumer goods, America's glamorous style of conspicuous consumption was the envy of Europe. And the prosperity that distinguished post-war America also distinguished Australia.

Prosperity in the first decades post-war ensured the expansion of the middle classes. Many more Australians had money to spend on houses, education and overseas travel. Commonwealth ties made for easy entry to the United Kingdom (work permits had not yet been made a requirement for a long stay) but Australians went also to France, Spain, Italy and northern Europe and a small, increasing number circled the globe via Canada and the United States.

Through the fifties and sixties Australian cities underwent an enormous change, their third transformation since the 1860s. Nearly every family had a car, and cars increasingly ruled the cities. This was the time of the Holden and big American cars – Fords, Dodges, Chevrolets and Pontiacs. The period saw the beginnings of freeways, glass-sided high-rise buildings, supermarkets, fast-food chains and vast new outer suburban developments.

The age profile of Australian society changed as the post-war baby boomers reached maturity and began to make their presence felt. Just as, in a statistical population graph, this generation was a decided bulge, so was it socially an aggressive new phenomenon. Youth declared its separateness from the older generation through a peer group style of speech (a featureless mumble of trailing sentences and hip jargon), music, clothes, hair and aggravatingly different politics. The baby boomers vetoed the older generation's decision to join the United States in its war against North Vietnam, they voted for the Labor Party and so helped to put the Liberal Party out of office for the first time in more than twenty years. Unlike their elders (and unlike their children) the baby boomers took financial security for granted and undertook a lifestyle of spending without feelings of guilt or anxiety. The American cult of youth made a big impression here. Young Australians listened to United States rock-n-roll, dressed American, watched Hollywood films and, in the 1960s, dressed in the pert style of London's Carnaby Street and listened to the Beatles and Rolling Stones. Films (especially American films) were a vital feature of youth culture. The drive-in, where from rows of darkened cars young people watched a film projected on a huge outdoor screen, was a short-lived feature of the age. Television, which was to be the universal medium of culture from the sixties onwards, arrived in 1955 – in time for the Olympic Games in 1956.

Australia participated in the worldwide expansion of university education and academic specialisation. In the 1950s and 1960s a spate of publications appeared with new interpretations of Australian history and the history of Australian art. Such were R.M. Crawford's *Australia* (1952), John Douglas Pringle's *Australian Accent* (1958), Russel Ward's *The Australian Legend* (1958) and *Australia* (1965). Bernard Smith's *European Vision and the South Pacific*, which was to be deservedly famous outside as well as within Australia, appeared in 1960. W.K. Hancock's *Australia* (1930) was reprinted twice, in 1961 and 1966. C.M.H. Clark's *A History of Australia* was published in 1962 and his *A Short History of Australia* in 1963. Others in an impressive list were Bernard Smith's *Australian Painting 1788–1960* (1962) and a new edition of his *Place, Taste and Tradition* (1963), Geoffrey C. Bolton's *A Thousand Miles Away: A History* (1963), Donald Horne's *The Lucky Country: Australia* (1964) and Geoffrey Blainey's *The Tyranny of Distance* (1966). Robert Hughes' *The Art of Australia*, published and suppressed in 1966, reappeared in 1970. In view of this spate of publications, the sixties could seem a latter-day age of reason when scholars promulgated myths of Australianness. It was also a period of biographical dictionaries. *The Australian Dictionary of Biography*'s first volume appeared in 1966, McCulloch's *Encyclopedia of Australian Art* in 1968. A.A. Phillips, Daniel Thomas, James Gleeson, Rex and Thea Rienits, Alan McCulloch, Margaret Plant and Patrick McCaughey made significant contributions to the discussion of Australian art and Australian culture in the period.

Australian art of the post-war decades again emphasised modernity: modern design, contemporary colours, modern life and youth. The vision was not specific to Australia: the urban settings could be any city in the western world, and the image of youth was western youth. On the whole the expression was ironic and otherwise was saved from sentiment by a certain impersonality. Similarities were noted in the figurative paintings of a young Sydney painter Charles Blackman (born 1928) and those of two older returned servicemen – John Brack (born 1920) of Melbourne and Robert Dickerson (born 1924) of Sydney. Blackman and Dickerson were taken up by John Reed, who showed their work at the Museum of Modern Art and Design in Melbourne. Post-war, the styles of abstraction and semi-abstraction became more expressionist in the paintings of Roger Kemp (Melbourne) and John Olsen (Sydney). Since Australia as a country, and Australian art, had entered a period when the tendency was to look beyond Australia – with place rather less important than it had been – it is curious that from the late 1950s the styles shared by artists of Sydney and Melbourne were debated as if Melbourne were to be identified by the figurative and Sydney by the abstract tradition.

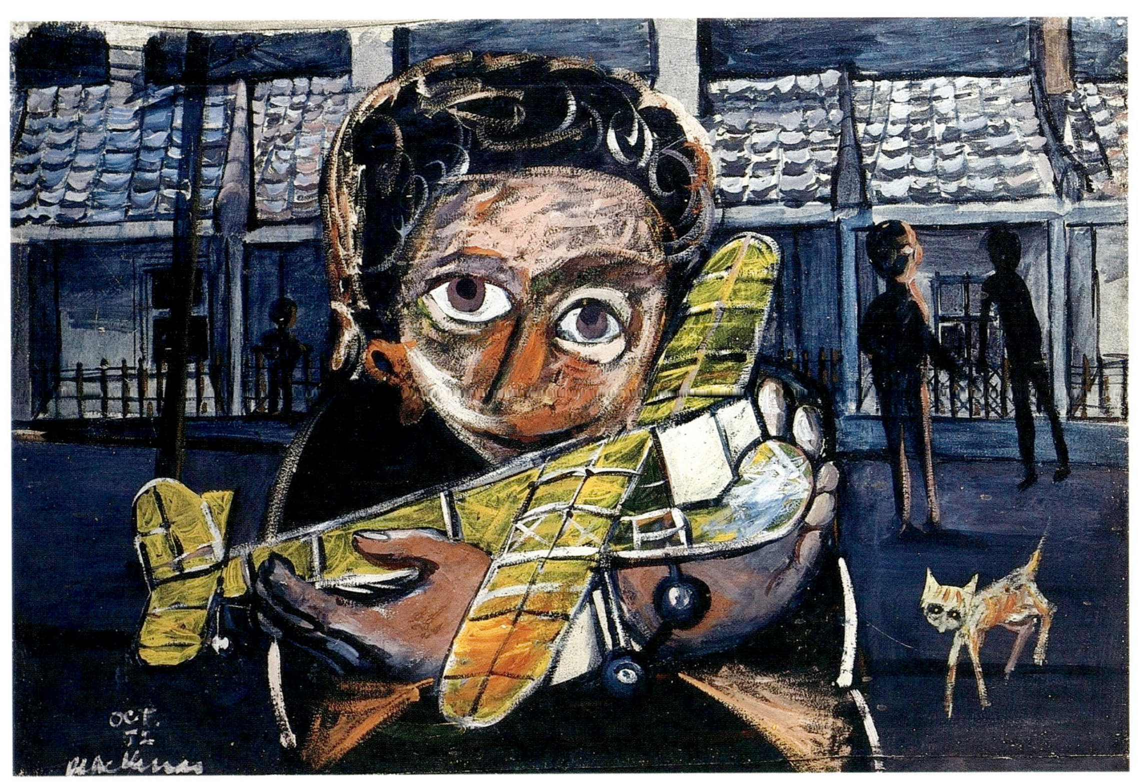

88   Charles Blackman
born 1928
Boy with model airplane 1952
tempera on canvas laid down on board
61.0 × 91.0 cm

Blackman's *Boy with model airplane* 1952 (plate 88) is far less threatening than his schoolgirl images of the same time. Whereas the schoolgirls are obscurely threatened by the black shadows in empty de Chirico-style cityscapes, the boy hugging his homemade aeroplane in an inner-city street is enjoying a child's pleasurable creativity. Blackman crafted his painting in a sympathetically childlike manner by cutting and pasting the canvas crooked on a masonite support and painting his image over the hems of canvas at top and bottom. The child's flesh, the balsa-wood aeroplane and the cat in the evening street are tenderly painted in layers of loosely applied, sweet colours.

Dickerson's dispassionate *The steps* c. 1958 (plate 89) is thinly painted, sparse in colour, and the image too is spartan. A flight of stone steps provides a theatrical motif on which the three figures, or rather three sets of figures, are separated from one another on different levels. At the bottom is a child in a ragged jersey eating a carrot. A derelict lies sleeping halfway up. At the top two figures – shoppers? – pass between the high walls of the city. The implication is that these people are separated not only from one another but from the modern city which is impersonal, hard and overscaled.

John Brack evolved an image of a type of Australian male, wooden headed, lantern jawed, serious faced (even when smiling) and inarticulate. The type is evident in his self-portraits and in drawings and paintings of people in the streets and about the town. His pencil drawing *Youth* 1954 (plate 90) could be Melbourne's version in the 1950s of Michelangelo's adolescent David – the same huge hands, strong neck, small head. A young spiv dressed up for the night and with brushed-back hair, *Youth* was observed by the artist, as by any casual observer in the public domain, hanging out on a street corner or riding on a tram. Brack showed the youth isolated during a moment of concentration, lighting a cigarette in his cupped hands. 'What I am interested in is people,' said Brack in 1962, 'how they live, how they behave, *how they get the faces they deserve*, how they can bear to put up with the life which seems so curiously tragic.'[1] He was a painter of ideas:

> Here we are . . . in Australia, made to think that a
> painter should be always passionately expressing his

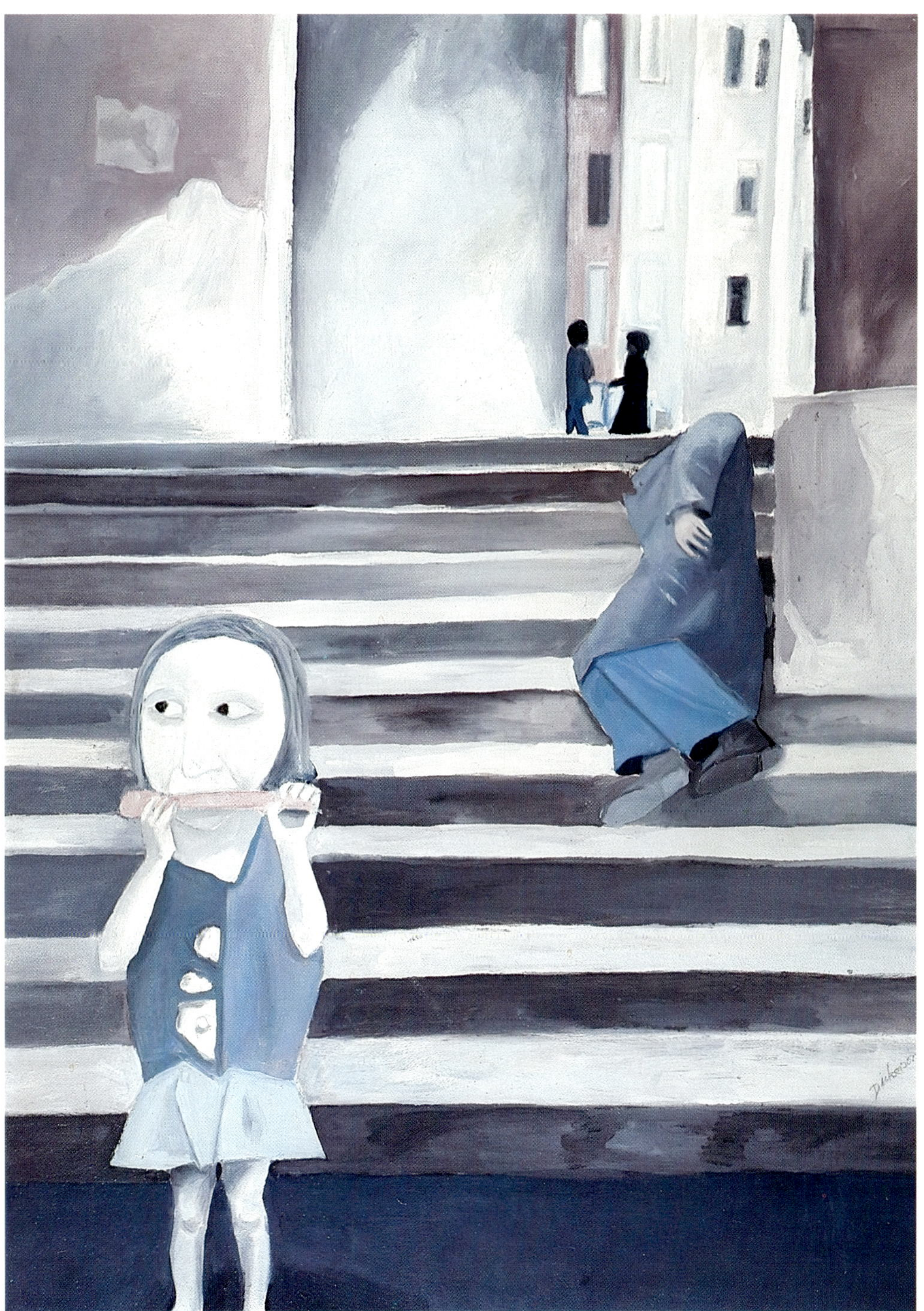

89   Robert Dickerson
born 1924
The steps (1958)
oil on board
120.5 × 88.5 cm

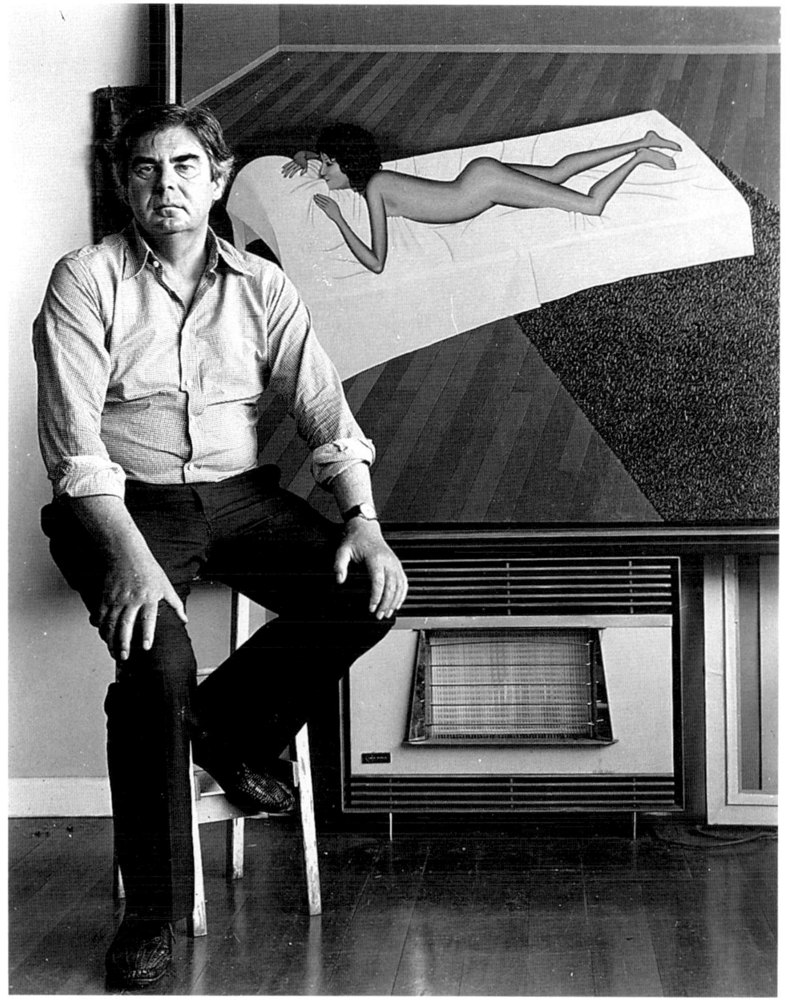

feelings, but I am for the side of the rational, and the form that I want to give to the picture is one which expresses the feelings and ideas that are associated with that subject.

He started with drawings of subjects that interested him. Not all resulted in completed paintings, perhaps because Brack did not invariably establish a form for his idea that he found aesthetically fitting. For example, there were few paintings of suburban streetscapes, although in the splendid drawing *Union Road* 1961 (plate 91) Brack had the perfect image of regimented life. Perhaps he did not see the suburbs as constricted. Union Road rises up the image into free space. The empty margin of the image

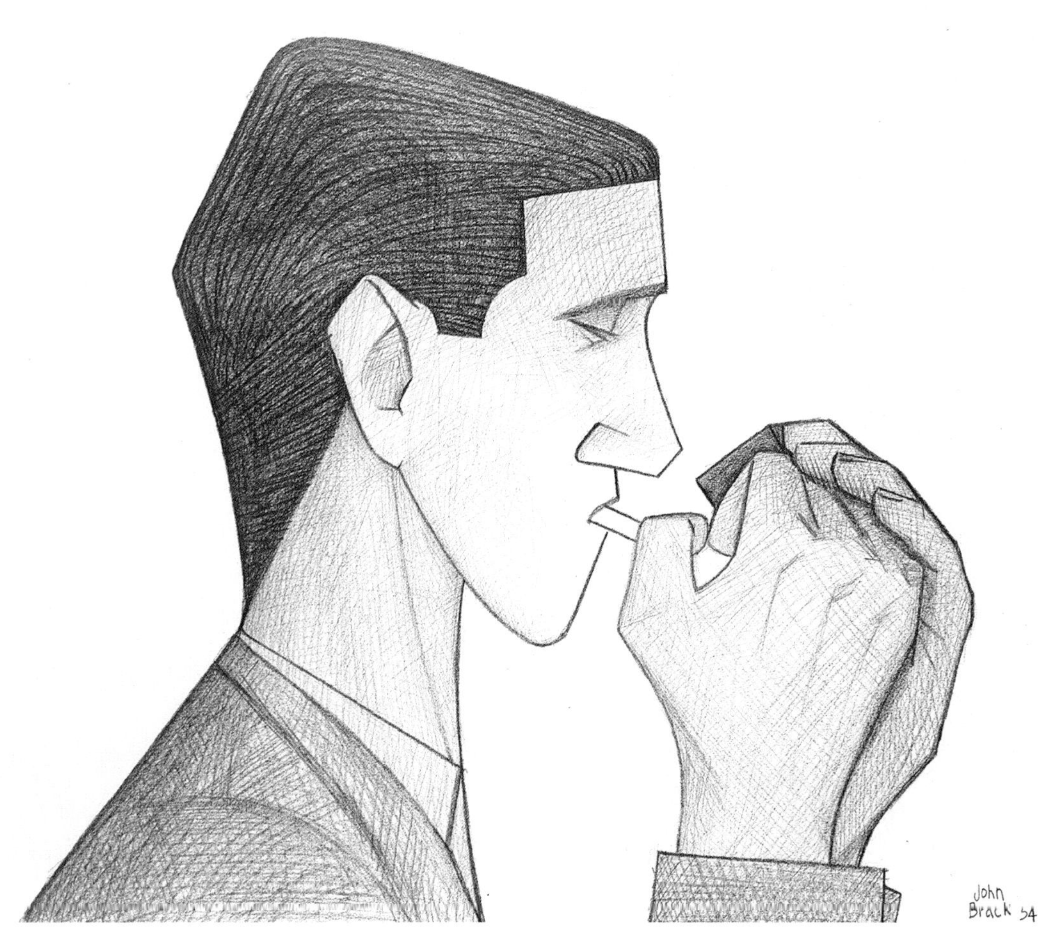

90   John Brack
born 1920
Youth 1954
pencil on paper
34.5 × 42.5 cm

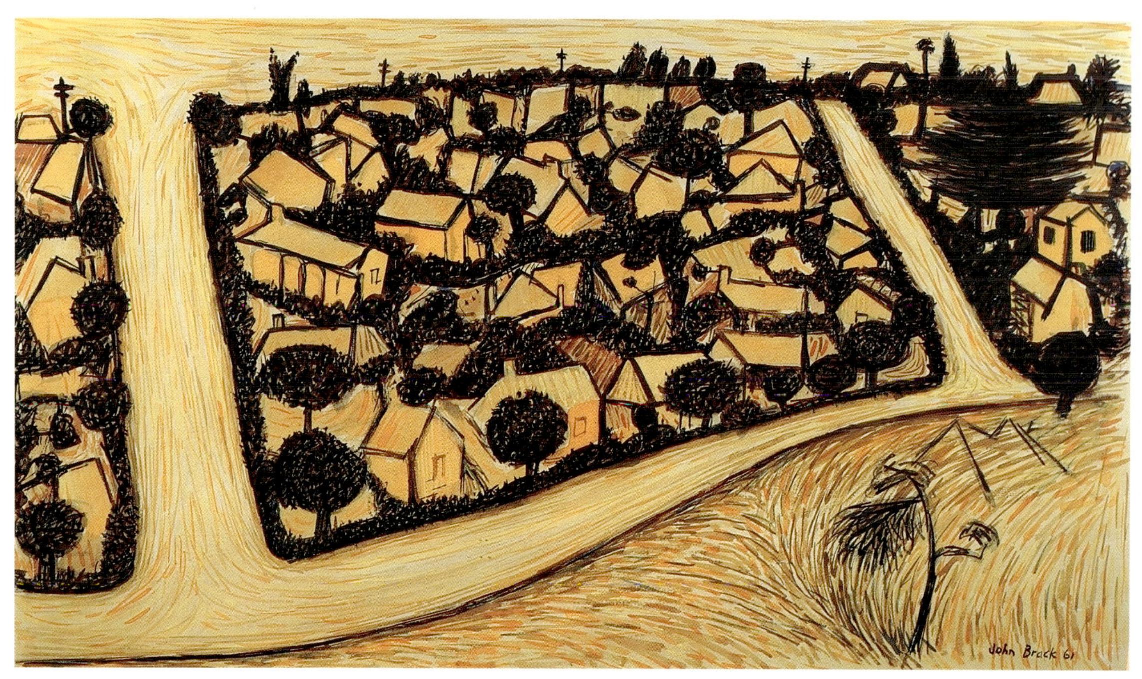

91   John Brack
born 1920
Union Road 1961
watercolour on paper
43.0 × 73.5 cm

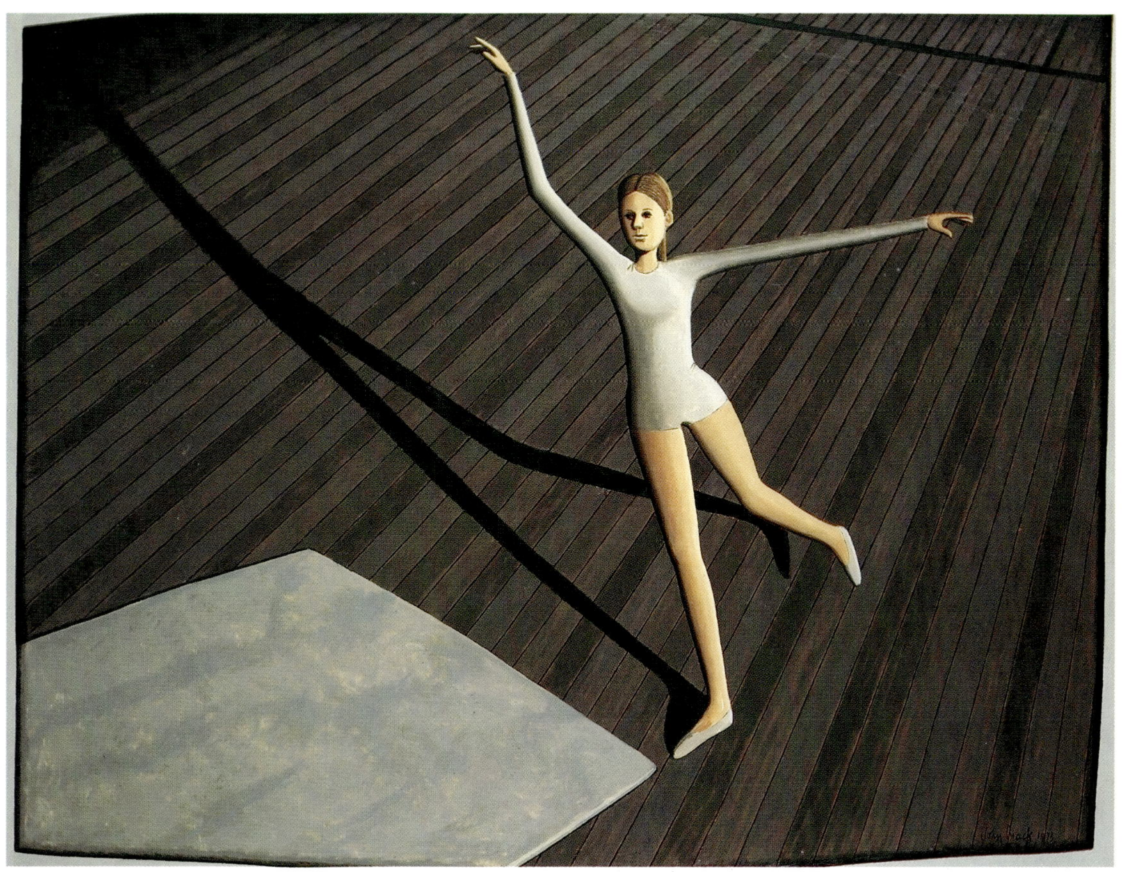

92   John Brack
born 1920
Arabesque 1973
oil on canvas
89.5 × 116.0 cm

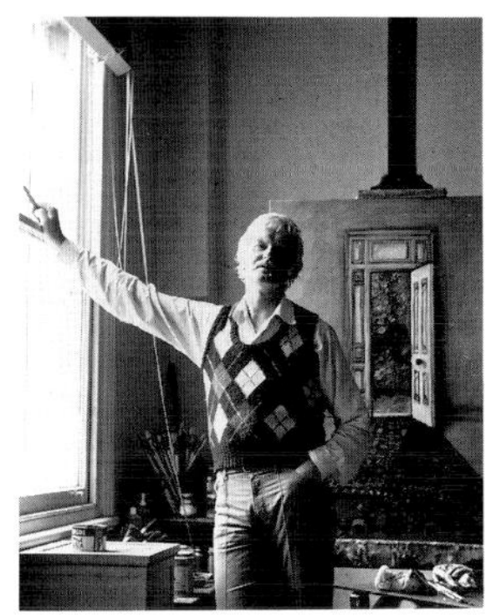

Michael Shannon in his studio in the 1970s.
Photograph by Richard Beck

contradicts the idea of an endlessly continuing garden suburb locked within a grid of roads, though ostensibly that was the main theme of the drawing.

Brack's career extended to art education. After serving in the artillery during the Second World War, he studied at the National Gallery School, sharing a city studio with Fred Williams, a fellow student. In 1949 he joined the staff of the National Gallery of Victoria, gave lunchtime lectures and accompanied a Travelling Art Exhibition around the country. For a decade between 1952 and 1962 he lectured regularly at the Council of Adult Education and University of Melbourne and was art master (part time) at Melbourne Grammar School. His published art criticisms and his art lectures – well thought out, incisive and indicative of an evolving aesthetic – addressed a broad cross-section of people in Melbourne. Brack's thinking, as well as his visual observation, was directed to the society in which he lived, exploring in particular its rituals. He held steadily to an unromantic approach. The accumulation over decades of works displaying his particular sardonic perception has had an evolutionary effect on Australian art and society which cannot be claimed for many artists who have looked to the art world rather than the larger community.

The girl gymnast in Brack's painting *Arabesque* 1973 (plate 92) is framed within the slightly bowed shape of a television screen. Her performance is one of those very many demonstrations of human skill and ingenuity which are the champion fare of television. Brack's pictures include whole series dealing with spectator sports in which he describes the performances of jockeys, ballroom dancers and nudes with clinical attention to the social genre they represented.

An air of dispassion is apparent in the studio interior *Composition with saw* 1958 (plate 93) by Michael Shannon (born 1927). Shannon was without Brack's curiosity about people and the set-pieces of their lives. In spite of its provocative title the work seems purely formal, a still-life arrangement. Shannon was one of a number of artists who studied with Jeffrey Smart in Europe after the war, taking lessons from Fernard Léger between 1949 and 1952. In this painting the hand saw (which in another artist's work could be a surreal note in an otherwise standard interior) is domesticated to conform with the modern austere lines, fashionable acid colours and thickly outlined

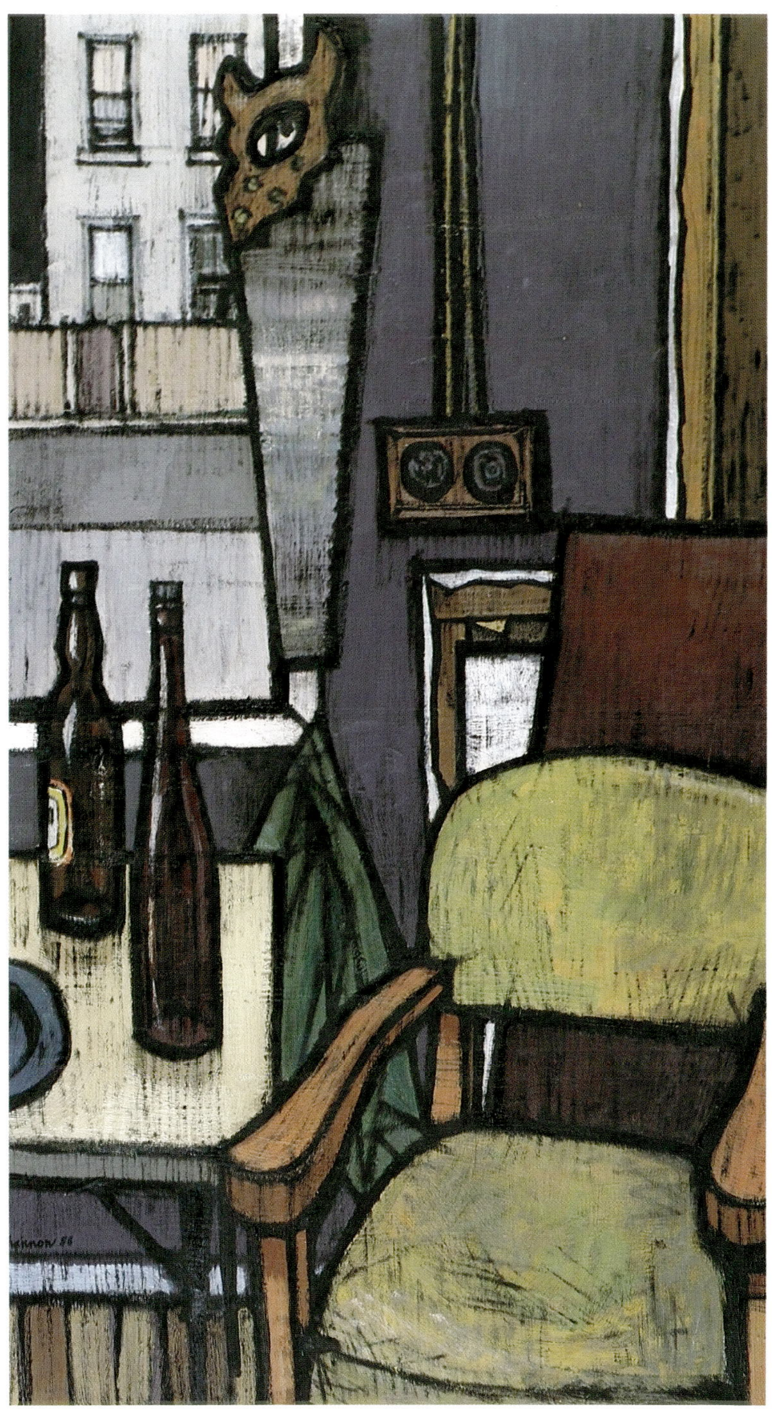

93   Michael Shannon
born 1927
Composition with saw 1958
oil on board
107.0 × 61.0 cm

shapes of the composition. Inserted in the composition as a design element to break the suggestion of depth between window and the street outside and so maintain the flatness of the image, the function of the hand saw is not literary but formal.

The passage of art in the fifties and sixties was marked by two events, the Antipodean group's exhibition of figurative art and their manifesto of 1959 and the Field exhibition of hard-edge, non-figurative paintings and sculptures at the National Gallery of Victoria in 1968. These events, nearly ten years apart, represented two positions on which contemporary artists were divided.

The Antipodean argument began in earnest in February 1959, when John Reed took to Sydney his exhibition 'Modern Australian Art: A Melbourne Collection of Paintings and Drawings' from the collection of the pretentious-sounding, actually quite small and informal, Museum of Modern Art of Australia. Sydney critics were not enthusiastic, and while to some readers in Melbourne the comments seemed fair, others found them downright critical. Wallace Thornton's remark that the art had 'a decadent, inbred, "hill-billy flavour" of tenth-rate German expressionism mixed with a dash of Picasso and at times reverting to the Australian primitive school'[2] was remembered by Bernard Smith whereas – as historian Gary Catalano subsequently pointed out – Elwyn Lynn's and Laurie Thomas' favourable responses to paintings by Arthur Boyd were not.[3]

The quarrel, starting in rivalry between Melbourne and Sydney, was argued as homegrown figurative versus imported abstract art. It could as well be seen as commencing in a difference of opinion between the humanist circle cultivated by John Reed and the outside practitioners of contemporary art. In the late 1950s Reed was active again in the art community after a quiet period. He had inherited some money, established the Museum of Modern Art of Australia, and was busily weaving a larger web of connections with artists and writers around Australia. His circle of artists included some whose style was non-figurative and others who did not live in Melbourne, however the tendency was figurative and the place Melbourne.

The historian Bernard Smith (who had moved from

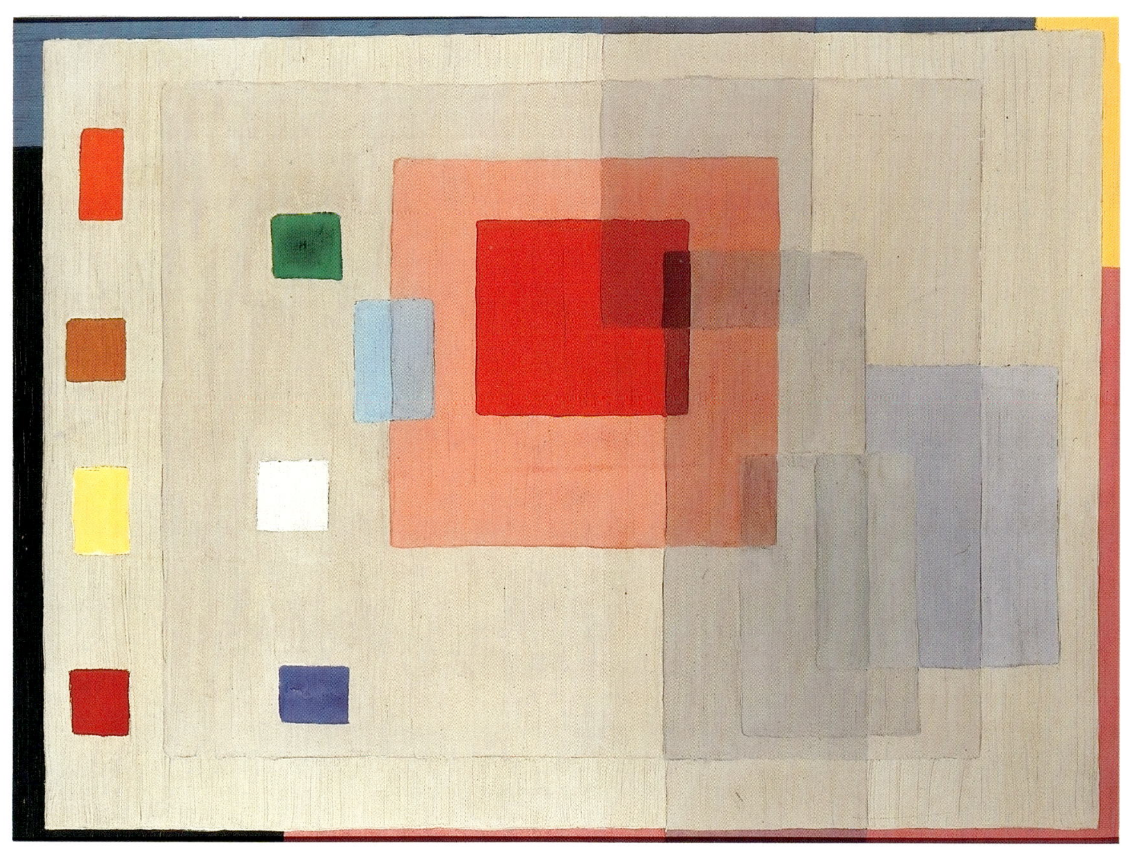

94   Ralph Balson
1890–1964
Constructive painting (1951)
oil on board
61.0 × 82.0 cm

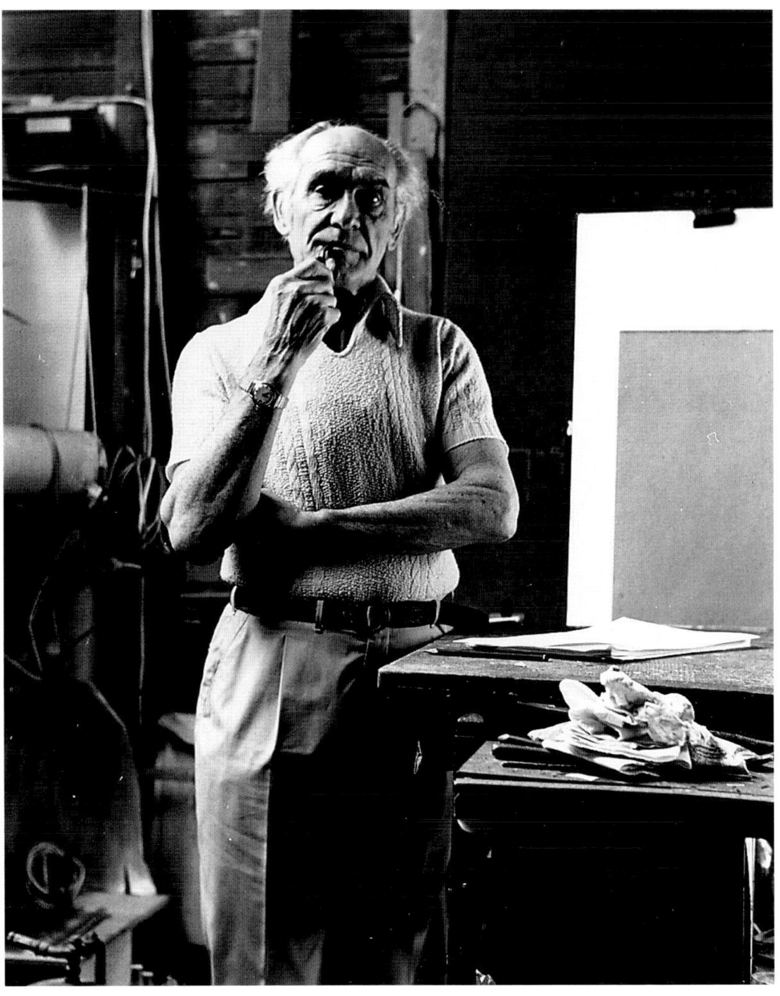

Sydney to Melbourne) became the spokesman for an
Australian figurative tradition:

> Several of us in Melbourne at the time felt that if
> figurative painting was going to survive in this
> country as a creative activity some sort of vigorous
> counter-attack was necessary, otherwise most of the
> individuality that had developed in Australian
> painting during the preceding twenty years would
> be swamped by a provincial form of American abstract
> expressionism with a good public relations machine
> behind it. Sydney was already beginning to look, in
> terms of its art, rather like a south-western suburb
> of San Francisco.[4]

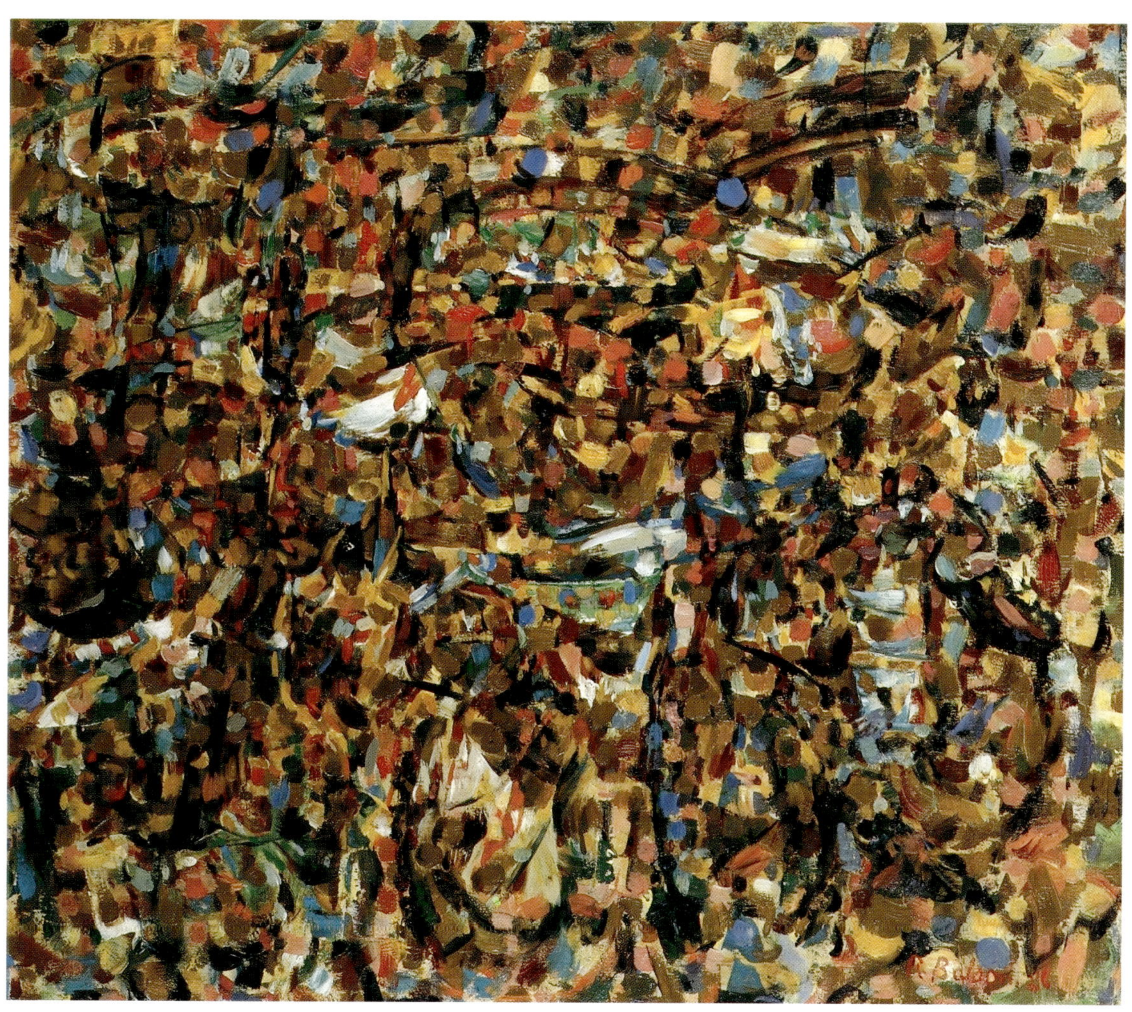

95   Ralph Balson
1890–1964
Non-objective painting 1956
synthetic polymer paint on plywood panel
63.0 × 73.4 cm

Smith got together the eight artists who formed the Antipodean group and wrote their manifesto. Far from the opposition having the better publicity machine, the Antipodeans had the edge. Because of Smith they had a cause, whereas the opposition was abstract – a concept advanced by Smith which in real life had to be a nebulous group without a central organisation.

The so-called imported styles opposed by the Antipodeans included the pure abstract art of older painter Ralph Balson (1890–1964), whose flat constructions of colour rectangles, painted in the 1940s and early 1950s, helped to establish the terms for hard-edge abstraction in the late 1960s. Space, in a work such as *Constructive painting* c. 1951 (plate 94), was a literal layering of transparent and opaque planes of colour over and beside one another: a step further towards controlling the potentially endless, illusory field which cubism had interrupted by geometric planes. (A similar literal depth was attempted by Robert Klippel in abstract–expressionist paintings of the 1950s in which space was actual layers of paint and glaze over paper.) In the mid-fifties Balson broke from geometry, painting fields of small patches of colour. The subject of *Non-objective painting* 1956 (plate 95) is the physical and visual effects produced by seemingly random clusters of colours, varying depths of illusory space, tighter and more open areas, and changes in weight and movement between parts of the composition. In reducing art to the physical object and the phenomena of vision, Balson anticipated the aesthetics of young 1960s artists.

Among the older artists who had been working in semi-abstract styles since the 1930s were the three Sydney painters Godfrey Miller, Frank Hinder (1906–92) and John Passmore. Hinder's style, as exemplified by the painting *Flight E. M. 513* 1956 (plate 96), was futurist (descriptive of movement) rather than cubist, and led into his own and others' kinetic sculpture rather than into the abstract painting styles of the 1950s and 1960s. John Passmore (1904–84) taught a number of the abstract and semi-abstract painters of the fifties and sixties, among them John Olsen, Brett Whiteley and Yvonne Audette. Works by Passmore, such as *Miller's Point* (plate 97), painted around 1952, were notably less tightly structured than the works of Cossington Smith, Hinder or Miller. Underneath the melting planes of muddy colours are the

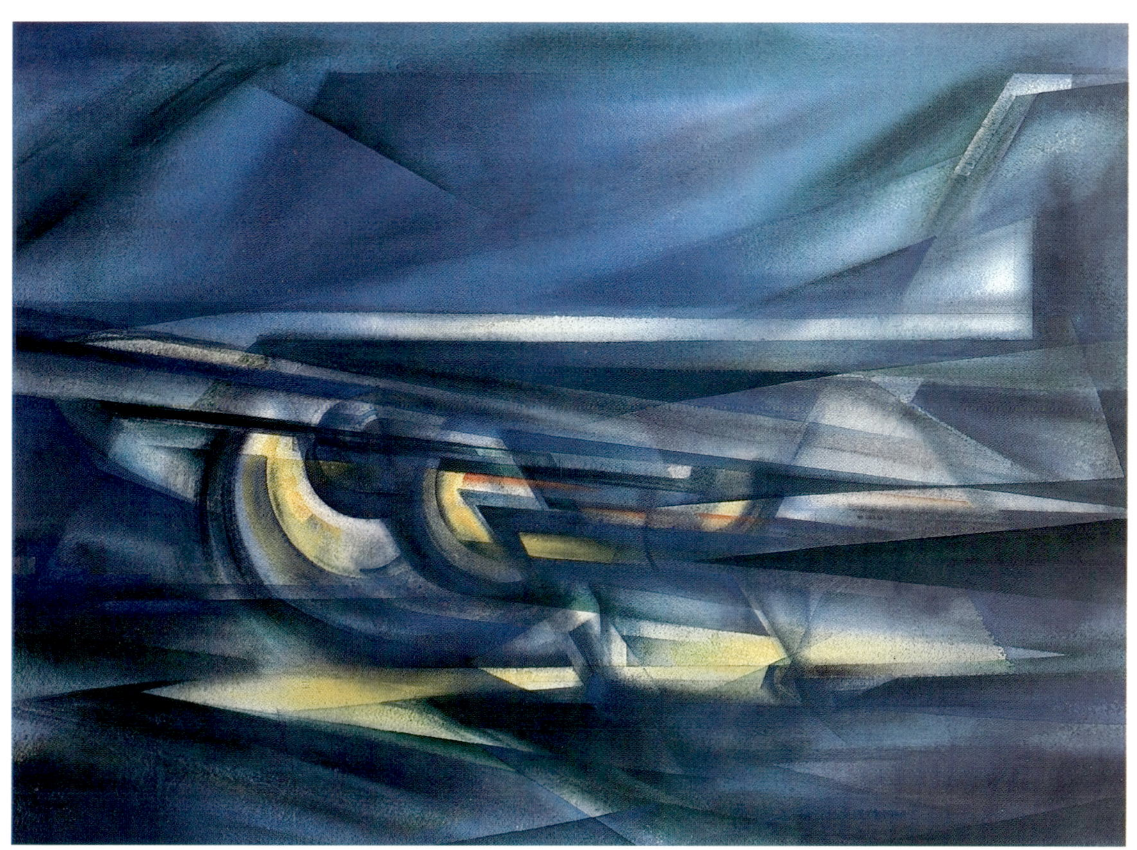

96   Frank Hinder
1906–92
Flight E.M. 513 1956
casein on paper
53.3 × 74.5 cm

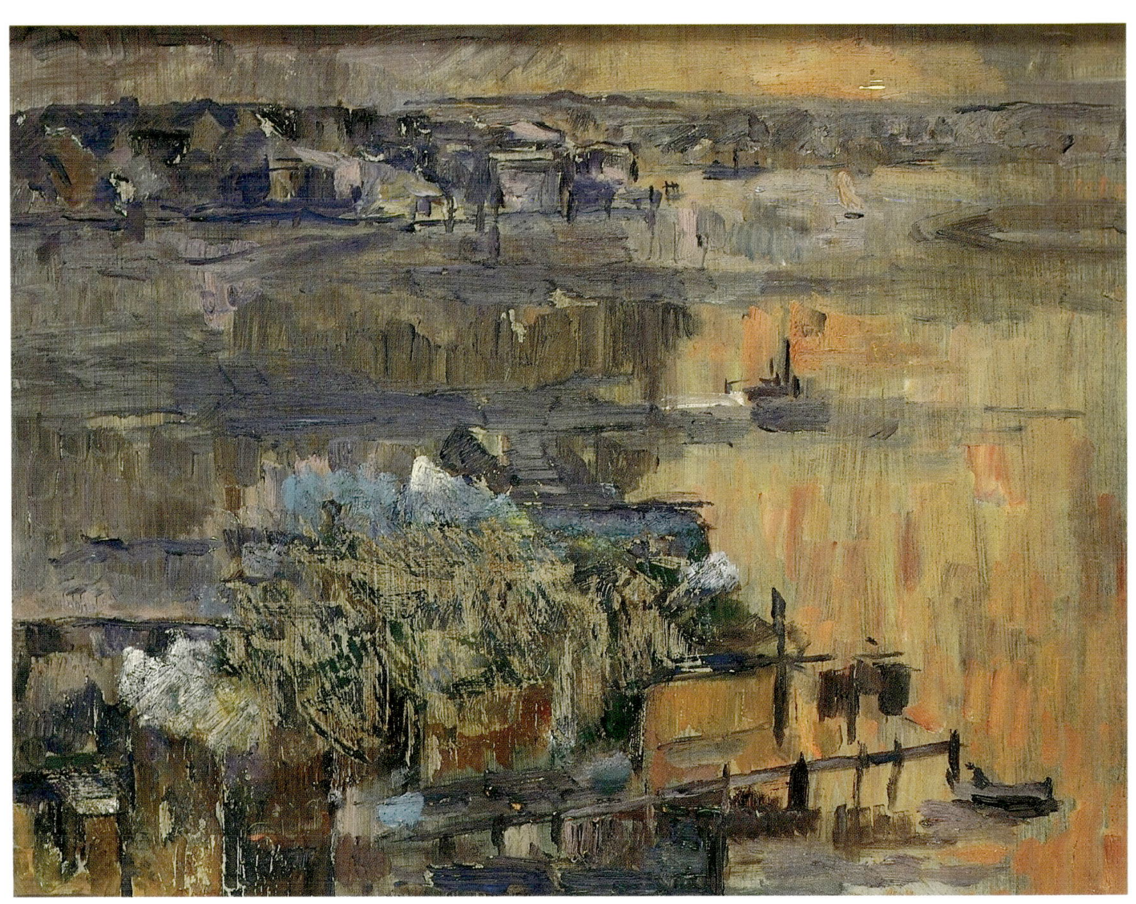

97 John Passmore
1904–84
Miller's Point (1952)
oil on board
46.0 × 60.5 cm

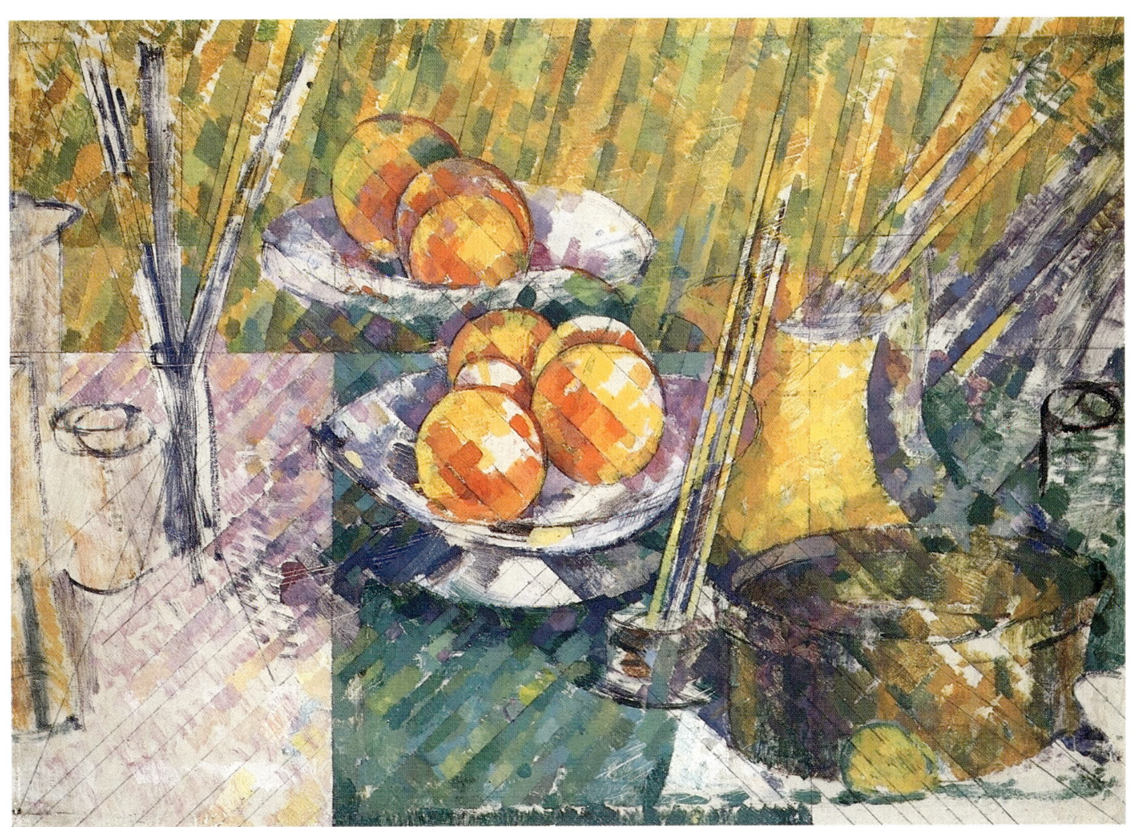

98   Godfrey Miller
1893–1964
Still life with fruit (1953)
oil on canvas
44.5 × 63.0 cm

Clifton Pugh in 1977.
Pugh often depicted
nature with a surreal or
naive guise.

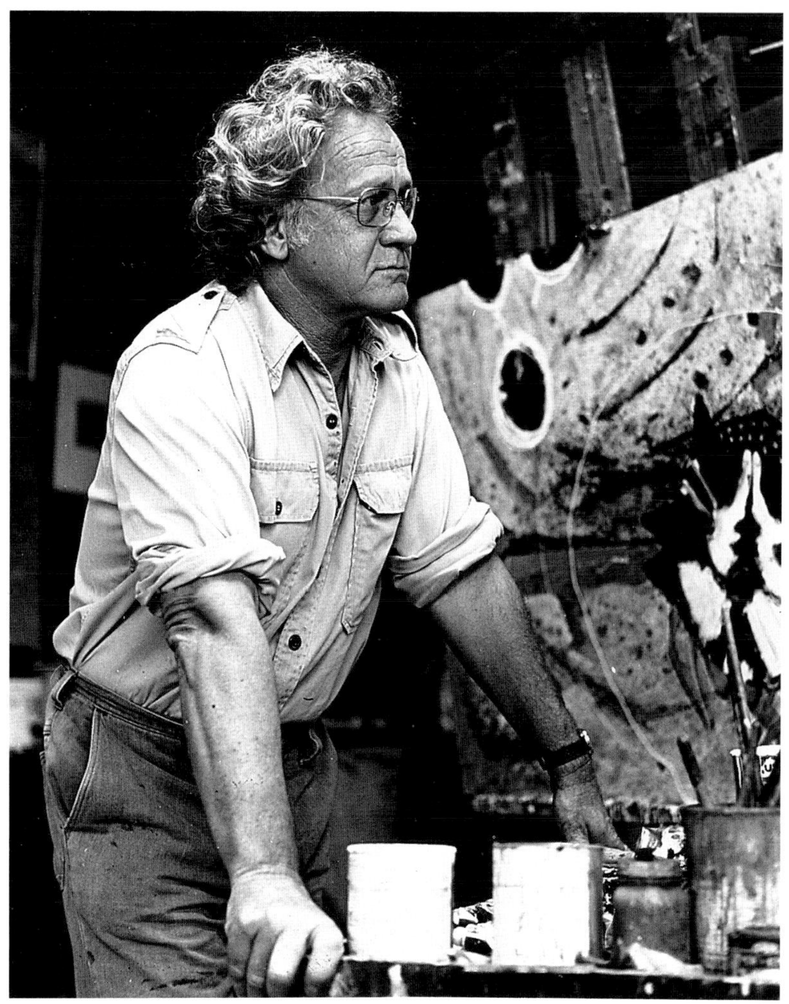

Photograph by Richard Beck

remnants of a Cezanne-derived system of planes. For the
younger painters the loose, comparatively formless
composition, the earth colours and accentuated textures
were stimulating influences.

Godfrey Miller (1893–1964) had the reputation of being
a lone and difficult man, one who was admired in Sydney
for the obsessive qualities of his work and life. Though
he painted physical objects of nude studies, still lifes, urban
and landscapes, the colours and forms were those he
decided. Nature was bypassed, an excuse for a passionate
delineation of tiny geometric planes. The energy of a work
such as *Still life with fruit* c. 1953 (plate 98) is from a force
outside the objects we recognise as 'natural'. Fruit,
casserole, jug and brushes are crystallised by the driving
force of myriads of parallel lines shafting through the

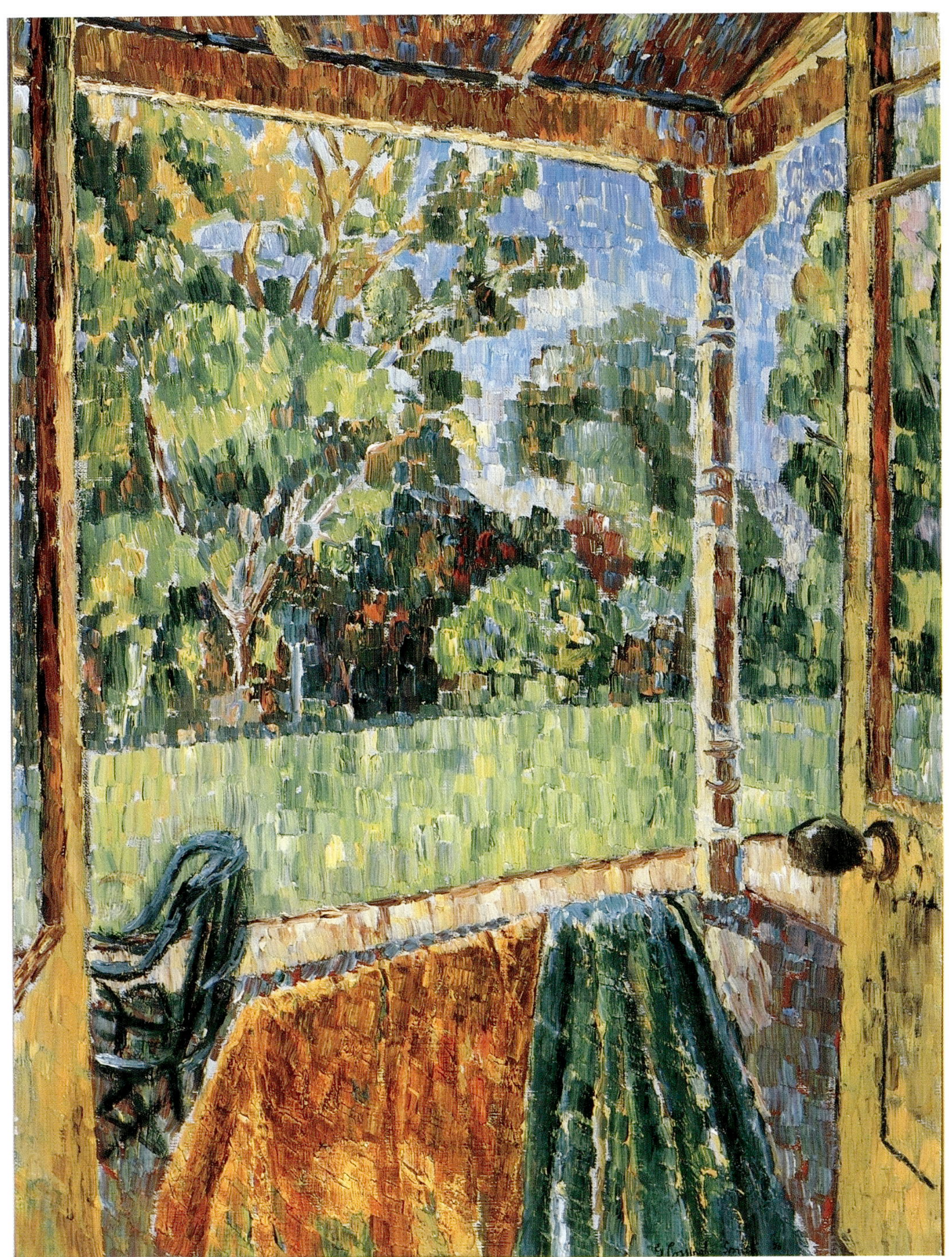

99   Grace Cossington Smith
1892–1984
(*The verandah and garden from the artist's bedroom*) 1956
oil on board
60.0 × 45.5 cm

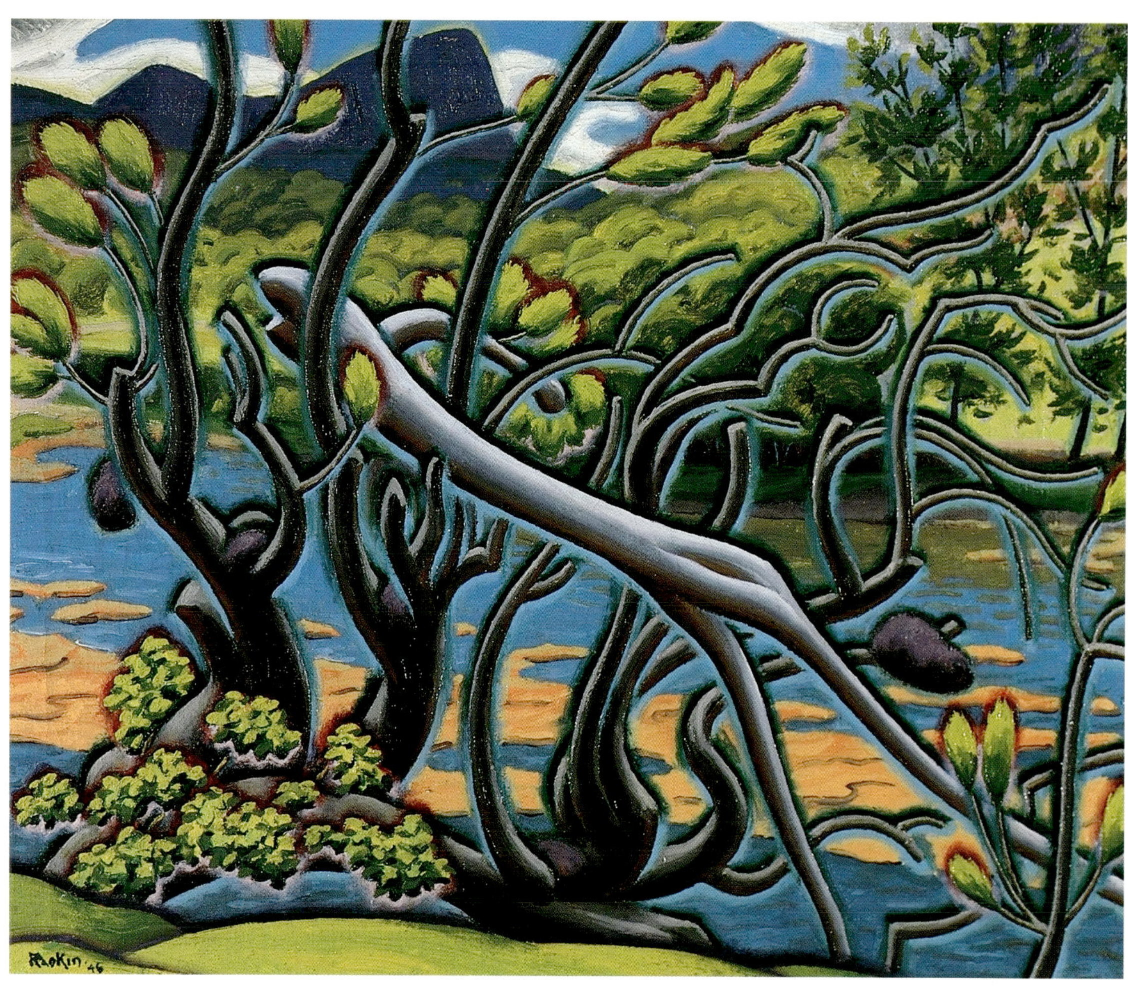

100   Weaver Hawkins
1893–1977
Burragorang landscape 1946
oil on canvas
51.0 × 60.8 cm

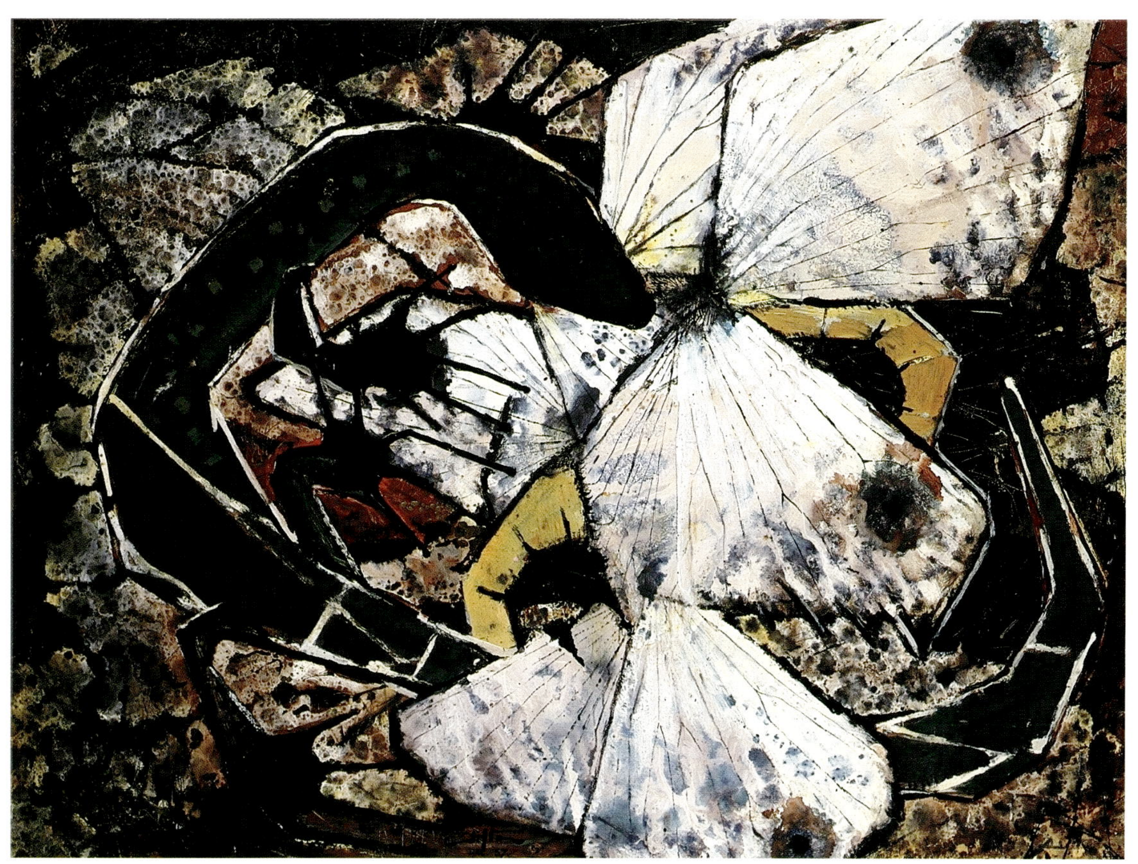

101　Clifton Pugh
1924–90
Lizard and butterflies 1957
oil on board
68.3 × 91.2 cm

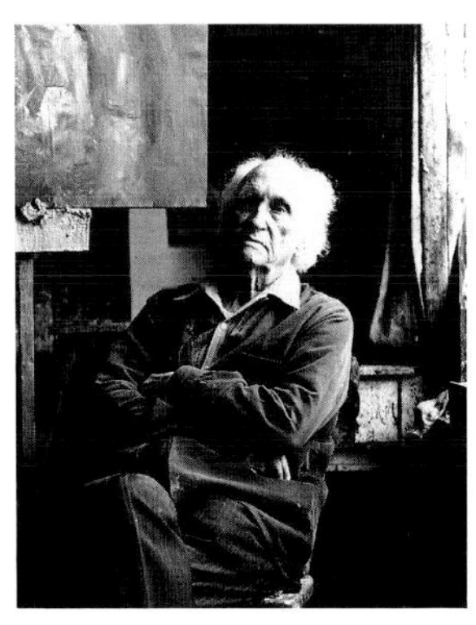

The grand old man,
Lloyd Rees, at 82,
photographed in 1976.
Photograph by Richard Beck

image. Another perception is that the fleshy objects of a typical still-life are suspended in space, creating an insubstantial, surreal illusion of coloured light.

The modern styles of the 1930s and 1940s had a plethora of propositions for analysing landscape and subject paintings. Grace Cossington Smith (1892–1984) structured *The verandah and garden from the artist's bedroom* 1956 (plate 99) according to the architectural lines of doorway and verandah and the small square units of colour. In the context of Miller's crystalline style hers appears relaxed and optimistic.

In the painting *Burragorang landscape* 1946 (plate 100) Weaver Hawkins (1893–1977) created an effect like tapestry using arabesque lines. The bright, close-toned colours are enlivened by a staccato repetition of adjacent light and dark tones. Hawkins created a work that was both mechanical and decorative: traits sought after by practitioners of one strand of modernism. At the other extreme Clifton Pugh (1924–90), in naively patterned bush subjects like *Lizard and butterflies* 1957 (plate 101), and John Perceval (born 1923), brought together the exuberance of a child's approach to image-making and an interest in the disciplined use of patterned strokes, a discipline in disorder that owed something to Vincent Van Gogh. The dark colours in *Fisherman's sights* (plate 102), a Williamstown marine painting of 1956, and *Winter landscape, Gaffney's Creek* 1958 (plate 103), form clots and the white strokes are dragged over the surface in open webs. Besides these various modernist interpretations by Cossington Smith, Hawkins, Pugh and Perceval there were Italian-Renaissance inspired subjects by Justin O'Brien (born 1917) such as *Three jugglers* c. 1955 (plate 104); old masterish landscapes by Lloyd Rees (1895–1988), who painted the *Winding road at Werri* 1958 (plate 105) as if it were the northern Italian landscape background to a *sacra conversazione*; and Arthur Boyd, who painted the summer *Eaglehawk landscape* 1956 (plate 106) in the fifteenth-century medium of tempera and with notations reminiscent of the mid-nineteenth-century illustrations of S.T. Gill. Later, in his Shoalhaven landscapes, Boyd looked back to the 1890s New South Wales paintings by Tom Roberts, as did the photorealist painter, William Delafield Cook (born 1936) in the 1982–3 work *The Hawkesbury* (plate 107). In other words there were various options in subject matter

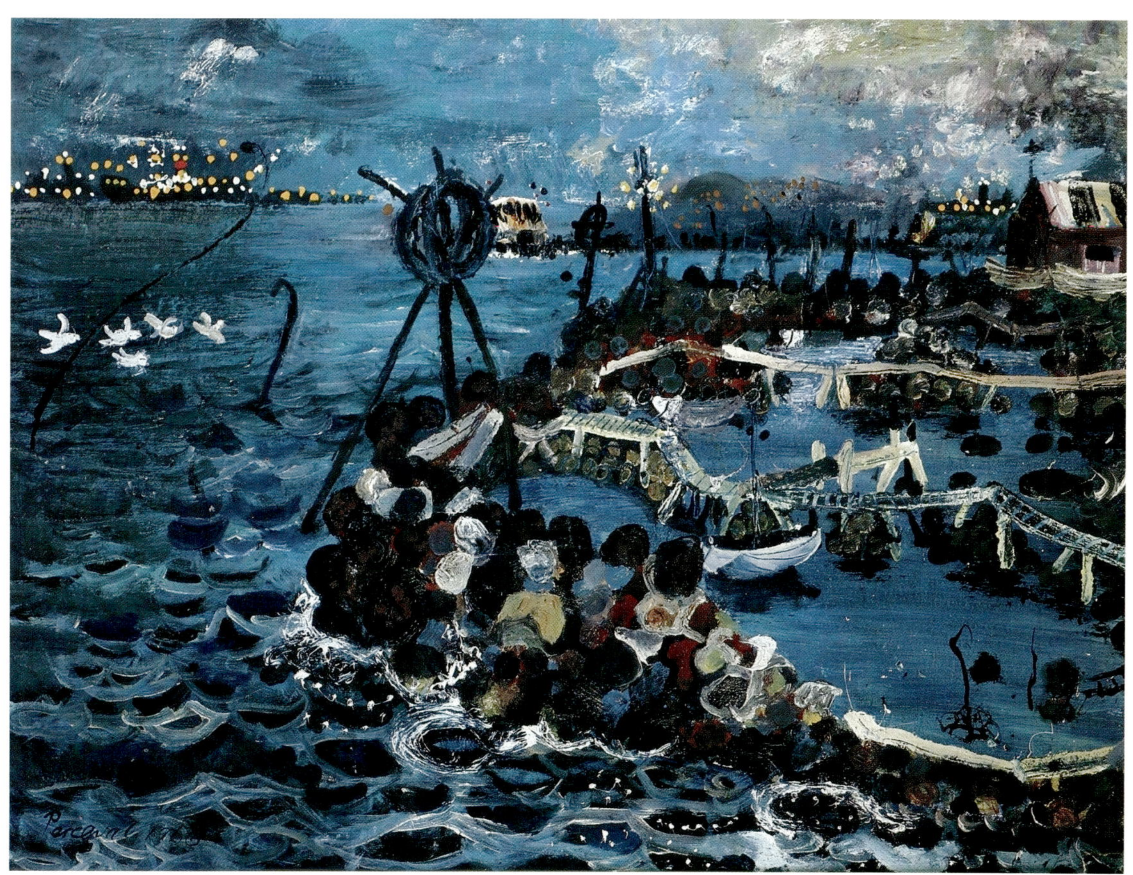

102   John Perceval
born 1923
Fisherman's sights 1956
oil on board
91.1 × 122.0 cm

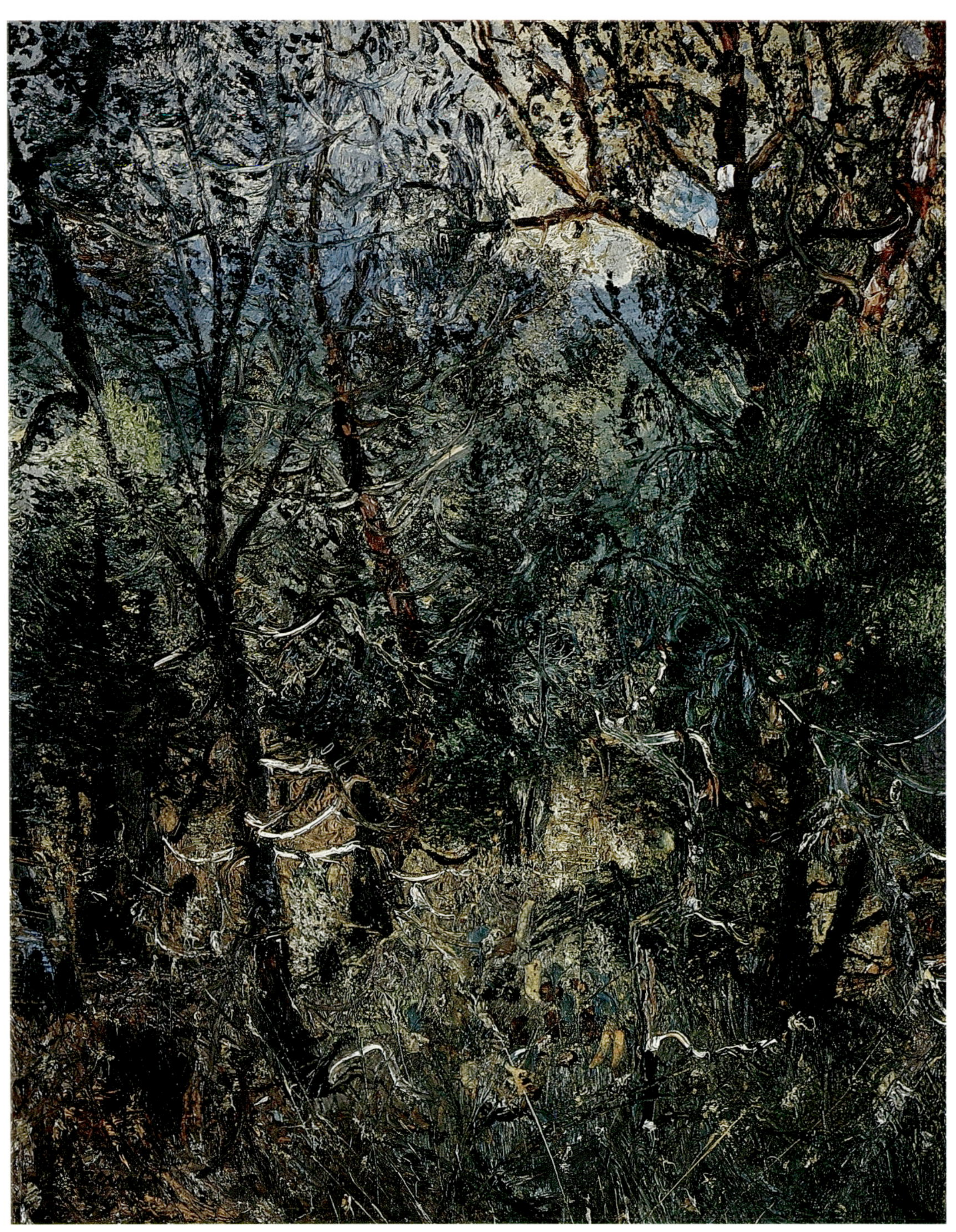

103   John Perceval
born 1923
Winter landscape, Gaffney's Creek 1958
oil on polystyrene panel
91.5 × 73.5 cm

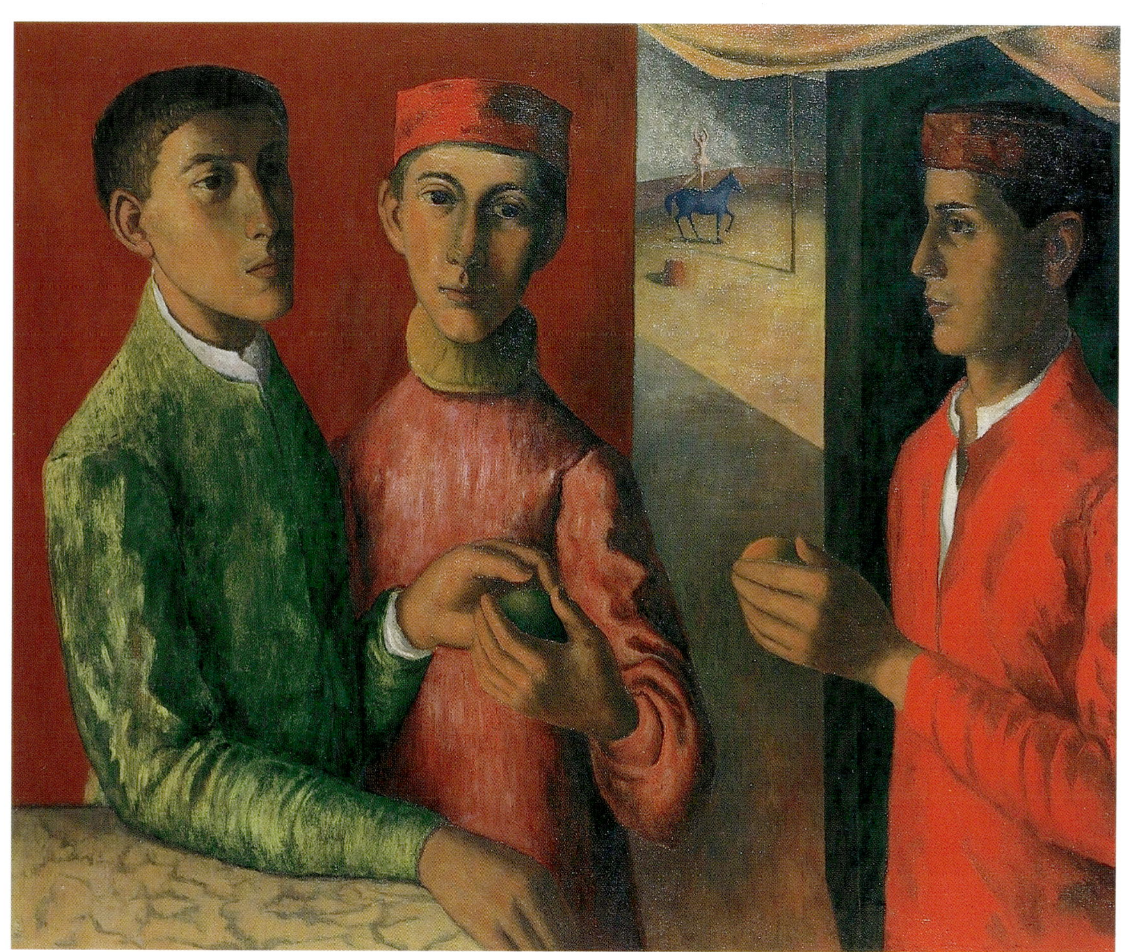

104   Justin O'Brien
born 1917
Three jugglers (1955)
oil on canvas
57.0 × 70.0 cm

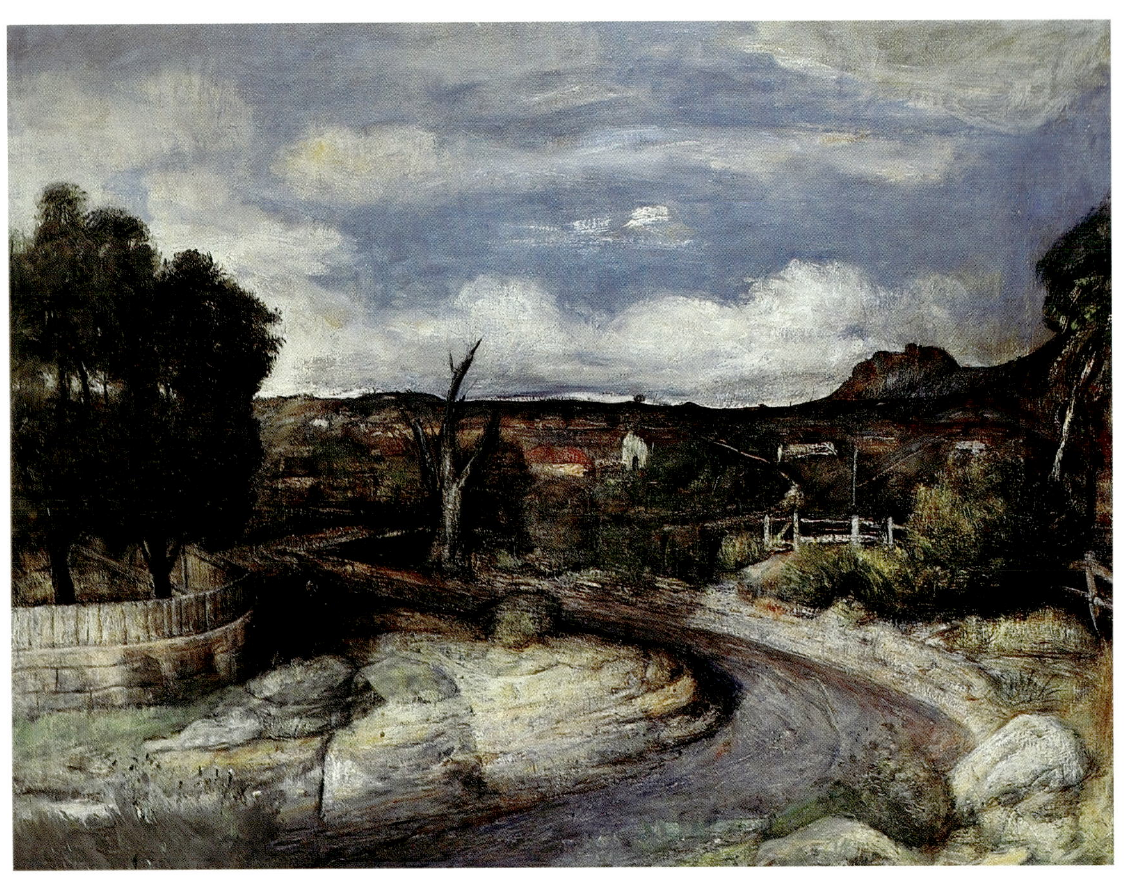

105 Lloyd Rees
1895–1988
Winding road at Werri 1958
oil on canvas
91.5 × 122.0 cm

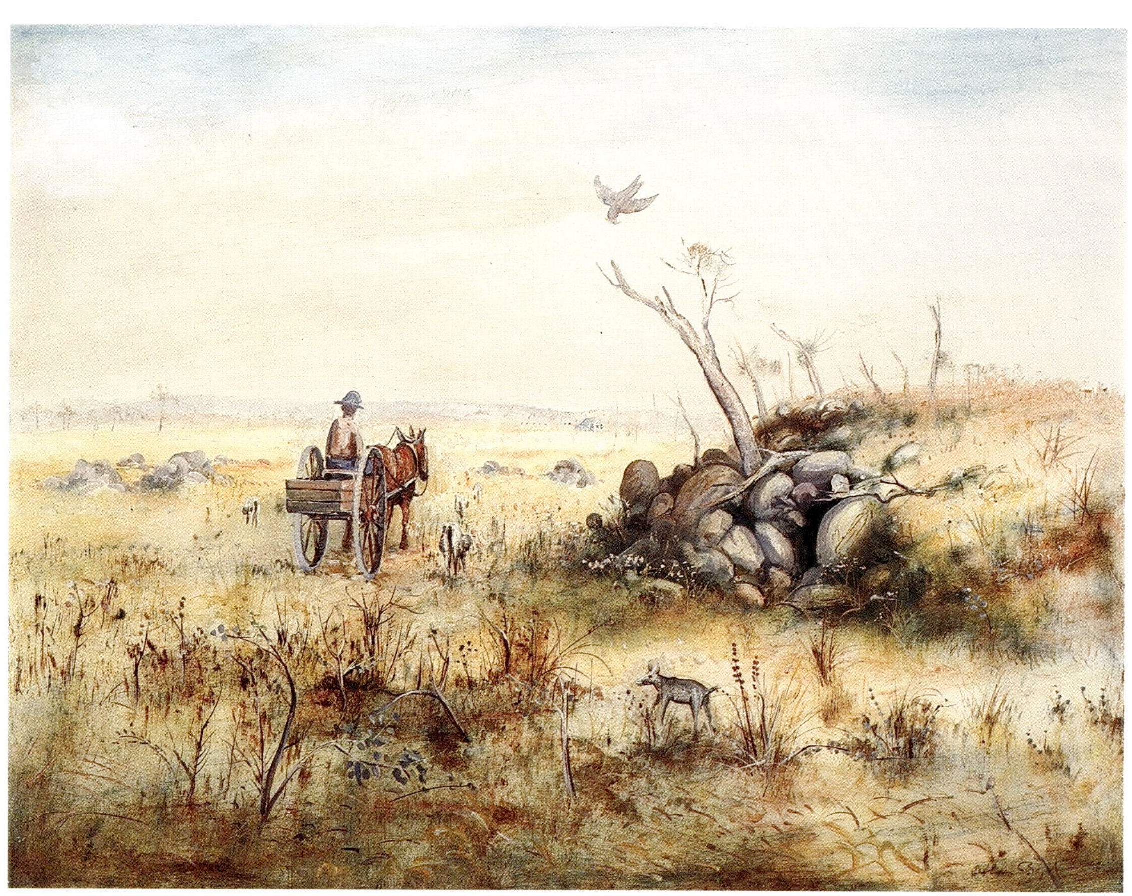

106   Arthur Boyd
born 1920
Eaglehawk landscape 1956
tempera on board
61.0 × 79.5 cm

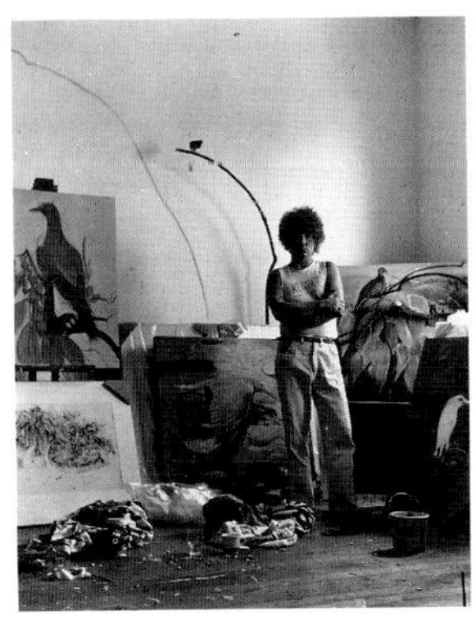

Brett Whiteley in 1979.
Photograph by Richard Beck

and numerous interpretations of the Australian landscape. Even the artists who were identified with their own unique interpretations, such as Boyd, Drysdale and Nolan, explored other ways of seeing.

Sydney, despite Smith's disparaging words, far from neglecting landscape painting, produced some of the most striking interpretations of the post-war period. Brett Whiteley (1939–92) and John Olsen (born 1928) produced memorable paintings. In the 1961 exhibition of 'Recent Australian Painting' at the Whitechapel Art Gallery in London, Whiteley showed semi-abstract works which in composition and style already looked like the Sydney Harbour paintings of later years. Shapes are large, colours uninflected, and the forms interlock like plates grinding together, lubricated by a few curving lines. The style was English in derivation. Years later the beige and white *Lavender Bay* 1980 (plate 108) was quieter in colour but otherwise within Whiteley's signature style. A stylistic continuity is recognisable in the shapes linked in ways reminiscent of sexual coupling, the disconcertingly upside-down composition and the exclusion of a stabilising point of reference. Map-making from above was the preferred mode of fifties and sixties landscapes by Whiteley, John Olsen, Sidney Nolan (in his Central Australian landscapes for example) and, from time to time, Fred Williams.

In the early 1960s John Olsen produced a series of extraordinary 'Journeys into You Beaut country' which were the strongest statements of a new vision of the country since Arthur Streeton seventy years earlier. He wished his paintings to describe a feast of sensations: expanding beyond visual perceptions to sensations of sound, smell and physical jostling. Olsen said, 'I am in the landscape and the landscape is in me.' Even the late landscapes, such as *The paddock of wattles* 1978–80 (plate 109), fit the ethos. In Patrick McCaughey's evocative image Olsen was an explorer who

seems content to follow his line wherever it will lead him. The landscape is not seen from a single viewpoint but as though, following his line, he moved into the landscape, around it, even above it. Always he is involved with it at first hand, in a close-up; he never loses his direct, immediate contact with it. The images,

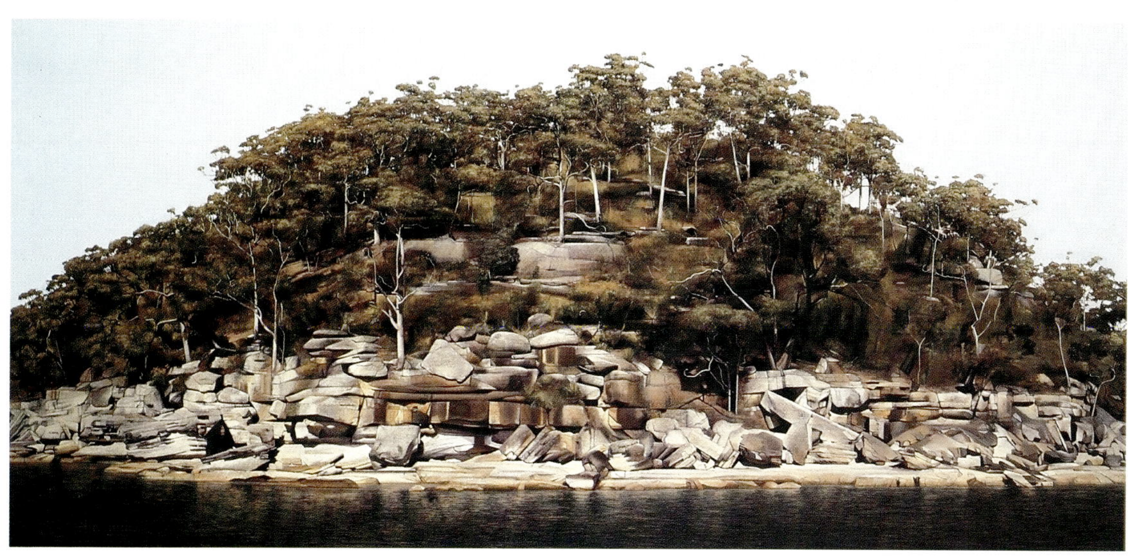

107   William Delafield Cook
born 1936
The Hawksbury 1982–3
synthetic polymer paint on canvas
88.8 × 195.5 cm

108 Brett Whiteley
1939–92
Lavender Bay 1980
synthetic polymer paint on canvas
122.0 × 81.0 cm

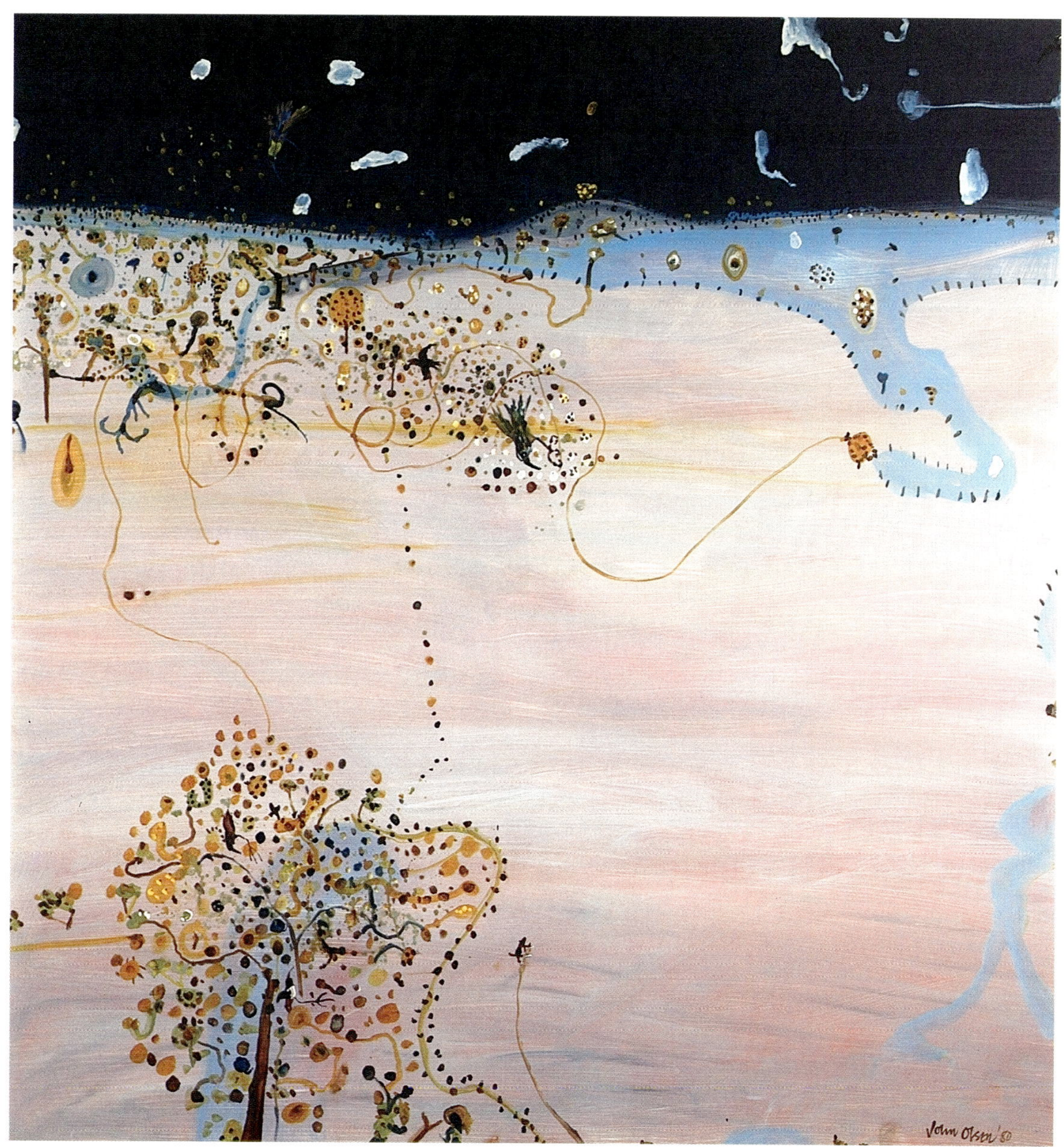

109 John Olsen
born 1928
The paddock of wattles 1978–80
oil on canvas
167.0 × 159.0 cm

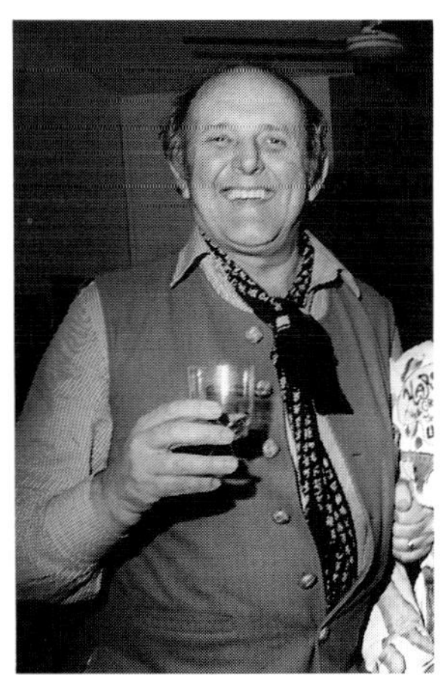
John Olsen in 1984.
Photograph by William Yang

the faces his line throws up for us, share this directness. They have the primitive immediacy and literalness of children's drawings.[5]

Detachment-in-involvement, a quality of Zen Buddhism, made Olsen's paintings easier to live with than, say, the angry or anxious landscapes of 1940s surrealism.

Another artist who made a major contribution to the diversification of Australian landscape imagery was Ken Whisson (born 1927). Although overlooked until the seventies and never within cooee of being recognised as an Antipodean, Whisson emerged as the artist who built most cogently upon the Melbourne figurative tradition of the forties. Like his precursors, Nolan and Boyd, he produced paintings that were essentially sketches recording a sequence of impressions and feelings. Forms are in lines of colour rather than built up as colour areas within a settled composition. An image such as *Spring tide* 1983 (plate 110) grew like Topsy, starting from one motif or more, isolated on the canvas and evolving by a process of doodling until the image encompassed a whole landscape. In the play of dislocations Whisson was more extravagant than most, though Olsen, Whiteley, John Firth-Smith, Gareth Sansom and others of that and the next generation made an art of the tense relationships between forms. The trend was general in art of the 1950s and 1960s. Visual art, whether by the Antipodeans Dickerson and Brack, the elderly abstract painter Balson, old hermit Fairweather or the young Dick Watkins, described flux and the territory between objects and people.

In 1974 Fred Williams (1927–82) painted *Forest pond* (plate 111), a work that is abstract *and* figurative. In August 1959 Williams, who had returned to Melbourne two years earlier from a long stay in England, was not represented in the first Antipodean exhibition, despite being a figurative painter and friend of many of the group. He felt the exclusion, which by implication defined artists like him as semi-abstract. Taking notice of what was said to be an Antipodean painting style – a protean style difficult to define but gutsy, straight-from-the-shoulder, tactile, and unaffected – and what were claimed to be Antipodean subjects – oblique myths connecting man and nature – he steered his art away from the realm of Antipodea. After

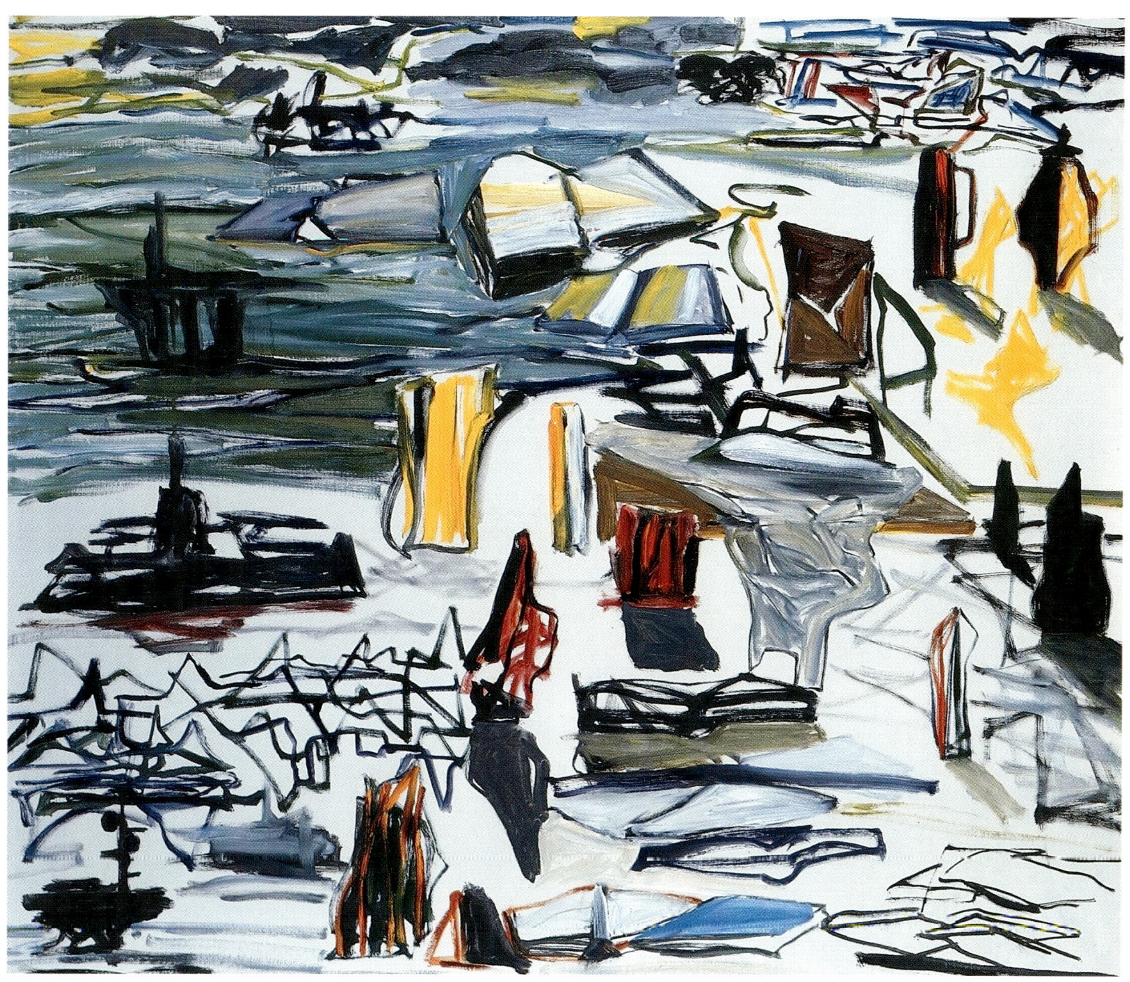

110   Ken Whisson
born 1927
Spring Tide 1983
oil on canvas
99.4 × 119.4 cm

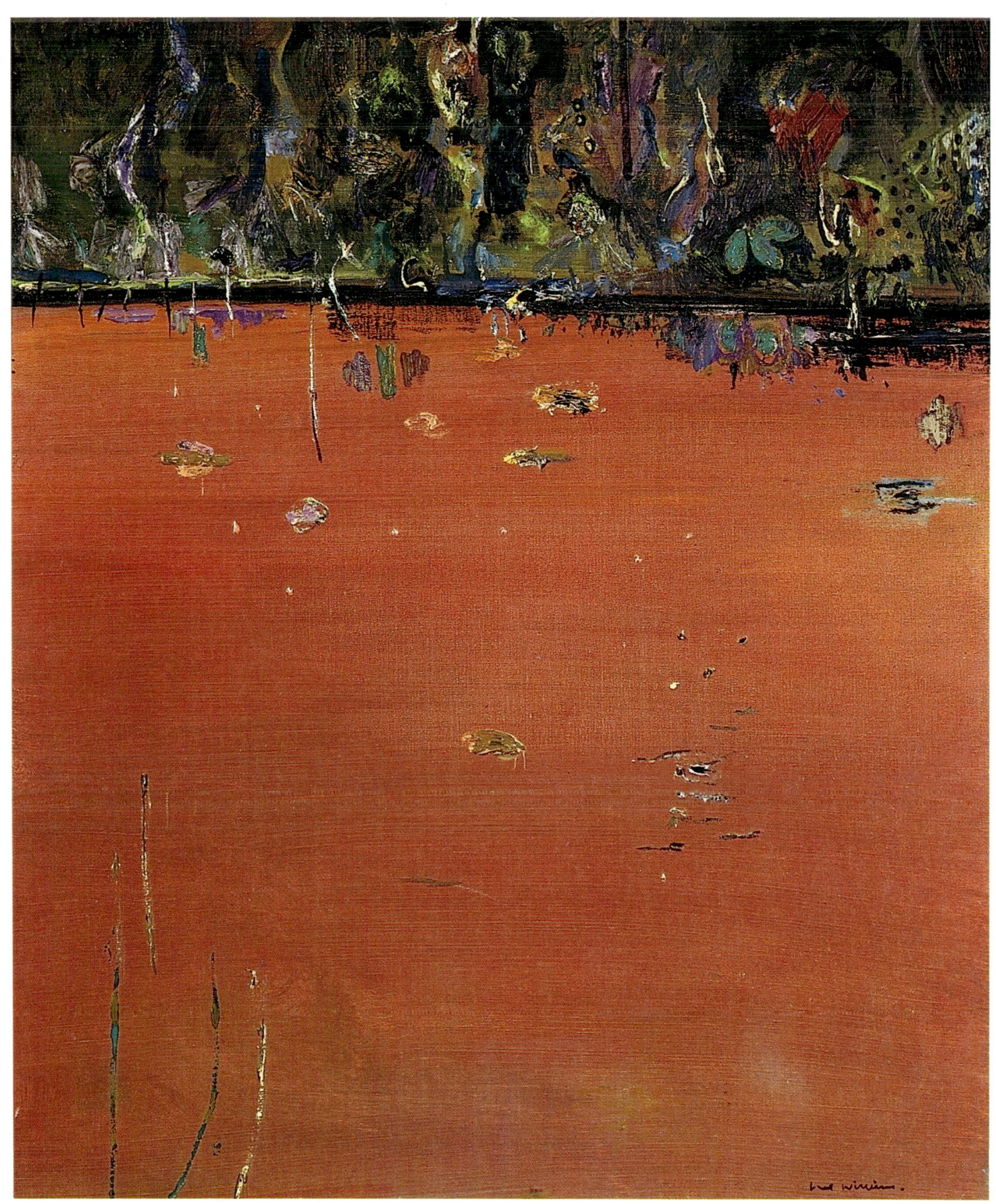

111 Fred Williams
1927–82
Forest pond 1974
oil on canvas
107.0 × 91.6 cm

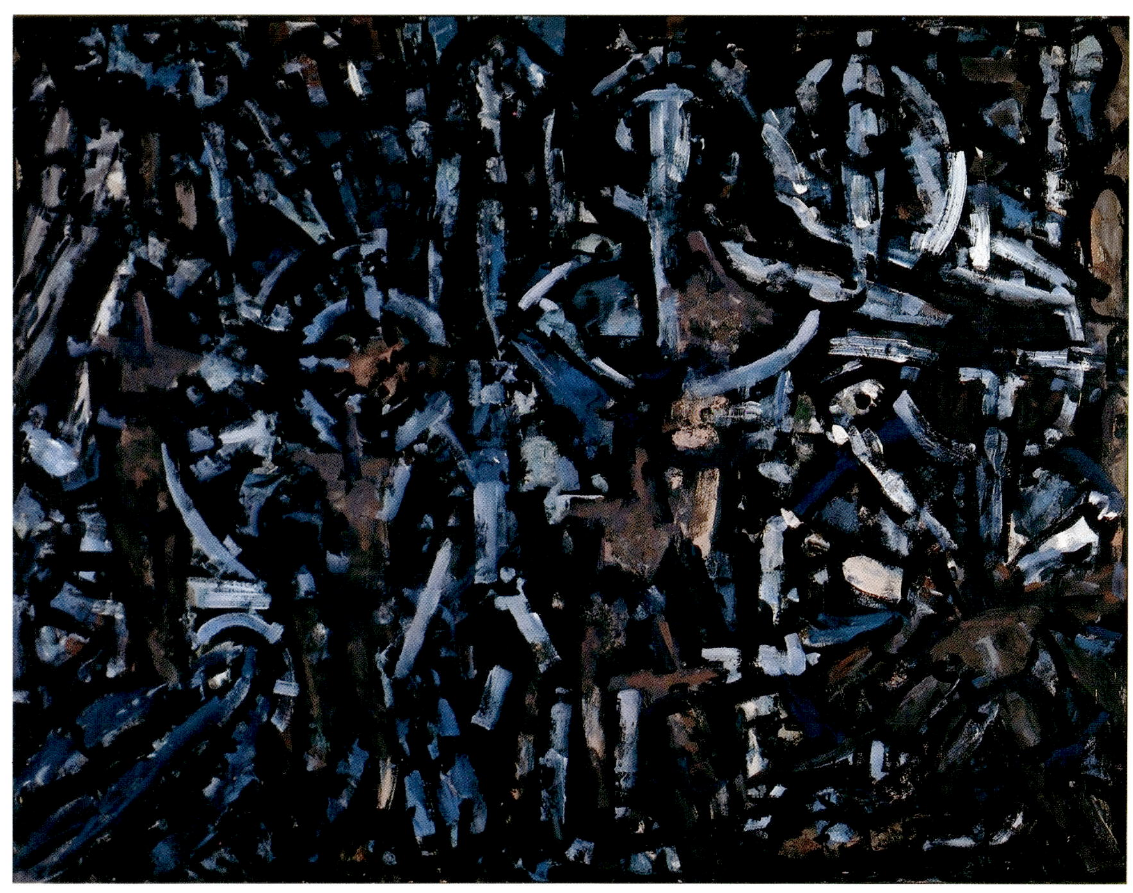

112 Roger Kemp
1908–87
Configuration 1965
synthetic polymer paint on board
137.0 × 183.0 cm

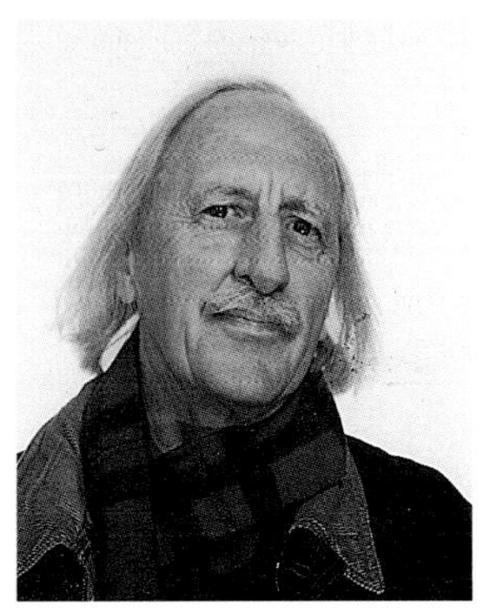

Ken Whisson in 1993.
Ken Whisson Collection

the single Antipodean exhibition Williams was invited to join the group and refused.[6]

He was not alone in disliking a definition of his work within style, subject or group. Almost every artist within the small Antipodean group expressed doubts about whether they could be said to share a common style. They refused to share an approach to subject matter, despite the initial efforts of Bernard Smith to define one that fitted them all.

It is time Australians put aside the Antipodeans as a historical red herring. Bernard Smith's exercise of defining a contemporary style-in-the-making posed a question about identity rather than analysed a trend in Australian art. The manifesto was written, the debate thundered on, but the question, though a burning one for cultural historians of the time, did not adequately fit the art of the period. There are other ways of interpreting the fifties and sixties. One tendency from the 1920s onward, through abstract and figurative styles, landscape and narrative subjects, was towards widening the vocabulary of visual expression. As styles became more varied, the formal aspects of art-making became apparent to the Australian public. Where once a work of art had been compared to its inspiration in nature – even the spiritual underpinning of much modern art had a scientific argument – from the fifties as a rule the sources of the style were noted and differences between styles codified. Many of the artists of the period worked eclectically, moving from one inspirational exemplar to another. Williams, Fairweather, Tuckson, Watkins, Hickey, Booth – most of the Field generation – worked in this way. They were the first generations to whom all art history was equally available, ready to be used at will.

The style of Roger Kemp (1908–87) of Melbourne developed from vivid landscape sketches in Fauve colours and with a Cezanne-inspired armature towards increasingly abstract and dynamic forms. Kemp's primary language was a circle and cross. From the 1940s to the 1980s he repeated these motifs in an incantatory way, finding in them the principles of cosmic energy. An image such as *Configuration* 1965 (plate 112) was the obverse of a finite statement bound within a concept of totality. It grew as a microcosm of something infinite. Not only the structure but the application of colour was steady, patient,

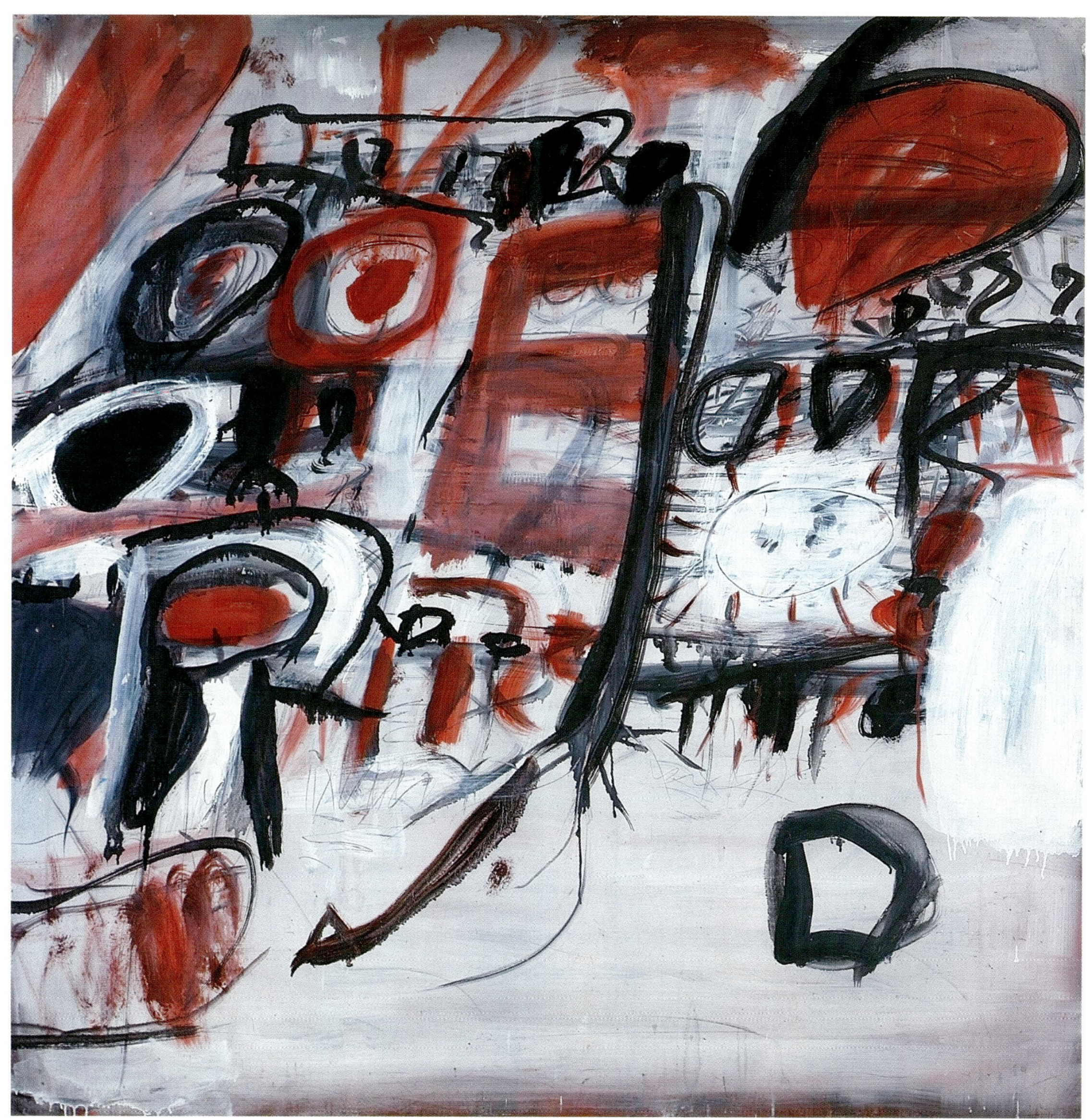

113   Tony Tuckson
1921–73
"E" (1962–5)
oil on board
122.0 × 122.0 cm

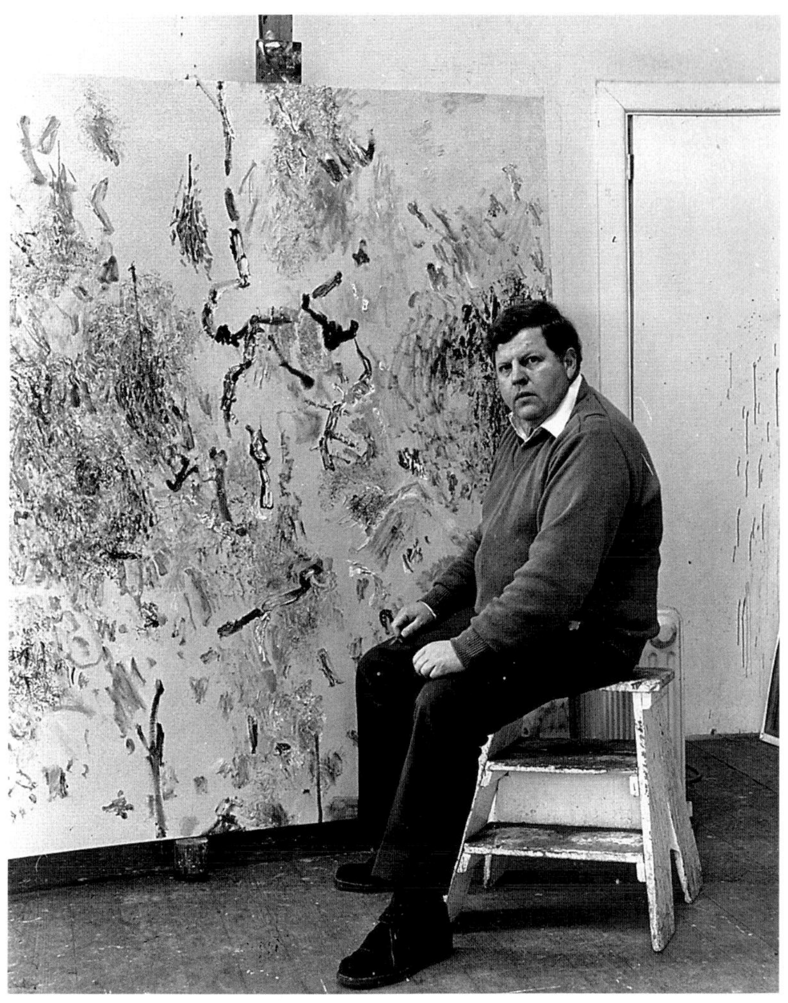

expansive. The inflexions of colour introduced space and implied a layering inwards as well as outwards. As Kemp pursued his sensation of an immanent truth, his paintings declared to others the possibility of an endless succession of light beyond vision.

Abstraction arose as a necessary expression of a mystical belief for Roger Kemp. On the other hand the friends of Tony Tuckson (1921–73), seeing his 1960s expressionist abstractions for the first time in exhibitions of the early seventies, found the paintings the perfect expression of the man they knew: unkempt, wild, clever and close. Endlessly talking about art, Tuckson did not discuss his own. Very few artists – those with long memories – knew about his practice as a painter, most people knew the collector and curator, not the closet painter. Privacy made

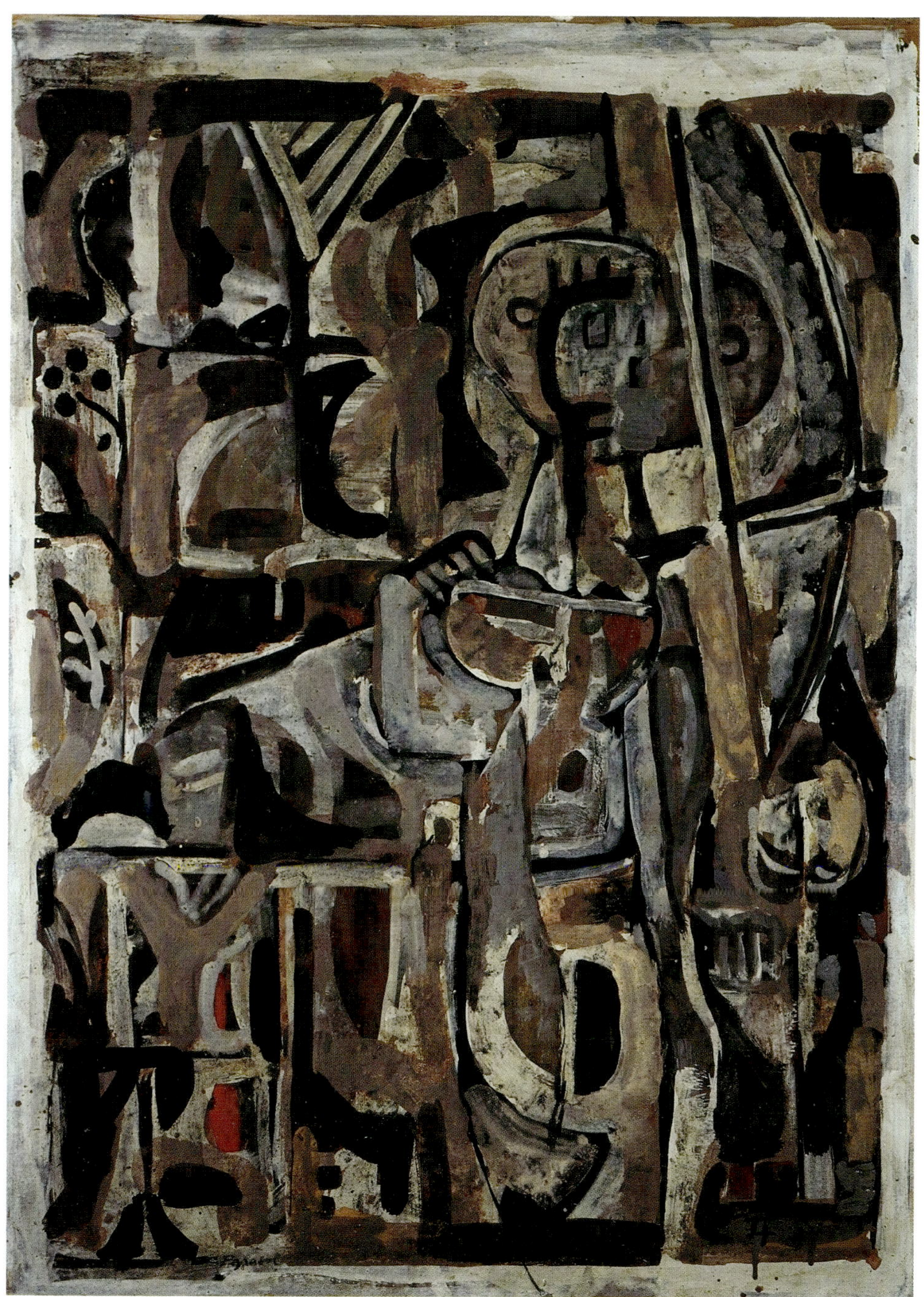

114 Ian Fairweather
1891–1974
Parasol 1957
gouache on cardboard
91.0 × 67.5 cm

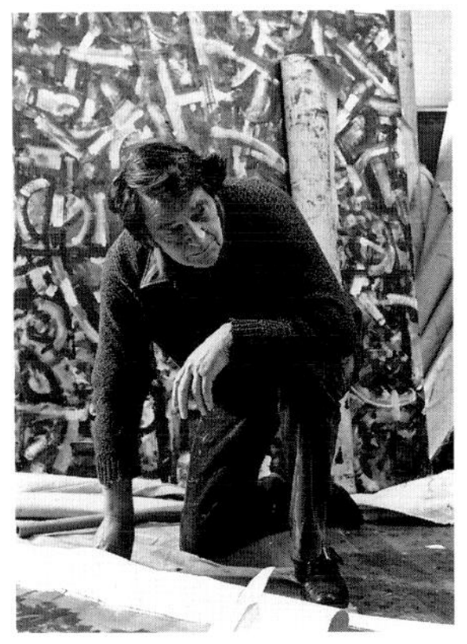

Roger Kemp in 1974.
Photograph by Richard Beck

all the difference. Tuckson was free to create his own frame of reference and, unhampered by the critical climate, market and audience of Sydney, he attacked subjects head-on, often using the poorest of materials and producing an image (on occasion) out of as little as two slashing gestures. Whether sketch or painting, drawing or mural, the categories mattered not at all to the painter working purely for himself against the highest standards of contemporary art. Most of Tuckson's production defies the standard categories. Neither did he share a language of forms with his Australian contemporaries. He saw their work and shared at least one stylistic habit, his way of weighting the top of an image, producing works which were top heavy. But he derived more from the few exhibitions of Italian, French, German and American art shown in Sydney through the fifties and sixties, and from close acquaintanceship with Aboriginal and New Guinea art. His various enthusiasms gave him media, techniques, social and pictorial conventions to explore in his own work.

"E" (plate 113) was painted between 1962 and 1965 in the larger studio of a new house, one of a number of works in the new medium of acrylic paint on four-feet (1.2m) square hardboard panels. Tuckson applied watery red and black in drunken dribbles. The thin wash dried to show fine veins. Over the top he overpainted some of the calligraphy in a solid black which stands out vividly against the thin ground. The image records his every gesture. Pencil scribbles, scored lines, sloshes of white and red, wash and paint, are to be read in a sequence just as Tuckson painted them. There seem to be letters perhaps forming words – food, look, poor, floor, flood, blood, ooe? Perhaps not. Is there a winged insect or a flying-machine in the upper centre? Tuckson was in the air force during the Second World War. The sequence suggests several images, words and letters, a landscape spread out in aerial perspective, an air battle, a grotesque gas-masked head, but no single theme is established. In the end, the fugitive process of working matches the elusive imagery, and Tuckson left the work untitled.

Tuckson was a friend and early patron of Dick Watkins who in the early sixties was exploring diverse styles (Rauschenberg, Jasper Johns, constructivism and so on). Both painters admired and studied the recent paintings

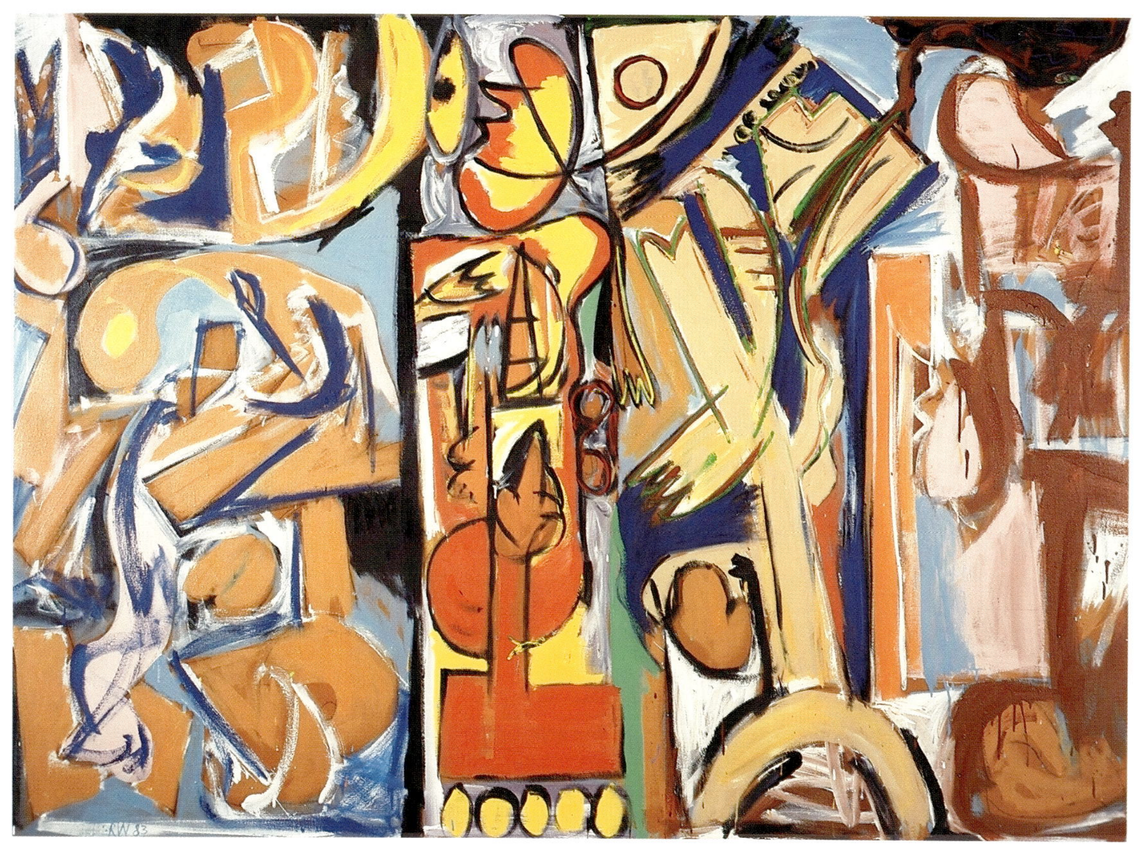

115 Dick Watkins
born 1937
Brief encounter 1983
synthetic polymer paint on canvas
173.0 × 244.0 cm

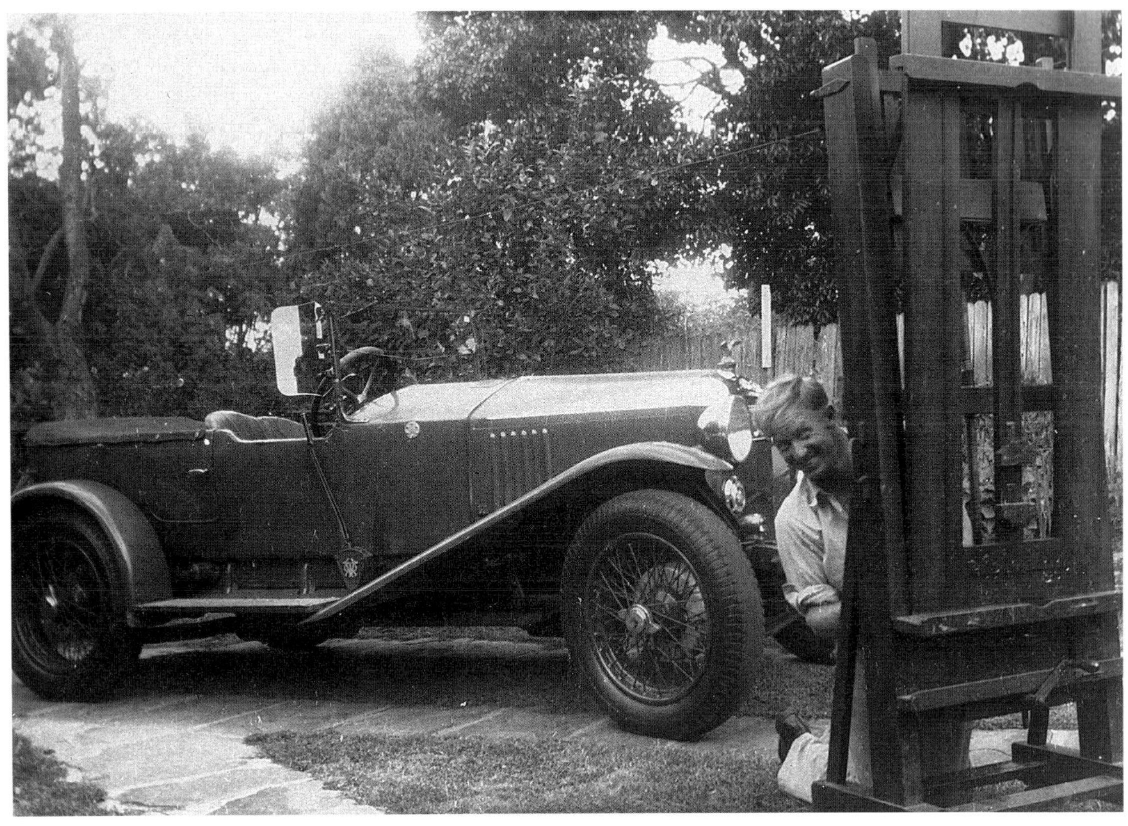

Tony Tuckson in 1949,
cleaning an easel he
had just bought
secondhand.

Photograph by Margaret Tuckson

of Ian Fairweather (1891–74). *Parasol* 1957 (plate 114) is one of Fairweather's last in the medium of gouache (his works, like Tuckson's, gained immensely in complexity after he began using the fast-drying acrylic medium in the late 1950s). The image, a complicated configuration of lines shifting angularly in space, came late in a series of cubist figures carrying parasols or wearing parasol-shaped coolie hats. The single figure is locked within a shallow box, bordered in white and surrounded by suprisingly substantial box shapes which, in turn, fit one inside the other, divided by quarter circles, crosses and smaller rectangles. The crowded image moves in depth from patches of light to shaped shadow. The colour is tonal, an array of dusky greys with a touch of red – surprisingly rich in effect against the prevailing greys. On the subject of colour, Fairweather used to quote a Chinese saying that 'colour is emptiness'. On final appraisal the only flatness in this calligraphic image is a fan-shaped bit of hatching, left over from the *Fan Dance* of the same year, two reminders of willow-pattern

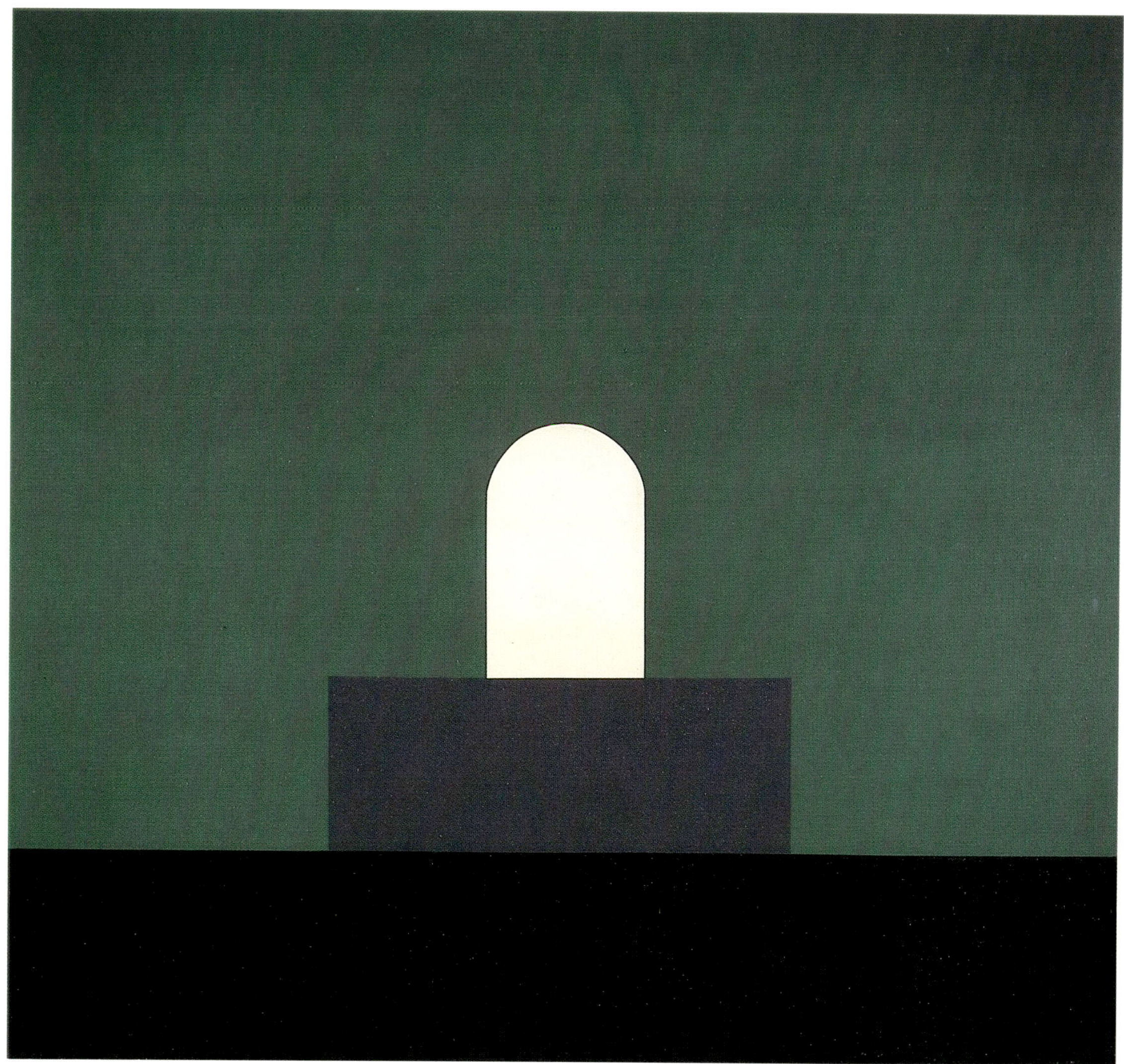

116 Dale Hickey
born 1937
Untitled painting 1968
synthetic polymer paint on canvas
152.5 × 165.0 cm

landscape, and bits of calligraphy which can be read as numbers or letters in an alphabet.

With Brack, the abstract-expressionist Tuckson, Fairweather and Dick Watkins, for the second time in Australian history the major subject was the figure rather than landscape. Watkins (born 1937) painted wildly but within a repertoire of gestures and forms. He was like a dancer for whom performance, practice and choreography were the elements of art. *Brief encounter* 1983 (plate 115) is divided into four vertical parts, each with its own figure, palette and style. As with a dance the four sections develop and expand a theme. The largest of the four figures is reminiscent of a primitive carving and the other figures are similarly dislocated, part cubist pattern, part sexual graffiti and with a suggestion of rods, wheels and pistons slightly reminiscent of Duchamp. The title 'Brief encounter' as well as supporting the thought of Duchamp, may refer to a famous film of 1945 about a chance romantic meeting of strangers on a railway station. In Australian terms the painting may seem to relate to Fairweather and Tuckson but for the artist the fusion was of Picasso and Pollock, with whose styles he vigorously competed.[7]

If the Antipodean manifesto was a red herring so, too, has been the Field exhibition in our understanding of the art of the 1960s. The Field forced the pace. This exhibition inaugurated the new building for the National Gallery of Victoria in August 1968. The style it celebrated was defined by the professional art establishment rather than created by artists. The Field set an expectation that artists could be led, it made reputations (something museum curators are supposed not to do) and established the pre-eminence of fashion art, last-wave art, and contemporaneity which has continued ever since. Above all, it ignored the perennial obsession of Australia with Australian identity. Sydney, Melbourne, Adelaide, Australian and non-Australian artists were represented without their differences being an issue. The only things that mattered were the stylistic theme – variously described as 'hard edge, unit pattern, colour field, flat abstraction, conceptual and minimal',[8] the art selected to establish that theme, and a prescribed way of looking.

The paintings and sculptures in the Field were well-designed rather than cerebral. And the artists were mostly temporary practitioners of hard edge. For Dick Watkins

117 Robert Hunter
born 1947
Untitled painting 1969
synthetic polymer paint on canvas
158.5 × 158.5 cm

it was one of a number of parallel explorations – not the most significant. The conceptual work of Mel Ramsden and Ian Burn sent from New York for the exhibition was recognised by fellow artists as 'different' from the other works on show. Robert Rooney and Dale Hickey based their seemingly abstract patterns on real-life objects. Janet Dawson, in her painting *Wall*, directly opposed the constraints of the style. Perhaps the only exhibitors adequately served by the Field were the architects Noel Dunn and Rollin Schlicht and designers Michael Nicholson and Paul McGillick. The arbitrary nature of their gathering was acknowledged in the catalogue essays. As had happened with the Antipodeans ten years before, the Field catalogue claimed that the artists shared no stylistic or other affiliations. Nonetheless the tenor of the exhibition and essays was overwhelmingly the other way.

In 1968, the year of the Field, Clement Greenberg visited Australia for a two-month lecture stint. His fellow (and rival) American critic Lucy Lippard had named Greenberg as the critic most responsible for promoting hard-edge/ colour-field painting at home in the United States. Australians expected to hear a strong defence of the style. Instead, during the tour, Greenberg expressed his opinion that avant-garde styles (by their nature) had a limited life span. The remark seemed significant coming from the senior advocate of the avant-garde style then being promoted with vigour in Australia. Because the hard-edge style was adopted rather late – it had begun in America in the fifties but was not practiced here in volume until the mid-sixties – the Australian movement had an artificial aspect, an adoption rather than a birth. Hard edge had legitimacy as an American movement. By the same token its fate was external to the Australian expression of hard edge. Just as no one cared to look back to a tradition of Australian abstraction, neither did it seem relevant to look forward to hard edge's local evolution into another style.[9] There *was* a local tradition of abstract colour painting by Balson, Crowley and others which could support and give richness to the style of hard edge, but this was ignored because young Australians were obsessed with an art history that was not their own. American hard edge was adopted wholesale. The growth stages were eliminated, the style flowered quickly and it was relatively short-lived. The Field exhibition, with its museum display, doctrinaire

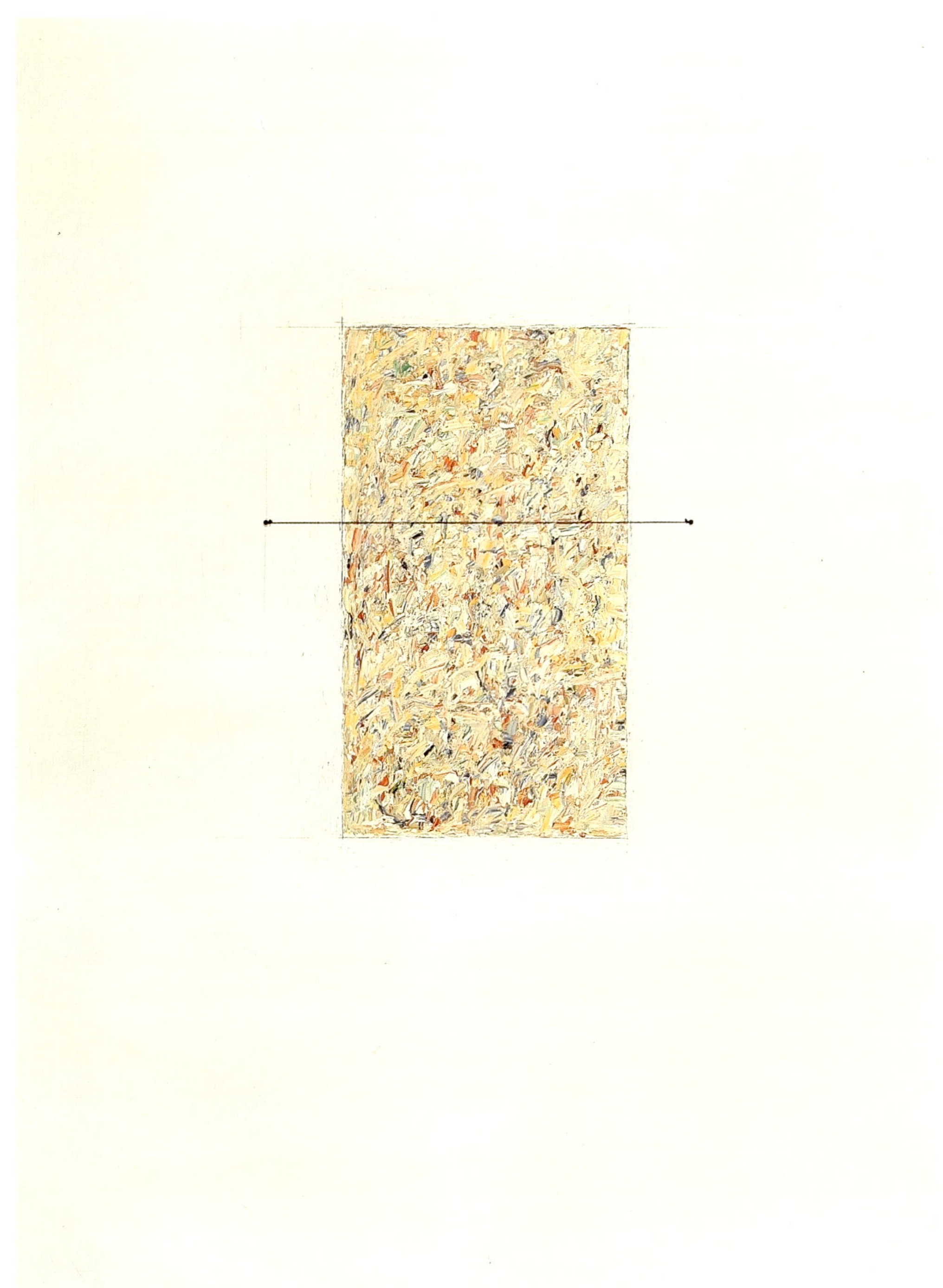

118   Paul Partos
born 1943
Untitled painting 1979
oil, pencil, metal pins and elastic cord on canvas
182.0 × 136.0 cm

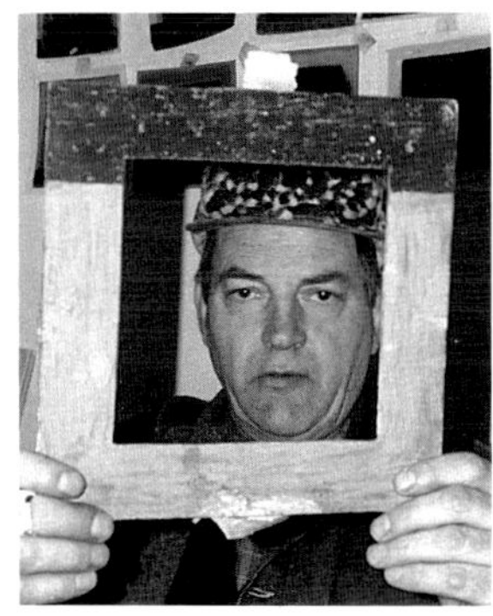

Dale Hickey in his
studio in 1993.

Photograph by Rosemary Hickey

catalogue essays and rigid selection of work, amounted
to a presentation of the style as the official contemporary
style.

In theory the Field painting expressed only itself. For
example, the bold design and flat paint of *Untitled* 1968
(plate 116) by Dale Hickey (born 1937) encouraged a view
of the object as a physical icon. But there was space and
illusion too. The image of a stark white arch in a field
of green suggested a window, or an altar, or a dressing-
table in an interior. The shock of recognition when the
viewer switched from seeing an abstract design to seeing
a subject was (and still is) Hickey's aim. By its translation
into a purely formal idiom the banal is made extraordinary,
even mystic. Hickey's sensibility was not ironic, unlike
that of his friend Robert Rooney. Pop art, which had a
similar transformative operation on reality, lacked the
slight element of the sacred which characterised Hickey's
imagery.

Totemic abstraction was a feature of the work of a
visiting American artist James Doolin, whose highly
patterned compositions had the dogmatic force of magic
symbols. In Melbourne between 1965 and 1967, Doolin
had considerable impact, as fellow American Clement
Greenberg noted in his essay for the Field catalogue.

Robert Hunter (born 1947), an ex-student of Dale Hickey
at Preston Technical College, made a 'dazzling debut'[10]
with an exhibition of thirteen square white paintings at
Tolarno Galleries, Melbourne in May 1968, some months
before the Field opened. He was the youngest artist in
the Field, one of the most gifted, and the only artist to
pursue a rich vein in minimalism in subsequent decades.
Untitled painting 1969 (plate 117) was one of the few which
introduced black. The beginnings of non-imagery in his
art stem from seeing paintings by Josef Albers and Ad
Reinhardt in the exhibition 'Two Decades of American
Art', which opened at the National Gallery of Victoria in
June 1967. A characteristic of western abstract painting
from the 1950s onwards has been its comparative
unreproducibility. Reproduction nullifies the physical
presence of the work of art and so makes the conditions
of viewing meaningless. For abstract art the unrepro-
ducible qualities of facture, scale and visual distance were
crucial. Knowledge about post-war abstraction necessarily
had to be gained through actual sighting, rumour or report,

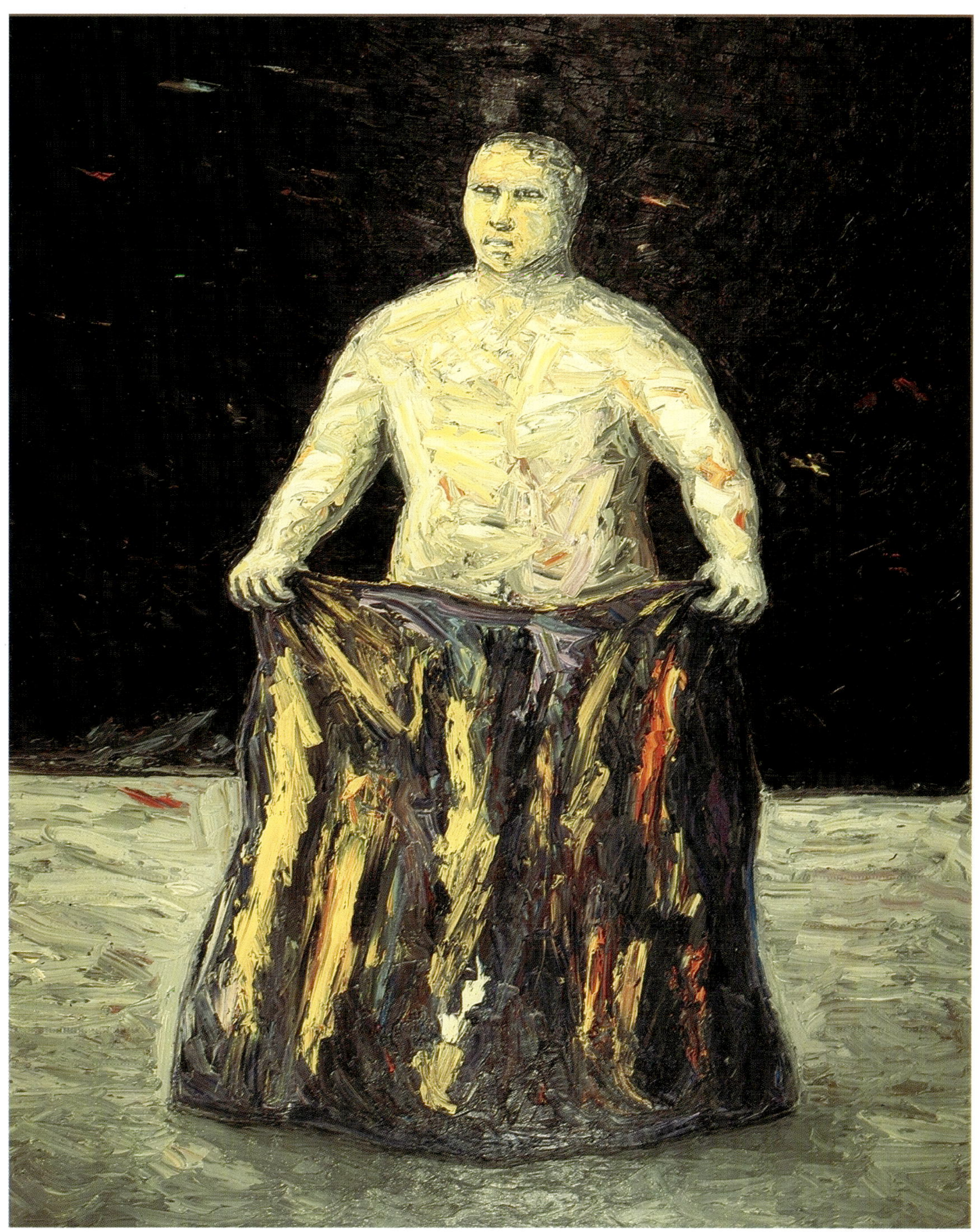

119 Peter Booth
born 1940
Painting 1989
oil on canvas
243.7 × 198.0 cm

or through painters following a set of instructions to produce their own models. Robert Hunter's paintings vanished entirely in reproduction, which could not represent their minimal shifts in hue and surface (for this reason his work was not reproduced in the Field catalogue). Even the viewer standing face to face with one of Hunter's paintings finds the image virtually imperceptible at first glance. The work actually never shows itself as a stable visual entity, but is revealed fugitively as a pattern of close relations.

Another veteran of the Field, Paul Partos (born 1943), deals with similar effects more overtly. Since the 1960s most of his paintings have had one set of references: a rectangle of thickly applied colours placed on a neutral rectangular ground. In paintings such as *Untitled painting 1979* (plate 118) the existence of an inner and an outer rectangle invites the question of where the image-object begins and ends. The uncertainty of the border is exacerbated or at least drawn to notice by the thread stretched across the image and into the field. Colour and texture are sensuous, the image is austere, nonetheless this handsome painting forces anxious questions about the stability of its borders and the alignment of the inner rectangle. The central rectangle may not be strictly aligned to the outer edges. It slips. The cross line is an unreliable measure. It may slope.

Peter Booth (born 1940) subsequently went a long way from the single, generously proportioned, geometric painting he showed in the Field. When, in the seventies, he began to paint hot red and orange strokes in the black the change perceived by reviewers was that the closed surface of his abstract paintings had split to reveal a volcanic world beneath.[11] (Booth himself corrected those who described his black paintings as doorways, saying they were more correctly solid boxes.) Soon after, the imagery became nightmarish, a science fiction of mutant bodies, flaming horizons, black skies and muddy seas. For more than fifteen years afterwards Booth transcribed dream-like revelations from the world of his imagination. *Painting 1989* (plate 119), a canvas of giant proportions, looms over the viewer and asserts the oppressive physical presence of Booth's inner world. The image is of a fattish giant who confronts the viewer and flourishes a cloth in the flapping gesture of a clumsy toreador. The world the

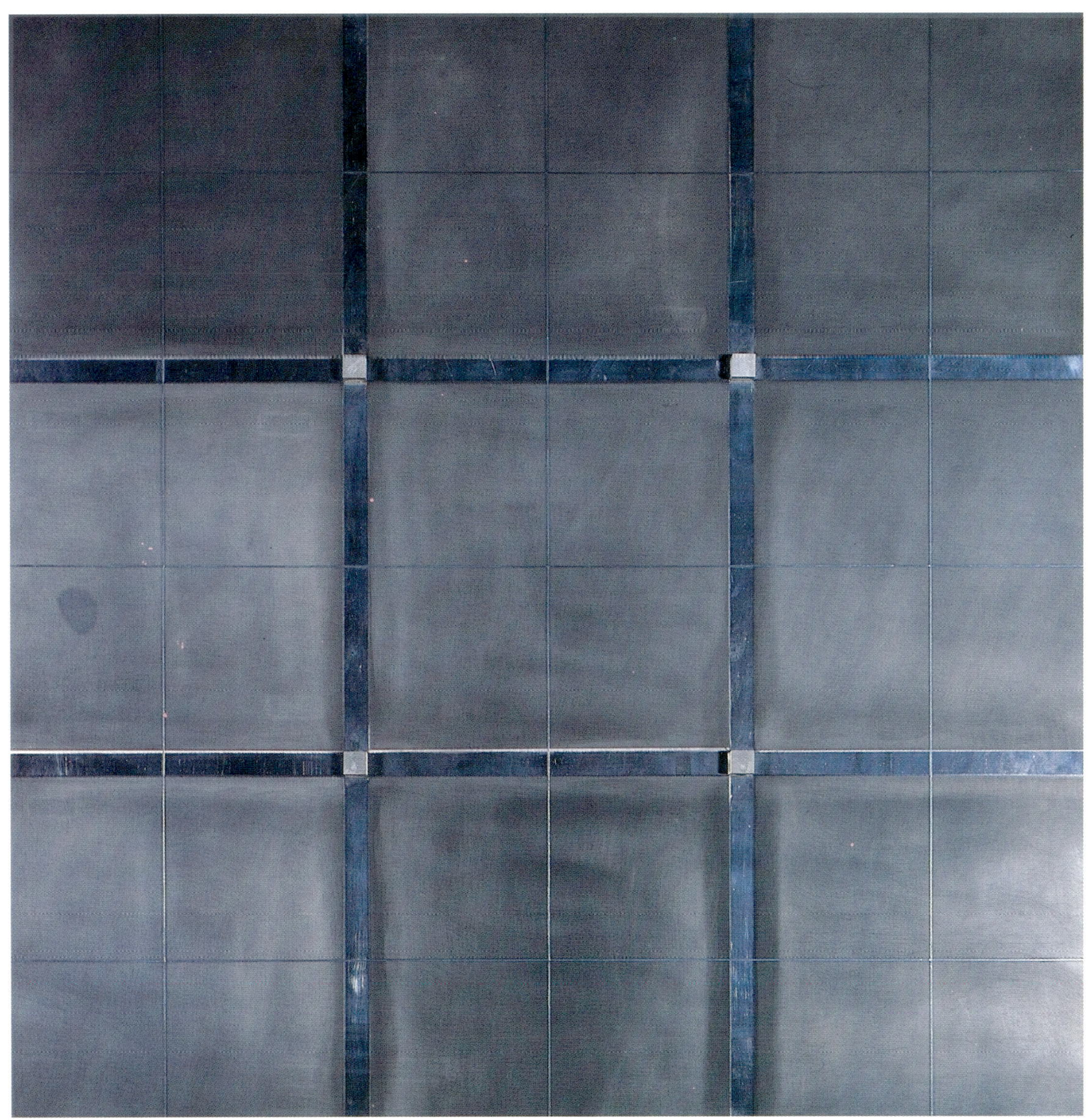

120   Robert Owen
born 1937
Stopover (1971)
aluminium, perspex, lead, wax and defraction grating
61.3 × 60.0 cm

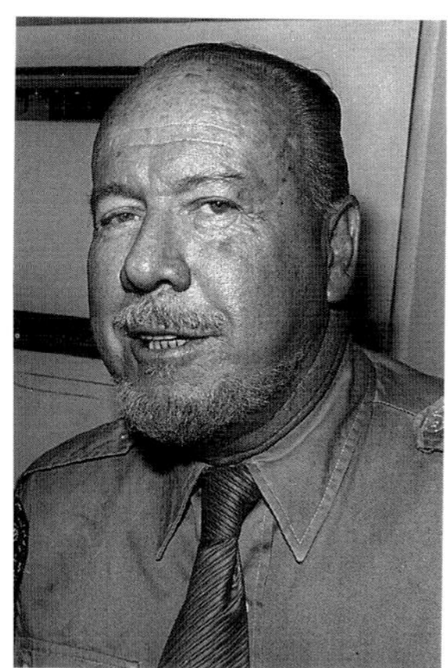

Jeffrey Smart on a trip
to Sydney in 1980.
Photograph by William Yang

giant fends off must be, has to be, ours.

Robert Owen (born 1937) likewise refers to a reality beyond the material world. *Stopover* c. 1971 (plate 120) is alchemical, its inspirational tradition seeming to be medieval mystical engineering or a modern philosopher's stone, rather than American hard edge or conceptual art. Strictly speaking *Stopover* is not a painting but a construction in metal. Owen ruled a grid of lines on a sheet of aluminium and rubbed graphite over the nine squares thus created, leaving the four grid lines to shine brightly in polished aluminium. The corners of the inner square were defined by raised cubes of metal. Lastly, very narrow strips of metal dissected the image into many smaller squares. Where light reflects off the metal the work gleams with brilliant rainbow colours which shift with every change of light or the viewer's angle of vision. Owen has explained that his constructions (so rigid yet visually so random) illustrated 'his feelings about individuals and their relations with one another, and nature'. The colours change constantly 'as we do' and each person sees them differently.[12] In a later exhibition he quoted the French anthropologist Claude Levi-Strauss, 'When we make an effort to understand we destroy the object of our attachment, substituting another whose nature is quite different.'[13]

One of the flourishing trends of art ignored by the Field was pop art. Imitation realism, or Australian pop, now seems among the strongest work of the time. The three painters whose work is represented here have not been identified with a group or even a style movement. Jeffrey Smart (born 1921) has lived in Europe for most of his adult life. Despite the gap of geographical distance and an introduction to art in the 1940s through the idiosyncratic sensibility of surrealism, his subjects have been sufficiently universal to strike a chord within our own society. In recent decades he has painted industrial landscapes, freeways, high-rise buildings, service industries, a world that is immediately recognisable for its dun-coloured expanses, bland shadows, lolly-coloured details, and figures which are at once individualised and puppet-like. *Public notice, Hove* 1969–70 (plate 121) is typical.

The second artist is Ivan Durrant (born 1947). He presents himself flamboyantly as a showman wearing two-tone shoes and with a salesman's patter. In the 1970s

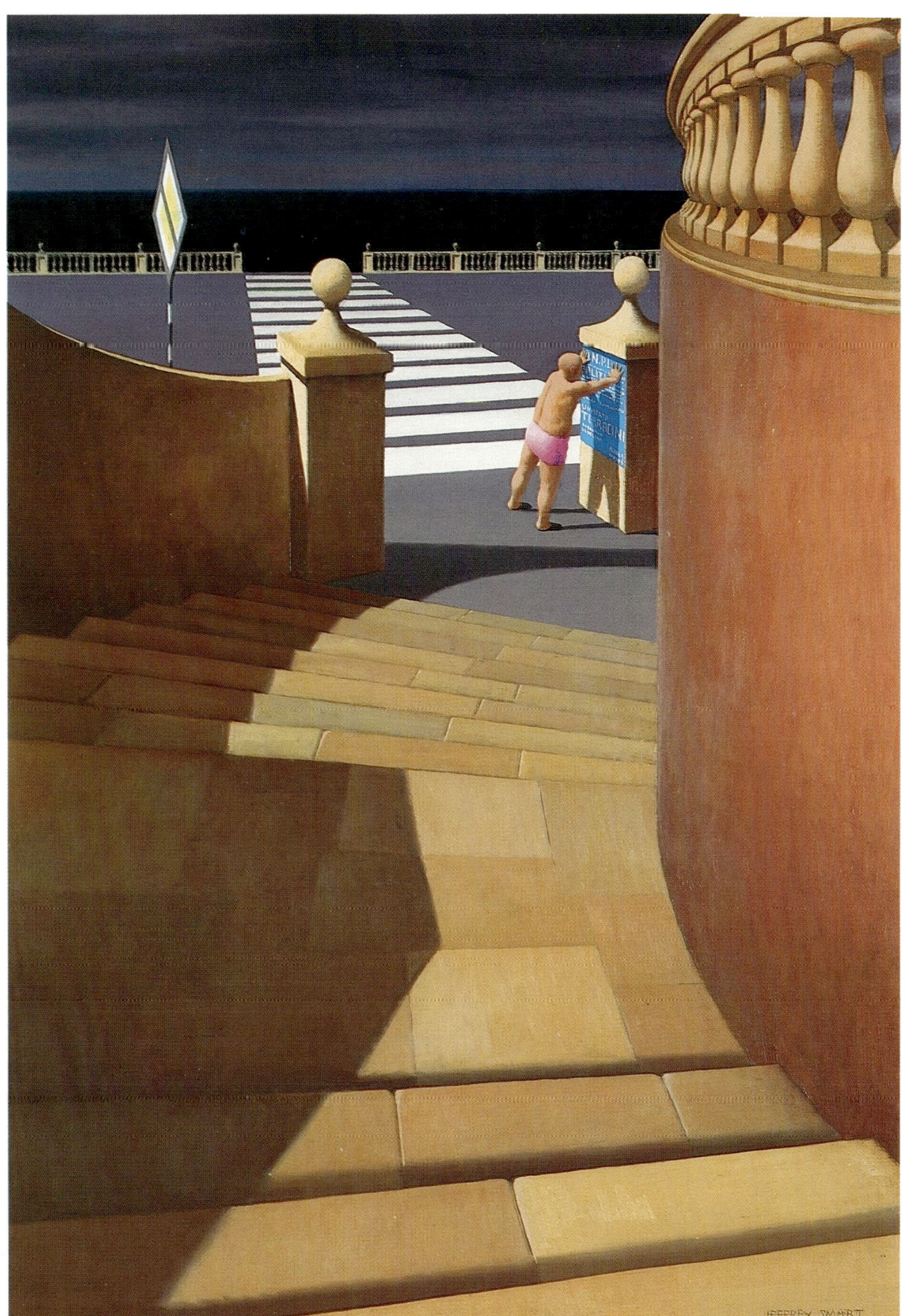

121 Jeffrey Smart
born 1921
Public notice, Hove 1969–70
oil on canvas
91.2 × 65.4 cm

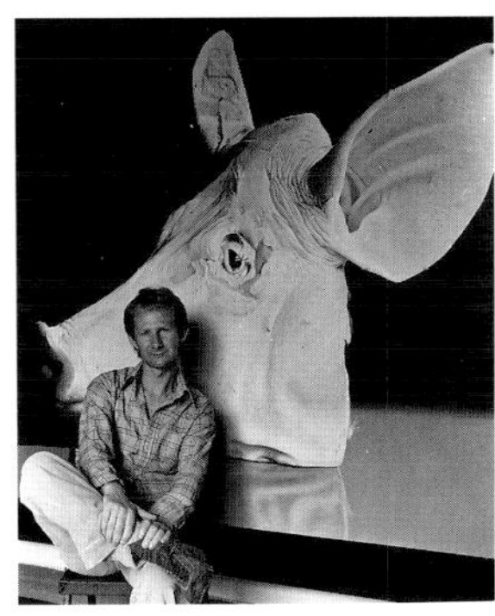

Ivan Durrant in the late 1970s, with a pig's head made from dental plastic.

Photograph by Richard Beck

Durrant left a dead cow on the steps of the National Gallery of Victoria. He crafted pink pig's heads out of dentist's plastic. And he sold a complete miniature butchery to the same Victorian Gallery. As well, he painted film stars with immaculate make-up and satin smooth smiles. *Humphrey Bogart* 1974 (plate 122) is debonair in grey suit and crisp white shirt. Because only Bogart's face and neck is spotlit, his hand in shadow poking forward towards us is grey – a glove? The carnation in his buttonhole is also grey. By the time one realises that the dead hue of hand and flower is shadow, the image has produced its sinister effect. Afterwards that grey disturbance hovers whenever one looks at the work, like an afterimage or a shadow in the mind.

The third in this small selection of Australian pop artists is Richard Larter (born 1929). Like the others he offers a mixed fare of blandness, exuberant delight and rude rebuff. *The Tinkling Eye of Marx* c. 1966 (plate 123) stares roguishly at the viewer from a tapestry of swirling colours and pert women. These, needless to say, are the obverse of stern Karl Marx. The best Australian pop has mirrored life, particularly the glorious icons of present-day consumption. But instead of standing back from these objects of delight, parading the detachment of a sociologist, the artists have shown their equivocal personal involvement. The female pin-up with legs crossed in Larter's painting is his wife Pat, whom he more often presents in the blatant poses of a centrefold.

Australian art over two hundred years has been marked by discontinuities perhaps as much as by the unfolding of certain favourite themes and approaches. In essence it has been migrant art made by and for people who are constantly on the move, either newcomers to Australia or Australians lightly rooted in their place of birth and ready to move on. It has been an art of the middle and lower classes, of people who enjoy prosperity and like to display it, though on the other hand they deny sophistication and are suspicious of any assumption of privilege. The expression has been in the vernacular rather than elevated in tone. Although religious feeling and rhetorical gesture have informed Australian art, there has been nothing like the piety of the United States or the imaginative flourish of France and Italy. Seemingly even the most spiritual interpretations have had a practical

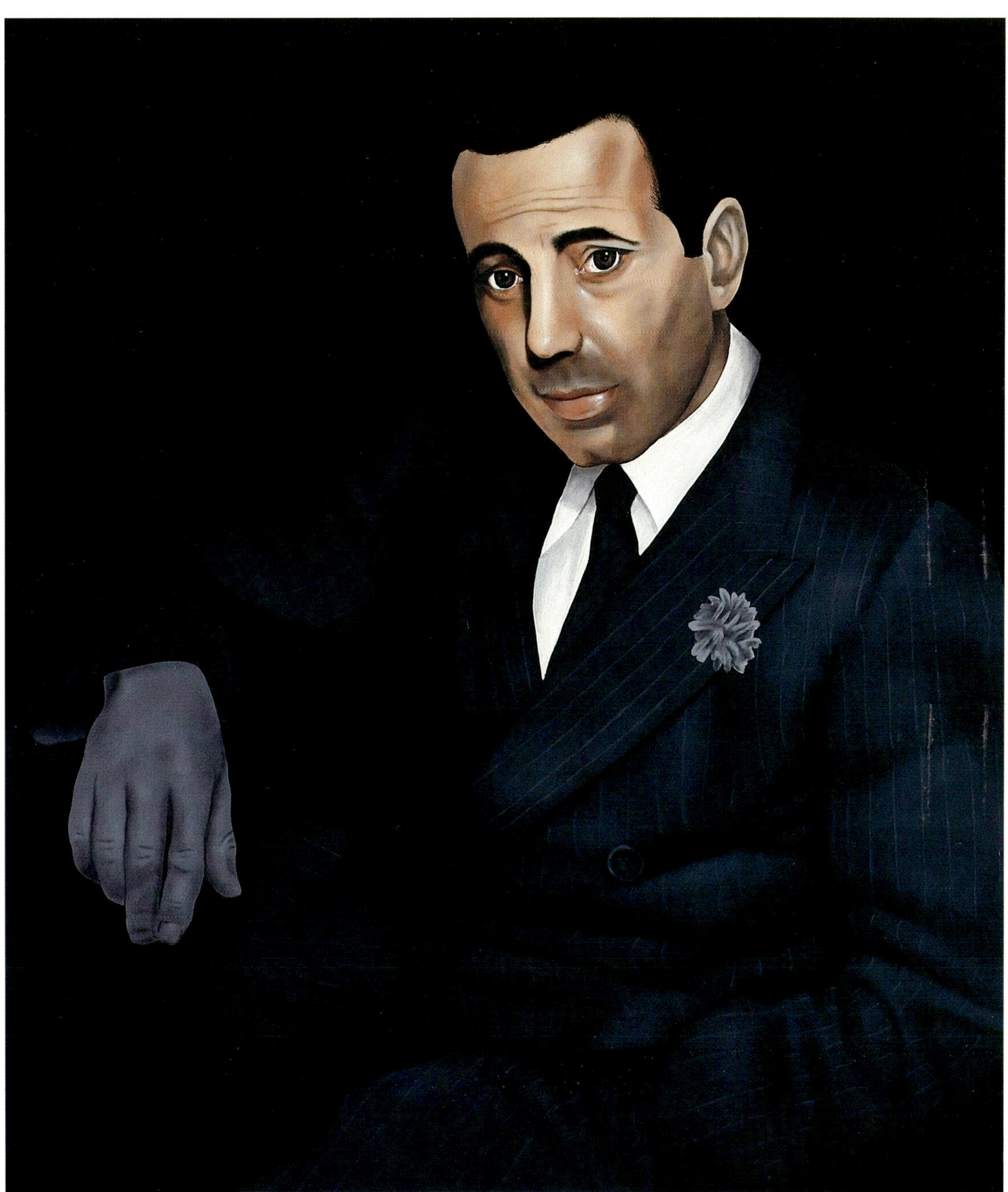

122   Ivan Durrant
born 1947
Humphrey Bogart 1974
synthetic polymer paint on board
122.5 × 106.8 cm

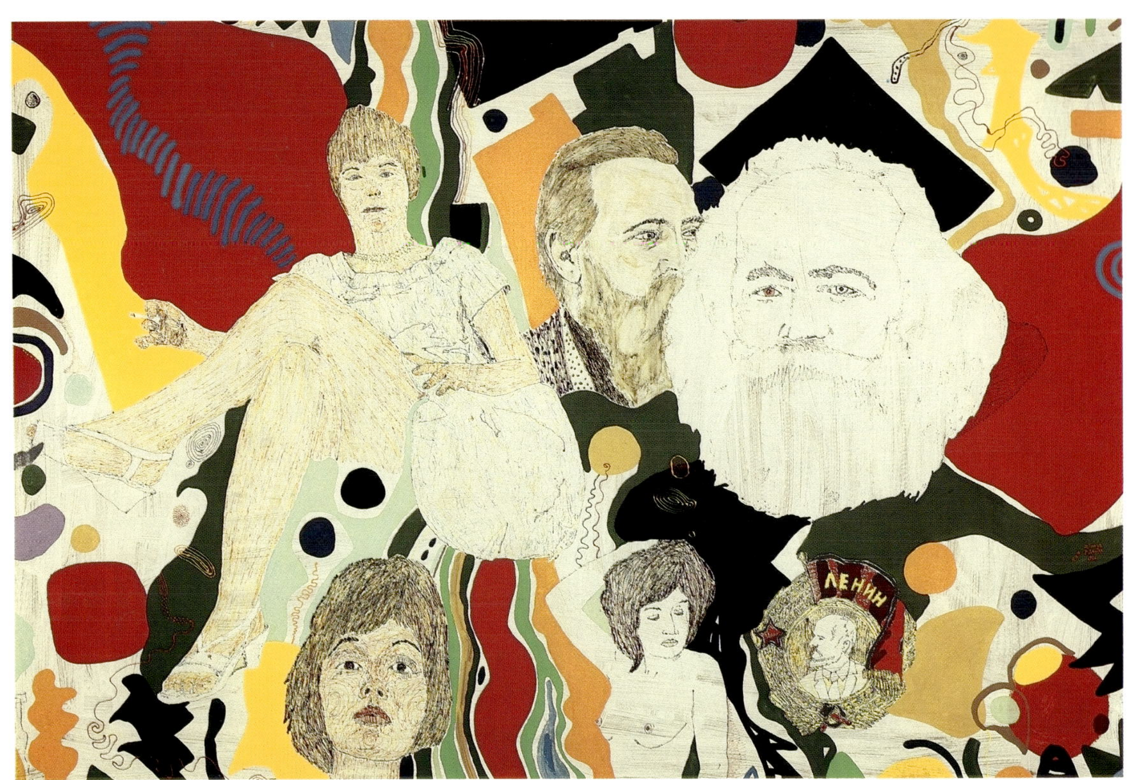

123   Richard Larter
born 1929
The Tinkling Eye of Marx (1966)
alkyd and epoxy resins on board
122.0 × 183.0 cm

purpose as well. Science has had a far greater hold than religion. Myths abound within Australian art but these have been stories about the exploits of ordinary people and jokes at the expense of pretentious leaders. There has been a constant, frank interest in material values. Early views of the landscape showed it as prime real estate. In the nineteenth century settlers commissioned portraits of themselves, wife and children for display in a new or refurbished home. Paintings, down to those produced today, were artefacts of expensive good taste in the size, medium, style and sophisticated subject.

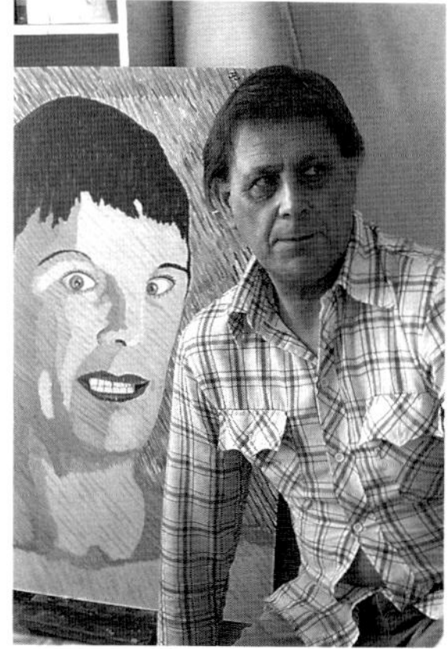

Richard Larter with a portrait of Pat in 1993. Pat Larter appears also in *The Tinkling Eye of Marx* (plate 123).

Photograph by Frank Watters

1 John Brack interviewed by Hazel de Berg, 9 August 1962, Hazel de Berg tapes, National Library of Australia. Italics are the author's.
2 *Sydney Morning Herald*, 18 February 1959, quoted in Bernard Smith *Australian Painting 1788–1970*, Oxford University Press, Melbourne, 1971, p. 328.
3 Gary Catalano, 'Childhood themes' in *The Years of Hope: Australian Art and Criticism 1959–1968*, Oxford University Press, Melbourne, 1981.
4 Bernard Smith, *Australian Painting Today*, John Murtagh Macrossan Lectures, 1961, University of Queensland Press, St Lucia, 1962, p. 30.
5 Patrick McCaughey, *Australian Abstract Art*, National Gallery Booklets, Oxford University Press, Melbourne, 1969, p. 8.
6 See discussion of Williams and the Antipodeans in Patrick McCaughey, *Fred Williams*, Bay Books, Sydney, 1980, pp. 120–2.
7 See Barbara Dowse, *Dick Watkins in Context: An Exhibition from the Collection of the National Gallery of Australia*, National Gallery of Australia, Canberra, 15 January–15 July 1993.
8 John Stringer, *The Field*, catalogue, National Gallery of Victoria, Melbourne, 1968, p. 3.
9 See Barbara Dowse, *Dick Watkins in Context*, National Gallery of Australia, Canberra, 15 January–15 July 1993 written some months after this text.
10 Patrick McCaughey, *Age*, Melbourne, 15 May 1968.
11 *Age*, Melbourne, 10 November 1976, 9 November 1978.
12 *Cosmopolitan*, October 1975.
13 Notes accompanying Robert Owen's exhibition 'Memory and Logic Units', Tolarno Galleries, October 1977.

CATALOGUE

Titles provided by someone other than the artist are given in parenthesis.

Dates in parenthesis are those that have been established by research rather than given in inscriptions.

1 J.W. Lewin
1770–1819
(*The opossum*) 1807
watercolour on paper
25.0 × 47.0 cm

2 Richard Browne
1776–1824
Burgun (1814–20)
watercolour on paper
29.6 × 24.0 cm

3 Joseph Lycett
c. 1775–1828
The Sugarloaf Mountain near Newcastle (1822)
watercolour on board
17.4 × 27.4 cm

4 Augustus Earle
1793–1838
Frederick Garling (1826)
oil on cedar panel
34.0 × 26.5 cm

5 Charles Rodius
1802–60
Neddy Noora, Shoalhaven 1834
lithograph on paper
20.7 × 14.8 cm

6 Charles Rodius
1802–60
Tooban, gin or wife of the Chief of the Shoalhaven Tribe 1834
lithograph on paper
24.0 × 20.0 cm

7 John Glover
1767–1849
Dinas Brann near Llangollen 1837
oil on canvas
76.0 × 114.0 cm

8 Conrad Martens
1801–78
(Road across the Blue Mountains with Mount Tomah in the distance) (1845)
watercolour on paper
45.5 × 65.2 cm

9 G.E. Peacock
1806 – after 1856
A suite of five views of Sydney
(from an original six)

a *View of Sydney and Port Jackson from the South Head Road, above Rose Bay* 1846
oil on board
15.5 × 20.8 cm

b *Port Jackson, New South Wales, view up the Harbour near Garden Island* 1846
oil on board
15.5 × 20.8 cm

c *View of Government House and Fort Macquarie from the Botanical Gardens* 1846
oil on board
15.5 × 20.8 cm

d *Port Jackson, New South Wales, view East
from the back of Government Domain,
Woolloomooloo Point, Darling Point and Point Piper
in perspective with Clarke's Island* 1846
oil on board
15.5 × 20.8 cm

e *Port Jackson, New South Wales, North West
view from the Lady Darling's Point with
Garden Island* 1846
oil on board
15.5 × 20.8 cm

10 Henry Gritten
1818–73
View of Hobart Town from Kangaroo Point (1854)
oil on canvas
36.1 × 53.2 cm

11 William Nicholas
c. 1807–54
*Masters William, Arthur and
Miss Augusta Campbell* 1851
watercolour on paper
26.0 × 27.5 cm (with arched top)

12 Robert Dowling
1827–86
Charles Kernot 1856
oil on board
31.0 × 25.0 cm

13 Robert Dowling
1827–86
Mary Kernot 1856
oil on board
30.0 × 25.0 cm

14 William Strutt
1825–1915
*The actor's cart, Black Thursday,
February 6th 1851* (1863)
oil on paper
22.1 × 39.2 cm

15 S.T. Gill
1819–80
Night concert, Main Road, Ballarat (1854)
watercolour on paper
26.5 × 37.0 cm

16 W.B. Gould
1803–53
(Still life: cat and fish) 1849
oil on canvas laid down on wood panel
41.5 × 61.0 cm

17 Eugene von Guérard
1811–1901
*View of the Wannon Springs in the Grampians,
with Mount Abrupt, Colony of Victoria* 1859
oil on canvas
56.0 × 73.0 cm

18 Eugene von Guérard
1811–1901
Wakatipu, with Mount Earnshaw 1878
oil on canvas
37.0 × 65.0 cm

19 Nicholas Chevalier
1828–1902
Sealers' Cove, Wilson's Promontory 1864
oil on canvas
42.9 × 68.6 cm

20 W.C. Piguenit
1836–1914
*Lake St Clair – the source of the River Derwent,
Tasmania* (1887)
oil on canvas
77.7 × 128.0 cm

21 Haughton Forrest
1826–1925
Mount Wellington from the Huon Road (1885)
oil on board
31.0 × 47.1 cm

22 Louis Buvelot
1814–88
Afternoon at Blackwood 1879
oil on canvas
46.0 × 68.5 cm

23 Tom Roberts
1856–1931
(Self portrait) 1889
from 'The 9 by 5 Impression Exhibition'
oil on wood panel
35.4 × 24.8 cm

24 Ugo Catani
1861-(19?)
St Kilda Pier 1886
oil on canvas
18.0 × 36.0 cm

25 Girolamo Nerli
1860-1926
*Looking towards Port Melbourne
from St Kilda* (1890-91)
oil on board
21.5 × 34.0 cm

26 Charles Conder
1868-1909
Fisherman's Bridge, Double Bay 1888
oil on wood panel
33.7 × 45.9 cm

27 Jane Sutherland
1855-1928
Little gossips 1888
oil on canvas
48.5 × 36.0 cm

28 Arthur Streeton
1867-1943
(Sunlight: the path to Podge Newton's) (1895)
oil on plywood panel
28.2 × 21.5 cm

29 Tom Roberts
1856-1931
Towards Millera 1894
oil on plywood panel
15.5 × 37.5 cm

30 Walter Withers
1854-1914
A Fallen Monarch 1890
oil on canvas
76.0 × 99.0 cm

31 Tudor St George Tucker
1862-1906
Ti trees near Sandringham 1896
oil on canvas
70.0 × 100.4 cm

32 Frederick McCubbin
1855-1917
At Macedon 1913
oil on canvas
51.8 x 61.2 cm

33 Sidney Long
1871-1955
The sheep pool 1898
oil on canvas
82.0 × 140.0 cm

34 Tom Roberts
1856-1931
The towpath, Putney 1904
oil on canvas
25.3 × 40.7 cm

35 Tom Roberts
1856-1931
The first basin, Lake Como 1913
oil on canvas
65.5 × 85.0 cm

36 Hans Heysen
1877-1968
(Late afternoon light, Hahndorf) 1915
pastel on paper
33.0 × 45.0 cm

37 David Davies
1864-1939
Cottages in snow, North Wales (1906)
oil on canvas
51.0 × 61.4 cm

38 John Russell
1858-1930
Races at Saint Tropez (1910)
watercolour on paper
25.8 × 35.8 cm

39 Iso Rae
1860-c. 1940
Roasted chestnuts, Etaples 1917
pastel and gouache on paper
46.0 × 53.0 cm

40 Max Meldrum
1875-1955
Portrait 1910
oil on canvas
49.0 × 59.0 cm

41 Hilda Rix Nicholas
1884-1961
Work (1909)
oil on canvas
162.0 × 130.0 cm

42 Ethel Carrick
1872–1952
Rue Mouffetard, Paris (1910)
oil on canvas
38.1 × 45.6 cm

43 E. Phillips Fox
1865–1915
(*Nude*) 1911
oil on canvas
65.0 × 81.2 cm

44 Rupert Bunny
1864–1947
Potiphar's wife 1920
colour monotype on paper
27.5 × 37.5 cm

45 Rupert Bunny
1864–1947
The letter (1914–16)
oil on canvas
73.3 × 60.2 cm

46 Rupert Bunny
1864–1947
A group of three south of France landscapes

a *The Capucin Monastery of St Feréol, Ceret*
(1926)
oil on paper mounted on plywood
21.0 × 24.0 cm

b (*St Paul du Var*) (1923)
oil on paper mounted on plywood
21.0 × 23.5 cm

c (*Near Sanary*) (1925)
oil on paper mounted on plywood
21.0 × 23.7 cm

47 Bessie Davidson
1879–1965
Still life (1913)
oil on board
44.8 × 72.8 cm

48 Kathleen O'Connor
1876–1968
Still life with white tulips (1935)
oil on board
76.0 × 63.0 cm

49 Blamire Young
1862–1935
(*Mariana*) (1910)
watercolour on paper
81.5 × 41.0 cm

50 Thea Proctor
1879–1966
The swing 1925
hand-coloured woodcut on paper
22.5 × 24.9 cm

51 Penleigh Boyd
1890–1923
Portsea Pier (1920)
oil on canvas
66.0 × 87.1 cm

52 Arthur Streeton
1867–1943
Blue and Gold, Olinda 1926
oil on canvas laid down on board
51.7 × 77.6 cm

53 Elioth Gruner
1882–1939
Yass landscape 1928
oil on canvas
50.5 × 60.5 cm

54 Elioth Gruner
1882–1939
Early morning, Cooma, New South Wales 1927
oil on canvas
32.5 × 39.0 cm

55 Roy de Maistre
1894–1968
The organist (1943)
oil on canvas
51.0 × 61.0 cm

56 Clarice Beckett
1887–1935
Taxi rank (1927)
oil on canvas on board
58.5 × 51.0 cm

57 Horace Trenerry
1899–1958
The road to Maslins (1940)
oil on board
48.5 × 57.0 cm

58   Grace Cossington Smith
1892–1984
The gully 1928
oil on board
110.5 × 82.5 cm

59   Margaret Preston
1875–1963
Hibiscus 1925
hand–coloured woodcut on paper
24.4 × 24.9 cm

60   Margaret Preston
1875–1963
Bottlebrush and angophora 1944
oil on canvas
54.5 × 45.5 cm

61   Margaret Preston
1875–1963
Native flowers on striped cloth 1932
oil on canvas
45.4 × 38.2 cm

62   Dorrit Black
1891–1951
(Nude with cigarette) (1930)
oil on canvas laid down on board
46.0 × 37.7 cm

63   Ian Fairweather
1891–1974
(Bathers) (1935)
oil and gouache on paper
35.5 × 43.0 cm

64   Eric Wilson
1911–46
Nude 1939
oil on canvas
76.0 × 56.0 cm

65   Eric Wilson
1911–46
Still life 1939
oil on canvas
54.5 × 75.0 cm

66   William Dobell
1899–1970
Derby Day (1938)
oil on paper on board
19.5 × 16.5 cm

67   William Dobell
1899–1970
James Cook 1942
oil on canvas
90.5 × 70.4 cm

68   Lina Bryans
born 1909
Alan McCulloch (1942)
oil on canvas on plywood panel
38.4 x 37.4 cm

69   William Frater
1890–1974
Sugarloaf, Plenty Ranges (1950)
oil on board
68.0 × 89.0 cm

70   Arnold Shore
1897–1963
Arthur's Creek 1949
oil on canvas
51.0 × 61.0 cm

71   Charles Meere
1890–1961
Still life 1958
oil on board
24.5 × 29.5 cm

72   Charles Meere
1890–1961
(Landscape) (1959)
oil on canvas on board
61.0 × 76.3 cm

73   Peter Purves Smith
1912–49
(Landscape near Cassis) 1933
oil on canvas
46.0 × 60.0 cm

74   Danila Vassilieff
1897–1958
A street in Fitzroy (1937)
oil on plywood panel
37.8 × 44.9 cm

75   Josl Bergner
born 1920
(Aboriginal family) (1943)
oil on board
37.0 × 42.0 cm

76 Vic O'Connor
born 1918
(*North Melbourne*) 1947–8
oil on board
37.5 × 53.3 cm

77 Sali Herman
1898–1993
(*Paddington back street corner*) 1947
oil on canvas
30.9 × 41.0 cm

78 John Perceval
born 1923
(*Woman pushing a crippled boy*) 1943
oil on board
65.0 × 49.0 cm

79 Arthur Boyd
born 1920
The Seasons 1944
oil on muslin laid down on board
63.5 × 76.2 cm

80 Albert Tucker
born 1914
Image of Modern Evil 1946
oil on board
80.0 X 120.0 cm

81 Herbert Badham
1899–1961
(*Bar scene*) 1940
oil on canvas
102.0 × 81.0 cm

82 Joy Hester
1920–60
(*Girl with hat*) 1955
ink on paper
73.5 × 48.5 cm

83 Russell Drysdale
1912–81
Ticket office, Albury 1943
gouache on paper
31.5 × 41.0 cm

84 Arthur Boyd
born 1920
Wheatfield, Berwick 1948
oil on canvas on board
54.0 × 65.0 cm

85 Sidney Nolan
1917–92
The Glenrowan siege 1955
synthetic polymer paint on board
91.5 × 71.0 cm

86 Russell Drysdale
1912–81
Maria 1950
oil on canvas
99.0 × 76.0 cm

87 James Gleeson
born 1915
Gardens of the Night 1947
oil on canvas
72.0 × 102.0 cm

88 Charles Blackman
born 1928
Boy with model airplane 1952
tempera on canvas laid down on board
61.0 × 91.0 cm

89 Robert Dickerson
born 1924
The steps (1958)
oil on board
120.5 × 88.5 cm

90 John Brack
born 1920
Youth 1954
pencil on paper
34.5 × 42.5 cm

91 John Brack
born 1920
Union Road 1961
watercolour on paper
43.0 × 73.5 cm

92 John Brack
born 1920
Arabesque 1973
oil on canvas
89.5 × 116.0 cm

93 Michael Shannon
born 1927
Composition with saw 1958
oil on board
107.0 × 61.0 cm

94 Ralph Balson
1890–1964
Constructive painting (1951)
oil on board
61.0 × 82.0 cm

95 Ralph Balson
1890–1964
Non-objective painting 1956
synthetic polymer paint on plywood panel
63.0 × 73.4 cm

96 Frank Hinder
1906–92
Flight E.M. 513 1956
casein on paper
53.3 × 74.5 cm

97 John Passmore
1904–84
Miller's Point (1952)
oil on board
46.0 × 60.5 cm

98 Godfrey Miller
1893–1964
Still life with fruit (1953)
oil on canvas
44.5 × 63.0 cm

99 Grace Cossington Smith
1892–1984
*(The verandah and garden
from the artist's bedroom)* 1956
oil on board
60.0 × 45.5 cm

100 Weaver Hawkins
1893–1977
Burragorang landscape 1946
oil on canvas
51.0 × 60.8 cm

101 Clifton Pugh
1924–90
Lizard and butterflies 1957
oil on board
68.3 × 91.2 cm

102 John Perceval
born 1923
Fisherman's sights 1956
oil on board
91.1 × 122.0 cm

103 John Perceval
born 1923
Winter landscape, Gaffney's Creek 1958
oil on polystyrene panel
91.5 × 73.5 cm

104 Justin O'Brien
born 1917
Three jugglers (1955)
oil on canvas
57.0 × 70.0 cm

105 Lloyd Rees
1895–1988
Winding road at Werri 1958
oil on canvas
91.5 × 122.0 cm

106 Arthur Boyd
born 1920
Eaglehawk landscape 1956
tempera on board
61.0 × 79.5 cm

107 William Delafield Cook
born 1936
The Hawksbury 1982–3
synthetic polymer paint on canvas
88.8 × 195.5 cm

108 Brett Whiteley
1939–92
Lavender Bay 1980
synthetic polymer paint on canvas
122.0 × 81.0 cm

109 John Olsen
born 1928
The paddock of wattles 1978–80
oil on canvas
167.0 × 159.0 cm

110 Ken Whisson
born 1927
Spring Tide 1983
oil on canvas
99.4 × 119.4 cm

111 Fred Williams
1927–82
Forest pond 1974
oil on canvas
107.0 × 91.6 cm

112   Roger Kemp
1908–87
Configuration 1965
synthetic polymer paint on board
137.0 × 183.0 cm

113   Tony Tuckson
1921–73
"E" (1962–5)
oil on board
122.0 × 122.0 cm

114   Ian Fairweather
1891–1974
Parasol 1957
gouache on cardboard
91.0 × 67.5 cm

115   Dick Watkins
born 1937
Brief encounter 1983
synthetic polymer paint on canvas
173.0 × 244.0 cm

116   Dale Hickey
born 1937
Untitled painting 1968
synthetic polymer paint on canvas
152.5 × 165.0 cm

117   Robert Hunter
born 1947
Untitled painting 1969
synthetic polymer paint on canvas
158.5 × 158.5 cm

118   Paul Partos
born 1943
Untitled painting 1979
oil, pencil, metal pins and
elastic cord on canvas
182.0 × 136.0 cm

119   Peter Booth
born 1940
Painting 1989
oil on canvas
243.7 × 198.0 cm

120   Robert Owen
born 1937
Stopover (1971)
aluminium, perspex, lead,
wax and defraction grating
61.3 × 60.0 cm

121   Jeffrey Smart
born 1921
Public notice, Hove 1969–70
oil on canvas
91.2 × 65.4 cm

122   Ivan Durrant
born 1947
Humphrey Bogart 1974
synthetic polymer paint on board
122.5 × 106.8 cm

123   Richard Larter
born 1929
The Tinkling Eye of Marx (1966)
alkyd and epoxy resins on board
122.0 × 183.0 cm

BLACK AND WHITE
ILLUSTRATIONS

Acknowledgements

The publisher would like to thank those people and organisations who have generously supplied illustrative material for this book. In particular thanks are due to Mary Lewis of the State Library of Victoria, Barbara Beck, Rosalind Hollinrake, Janine Burke, Eve Sainsbury from Sally Milner Publishers, Margaret Tuckson and Rosemary Hickey. A special thank you is due to Albert Tucker.

La Trobe Collection, State Library of Victoria
Pages 54, 72, 83, 84 and 120; Photographer unknown: pages 82, 96, 105, 164; Photograph by Stewart and Company: page 52; Photograph by Foster & Martin: page 64; Photographs by J.K. Moir: pages 67 and 97: Photograph by H. Walter Barnett: page 74; Photograph by Mina and Max Moore: page 150; Photograph by A. Wilkinson, *The Home*, 1/12/21: page 152; Photograph by Bernice Agar, *The Home*, 1/10/27: page 142; Photograph by Judith Fletcher, *The Home*, 1/12/ 21: page 166; Photographs by Richard Beck: pages 226, 230, 234, 240, 244, 250, 260, 262 and 276.

Albert Tucker Collection
Pages 188, 194, 196, 198, 202, 204, 206 and 210.

Rosalind Hollinrake Collection
Page 158.

William Yang Collection
Pages 254 and 274.

Janine Burke Collection
Pages 123, 162 and 184.

Rosemary Hickey Collection
Page 270.

David Moore Collection
Pages 176 and 208.

Margaret Tuckson Collection
Page 264.

Ken Whisson Collection
Page 258.

Tasmanian Museum and Art Gallery
Page 50: W.B. Gould *Self portrait* 1838; oil on canvas 68.7 x 59.2; signed,
    dated and inscribed 'Wm Buelow Gould/Painter 1838 VDL' on verso
    of canvas (purchased 1920).

National Gallery of Victoria
Page 170: photograph by Russell Drysdale 1912–1981
Women students at the George Bell School 1939
Gelatin silver photograph, printed 1980s
Presented by Lady Drysdale 1982
National Gallery of Victoria, Melbourne.

Ian Fairweather
Page 172: photograph from *Ian Fairweather* by Murray Bail, Bay Books,
    Sydney, 1981.

Niagara Gallery
Page 279: photograph by Frank Watters, courtesy of Niagara Galleries,
    Melbourne, & Watters Gallery, Sydney.

Bold type refers to illustrations